Toward a Global History of
Latin America's Revolutionary Left

Toward a Global History
OF LATIN AMERICA'S
REVOLUTIONARY LEFT

Edited by Tanya Harmer
and Alberto Martín Álvarez

University of Florida Press
Gainesville

First cloth printing, 2021
First paperback printing, 2025

30 29 28 27 26 25   6 5 4 3 2 1

Library of Congress Cataloging-in-Publication Data
Names: Harmer, Tanya, editor. | Martín Álvarez, Alberto, editor.
Title: Toward a global history of Latin America's revolutionary left /
    edited by Tanya Harmer and Alberto Martín Álvarez.
Description: Gainesville : University of Florida Press, [2021] | Includes
    bibliographical references and index.
Identifiers: LCCN 2020038260 (print) | LCCN 2020038261 (ebook) | ISBN
    9781683401698 (hardback) | ISBN 9781683401964 (pdf) | ISBN 9781683405139 (pbk.)
Subjects: LCSH: Revolutions—Latin America—History—20th century. | Right
    and left (Political science)—Latin America—History—20th century. |
    Latin America—Foreign relations—Europe. | Latin America—Foreign
    relations—Asia. | Latin America—Foreign relations—Africa.
Classification: LCC F1414.2 .T687 2021 (print) | LCC F1414.2 (ebook) |
    DDC 980.03—dc23
LC record available at https://lccn.loc.gov/2020038260
LC ebook record available at https://lccn.loc.gov/2020038261

University of Florida Press
2046 NE Waldo Road
Suite 2100
Gainesville, FL 32609
http://upress.ufl.edu

UF PRESS

UNIVERSITY
OF FLORIDA

GPSR EU Authorized Representative: Mare Nostrum Group B.V., Mauritskade 21D, 1091 GC Amsterdam,
The Netherlands, gpsr@mare-nostrum.co.uk

Contents

Illustrations

Abbreviations

AAPSO	Afro-Asian Peoples' Solidarity Organization (see also OSPAA)
AFL-CIO	American Federation of Labor-Congress of Industrial Organizations, USA
AI	Amnesty International
ALN	National Liberation Alliance, Brazil
BPP	Black Panther Party for Self Defense, USA
CAM	Ambrosio Mogorrón Committee, Nicaragua
CCFD-Terre Solidaire	Catholic Committee against Hunger and for Development
CC.OO	Workers' Commissions, Spain
CCP	Chinese Communist Party
CCSN	Catalan Solidarity Co-ordinating Committee in Support of Nicaragua
CESN	State Solidarity Co-ordinating Committee in Support of Nicaragua
Cfdt	Democratic Confederation of Labor, France
CGT	General Confederation of Labor, France
CGUP	Guatemalan Committee for Patriotic Unity
CIA	Central Intelligence Agency, USA
CNASP	Nicaraguan Council of Friendship, Solidarity and Peace
CNUS	National Committee for Trade Union Unity, Guatemala
COSOCAN	Catalan Solidarity Committee in Support of Nicaragua
COTRAM	Commission for Broad Mass Work, EGP, Guatemala
CPSU	Communist Party of the Soviet Union
CSARG	Guatemalan Refugee Support Group
ČTK	Czechoslovak News Agency
CUC	Peasant Unity Committee, Guatemala
CVSN	Basque Solidarity Co-ordinating Committee in Support of Nicaragua

DCG	Guatemalan Christian Democracy
DN	National Direction, EGP, Guatemala
DRI	Department of International Relations, FSLN, Nicaragua
DRV	Democratic Republic of Vietnam
EGP	Guerrilla Army of the Poor, Guatemala
ERP	People's Revolutionary Army, Argentina
ETI	International Work Team, EGP, Guatemala
FALN	Armed Forces of National Liberation, Venezuela
FAR	Rebel Armed Forces, Guatemala
FDCR	Democratic Front against Repression, Guatemala
FDR	Democratic Revolutionary Front, El Salvador
FMLN	Farabundo Martí National Liberation Front, El Salvador
FO	Force Ouvrière, France
FPL	People's Liberation Forces, El Salvador
FSLN	Sandinista National Liberation Front, Nicaragua
FUR	United Front of the Revolution, Guatemala
GDR	German Democratic Republic (East Germany)
GFE	Giangiacomo Feltrinelli Editore
JPT	Patriotic Labor Youth, Guatemala
KGB	Soviet Committee for State Security
LCR	Revolutionary Communist League, France
M-19	Movement April-19, Colombia
M-26-7	26 July Movement, Cuba
MAS	Movement toward Socialism, Venezuela
MCE	Communist Movement of Spain
MINREX	Foreign Affairs Ministry, Cuba
MIR	Movement of the Revolutionary Left, Chile/Peru/Venezuela
MIR-Praxis	Movement of the Revolutionary Left-Praxis, Argentina
MLN	National Liberation Movement, Mexico
MLN-T	National Liberation Movement-Tupamaros, Uruguay
MNR	National Revolutionary Movement, El Salvador
MR-13-M	March 13 Students' Directorate, Cuba
MRT	Movimento Revolucionário Tiradentes
NAM	Non-Aligned Movement
OAS	Organization of American States
OLAS	Latin American Solidarity Organization
ORM-Polop	Revolutionary Marxist Organization-Workers' Policy, Brazil

ORPA	Revolutionary Organization of the People in Arms, Guatemala
ORT	Workers' Revolutionary Organization, Spain
OSPAA	Afro-Asian People's Solidarity Organization (see also AAPSO)
OSPAAAL	Organization of Solidarity with Peoples of Africa, Asia, and Latin America, or Tricontinental (AALAPSO in English)
PCB	Brazilian Communist Party
PCBR	Revolutionary Brazilian Communist Party
PCdoB	Communist Party of Brazil
PCE	Spanish Communist Party
PCE(m-l)	Spanish Communist Party (Marxist-Leninist)
PCF	French Communist Party
PCI	Italian Communist Party
PCPE	Communist Party of the Peoples of Spain
PCV	Venezuelan Communist Party
PdUP	Proletarian Unity Party, Italy
PGT	Guatemalan Party of Labor
PRT	Workers Revolutionary Party, Argentina
PSB	Belgian Socialist Party
PSD	Democratic Socialist Party, France
PSF	French Socialist Party
PSI	Italian Socialist Party
PSOE	Spanish Socialist Workers' Party
PSP	Popular Socialist Party, Cuba
PSU	Unified Socialist Party, France
PTB	Brazilian Labor Party
PTE	Spanish Labor Party
RUOG	Unitary Representation of the Guatemalan Opposition
SI	Socialist International
SPD	Social Democratic Party, Germany
UGT	General Workers' Union, Spain
UN	United Nations
UNAN	National Autonomous University of Nicaragua
URNG	Guatemalan National Revolutionary Unity
WFDY	World Federation of Democratic Youth

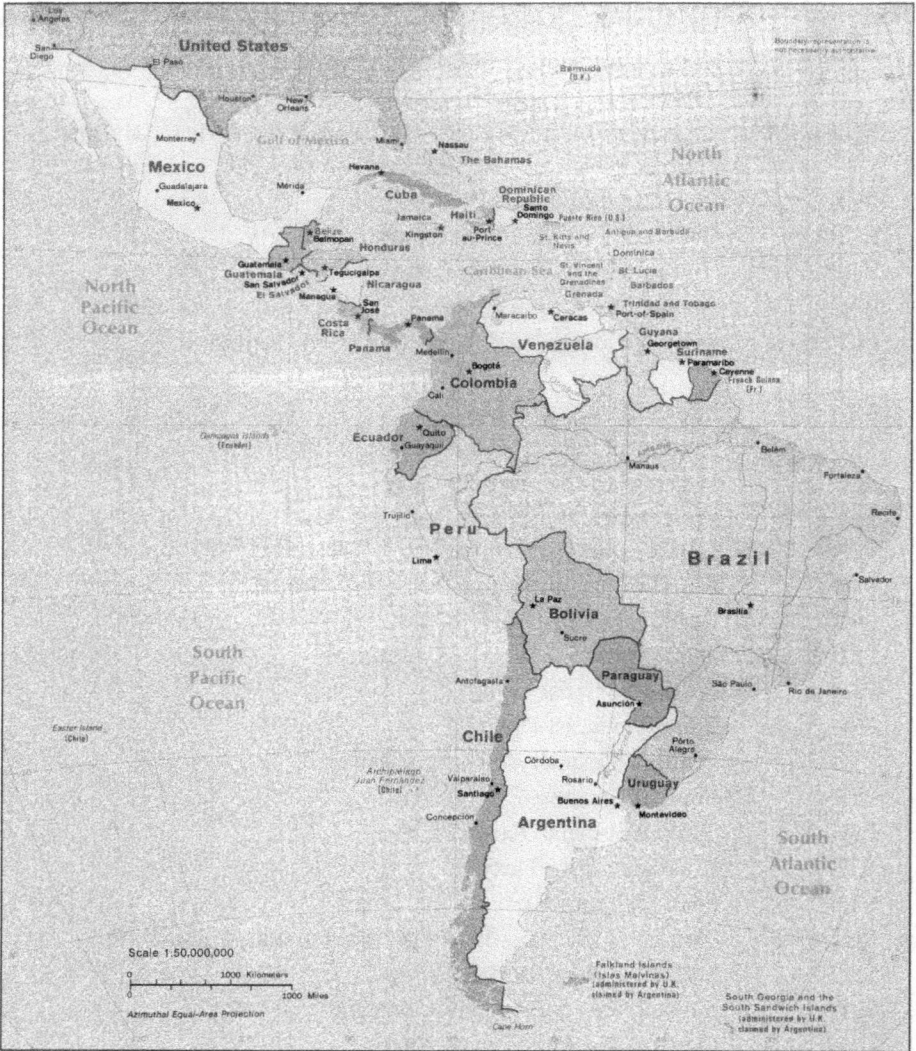

Figure 0.1. Map of Latin America. Courtesy University of Texas Libraries.

Introduction

Globalizing Latin America's Revolutionary Left; Historiography, Approaches, and Context

TANYA HARMER AND ALBERTO MARTÍN ÁLVAREZ

"Cuba and Latin America are part of the world," Fidel Castro proclaimed to over a million Cubans gathered at the *Plaza de la Revolución* in Havana on February 4, 1962. In what would become known as the "Second Declaration of Havana," he rejected any notion that Latin Americans should consider themselves separate from a global revolutionary project. "The movement of the dependent and colonial peoples is a phenomenon of universal character which agitates the world and marks the final crisis of imperialism," he declared, "Our [Latin Americans'] problems form part of the problems engendered by the general crisis of imperialism and the struggle of the subjugated peoples—the clash between the world that is being born and the world that is dying."[1]

Indeed, it is hard to understand Latin America's Revolutionary Left without grasping its global, transnational influence and ambition. Left-wing revolutionaries in the region drew inspiration and strength from contemporaneous struggles far from their local environments: the Chinese Revolution and its example, Algeria's War of Independence, the Vietnam War, Palestine, or anticolonial struggles in Lusophone Africa. Collaboration was also often fundamentally important to the existence, evolution, and survival of revolutionary leftist organizations. Especially when groups found themselves in open conflict with the state, vital resources, funds, and logistical assistance from abroad were essential. A quick glimpse of who attended the "Tricontinental" meeting of revolutionaries from Africa, Asia, and Latin America in Havana in January 1966—a remarkable and unprecedented gathering—similarly underlines the interconnectedness of revolutionary currents across the globe. And it is noteworthy that Europeans (from East and West) also attended the same conference, being among Latin American revolutionaries' most ardent supporters. Cuba, more than any other country in Latin America, therefore intentionally and effectively broke free of the Monroe Doctrine, building bridges beyond the Western Hemisphere and inviting revolutionaries from within and beyond it to engage with each other. From the 1960s, left-wing groups in the region thus very often discovered the world beyond the Americas via Cuba. Through its interaction with countries and peoples in Africa and Asia, especially, Cuba made the Third World relevant, intelligible, and relatable for Latin American audiences. Its involvement in Africa, particularly when it came to assisting the anticolonial struggle in Angola, Mozambique, and Guinea Bissau against the Portuguese and then South Africa in the 1970s and 1980s, is also notable for its significance, audacity, and results.[2]

But it was not only Cuba's revolutionary regime that facilitated and forged such connections. Revolutionary Left publications throughout the region echoed proclamations of solidarity and denunciations of imperialism across the world, urging readers to identify with people living and fighting for a similar future beyond the Americas. Young Latin American revolutionaries marched to protest the United States' intervention in South East Asia and clashed with national police forces for the same reason; they traveled abroad to learn or to disseminate news of their own struggles and ask for support. They imbibed and generated new cultural influences that were exchanged and transferred across regions. The development of "Dependency Theory" within Latin America in the 1960s—and its appropriation by the Left as an explanatory framework for understanding the revolutionary potential for the region—situated local phenomena in a global context and increasingly shaped international debates on development and trade in the 1970s.[3]

So, why do we not know more about the global dimensions of Latin America's Revolutionary Left? In part, the answer to this question is rooted in a much deeper "disconnect" between global—or world—history and Latin America. As Matthew Brown has lamented, the region "rarely shines brightly, is often overlooked, and has remained on the periphery of a way of writing about history that consciously seeks networks and connections, and aspires to overcome older imperial and colonial exclusionary narratives."[4] Brown suggests multiple reasons for this, including Latin Americanist historians' "anxiety" about the "loss of culture-specific knowledge and of the potential homogenization of the historical discipline"; prevailing historiographical attention to the micro and local in histories of the region; and the tradition within Latin America of teaching *"historia nacional"* as separate from *"historia universal."*[5] Other historians have also lamented the institutional, financial, and structural impediments to conducting global histories. As Aldo Marchesi notes, writing global history is "expensive." It requires global research and libraries. Language expertise has meanwhile separated scholars of different regions of the world and, in many cases, led global historians to work using colonial archives (or in the case of twentieth-century Latin America, U.S. archives) as a means to bridge divides.[6]

However, perhaps the biggest problem, Brown notes, has been the tendency to write global history as the teleological history of our contemporary globalized world, privileging the events and actors that ultimately won out and determined the way history unfolded as it did. This approach marginalizes groups and processes that were overcome and defeated, the Revolutionary Left included. Global historians' attention, instead, tends to fall on ascending globalizing forces, the rise of a neoliberal world order, and power shifts among Asia, Europe, and the United States, with Latin America consigned to the periphery.[7] As Richard Drayton and David Motadel have acknowledged, global history as a field largely "remains driven covertly by Western priorities . . . returning us often by non-Western routes to the idols of the old 'Rise of the West' historiography" and remaining "dominated by Anglophone historians who seem unable or indisposed to read history written in other languages."[8]

When it comes to histories of the "Global Cold War"—first propagated by Odd Arne Westad in his seminal book *The Global Cold War: Third World Interventions and the Making of Our Times*—Latin America has also remained somewhat on the margins relative to other parts of the globe. Westad's own *Global Cold War* zoomed in on revolution in Cuba and Nicaragua but spent far more time examining the superpower's interaction with Africa and Asia.[9]

There were good reasons for this. For one, Latin America did not share the fundamental narrative of decolonization, which has resulted in what Christy Thornton has called a historiographical "decolonization divide" in scholarship of the Global South.[10] Latin America's proximity to the United States and distance from the Soviet bloc did not make it a theater of direct superpower competition, except in the Cuban and Nicaraguan cases. Latin American governments' entanglements with the United States through international organizations and security pacts also complicated its relationship with the Third World and Non-Aligned Movement. Intra-regional and inter-American currents of exchange and contestation, not to mention the violent civil wars that left hundreds of thousands dead or disappeared, also served to give Latin America its own distinct *hot* character.

Yet, Latin Americanist experts, global historians, and Cold War scholars have also shown a degree of unwillingness to engage in global histories of Latin America's recent past, and this needs to be remedied. For one reason, not to engage with the global is ahistorical; it ignores the very real and significant ties that existed between local phenomena and transnational or international influences. It also distorts the way the "global" is imagined. Consider, for a moment, studies of "the Global 1968" or the "the Global Sixties" and the relative lack of engagement with "the active role that peripheries [played] in ideas and repertoires of protest."[11] As Marchesi laments, the tendency to reduce global upheavals in 1968 to French protests in May of that year—or even May and October, to incorporate the Mexican Tlatelolco massacre that often figures as *the* Latin American case study in global histories of that year—ignores a much richer and complex history of protest and change in the region and its interaction with other areas of the world. Calling on historians to study "multiple epicentres of the geographies of the turbulent sixties," he questions "why, in our global historical memory" May 1968 in France still "epitomizes a process that transcends it and did not actually revolve around it."[12]

The answer, of course, is that, as in the case of other eras, the "global" has predominantly been linked to, and written by scholars working in, Europe and North America. As Marchesi argues, transnational Cold War histories that *have* incorporated Latin America have tended toward using the region to explain U.S. power rather than Latin America's role in shaping events, ideas, and processes. When it comes to ideas about development and modernity, he also argues that far too much emphasis has been placed on ideas that penetrated Latin America from outside the region and not enough on local ideas and theorization within the region that in turn shaped global debates. And, like others, he notes a "paradoxical" tendency to confine studies of left-wing political movements and intellectuals who were deeply associated with internationalist traditions within national borders.[13] Christy Thornton, in her work on the Third World's push for a New International Economic Order—after all, inspired and promulgated by Mexican initiatives—has also observed Latin America remains on the periphery of understanding global impulses for change. "Even as renewed interest in the history of the global has pushed scholars to take seriously interventions from the South," she laments, "a curious divide has emerged in this literature: Latin America is frequently left off the maps scholars have drawn."[14]

The picture nevertheless seems to be changing—at least as far as historians of Latin America are embracing global lenses and questioning national or region frameworks of the past.[15] Major international conferences of Latin Americanists have recently been framed in relation to the region's relationship with the global.[16] Significant efforts by scholars such as Alexandre Moreli and Stella Krepp have attempted to stimulate a broader conversation about global history and to move beyond "the North Atlantic axis" that has dominated the field. As Moreli notes in a special issue of the Brazilian journal *Estudos Históricas* arising from two conferences on global histories of the region he and Krepp organized in Bern and Rio de Janeiro, the task ahead is to re-imagine global history from "the axis of the Americas and their channels of communication."[17]

With regard to global histories of Latin America's Cold War, as with global history further afield, historians have been concerned primarily with looking at comparisons and connectivity, either when it comes to state-led diplomacy (international ties) or non-state relations (transnational networks).[18] Although there is far more to learn, they are building on comparative studies of development strategies that have shown Latin America was part of a broader global contestation of modernity.[19] Scholars like Kyle Burke have also striven to explain the networks of right-wing counter-revolutionary groups that connected Latin American Cold Warriors to counterparts further afield.[20] On the left, Piero Gleijeses's ground-breaking studies of Cuban involvement in Africa—perhaps *the* most obvious and extensive example of Latin America's direct interaction and relevance for global histories of the Cold War—have stimulated new interest in significance of examining South–South interactions during the Cold War.[21] In particular, histories of transnational solidarity movements and exile have forced historians to rethink geographies, agency, and identity when dealing with Latin America's recent past.[22] Jessica Stites Mor's work on Argentine revolutionary groups' solidarity with Palestine's Liberation Organization and the links Argentinean members of guerrilla groups made between Argentina, Vietnam, and the PLO is just one example of transnationalism routed beyond European and North American capitals.[23] And in this context "transnational spaces"—beyond the nation-state and imperial structures, inside and outside the Americas—have become increasingly important objects of study.[24] Diplomatic historians such as Vanni Pettinà, Stella

Krepp, and Carlo Patti have meanwhile begun to seriously explore the extra-hemispheric state-to-state ties that existed between Latin America and other regions of the world.[25]

The literature on Latin America's Revolutionary Left, about which more below, is meanwhile relatively abundant, but irregular.[26] There are good studies on certain national cases, while the bibliography is very scarce for others.[27] Even so, some excellent works have tried to offer an overarching view of the region's Revolutionary Left, either over a particular period in its various stages of development,[28] or focusing on the revolutionary organizations of a particular subregion within America Latina,[29] or the region as a whole.[30]

This body of literature has helped us to understand the processes by which the Revolutionary Left emerged, developed, and disappeared in different Latin American countries, the factors that explain its few successes, and the reasons for its multiple failures in taking power. Historians have also spent considerable time examining the position of the Cuban government toward this political movement.[31] However, we have much to learn when it comes to global perspectives on the links built by Latin American Revolutionary Left organizations and movements with movements, parties, or organizations outside the region.[32] We also need many more comparative studies of Latin America's Revolutionary Left as compared to other regions' revolutionary trajectories—as Van Gosse provides a model for in the afterword of this volume—so as to understand specificity and difference as it existed across the globe. In essence, and with some partial exceptions, the history of Latin America's Revolutionary Left has been built in a national or (at best) a comparative perspective. So far, no attempt has been made to reconstruct the history of this broad political movement from a perspective that emphasizes the symbolic or material relations of the Revolutionary Left with people, organizations, movements, and governments outside Latin America.

Indeed, despite advances in recent years, much clearly remains to be done. We have only really begun to scratch the surface when it comes to understanding Latin America's relationship with the wider world in the twentieth century, its particularities and uniqueness, the way its inhabitants interacted with counterparts from other regions, and the circulation of ideas that flowed to and from it. And we are certainly far from understanding the picture as a whole as opposed to the sum of different case studies and perspectives. At a juncture when historians of Latin America's recent past are embracing the global turn, it is therefore worth taking stock of where we are and pausing to consider where we are and where we are going. Focusing tightly on Latin America's Revolutionary Left, this volume aims to do just that. It does not purport to present a complete picture. To the contrary, it identifies significant gaps in our knowledge that we hope researchers will consider as they move toward a fuller global history of the region's Revolutionary Left. In short, what follows aims not to define an established field but to map the direction scholars are only recently taking, to reflect on their findings, and to tentatively propose suggestions for the future.

Latin America's Revolutionary Left

Before moving to the contributing chapters, their conclusions, and the wider significance of what they tell us about the results and potential for global histories of Latin America's Revolutionary Left, a few words are necessary on what it is we mean by the "Revolutionary Left" and the context in which it arose. Primarily, this volume treats the Revolutionary Left as comprising groups that, from the late 1950s and early 1960s, shared criticism of what they articulated as being the "Reformist" Left (comprising both orthodox Communist and Social Democratic Parties); identified with the Cuban and Algerian revolutions; supported North Vietnam and the National Liberation Front in South Vietnam; espoused faster, immediate overthrow of the existing order; and sympathized or adhered to the idea of armed struggle. Organizations did not necessarily have to practice armed struggle to support it elsewhere. Marxism-Leninism did not always underpin support for leftist groups and national liberation movements (especially in Latin America and Africa). Moreover, as Vania Markarian notes, the "revolutionary" versus "reformist" Left labels constructed by members of the Revolutionary Left all too often established a false dichotomy that simplified the objectives and relationships between and within left-wing groups.[33] But such constructs and broad ideas were central components of what it meant to identify with the Revolutionary Left.

Many of the contributors in this volume shift between the terms "Revolutionary Left" and "New Left." Yet it is worth noting that however synonymously and interchangeably these terms tend to be used, there are differences between them that explain why we chose "Revolutionary Left" as the overarching term for this volume. Specifically, Van Gosse and Eric Zolov have contended the Revolutionary Left as being part of the much broader and diverse category of a New Left. As Zolov contends, reference to Latin

America's New Left that deals only with *foquismo* and arms is too narrow, ignoring a range of countercultural, social, and generational influences that fed into the idea of New Left.[34] From this point of view, the New Left was a broad and heterogeneous "movement of movements" whose organizations shared a series of essential basic features, but which, at the same time, also maintained a number of differences among them. In this framing, the Revolutionary Left was therefore one of many currents within the New Left. And it is therefore worth underlining that our focus here—as well as in the chapters that follow—is not on this broader, heterogeneous New Left, which undoubtedly had its own global dimensions, but on the specificities of the Revolutionary Left within it.

In a Latin American context, the Revolutionary Left predominantly arose after the triumph of the Cuban Revolution, although it had begun to develop in the late 1950s and was rooted in crises and change at the end of that decade.[35] To a large extent, its emergence was a reaction to the strategy of existing Left or Center-Left parties. Within this context, and a questioning of strategies for effecting decisive change, Cuba's emphasis on the need for revolutionary violence and, in particular, the elevation of guerrilla warfare to the category of main instrument in the struggle for the seizure of state power, coupled with the declaration of the socialist character of the revolution in 1961, strongly contributed to a questioning of left-wing strategies—and particularly those of Latin American Communist Parties—to that point. While Communist Parties had defended the need for collaboration with the progressive sectors of the national bourgeoisie of each country to carry out a democratic revolution that would eliminate "feudal remnants" as the first step toward the future attainment of a socialist revolution, Cuba showed that the immediate objective of the revolution was socialism, and that to achieve it the most important thing was the will of the revolutionaries themselves. At the same time, although most Communist Parties recognized, at least rhetorically, the inevitability of the use of violence as an eventually necessary step for the seizure of state power, they used peaceful strategies of "accumulation of forces" and developed organizing activities—open or clandestine—among workers, students, and peasants, while waiting for "objective conditions" for revolution to develop.

For the most radical sectors of left-wing youth, the Cuban example provoked criticism that the majority of Latin American Communist Parties denied the possibility of revolution by placing it at an indeterminate moment in the future. This was not a reflection of a continuous strategy held since the founding of Communist Parties in the 1920s. To the contrary, the communist movement had undergone significant shifts and turns in its approach to revolution that had included immediate (disastrous) insurrection in the past. However, in the postwar years the adoption of a gradualist strategy for winning influence and power predominated, which was increasingly challenged from the late 1950s onward. A similar reaction to that of some young left-wing groups occurred among the youth of Christian Democratic, or even among leftist nationalist parties, whose reformist agendas appeared to be insufficient or irrelevant when contrasted to the depth of problems—poverty, inequality, "underdevelopment," representation, repression—the region faced and the changes taking place in Cuba after 1959. That Cuba's revolutionary leaders nurtured the organizations of the Revolutionary Left through the dissemination of information, regional conferences, and direct training of militants accelerated the search for alternatives even more so than might otherwise have been the case. In this context, the armed struggle as a strategy for seizing power, as purportedly exemplified by Cuba's example and disseminated by the island at least for the first decade after 1959, was increasingly a characteristic feature of Latin America's Revolutionary Left.

In addition to the significance of Cuba's example when it came to armed struggle, the influence of African or Asian liberation movements was to make anti-imperialism—understood as the rejection of the presence of the United States—one of the main ideological features of the Revolutionary Left. U.S. power was considered to be the guarantor of the interests of the bourgeoisie and the armies of the region. Thus the aspiration of the revolutionaries was to free their societies from U.S. guardianship. This had long been a part of communist parties' ideology. But the Revolutionary Left seized on it more vocally and more urgently than the latter advised, regarding cutting ties with the United States as synonymous with national liberation. Indeed, in keeping with this imaginary of the Revolutionary Left, a number of revolutionary organizations included these two words in their own name. But national liberation also meant the liberation of the exploited people or "*el pueblo*"—identified with the true nation—from the domination of a class or class alliance (bourgeoisie, oligarchies) that they characterized as an exploitative or parasitic class, dependent on imperialists' cultural and economic patterns and interests.

The idea of revolution was another key ideological feature of the New Left's "movement of movements," although there were significant differences around its meaning. On the Revolutionary Left, organizations identified the revolution with the seizure of state power through armed struggle, as the first step toward building a socialist society in the future. Anti-capitalism was also a central feature for the majority of the organizations and movements of this Left, but not necessarily for all of them (the M-19 in Colombia, for example). There were other revolutionary movements that proposed an agenda of radical changes but did not necessarily have among their objectives the construction of socialism; rather, they wanted a more democratic society freed from the dominance of economic elites and American guardianship.

In sum, these tenets—armed struggle, revolution, national liberation, anti-imperialism, and anti-capitalism—made up the defining features of the ideological framework of the Revolutionary Left. These same features allowed it to establish connections with movements, parties, organizations, and radical or revolutionary governments that shared all or part of these same principles, as shown in the breadth of the chapters in this book.

What, then, did this mean when it came to revolutionary praxis and reach? In Latin America, the Cuban triumph, but also the Algerian revolution and the Vietnamese struggle, offered models of organization and repertoires of action for those radical transformation of politics and society. It must be borne in mind that, in the early 1960s, with a few exceptions, most Latin American political regimes were authoritarian and exercised their power over highly unequal and excluding societies. Opportunities for decisive change were thus invariably constrained. Even in democratic countries, frustrations with the pace of change and restrictive patterns of inclusion were growing by the 1950s.

The militants of the Revolutionary Left came from Communist Parties, from groups on the moderate Left, leftist nationalist organizations, or reformist Centrist parties, including those of a Christian Democratic character. Many of them began their militancy in universities that at this time became nodal centers of political socialization, intellectual exchange, and mobilization.[36] There's not space enough here to register all the organizations of the Revolutionary Left in the continent, but we can cite some of the most influential. For example, and because of its pioneering character, we can cite, for instance, the Argentine Movement of the Revolutionary Left-Praxis (MIR-Praxis) led by Silvio Frondizi, a forerunner in the search for a new Marxism far from Soviet orthodoxy, and also the Brazilian Revolutionary Marxist Organization-Workers' Policy (ORM-Polop) of Ruy Mauro Marini and Theotonio dos Santos. Although appearing later, the Chilean Movement of the Revolutionary Left (MIR) is also worth mentioning due to the projection it had throughout the region. In addition to these, throughout the sixties, seventies, and eighties a myriad of leftist armed groups emerged. Here, to name only some of the most relevant, we can mention the Movement of the Revolutionary Left (MIR) in Venezuela, the National Liberation Movement (MLN)-Tupamaros in Uruguay, the Rebel Armed Forces (FAR) in Guatemala, the Movement April-19 (M-19) in Colombia, the People's Revolutionary Army (ERP) in Argentina, the Sandinista National Liberation Front in Nicaragua (FSLN), and the Farabundo Martí National Liberation Front (FMLN) in El Salvador.

Beyond Latin America, the Revolutionary Left had different expressions, but in almost all cases the armed struggle had a much smaller specific weight. Even so, whatever its position on the use of armed struggle in its own territory, the organizations of the European or North American Revolutionary Left lent political and sometimes material support to their comrades in Latin America. As shown, for example, by Arturo Taracena's chapter in this volume, the neo-Trotskyist and French Maoist organizations lent solidarity to the Latin American revolutionaries for years. By contrast, collaboration with armed groups of the European Left was not desirable or truly important for Latin American revolutionaries.

When it comes to chronology, the energy of the Revolutionary Left in the Southern Cone was exhausted to a large extent by the mid-seventies. Overall, Latin American revolutionary movements of the 1960s were systematically defeated by the armed forces of their respective countries. Then, in the mid-seventies, the military dictatorships of Brazil and other Southern Cone countries liquidated some of the most important surviving organizations. At the end of the seventies, throughout the eighties, and in the early nineties, only Central America, Peru, and Colombia were important foci of Revolutionary Left activity. And this activity was encouraged largely by the Sandinista's revolutionary triumph in Nicaragua in July 1979, which had enormous pull and prestige across the world, and left-wing spectrums, as discussed in José Manuel Ágreda Portero's chapter. However, for the most part, the cultural energy, the seductive capacity that its political project had, had been lost in the long 1960s.

Indeed, by the mid-1970s in South America and the late 1980s in Central America, the Revolutionary Left was in retreat—under siege and defeated by a powerful coalition of interests and forces ranged against it. Those bent on defeating it sought to undo many of the transnational and international links forged by the Revolutionary Left in preceding years, destroying the global maps and imaginaries that its members had forged in the process. In their place came a realignment to the United States, a neoliberal model of globalization, and triumph—at least for the immediate decades after the collapse of the Soviet Union and Central American peace processes—of a particular form of democracy that excluded the Revolutionary Left of previous decades and emphasized stability, compromise, and moderation over change.

Contributions and Future Directions

What, then, does a global perspective—or at least the beginnings of one— offer by means of understanding Latin America's Revolutionary Left? As the chapters in this volume demonstrate, expanding our horizons beyond the Americas has the potential to explain what happened within the region as well as why and with what consequences. This does not mean substituting local knowledge and expertise for outside frameworks and logics, but instead following the concrete historical tracks that lead us to understand how Latin America's Revolutionary Left conceptualized the world around them, how they operated, with what purpose, and effect. It also raises a number of significant avenues for further research when it comes to understanding the global Revolutionary Left as a whole, including a call for examining what Latin America's particular experience might teach us about other regions by way of contrast and raising questions. Van Gosse's reflective Afterword on the comparisons between Latin America and the United States is an example of how this can work well. Rather than the all-too-familiar global histories of Latin America that use the region to explain U.S. power, it turns the relationship on its head to look at what Latin American global perspectives can tell us about the comparative fragility and isolation of U.S. left-wing movements. This in turn raises questions about how we conceptualize and contextualize the power, breadth, and scope of Latin American revolutionary networks.

Moving to the volume as a whole, the first set of contributions the chapters make unsurprisingly relate to Cuba. It is hard to conceive of Cuba not being a central focus of any study of the Revolutionary Left, Latin American or otherwise. Not only did it propagate a new model of revolutionary development, but its leaders also explicitly called on others to follow its example, building networks across the globe to fight what they considered to be a worldwide revolutionary struggle. In this respect, Cuba was quite simply a game changer, a fulcrum of history, and a reference point, as well as a topic of sharp disagreement. It is therefore where many of our contributors focus their analysis. And yet, collectively, the chapters in this volume show that

Cuba could not have had the pivotal influence it did alone. Eduardo Rey's chapter on radical European publishing houses reveals the significance of interlocutors outside Cuba who helped disseminate the Revolution's ideas and how these intersected with an existing revolutionary context derived from other events beyond the Americas, first and foremost Algeria's struggle for independence. Michal Zourek's examination of Czechoslovak intelligence sources meanwhile underlines the significance of Prague in facilitating Cuba's revolutionary ventures in Latin America, albeit noting the tensions that existed in such a relationship and confirming Cuba's autonomy—resented and maligned by its Soviet bloc counterparts—in determining its foreign policy.

Nor was there anything automatic or predetermined about Cuba's outreach. As Blanca Mar León's chapter on the organization of the Trincontinental conference shows, the Cuban revolutionary regime's conscious efforts to re-map the world, and more specifically Latin America's place within the Third World, were far from straightforward. At a moment when the logic of world governance was being challenged by Third Worldist groupings, Cuban representatives fought persistently to have a seat at the table and assert leadership from such a position. As León reveals, there are a number of instances when, had it not been for such Cuban insistence, the global character of the Revolutionary Left—with Latin America influenced by and influencing other regions—would have been different. In sum, if the Tricontinental became emblematic of Latin America's driving influence over a global Revolutionary Left, it is now clear this resulted as much from contingency and perseverance in the face of resistance as from an automatic recognition of Havana's place as a capital of worldwide revolution.

From the perspective of Latin America and the socialist world, rather than Third World groupings, Cuba's legitimacy and leadership were far more obvious early on. As James Hershberg shows in his chapter, on competing Brazilian revolutionary groups and strategies, Fidel Castro's approval was considered immensely important to leaders of competing left-wing factions. He also shows the local power derived from association with Cuba and from championing Cuba's cause through his examination of competing plans to host a Cuba solidarity congress. To date, we know considerably more about Cuban foreign policy and revolutionary goals than about how these were received.[37] Hershberg's chapter thus adds to a growing interest in evaluating Cuba's reach and significance outside the island.[38]

In both respects—that of Cuba's diplomatic forays into Third World politics and revolutionary groups' search for Castro's support—a striking feature of Blanca Mar Leon's and Hershberg's chapters is the insight they shed on character of interactions. Although we tend to think of Cuba's revolutionary regime as epitomizing a new style of politics and state building, with its young, bearded leaders as the very antithesis of establishment figures and global statesmen, the reality was that institutional diplomacy, protocol, and state tools of recognition were at least partly central to the way in which Cuba's leaders conducted themselves, built alliances, and established their positions as authorities of the global Revolutionary Left.

A second contribution of this volume is to help scholars better understand the circuits, global maps, and imaginaries that underpinned the Revolutionary Left. This is not simply a function of the journeys that its constituent members made or the logistical support networks that they established, although both of these aspects are important. As the chapters by Gerardo Leibner and Eduardo Rey demonstrate, lived experience, formative influences, and affective ties also shaped individuals' conduct and interactions. When it comes to mapping the global contours of Latin America's Revolutionary Left, as part II of this volume shows, Western Europe was meanwhile conceived as a pivotal source of support and dissemination of ideas.[39] Arturo Taracena's testimony of Guatemalan revolutionary groups' strategies for mobilizing solidarity and awareness serves as a key source—as well as a historical account—on the agency and ideas driving Latin American Revolutionary Left groups' global agendas. On the other side of the story, José Manuel Ágreda and Eduardo Rey offer a European perspective to show how crucial ideas coming from Latin America, and interactions with the region, were to forging European revolutionary left-wing identities and ideas within a domestic and international context far from the Americas.

This latter point is an important corrective regarding our understanding of the direction ideas and influence traveled, speaking to Marchesi's concerns with existing global history cited above. Back in the 1990s, Forest Colburn wrote of a "Vogue of Revolution in Poor Countries," shaped by strikingly similar repertoires, programs, and revolutionary *mentalité.* Significantly, he posited this revolutionary zeal came not so much from the Soviet bloc, but from former imperial capitals in Europe. The direction of travel of such ideas, in other words, spanned outward from these metropoles to Africa, Asia, and Latin America.[40] While much of his argument, based on examining the trajectories and experiences of revolutionary leaders, remains persuasive, it is now abundantly clear that ideas also traveled in opposite directions, blending and interacting with those they encountered and overlaying each other. Latin America's revolutionary developments were key in this regard, providing the basis for a new corpus of ideas and strategies. Visitors from Asia and Africa—or indeed from other parts of Latin America—to Europe may have joined the revolutionary bandwagon while in Europe, but the shared *mentalité* that underpinned the Vogue of Revolution was at least in part comprised of influences from outside Europe.[41]

Third, chapters in this volume collectively underline the division and disjuncture that accompanied—or directly resulted from—connectivity, interaction, and exchange. In this respect, the global story of the Revolutionary Left shares common ground with other global histories, which have unearthed "fractures" as much as "seamless and coherent convergence." As Drayton and Motadel have argued, "Studying interruptions and connections are not mutually exclusive."[42] If a first wave of histories on South–South connections romanticized them as proving challenges to the dominant world order (and historical depictions of it) existed, new research has begun questioning what such processes amounted to, why, and with what consequences. "Seeing the connection may be the easy part," Jeremy Adelman cautions. "It is just the start. But for too many global historians it is taken as the end in itself, as if it were self-evident how crossing boundaries worked to produce something different, as if . . . connecting meant fusing and integrating . . . [But] connection might lead to detachment, aversion, withdrawal, exist from entanglement."[43]

Certainly, as subsequent chapters show, tensions and problems, derived at least in part from the comparisons and competition that accompanied connectivity, caused considerable problems for Latin America's Revolutionary Left. When it came to devising revolutionary strategies or countering opposition, mobilizing support, or analysing contemporary politics and society, sectarianism and difference proved alluring ways to demonstrate revolutionary credentials. Very often, as we see in the case of all chapters in this volume, left-wing factions expended energy and time confronting each other and trying to assert authority. Arguments revolved around who best understood revolutionary theory and praxis—who held the key to the future—rather than how to work together to resolve common obstacles and withstand mutual enemies on the center and right-wing of the political spectrum.

And yet, as Gerardo Leibner cautions in his chapter on Brazilian guerrilla groups' links with the Italian Communist Party, we need to avoid simplistic assumptions and generalizations about the character of left-wing divisions and blocs. What is striking about his examination of the PCI's relationship with Brazilian guerrilla groups is that beyond doctrinal debates and strategic differences, personalities and affective ties mattered when determining alliances. And in this respect, the way that interactions occurred, through what channels, is important. The role of gatekeepers and individuals in establishing networks and ties was key, as is clear also from Taracena's recollections of Guatemalan revolutionary organizing in Europe. Michal's Zourek's chapter meanwhile shows that for all the tensions that existed between the Soviet bloc and Cuba with regards to revolutionary strategy, it is simply ahistorical to suggest the former did not support the Revolutionary Left.

*   *   *

Much remains to be done as we move toward a global history of Latin America's Revolutionary Left. As Sebastian Conrad writes, global history's "core concerns are with mobility and exchange, with processes that transcend borders and boundaries. It takes the interconnected world as its point of departure, and the circulation and exchange of things, people, and institutions are among its key subjects."[44] Given what we know already about the Revolutionary Left's internationalist character and goals, it is imperative that future historians embrace a more global perspective when trying to discern its characteristics, composition, strengths, and weaknesses. Rather than forcing a subject into a global framework where it doesn't fit, the Revolutionary Left is a prime example of where the global should be a point of departure rather than an afterthought in historians' predilection for national frameworks.

So, where now? When it comes to areas ripe for future research, at least two historiographical gaps are worth noting. Surprisingly, very little work has been conducted either on direct links between Vietnam and Latin America or the ideas and influences that traveled between them. Although Soviet bloc archives are rich with materials for research on connections with Latin America, as demonstrated by Zourek's and Hershberg's chapters, much remains to learn about these ties.[45] The reason these connections are important is that we already know they played a concrete role in determining the shape and character of Latin America's Revolutionary Left, and vice versa. Cuba and Vietnam were central to a global Revolutionary Left, but we know remarkably little about how revolutionary projects in both countries intersected with each other. There are obviously other historiographical gaps, most notably related to Africa and the Middle East, where more work has been conducted but further research is needed.[46] To be sure, global history does not require planetary coverage and should never be a quest to cover all corners of the globe purely for the sake of it. With this volume we do not purport to offer a picture of an already fully defined map, but rather to move toward a more globalized picture of the Revolutionary Left's geographical reach and significance. In other respects, a broader global history will also probe the different types of connectivity that existed: the flow of ideas, the flow of money and resources, the example of praxis, the circulation of imagery, and the physical movement of people and the experiences these travels engendered.

The challenges of regional and linguistic expertise mean we are impelled to pursue such a path collaboratively and comparatively. In doing so, we must also question how different cases connect to each other and what they tell us more broadly about the Revolutionary Left project as a whole in the mid-to-late twentieth century. As Drayton and Motadel contend, "Global history is not a federation of national and area studies history, as important and sovereign as these levels of analysis are. It is the product of engagements with the problem of the global, based on inspired comparative and connective thinking." If we are to move to a global history, looking up from our own specific case studies and reflecting on what they together can elucidate and complicate about Latin America's place in a global moment of revolutionary upheaval is key. We sincerely hope this volume will stimulate further debate, reflection, and research toward this end.

Acknowledgments

Compiling an edited volume bringing together historians working in six different countries has been an exciting collaborative venture. However, it would not have been possible without the generous support and encouragement we have received. First and foremost, we would like to thank the British Academy Newton Mobility Fund for providing the framework that allowed Tanya Harmer and Alberto Martín Álvarez to collaborate on a project to examine Latin America's Revolutionary Left in a global and transnational perspective. It provided the impetus to work on such a project, the means for us to visit each other's institutions, and to hold a series of seminars in London and Mexico City, bringing scholars together from across the world to discuss their findings. In addition, Alberto Martín Álvarez thanks the Instituto Mora in Mexico, where he was based when the project began, for the valuable support it provided for the conception and development of this book. Tanya Harmer is grateful to the Department of International History for its support in running these seminars and its Staff Research Fund for assisting with the costs of translation. In particular, she would like to thank Bastiaan Bouwman, Susana Carvalho, Demetra Frini, and Eline van Ommen. For his translation of Arturo Taracena Arriola's chapter, thanks also to Thomas McFarlane. For her help and advice when it came to selecting the cover image, we would like to thank Patricia Calvo.

We extend our sincere gratitude to Stephanye Hunter at the University of Florida Press for believing in the project and for her enduring patience and support while we pulled the volume together. We thank John Wentworth for his careful copyediting. We are all also enormously grateful to the two reviewers of this book, Aldo Marchesi and Jessica Stites Mor. Their incisive comments, expertise, and suggestions helped us all improve its contents.

In addition to these acknowledgments, José Manuel Ágreda Portero wants to express his gratitude to members of the Histamérica research group, especially Eduardo Rey Tristán, for their support. James Hershbreg thanks Sergey Radchenko (Cardiff University) for providing and translating Chinese documents, and also thanks Gianfranco Caterina, Paulo R. Almeida, Felipe Loureiro, Milorad Lazic, Renata Keller, Jonathan C. Brown, Luiz Alberto Moniz Bandeira, Joseph A. Page, Balazs Szalontai, Malcolm Byrne, Elidor Mëhilli, and Oldřich Tůma. Blanca Mar León would like to acknowledge Jeremy Friedman and Alexis Anagnan for their enormous generosity in sharing archival documents and the results of their research. She dedicates her chapter to Cuban researchers, experts for Asian and African affairs, Luis Mesa Delmonte (recently deceased) and Domingo Amuchástegui Alvarez, her teachers and accomplices in the study of the influences of the Cuban Revolution in the Third World. Gerardo Leibner extends a special thanks to the staff at the Archivio Fondazione Gramsci (AFG) in Rome. Michal Zourek wishes to acknowledge support from the Internal Grant Agency of the Faculty of Regional Development and International Studies of Mendel University under Grant FRRMS_IGA_2019/007.

Notes

1. Fidel Castro, "The Second Declaration of Havana," 4 February 1962, online at www.walterlippmann.com/fc-02-04-1962.pdf

2. Gleijeses, *Conflicting Missions*; *Visions of Freedom*; Hatzky, "Cuba's Concept of 'Internationalist Solidarity.'"

3. Marchesi, "Southern Cone Cities," 66–67.

4. Brown, "Global History of Latin America," 365, 367. On Latin America's marginalization in global history, see also, Thornton, "A Mexican International Economic Order?" 391–393.

5. Brown, "Global History of Latin America," 365, 373, 374.

6. Marchesi, "Escribiendo la Guerra Fría," 189; Drayton and Motadel, "Discussion," 8, 15.

7. Brown, "Global History of Latin America," 368–369.

8. Drayton and Motadel, "Discussion," 8.

9. Westad, *Global Cold War*.

10. Thornton "Mexican International Economic Order?" 393.

11. Marchesi, "Escribiendo la Guerra Fría," 197–198.

12. Marchesi, "The May '68 That Was Not May '68."

13. Marchesi, "Escribiendo la Guerra Fría," 193, 196–197.

14. Thornton, "Mexican International Economic Order?" 391.

15. For the most recent and significant contribution to global perspectives of Latin America during the Cold War, see Field, Krepp, and Pettina, *Latin America and the Global Cold War*.

16. See, for example, LASA's 2018 conference in Barcelona titled "Latin American Studies in a Globalized World" and AHILA's 2014 conference in Berlin titled "Entre Espacios: La historia latinoamericana en el contexto global"; Brown, "Global History of Latin America," 372.

17. Moreli, "Life (and death?) of Global History," 13–14.

18. Drayton and Motadel, "Discussion," 3; Conrad, *What Is Global History?*

19. See, for example, Connelly, *Fatal Misconception*; Latham, *Right Kind of Revolution*; Thornton, "Mexican International Economic Order?"

20. Burke, *Revolutionaries for the Right*.

21. Gleijeses, *Conflicting Missions*; Gleijeses, *Visions of Freedom*.

22. See, for example, Rojas and Santoni, "Geografía Política del Exilio Chileno."

23. Stites Mor, "The Question of Palestine," 189.

24. Marchesi, "Escribiendo la Guerra Fría," 195.

25. Krepp, "Brazil, Non-Alignment, and the Struggle for the Region's Role in the Global Order"; Patti, "Origins of the Brazilian Nuclear Programme"; Pettinà, "Global Horizons."

26. Oikión, Rey, Ávalos, *El estudio de las luchas revolucionarias en América Latina (1959–1996): Estado de la cuestión*. For recent studies of transnational ties on the Revolutionary Left within the Americas, see Cortina, "Internacionalismo y Revolución Sandinista"; Reyes, "La cultura de la revolución en los Andes."

27. Among the Revolutionary Left movements studied most widely are those that existed in Cuba, Chile, Argentina, Uruguay, Nicaragua, and El Salvador. Among the revolutionary movements that require more attention are those that existed in Venezuela, the Dominican Republic, Honduras, and Paraguay. For a detailed examination of an internationalist guerrilla movement in a national, international, and transnational context, see, for example, Rodriguéz Ostria, *Teoponte*.

28. See, for example, Gott, *Guerrilla Movements in Latin America*; Castro, *Revolution and Revolutionaries.*

29. See, for example, Kruijt, *Guerrillas. War and Peace in Central America*; Marchesi, *Latin America's Radical Left.*

30. See, for instance, Kruijt, Rey, and Martín Álvarez, *Latin American Guerrilla Movements: Origins, Evolution, Outcomes*; Wickham-Crowley, *Guerrillas and Revolution in Latin America: A Comparative Study of Insurgents and Regimes since 1956*; Castañeda, *Utopia Unarmed*; Young, *Making the Revolution.*

31. Suárez Salazar and Kruijt, *La Revolución Cubana en Nuestra América*; Kruijt, *Cuba and Revolutionary Latin America*; Brown, *Cuba's Revolutionary World*; Suárez Salazar (ed.) *Manuel Piñeiro*; Suárez Salazar, "The Cuban Revolution and the New Latin American Leadership."

32. Recent contributions to global histories of Latin American revolutionary movements have tended to focus predominantly on solidarity movements. See, for example, Christiaens, "Between Diplomacy and Solidarity"; Helm, "Booming Solidarity" and *Naveg@merica*'s 2016 special issue on solidarity with Central America in the 1970s and 1980s, including Blecha, "¡Vietnam en América Latina!"; Camacho Padilla and Ramírez Palacio, "Las imágenes de las guerrillas centroamericanas en las redes de la solidaridad internacional de Suecia" and Van Ommen, "La Revolución Sandinista en los Países Bajos."

33. Markarian, *Uruguay, 1968*, 77.

34. Gosse, *Rethinking the New* Left; Zolov, "Expanding Our Conceptual Horizons"

35. On the chronological framing of the "long sixties," see, for example, Casals, *El alba de una revolución*; Manzano, *The Age of Youth*; Pensado, *Rebel Mexico*; Salgado, "Making Friends."

36. See, for example, Purcell and Casals, "Espacios en disputa."

37. Brown, *Cuba's Revolutionary World*; Kruijt, *Cuba and Revolutionary Latin America.*

38. See, for example, Gronbeck-Tedesco, "The Left in Transition"; Marchesi, *Latin America's Radical Left.*

39. On West Europe's significance, see also Van Ommen, "Sandinistas Go Global."

40. See, for example, Colburn, *Vogue of Revolution*

41. On this point, see also Marchesi, "The May '68 That Was Not May '68" and Eugenia Palieraki, "Revolutions Entangled: Chile, Algeria, and the Third World." Palieraki argues Algeria revolutionaries learnt much about the concept of a Second (economic) Independence from direct travels to Latin America.

42. Drayton and Motadel, "Discussion," 9–10.

43. Jeremy Adelman in Drayton and Motadel, "Discussion," 20.

44. Conrad, *What Is Global History?*, 5.

45. Existing work drawing on Soviet bloc archives when it comes to Latin America, includes Ulianova, "La Unidad Popular y el golpe militar"; Storkmann, "East German Military Aid to the Sandinista Government"; Pettinà, "Mexican-Soviet relations, 1958–1964"; Zourek, *Checoslovaquia y el Cono Sur.*

46. For some of the newest research on Latin America's ties with Africa and Asia, see Field, Krepp, and Pettinà, *Latin America and the Global Cold War.*

Bibliography

Blecha, Laurin. "¡Vietnam en América Latina!" *Naveg@mérica. Revista electrónica editada por la Asociación Española de Americanistas* 17 (2016).

Brown, Jonathan C. *Cuba's Revolutionary World*. Cambridge, MA: Harvard University Press, 2017.

Brown, Matthew. "The Global History of Latin America." *Journal of Global History* 10, no. 3 (2015): 265–386.

Burke, Kyle. *Revolutionaries for the Right: Anticommunist Internationalism and Paramilitary Warfare in the Cold War*. Chapel Hill: University of North Carolina Press, 2018.

Camacho Padilla, Fernando, and Laura Ramírez Palacio. "Las imágenes de las guerrillas centroamericanas en las redes de la solidaridad internacional de Suecia." *Naveg@mérica. Revista electrónica editada por la Asociación Española de Americanistas* 17 (2016).

Casals Araya, Marcelo. *El alba de una revolución. La izquierda y el proceso de construcción estratégica de la vía chilena al socialism, 1956–1970*. Santiago: LOM, 2010.

Castañeda, Jorge. *Utopia Unarmed: The Latin American Left after the Cold War*. New York: Knopf, 1993.

Castro, Daniel, ed. *Revolution and Revolutionaries: Guerrilla Movements in Latin America*. Oxford: SR Books, 1999.

Christiaens, Kim. "Between Diplomacy and Solidarity: Western European Support Networks for Sandinista Nicaragua." *European Review of History: Revue Européenne d'histoire* 21, no. 4 (2014).

Colburn, Forest. *The Vogue of Revolution in Poor Countries*. Princeton, NJ: Princeton University Press, 1996.

Connelly, Matthew. *Fatal Misconception: The Struggle to Control World Population*. Cambridge, MA: Belknap Press, 2008.

Conrad, Sebastian. *What Is Global History?* Princeton, NJ: Princeton University Press, 2017.

Cortina, Orero, Eudald. "Internacionalismo y Revolución Sandinista: proyecciones militantes y reformulaciones orgánicas en la izquierda revolucionaria argentina." *E.I.A.L.* 28, no. 2 (2017): 80–103.

Drayton, Richard and David Motadel. "Discussion: the Futures of Global History." *Journal of Global History* 13, no. 1 (2018):1–21.

Field Jr., Thomas, Krepp, Stella, and Vanni Pettinà eds. *Latin America and the Global Cold War*. Chapel Hill: University of North Carolina Press, 2020.

Gleijeses, Piero. *Conflicting Missions: Havana, Washington, and Africa, 1959–1976*. Chapel Hill: University of North Carolina Press, 2002.

———. *Visions of Freedom. Havana, Washington, Pretoria and the Struggle for Southern Africa, 1976–1991*. Chapel Hill: University of North Carolina Press, 2013.

Gosse, Van. *Rethinking the New Left. An Interpretative History*. New York: Palgrave Macmillan, 2005.

Gott, Richard. *Guerrilla Movements in Latin America*. London: Nelson, 1970.

Gronbeck-Tedesco, John A. "The Left in Transition: The Cuban Revolution in US Third World Politics." *Journal of Latin American Studies* 40, no. 4 (2008): 651–673.

Hatzky, Christine. "Cuba's Concept of 'Internationalist Solidarity': Political Discourse, South-South Cooperation with Angola and the Molding of Transnational Identities." In *Human Rights and Transnational Solidarity*, edited by Jessica Stites Mor. Madison: University of Wisconsin Press, 2013.

Helm, Christian. "Booming Solidarity: Sandinista Nicaragua and the West German Solidarity Movement in the 1980s." *European Review of History: Revue Européenne d'histoire* 21, no. 4 (2014)

Krepp, Stella. "Brazil, Non-Alignment, and the Struggle for the Region's Role in the Global Order, 1961–1964." Paper presented at LASA, Barcelona, 2018.

Kruijt, Dirk. *Cuba and Revolutionary Latin America: An Oral History*. London: Zed Books, 2017.

———. *Guerrillas: War and Peace in Central America*. London: Zed Books, 2008.

Kruijt, Dirk, Eduardo Rey Tristán, and Alberto Martín Álvarez, eds., *Latin American Guerrilla Movements: Origins, Evolution, Outcomes*. New York: Routledge, 2020.

Latham, Michael E. *The Right Kind of Revolution: Modernization, Development, and U.S. Foreign Policy from the Cold War to the Present*. Ithaca, NY: Cornell University Press (2011)

Manzano, Valeria. *The Age of Youth in Argentina: Culture, Politics, and Sexuality from Perón to Videla*. Chapel Hill: University of North Carolina Press, 2014.

Marchesi, Aldo. "Escribiendo la Guerra Fría latinoamericana: entre el Sur 'local' y el Norte 'global.'" *Estudos Históricos* 30, no. 60 (2017): 187–202.

———. *Latin America's Radical Left: Rebellion and the Cold War in the Global 1960s*. New York: Cambridge University Press, 2018.

———. "Southern Cone Cities as Political Laboratories of the Global Sixties: Montevideo (1962–1968); Santiago de Chile (1969–1973); Buenos Aires (1973–1976)." *E.I.A.L.* 27, no. 2 (2018): 54–79.

———. "The May '68 That Was Not May '68: Latin America in the Global Sixties." Verso Blog, 24 May 2018: www.versobooks.com/blogs/3846-the-may-68-that-was-not-may-68-latin-america-in-the-global-sixties

Markarian, Vania. *Uruguay, 1968: Student Activism from Global Counterculture to Molotov Cocktails*. Oakland, University of California Press, 2017.

Moreli, Alexandre. "Life (and Death?) of Global History." *Estudos Históricos* 30, no. 60 (2017): 11–16.

Oikión, Veronica, Eduardo Rey Tristán and Martin López Ávalos. *El estudio de las luchas revolucionarias en América Latina (1959–1996): Estado de la cuestión*. Santiago de Compostela: Universidad de Santiago de Compostela. Servicio de Publicaciones e Intercambio Científico, 2014.

Palieraki, Eugenia. "Revolutions Entangled: Chile, Algeria, and the Third World in the 1960s and 1970s" in *Latin America and the Global Cold War*, edited by Thomas Field Jr., Stella Krepp, and Vanni Pettinà (Chapel Hill: University of North Carolina Press, 2020): 274–300.

Patti, Carlo. "The Origins of the Brazilian Nuclear Programme, 1951–1955." *Cold War History* 15, no. 3 (2015): 353–373.

Pensado, Jaime M. *Rebel Mexico: Student Unrest and Authoritarian Political Culture during the Long Sixties*. Stanford, CA: Stanford University Press, 2013.

Pettinà, Vanni. "Global Horizons: Mexico, the Third World, and the Non-Aligned Movement at the Time of the 1961 Belgrade Conference." *The International History Review* 38, no. 4 (2016): 741–764.

———. "Mexican-Soviet relations, 1958–1964: The Limits of Engagement." Cold War International History Project E-Dossier 65: www.wilsoncenter.org/publication/mexican-soviet-relations-1958–1964-the-limits-engagement

Purcell, Fernando, and Marcelo Casals. "Espacios en disputa: El Cuerpo de Paz y las universidades sudamericanas durante la Guerra Fría en la década de 1960." *História Unisinos* 19, no. 1 (2015): 1–11.

Reyes, Miguel Angel. "La cultura de la revolución en los Andes: aproximación a las relaciones transnacionales entre el M-19 y AVC en la década de 1980" *E.I.A.L.* 28, no. 2 (2017): 104–128.

Rodriguéz Ostria, Gustavo. *Sin tiempo para las palabras: Teoponte, la otra guerrilla guevarista en Bolivia*. Cochabamba: Grupo Editorial Kipus, 2006.

Rojas Mira, Claudia, and Alessandro Santoni. "Geografía política del exilio chileno: los diferentes rostros de la solidaridad." *Perfiles latinoamericanos* 21, no. 41 (2013): 123–142.

Salgado, Alfonso. "Making Friends and Making Out: The Social and Romantic Lives of Young Communists in Chile (1958–1973)." *The Americas* 76, no. 2 (2019): 299–326.

Stites Mor, Jessica. "The Question of Palestine in the Argentine Political Imaginary: Anti-Imperialist Thought from the Cold War to Neoliberal Order. *Journal of Iberian and Latin American Research* 20, no. 2: 183–197.

Storkmann, Klaus. "East German Military Aid to the Sandinista Government of Nicaragua, 1979–1990." *Journal of Cold War Studies* 16, no. 2 (1 April 2014): 56–76

Suárez Salazar, Luis and Kruijt, Dirk, eds. *La Revolución Cubana en Nuestra América: El internacionalismo anónimo*. Havana: Ruth Casa Editoria, 2015.

Suárez Salazar, Luis. *Manuel Piñeiro: Che Guevara and the Latin American Revolutionary Movements*. Melbourne: Ocean Press, 2001.

———. "The Cuban Revolution and the New Latin American Leadership: A View from Its Utopias," *Latin American Perspectives* 36, no. 114 (2009): 114–127.

Thornton, Christy. "A Mexican International Economic Order? Tracing the Hidden Roots of the Charter of Economic Rights and Duties of States." *Humanity* 9, no. 3 (2018): 389–421.

Ulianova, Olga. "La Unidad Popular y el golpe militar en Chile: Percepciones y análisis soviéticos." *Estudios Públicos* 79 (2000): 83–171.

Van Ommen, Eline. "La Revolución Sandinista en los Países Bajos," *Naveg@mérica. Revista electrónica editada por la Asociación Española de Americanistas* 17 (2016).

———. "Sandinistas Go Global: Nicaragua and Western Europe, 1977–1990." PhD Dissertation, London School of Economics and Political Science, 2019.

Westad, Odd Arne. *The Global Cold War: Third World Interventions and the Making of Our Times*. Cambridge/New York: Cambridge University Press, 2005.

Wickham-Crowley, Timothy P. *Guerrillas and Revolution in Latin America: A Comparative Study of Insurgents and Regimes since 1956*. Princeton, NJ: Princeton University Press.

Young, Kevin, ed. *Making the Revolution: Histories of the Latin American Left*. Cambridge: Cambridge University Press, 2019.

Zolov, Eric. "Expanding Our Conceptual Horizons: The Shift from an Old to a New Left in Latin America." *A Contracorriente* 5, no. 2 (2008): 47–73.

Zourek, Michal. *Checoslovaquia y el Cono Sur 1945–1989. Relaciones políticas, económicas y culturales durante la Guerra Fría*. Prague: Karolinum 2014.

PART I

Latin America's Revolutionary Left in the Age of the Tricontinental

1

Czechoslovakia and Latin America's Guerrilla Insurgencies

Secret Services, Training Networks, Mobility, and Transportation

MICHAL ZOUREK

Throughout the 1960s, Latin America's Revolutionary Left was heavily dependent on financial and logistical assistance from abroad, particularly from Cuba. However, the efforts made by Castro's regime to promote its revolutionary model and support local left-wing movements were significantly disrupted by the island's diplomatic isolation, which accelerated after 1961. First, the United States and subsequently several other Latin American states canceled diplomatic relations with the Cuban government, the climax being in January 1962 when Cuba was expelled from the Organization of American States (OAS). In October of the same year, as a consequence of the missile crisis, logistical isolation also deepened. Cuba faced a blockade, and air links with the island were heavily restricted.

Immediately after this crisis, cooperation between Cuba and the Soviet Bloc also deteriorated. As a result, Cuba's revolutionary government decided to seek support further afield, in particular from Mao Zedong's China. However, Cuba remained dependent on the assistance from Eastern European countries in many ways, including the help that it received to support Latin America's guerrilla insurgencies. After the missile crisis, for example, one of the few ways of leaving Cuba was via air link to Prague. And, by the end of 1962, this link had become the basis for an intensive logistical cooperation between the Czechoslovak and Cuban secret services that would have extraordinary regional and global significance.

After the establishment of Cuba's revolutionary government, Moscow's leaders had seen the island as unpredictable, with few Soviet analysts expecting Castro to stay in power for long. Similarly, the Cuban leadership had been extremely cautious about establishing relations with the Eastern Bloc. It feared Washington's reaction, and so proceeded gradually in forging relations with socialist states.[1] Under these circumstances, Czechoslovakia was to play the role of "ice-breaker" for the socialist camp in Cuba.[2] And it was the Cuban side that took the initiative in this regard. Severo Aguirre, representative of Cuba's Popular Socialist Party, proposed this possibility in March 1959 during his visit to Prague, suggesting that Czechoslovakia should send its diplomats to Havana soon, that it should deliver weapons, and that it should also send its experts to help build socialism.[3] This recommendation soon turned to fruition. Czechoslovakia normalized relations with Cuba in June 1959 and from then on became more actively involved on the island, and also with other countries in the region. In May 1960, Czechoslovakia was the first Soviet Bloc country to open an embassy in Havana.[4]

Czechoslovakia was not only one of the most economically developed communist countries, but unlike the other countries of Eastern Europe, it had maintained close relations with Latin America in the interwar period, meaning it had a wide network of embassies and trade with the region. Therefore, in the 1950s and early 1960s, Prague helped other Eastern European countries whose positions in Latin America were not strong enough to open relations.[5] Czechoslovakia also worked actively in other areas of the world. At the end of the 1940s, it provided arms and support to Israel, and in the 1950s it engaged strongly in the Middle East.[6] In this respect, during the 1960s its main focus of attention was Africa.[7]

It was in this context that Czechoslovakia also became the principal mediator of Soviet influence in Cuba. Initially, Czechoslovak products accompanied the export of the Soviet ideology and, later, it became an essential part of the so-called international assistance that the Soviet Bloc provided to Castro's regime. The country also placed a specific role for Cuba in the international field. Indeed, when Washington broke diplomatic relations with Havana in January 1961, it was Prague that served as the representative and advocate of Cuba's interests in the United States.[8] Czechoslovakia would later play a similar role in other Latin American countries.

Meanwhile, the Soviet leadership gradually began to recognize Cuba's remarkable geopolitical value. As early as September 1960, Khrushchev expressed the hope that Cuba would become a beacon for socialism in Latin

America. Extraordinary enthusiasm triggered by Castro´s regime was to be used to support the Soviet Bloc penetrate and permeate further into Latin America. Despite numerous political conflicts, the Soviet Union did not want to lose its position of influence on the island. In order to facilitate this, and within the context of the Cuban leadership's anger at the resolution of the missile crisis, the Soviets subsequently provided many concessions.[9]

One of those concessions was logistical support for its revolutionary ventures abroad, with Czechoslovakia being the key player in this endeavor. Henceforth, Prague became a location of numerous secret operations in the following years, a paradise for spies and secret services. In the 1960s, thousands of Latin Americans traveled between Prague and Cuba by air, with many of them engaging in anti-government armed struggles in the region after returning to their home countries. Certainly, more than a thousand were dispatched to Latin America with the help of Czechoslovakia's secret service, which also "removed" the trace of their stay in Cuba from their records. Beyond this, Operation Manuel—as this highly secret operation was named—also provided cover for revolutionaries in Czechoslovakia while they awaited instructions from Latin America.

* * *

This chapter is devoted to an analysis of this Czechoslovak logistical support. It draws on documents from the Czech Security Services Archives (*Archiv bezpečnostních složek*), based at the Institute for the Study of Totalitarian Regimes (*Ústav pro studium totalitních režimů*) in Prague.[10] In recent years, these archives have been digitalized, which has provided access to a vast number of materials on Czechoslovak secret service activity in Latin America, including reports on the monitoring of enemy embassies or persons of interest. The relative inaccessibility of Russian and Cuban intelligence archives makes these documents all the more unique as a source of information for beginning to reconstruct and understand the global history of Latin America's Revolutionary Left, as well as the way that its members traveled and communicated with each other.

In terms of Operation Manuel, Volume 80723 in the Czech Security Services Archives is of key importance. The volume contains operational correspondence on the cooperation with the Cuban intelligence service for the period 1962 to 1970. Thousands of pages relate to reports submitted to the Cubans by the Prague headquarters, and vice versa from the Cuban side, information on the state of what were known at as "national liberation movements" in Latin America, and the progress of the Cuban Revolution.

Several researchers have already provided insights into the issue of the transfer of Latin American nationals from Cuba through Prague. The first historian to write about the existence of Operation Manuel was Prokop Tomek.[11] Daniela Spenser then brought the issue to the attention of an international audience.[12] She is also credited with making several documents relating to the operation accessible in English through her participation in the Cold War International History Project.[13] These published documents, from the National Archives (*Národní archiv*) in Prague, reflect the viewpoints of the highest authorities at that time, namely the Czechoslovak Communist Party and the Czechoslovak Ministry of the Interior.

The Argentinian historian Juan Yofre also presented some aspects of the cooperation between the Czechoslovak and Cuban secret services to Latin American audiences in 2014.[14] Yofre's book, which is based on an impressive number of documents, including those from Czech archives, met with great acclaim. However, as a former head of the Secretariat of Intelligence (SIDE), his work was not impartial. His interpretation had the clear goal of exposing Soviet intervention in Latin America as a one-way and sinister operation. The strong anti-Castro discourse is reflected in the author's statement that he obtained the Czechoslovak archival documents from Cuban exile representatives.[15]

Contrary to Yofre's account, Operation Manuel reveals the very complex dynamics of relations between the Soviet Bloc and Cuba. Often, it was a relationship of mistrust, with the main bond between them being the struggle against a common enemy symbolized by the United States. The remarkable story of Operation Manuel, which lasted for more than seven years (1962–1970), also relativizes the thesis that the Soviet Bloc did not provide support for armed revolution. However, as this chapter suggests, the circumstances of its support were complicated. The main focus of the study is on the Czechoslovak's approach to logistical assistance for Cuba and how this approach gradually evolved. It also addresses questions regarding the extent to which the Czechoslovak leadership was able to take an autonomous position on the whole issue, questions about the importance they attached to Operation Manuel, and whether they were aware of its implications.

At the same time, the study focuses on what extra-regional interactions can tell us about Cuban revolutionary policy toward Latin America and the region's Revolutionary Left overall. The data contained in archival documents, such as the real names of the people who passed through Prague from Cuba, their nationality, date of arrival and departure, the place where they were accommodated, as well as the routes the "Manuelistas" used when returning to their home countries, allow us to move on to some more general conclusions about Latin America's Revolutionary Left, its priorities, strengths, and limitations. Based on the sample of more than a thousand people, for whom data exists, for example, we gain insight into Cuba's revolutionary priorities and their evolution over time. Building on previous studies of Latin America's left-wing in the 1960s, we also gain insight into the changing political orientation of those who collaborated with Cuba during this decade. In this regard, Czechoslovak archival sources are of utmost importance for our understanding of the global and transnational dynamics of Latin America's Revolutionary Left.

Czechoslovakia and the Cuban Revolution: The Early Years and the Initiation of Cooperation between the Secret Services

In the early 1960s, prior to Operation Manuel, the Czechoslovakian government provided Castro with considerable help. It supplied large industrial works and weapons (albeit largely obsolete), welcomed Cubans to join training programs, and sent its own experts to the island. In the years 1960–1961, it also secretly printed new banknotes and minted new coins and transported them by sea to Cuba.[16] Czechoslovakia was also heavily involved in setting up the Cuban-led Prensa Latina press agency. The Czechoslovak News Agency (ČTK) became the pillar of international political news disseminated throughout Latin America.[17] Given the strategic importance of the island, Prague maintained a "highly political approach" at the economic level. The needs of the Czechoslovak economy were not taken into consideration. For example, the main import from Cuba was sugar, although Czechoslovakia was one of the world's largest exporters of beet sugar. The trade balance was considerably unbalanced, and the Cuban debt to Czechoslovakia grew.

Another pillar of this assistance was intelligence cooperation. In May 1960, a Czechoslovak secret service station (*rezidentura*) was opened in Havana at the same time as the embassy.[18] In the 1950s, Czechoslovakia had already opened several secret service stations on the American continent: in New York, Washington, Montreal, Ottawa, Buenos Aires, Rio de Janeiro, and Mexico. Havana soon became not only the center of the Czechoslovak secret service's operations in Latin America, but, as a report underlined, also "one of the most politically important Czechoslovak stations and one of the most complex ones in terms of working tasks" in the world.[19]

Following Havana, other intelligence posts soon followed. In 1961, for example, a station was established in Montevideo, with subsequent ones being established in La Paz, Bogotá, Caracas, and Santiago a year later. Their main priority was to monitor and disrupt U.S. activities by means of disinformation and confrontational actions. However, the Latin American stations also focused on "consolidating and defending the Cuban Revolution and organizing a movement to protect the Cuban Revolution in Latin America and other countries using available means."[20]

What had been a relatively autonomous Czechoslovak venture in Cuba did not last long. Moscow had become quickly aware of the strategic importance of the island and the undesirable nature of the excessive convergence of the Czechoslovak and Cuban intelligence services. In July 1961, the KGB therefore limited the Czechoslovak secret service's authority and made it completely subordinate. As a consequence, Czechoslovakian intelligence subsequently had to consult with the Soviets on everything.[21] The division of powers between Soviet and Czechoslovak secret services in relation to Cuba became evident for the first time at the end of 1961, with the role of the latter being practically limited to the island's international relations and, in particular, the receipt of reports from the Czechoslovak stations in Latin America.

In this respect, Czechoslovakia, which invariably had a better political position than the Soviet Union in the region, worked very actively.[22] In January 1964, Manuel Piñeiro, Cuba's chief external intelligence and counter-intelligence body, assessed the level of Czechoslovak reporting as being very high, adding that its information was of better quality than that of the Soviets.[23] The privileged position Czechoslovakia held among the countries of the Socialist Bloc in terms of its relationship with Castro's regime helped it to establish close relations with representatives of the Latin American non-communist Left. Shared common objectives resulted in Czechoslovak Intelligence cooperating with several influential personalities, through whom it financed the publication of books and articles promoting the Cuban Revolution and condemning U.S. activities.[24] However, Czechoslovak agents and collaborators in capitalist countries were not allowed to be recruited from local Communist Parties or the organizations under their direct influence. As mentioned in the Czech archives, this was a task for the KGB.[25]

Initiation of Operation Manuel

Prague's geographical position predetermined its role as the "bridge" between West and East and made it an obvious city to consider when establishing an air link between Cuba and the Eastern Bloc. As the Czechoslovak Ambassador in Havana, Vladimír Pavlíček, reported, it was also clear that the Cubans initiated conversations regarding an air link with Prague. In October 1960, he informed his superiors back in Czechoslovakia that "having to continuously respond to the questions and demands of Fidel, Raúl Castro, and Guevara to establish an air link is embarrassing."[26]

The Havana-Prague air link, the first between Latin America and the socialist camp, was eventually launched in April 1961. Weekly flights along the route, which went via Bermuda and Santa Maria (Azores), were secured by Cubana de Aviación. Flights later increased to twice weekly.[27] The following year, Cubana rented two Bristol Britannia 318 aircraft to Czechoslovak Airlines (CSA). This arrangement was meant to prevent possible complications during over flights and stopovers due to the controversial international position of Cuba. In addition, a once-weekly Prague-to-Havana service via Shannon (Ireland) and Gander (Canada) started in February 1962.[28] Aeroflot's Havana-Moscow service was officially launched as late as January 1963.

After the missile crisis, the regular daily Pan-American Airways and KLM links from Havana were canceled. The connection to Mexico (Mexicana de Aviación), which maintained diplomatic relations with Cuba, remained. At the same time, flights to Madrid (Iberia) were preserved despite U.S. pressure on Spain, as Madrid did not want to lose its connection with its former colony where the large expat community lived.[29] However, people and goods transported on these two lines were under close supervision. At Mexico City airport, on the instructions of the CIA, passports were photographed and copies of passenger lists handed over. There was also a CIA observation post with cameras, microphone monitoring, and car checks in front of the Cuban Embassy in Mexico City.[30]

An allied socialist country represented a much safer option, and the link to Prague thus gained an exceptional position. And in October 1962 the Cuban Ministry of the Interior was already indicating that the Havana-Prague air link could play an important role in the transit of Latin American revolutionaries. As a report of the representatives of Czechoslovak and Cuban intelligence revealed: "It cannot be ruled out that the leaders of the Latin American revolutionary movement will have no direct access to

Cuba due to American actions, and as a result, they will have to choose a detour across Europe. In this case, Prague would be a key place."[31]

One such important transit via Prague occurred at the end of November 1962 when a seven-member group arrived in the city. Headed by the Argentine Jorge Ricardo Masetti, the group all had false passports. Prior to this, Masetti had been the first director of Prensa Latina, but in 1961, mainly due to the growing pro-Soviet orientation of the agency, he had resigned from his position. The Czechoslovaks, who had been critical of him, and who referred to him as an irresponsible alcoholic, were now willing to help him.[32] His men stayed in a snow-covered hotel near Prague and underwent physical training there. The group left Czechoslovakia on December 30, 1962, headed for Algeria and later Bolivia, which was to become the gateway to Argentina.[33] In an attempt to change the Andean cordillera into the "Sierra Maestra of South America," the group led an unsuccessful partisan struggle in the Salta Province in 1963–1964.

Although much is known about the Salta expedition, its Czechoslovak dimension is important. It shows that Cuba's influence at that time was not only regional but also already global. When it comes to this Soviet Bloc involvement, new evidence tends to support narratives, such as Yofre's aforementioned, that suggest the Soviet Bloc lay behind all revolutionary activity in Latin America. And yet, this case also clearly shows what position Czechoslovakia had in dealing with the Cubans. Although the Czechoslovaks had a negative experience with Masetti in the recent past, in accordance with the policy of the Soviet Union, they were forced to accept Cuban demands and to support the expedition. At the same time, however, the Czechoslovak authorities took a passive approach to the matter, with Masetti's stay remaining under the control of Cuban agents. The Czechoslovak side did not have any further information about the Argentinean's other targets, nor did they think about acquiring it, because they did not consider themselves to have the right to do so. The Soviet Bloc was therefore involved but not in control of operations, which remained very much in the hands of the Cubans and their regional allies. Indeed, as we will see later, this position characterized the Czechoslovak approach to logistical support for Latin American revolutionaries throughout the 1960s.

On 17 December 1962, Carlos Chaín Soler, the deputy head of the Cuban intelligence service, then contacted Zdeněk Vrána at the Czechoslovak station in Havana with a request for assistance within the framework of cooperation between the ministries of the interior of both countries. Specifically, Chaín Soler asked Vrána to help seven Venezuelans, who had undergone guerrilla training in Cuba, return home. Vrána accepted the request, and the Venezuelans left the island the following day. In Prague, they handed in their false passports and, using their real documents, continued their journey through several transit countries without any trace of their stay in Cuba.[34] This unobtrusive route would be crucial in the coming years for linking Cuba and Latin America's Revolutionary Left and inaugurated Operation Manuel.

A little over a month after Chaín Soler's request, on January 25, 1963, the term "Operation Manuel" first appeared in documents of the First Directorate of the Ministry of the Interior (Intelligence Department) as a code name for arranging visa-free transits for Latin American nationals who had arrived in Prague from Havana. Naturally, there were transfers both to and from Prague. However, Czechoslovakia's secret service was only in charge of transits from Cuba to Latin America. Broadly speaking, it was about helping to secure a safe return home. The journey to Havana was meanwhile administrated by Cuban agents in Prague, was not a part of Operation Manuel, and, according to available documents, the Czechoslovak intelligence service does not appear to have had any information on these journeys.

The First Directorate of the Ministry of the Interior immediately informed the KGB representative in Havana and the Soviet representative in Prague about the whole operation in detail. In fact, the Soviets recommended the Czechoslovaks should "be willing to provide any assistance to its Cuban friends in this operation."[35] In this case, it was not so much that Moscow preferred to pass a high security risk onto its satellite, but simply that the Soviet Union was not geographically well placed to deal with such transits. There were fewer direct air links between Moscow and the West European countries from which Latin Americans returned home. Most of the stopovers had to be made in Prague. The journey through the Soviet Union would be a detour, especially as Soviet authorities could function comfortably in the Czechoslovak metropolis and have an overview of the whole operation.

This logistical support clearly shows how a small island had a major influence on Soviet policy toward Latin America and the United States through involving it logistically in its operations. The Soviet leadership sought to avoid losing influence on the island, and Czechoslovakia, which was subordinate to the Soviet Union's interests, was thus forced to comply with Cuban demands. Stanislav Svoboda, a high-ranking diplomat in Czechoslovakia at the time, noted as much in a recent interview that covered Operation Manuel: "We worked on the assumption that it was necessary to maintain good relations with Cuba. . . . If we had taken a negative attitude toward the request for cooperation in any sense, it would have noticeably altered mutual relations."[36] The logistical assistance that enabled Cuba to pursue its foreign policy objectives reflects Czechoslovakia's extraordinary importance in the Global Cold War competition.

Forms of Czechoslovak Assistance

In Prague, Operation Manuel was seen as helping the Cuban intelligence service rather than supporting revolutionary movements. This was based on the simple fact that Latin American nationals who had completed their stay in Cuba would not have been able to return home without going through Prague. Operation Manuel fulfilled Cuba's objectives entirely, and the Czechoslovak approach can therefore be evaluated as relatively mechanical and instrumental. Envisaged as a temporary arrangement, the aim was to follow instructions and to simultaneously push the Cubans to improve its operations with regard to greater compliance with security principles.

However, Czechoslovakia and Cuba never signed a formal agreement that would have unequivocally specified the function, power, and responsibility of each party in the operation. As an official Czechoslovak evaluation of the operation from March 1964 states:

> A problem with the operation, which has lasted throughout its entire course, is the fact that from its early beginnings it was envisaged to be short-term. On this basis, no official discussions took place with the representatives of Cuban intelligence, not even on the basic conditions of the cooperation. To this day, our Cuban friends have not even outlined the global goals which they pursue in this operation and have not familiarized us with the intended impact of the entire operation in Latin America. Our station in Havana has become the only intermediary for transferring sub-tasks and critical comments from our side. This communication is virtually limited to brief telegraphic messages between the headquarters and our station and to a more detailed analysis sent monthly by courier.[37]

The Czechoslovak assistance was therefore purely technical. It consisted of passport check-in services at the airport and arranging accommodation. On the basis of information on customs and passport regulations at European airports, Prague also provided instructions on the most appropriate routes to Latin America. And, initially, the "Manuelistas" (as the travelers were referred to in documents of the First Directorate from 1965 onward) traveled to their homeland almost exclusively through Paris and Zurich.[38]

The Czechoslovak side never formally gave any instructions for the activities or provided any funding. According to the Czechoslovak archive documents, the Cubans financed the whole operation using their own resources, including accommodation in Prague hotels. Naturally, we do not know for sure whether the Soviets or Czechoslovaks provided money behind the scenes to give to "Manuelistas." However, it does not seem to be of high probability. This is confirmed by Alfredo Helman, who left the Communist Party of Argentina at the end of 1966 and subsequently collaborated with the Armed Revolutionary Forces (FAR). He was in Cuba in 1964 and 1966. On his return journey home after his second visit, he was dispatched with Czechoslovak help. And, as a result, his name appears on a Czechoslovak list of "Manuelistas."[39] "I went to Cuba twice during this period, and each time via Prague," he remembered: "As far as I know, all of us from Argentina went to Cuba through Paris and Prague. I am not aware of any other routes. The trips were funded by the Cubans. I had to go to the local Cuban embassy in Paris. They gave me a false Cuban passport, a ticket to Prague, and said, 'You will fly from there!' I spent one or two nights in a hotel in Prague where only Cubans were."[40]

Even so, the Czechoslovak station in Havana played a key role in coordinating events. It cross-referenced information about the arrival of participants in Prague with the necessary report from the Cuban intelligence service. According to the instructions from headquarters, and in conjunction with Cuban leaders, it dealt with the problems and failings of the operation. On December 29, 1962, for example, the central office of the First Directorate of the Ministry of the Interior issued the first set of instructions to the station in Havana on how to proceed in the dispatching of "delegations" to Latin America via Prague:

Each group must have its own leader, who, after arriving in Prague, will call (if not contacted themselves at the airport) a designated phone number, introduce themselves using the name in their false Cuban passport and ask for Gonzales. They will pass on greetings from Manuel ("Saludos de Manuel"), to which the person on the other end will respond by asking about Augusto ("¿Qué hace Augusto?").

The callers will then make an appointment. The Embassy of Cuba in Prague or other institutions are not to be involved in this dispatch. At the meeting, the group leader will hand in the Cuban passports, which will then be returned to Havana. The station in Havana will inform headquarters about all groups prior to their arrival in the country. Only announced groups will be dispatched. Requests made by participants on the spot will receive no response.[41]

The logistical assistance can be perceived as indirect support for the armed struggles that were taking place. Czechoslovak engagement was limited, as too was the profit from participation in Operation Manuel. As one of the participants, Alfredo Helman, speculated: "I think neither Czechoslovakia nor the Soviet Union made any profit from the transfers. It was just about keeping influence over Cuba and having some control over the guerrilla groups. Getting to know them better."[42] Helman's statement that Operation Manuel served as a source of information for the Eastern Bloc is confirmed by information in documents held in Czech archives. As an intelligence report from May 1964 reflected: "It was only with the passing of time, on the basis of interviews, discussions and polemics with the passing Latin American nationals, from highlanders to students, and youngsters up to members of the central committees of the liberation movements, that we began to put together the mosaic of tasks of the revolutionary movements in Latin America."[43]

* * *

Within this context, it is clear that the main argument of Yofre's book—that is, that the Soviet Union and Czechoslovakia organized a revolution in Latin America—is therefore greatly overstated. Isidoro Gilbert, an Argentine correspondent for the Soviet TASS agency between 1962 and 1989 who had very detailed information about Soviet intentions in Latin America, made the following claims in a recent interview about Operation Manuel:

> It is clear that Prague was only a transport destination, not a political one. Yofre highlights information about the transits. At that time, there was simply no other way to get to Havana. One had to go over Prague or Moscow, or via Mexico or Madrid. Fullstop. Prague was the place where it was necessary to transfer; it was indispensable. But what did he discover? He talks about the Cuban Revolution being organized by Moscow, but that is a mistake. He claims that Cuba launched an invasion of Argentina through the Communists. But

of course the Communist Party of Argentina did not support this policy because people like Masetti were dissidents. Yofre's vision is very tendentious.[44]

Cuba and local Latin American organizations proceeded independently of the Soviet Bloc, even though the logistical assistance they received in Prague was necessary for the implementation of the revolutionary policy. This assistance was based on the Soviet Union's obligations to Cuba, and as it will be shown later, the Czechoslovak authorities perceived it as a necessary evil. With the existence of the Havana-Prague air link, it was not possible to prevent transfers and the involvement of the Czechoslovak secret services, and it was all executed with the particular efforts to reduce the security risk. And by relying on their allies in this way, the Cubans and Latin American revolutionary movements inevitably opened up their operations to the Soviet Bloc.

Prague as the Informational Channel between Latin America and the Eastern Bloc

As previously mentioned, the Cuban intelligence services concealed a number of important aspects of Operation Manuel from their Czechoslovak counterparts, which was therefore largely dependent on information provided by their foreign secret service stations or the Manuelistas themselves. However, with the latter, Prague maintained some restraint. "We considered the Latin American nationals to be, to a certain extent, illegals of the Cuban intelligence service and presumed that it would not be tactful to inquire about their training in Cuba or about the tasks that were awaiting them in their countries."[45] It was therefore not a systematic effort, but rather the gathering of random pieces of information.

Naturally, the Czechoslovak authorities had the closest contacts with the members of the Communist Parties. Prague was the seat of many Soviet-fronted organizations in which high-ranking party functionaries from all over the world worked. In 1946, for example, the International Union of Students and the International Federation of Journalists were founded there. In 1950 the International Radio and Television Organization also moved from Brussels to Prague. And in 1956 the Secretariat of the World Federation of Trade Unions moved from Vienna to the Czechoslovak metropolis. From 1958 on, the editorial office of the international communist magazine *World Marxist Review* was also in Prague. The activities of

Communist funtionaries within these organizations were mostly formal and served to legalize their stay. They also often fulfilled the role of unofficial "ambassadors" with responsibility for representing the interests of their Parties in negotiations with the representatives of the international communist movement, as well as deputizing for their Party colleagues abroad. Staff at these organizations were mostly also strongly pro-Soviet, which is why little information is available in Czech archives. They fell within the field of the KGB's interests, so the Czechoslovak secret service did not pay attention to them.

Meanwhile, some of these Communist functionaries from Latin America in Prague had links to various revolutionary movements, and these people played an important role of liaison between the revolutionary groups and communist states' leaderships. For example, the representative of the World Federation of Trade Unions, Jerónimo Carrera, was a member of the Central Committee of the Communist Party of Venezuela and, as such, was in charge both of matters of his party and, between 1964 and 1965, the Armed Forces of National Liberation (FALN). And, given the high number of Venezuelans passing through Prague, the Czechoslovak intelligence service also communicated frequently with Carrera. A large number of these "ambassadors" also worked at the editorial office of *World Marxist Review*. For instance, the prominent exiled leader of the Guatemalan Party of Labor (PGT), José Manuel Fortuny, who worked for the journal, administered Guatemalan affairs in Czechoslovakia. Both Carrera and Fortuny, were understood as the Cuban intelligence service's confidential contacts.[46]

However, especially in the second half of the 1960s, when relations between the pro-Soviet Communist Parties and Cuba cooled down, the importance of connection between the "Manuelistas" and international organizations in Prague decreased significantly. Persons passing through did not actively seek help from their compatriots. On the contrary, they were often concerned about having any contact with them at all. This is confirmed by the testimony of Alfredo Helman. "We did not seek the help of Argentines in these organizations. All of them were people from the party who did not have much to do with us, on the contrary, we tried to prevent them finding out about our presence."[47] Indeed, the "Manuelistas" were increasingly distrustful of the Communist organs, and Czechoslovak intelligence agents thus found it more and more difficult to gain valuable insights from the persons passing through. As a result, the already poor grasp of Cuban revolutionary plans became even more profound.

Numbers of "Manuelistas" According to Nationality

Archival documents suggest that in total 1,179 people were dispatched to Latin America via Prague as part of Operation Manuel between 1962 and 1969 (see tables 1.1 and 1.2). However, this number includes only those the Czechoslovak intelligence service helped. Some groups were dispatched with the assistance of Cuban agents or the staff of international organizations. The number of people heading from Cuba to other Latin American countries with special tasks was therefore probably several times higher. According to CIA estimates, it is also worth remembering that between 1,500 and 2,000 Latin Americans were trained by Cuba during 1961–1964 alone.[48] And, given the difficulties of traveling to and from Cuba, it can be assumed that a significant majority of those trained flew via Prague. Indeed, a representative of the Cuban secret services stated during his stay in Czechoslovakia in September 1964 that the number of people who had passed through Prague within the framework of Operation Manuel represented a mere third of those who had undergone training in Cuba.[49]

Although the numbers of dispatched people that the Czechoslovak intelligence service had is only illustrative, they are important. On one level, the increase and decrease in the numbers of "Manuelistas" during specific periods show us how the revolutionary operations were proceeding in Latin America. The proportion of individual nationalities also demonstrates where Cuba's attention was focused in its efforts to promote its revolutionary model abroad. Much of this information confirms what we already know but adds to our understanding of Cuba's interaction with, and influence over, Latin America's Revolutionary Left.

In January 1964, for example, Manuel Piñeiro communicated to the head of the Czechoslovak station in Havana that a major expansion of revolutionary activities was planned for the same year. In particular, he indicated that there would be a supply of arms from Cuba to Venezuela by air.[50] The first half of 1964 subsequently saw the largest number of "Manuelistas" dispatched through Prague (155). As is well known, Venezuela was a focal point of interest for Havana during the 1960s, but Operation Manuel statistics helps give a sense of how significant it was. In total, for example, in the period 1962–1969, 236 passengers, equivalent to one-fifth of the total number of passengers transported under Operation Manuel, originated from Venezuela. During 1963–1965, the Communist Party of Venezuela also took the lead in providing Soviet-backed financial support to the communist parties in Latin America.[51] The fact that it was an organization supporting armed struggle reflected Moscow's desire to regain credibility as the leader of the Communist world after different revolutionary models and revolutionary Third Worldism at the beginning of the 1960s gained more traction.

The second largest group of passengers were Argentinians: in total 187 people, or 15.9 percent of the total number. Argentinia had a privileged position in Cuban plans. Che Guevara, deeply affected by the failure of Masetti's guerrilla insurgency in Salta, considered going personally to start a revolutionary struggle in his country of birth.[52] These two groups were followed by Dominicans (122, or 10.3 percent), Guatemalans (100, or 8.5 percent), Colombians (79, or 6.7 percent), and Peruvians (76, or 6.5 percent). The numbers of people of individual nationalities clearly reflected Cuba's foreign policy line. During a visit to Prague in May 1964, Manuel Piñeiro explained that Cuba was not supporting revolutions in those countries that maintained diplomatic relations with Cuba—that is, Uruguay, Mexico, Bolivia, Brazil, and Chile.[53] This did not mean no contact whatsoever. But Havana's caution when it came to to getting involved is reflected in the low numbers of people from these countries dispatched during the first eighteen months of the operation (i.e., by mid-1964): two people each from Brazil,[54] Mexico, and Chile, and only one from Uruguay (see table 1.1).

Over the following months the situation changed dramatically. A military coup d'état in Brazil deposed President João Goulart and on May 13, 1964, the dictatorship that followed very quickly broke diplomatic relations with Cuba.[55] After July, following the "discovery" of a cache of Cuban arms in Venezuela, other states came under mounting pressure from the Organization of American States (OAS) and from Lyndon Johnson's administration in the United States to break relations with Cuba.[56] At an OAS meeting in July, Cuba was condemned for aggressive behavior and intervention against the territorial and political independence of a sovereign country on the basis of the arms discovered. As a result, the number of ships heading to the island fell sharply, as did Cuba's trade with Latin America. By September 1964, Mexico was the only country to maintain relations with Havana. Testimony to the rules governing Cuba's commitment to supporting revolutionary movements, numbers of Uruguayan, Bolivian, Chilean, and especially Brazilian "Manuelistas" significantly increased after mid-1964.

At the same time, Cuba's revolutionary government began to lose the support of other Communist Parties, who had to acknowledge that the damage caused by state repression and paramilitary forces had only produced minimal results. While the Havana Conference of Latin American Communist Parties held in December 1964 still referred to a compromise

Table 1.1. Numbers of people (according to nationality) dispatched under Operation Manuel from 1962 to 1965

	17/12/1962– 4/6/1963	5/6/1963– 31/12/1963	1/1/1964– 11/6/1964	12/6/1964– 11/11/1964	12/11/1964– 14/6/1965	15/6/1965– 31/12/1965
Argentina	—	5	45	10	1	8
Bolivia	—	—	2	2	—	—
Brazil	1	—	1	—	4	8
Chile	1	—	1	—	1	2
Colombia	5	13	11	1	4	27
Costa Rica	1	—	—	—	—	—
Cuba	2	1	1	—	—	—
Dominican Republic	24	2	17	9	9	8
Ecuador	11	2	2	3	4	5
El Salvador	9	18	—	1	—	—
Great Britain	1	—	—	—	—	—
Guatemala	1	6	15	16	6	3
Haiti	—	—	—	1	—	—
Honduras	—	9	1	5	7	1
Mexico	1	—	1	—	—	—
Panama	—	1	6	—	—	—
Paraguay	—	7	26	2	1	—
Peru	10	11	4	4	2	1
Puerto Rico	—	2	—	—	3	—
Spain	1	—	—	—	—	—
Uruguay	—	—	1	3	1	1
USA	—	—	1	—	1	—
Venezuela	24	29	20	21	25	36
Groups				50	58	73
Persons	92	106	155	78	69	100
Total	92	198	353	431	500	600

Source: ABS, 80723/100.

between armed struggle and more pragmatic pro-Soviet strategies, most of the orthodox Communist Parties were not even invited to the subsequent Tricontinental Conference for revolutionary movements from Africa, Asia, and Latin America held in Havana in January 1966.[57]

The impact of this sea change was also reflected in the ever-declining involvement of these parties in the selection of recruits for armed training. Indeed, when it came to Operation Manuel, the backgrounds of the travelers consequently changed. The share of members from communist

Table 1.2. Numbers of people (according to nationality) dispatched under Operation Manuel from 1966 to 1969

	1/1/1966–31/5/1966	1/6/1966–31/12/1966	1/1/1967–30/6/1967	1/7/1967–31/12/1967	1/1/1968–30/6/1968	1/7/1968–31/12/1968	1/1/1969–30/6/1969	1/7/1969–31/12/1969
Argentina	3	12	20	22	46	–	8	7
Bolivia	2	2	–	–	1	–	–	9
Brazil	4	13	7	2	–	1	5	2
Chile	–	1	1	3	4	–	4	1
Colombia	3	4	2	7	–	–	1	1
Costa Rica	–	–	–	–	1	1	8	–
Cuba	–	–	–	–	–	–	2	1
Dominican Republic	9	11	14	9	1	2	6	1
Ecuador	1	–	1	7	3	–	2	–
El Salvador	–	3	–	2	–	2	–	1
Guadeloupe	–	–	–	1	1	1	1	–
Guatemala	10	15	11	8	4	2	2	1
Haiti	–	–	–	2	6	10	12	4
Honduras	5	3	1	1	–	–	1	1
Iran	–	–	12	–	–	–	–	–
Jordan	–	–	–	–	–	–	5	–
Mexico	–	–	–	–	–	–	1	–
Nicaragua	–	–	–	1	–	1	9	–
Panama	–	–	7	11	2	–	1	–
Paraguay	–	–	–	–	–	2	–	–
Peru	3	7	9	4	7	2	11	1
Switzerland	–	–	–	–	–	1	–	–
Uruguay	2	–	1	–	4	5	2	–
Venezuela	13	30	8	10	2	8	9	1
Groups	44	56	52	51	41	17	15	10
Persons	55	101	94	90	82	38	90	29
Total	655	756	850	940	1,022	1,060	1,150	1,179

Source: ABS, 80723/100.

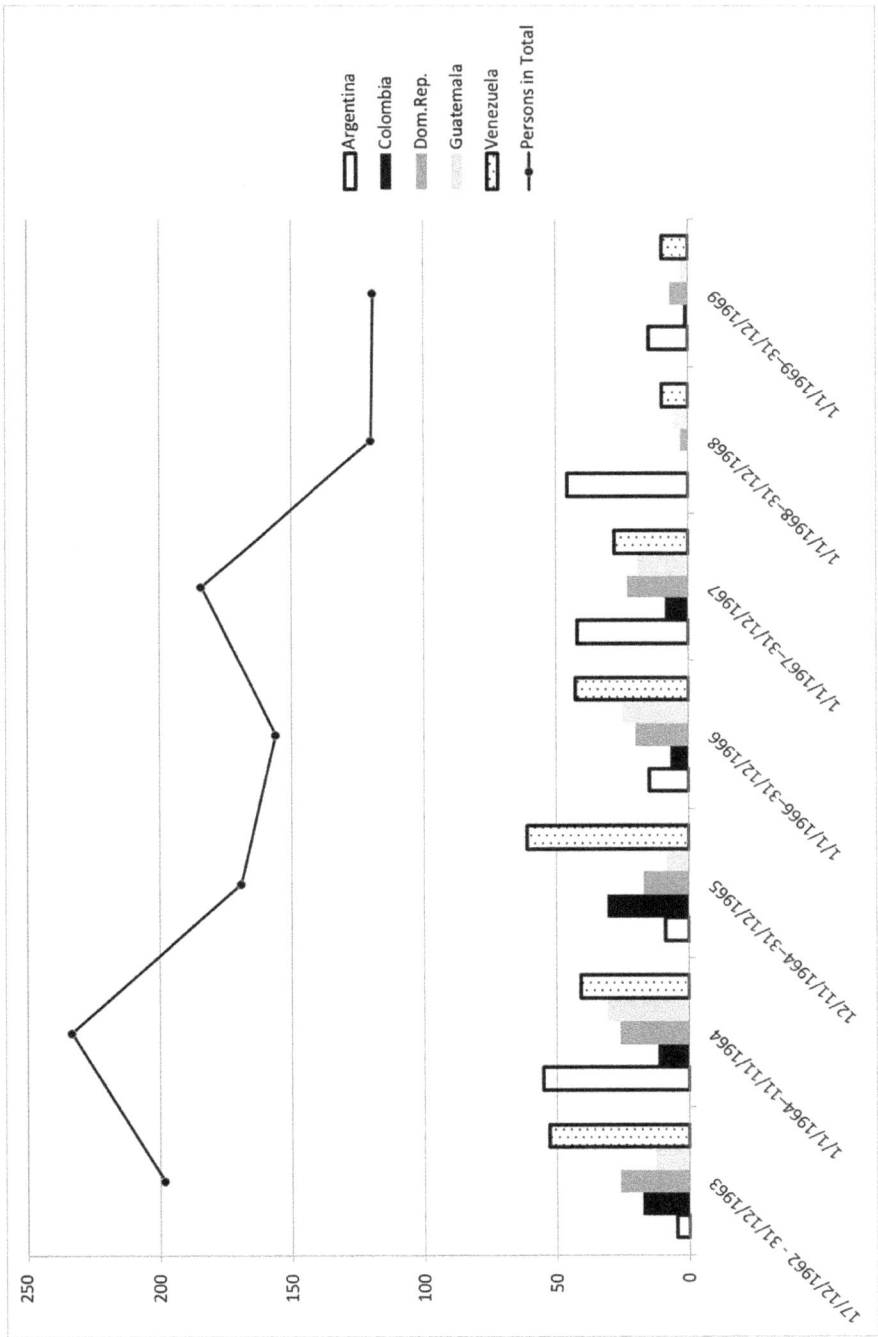

Figure 1.1. Numbers of people dispatched under Operation Manuel (Total number for a given period and nationality)

parties gradually declined, whereas the number of members from radical far left-wing groups—or the Revolutionary Left—rose. This therefore led to a decrease in the number of Venezuelans and Colombians, and to an increase in the number of people from Central America and the Caribbean.

It must be recognized that Latin American nationals were not the only ones flying through Prague after stays in Cuba. During the first quarter of 1967, a total of twelve Iranians in three groups, who were returning from the island to Iran after completing eight months of guerrilla training, flew through Prague.[58] In addition, and beyond the scope of Operation Manuel, a group of ten Eritreans was dispatched to Cuba. They flew on December 5, 1968, from Damascus to Prague, using Syrian passports, before departing for the island, where they were to be trained. The Czechoslovak intelligence service was accidentally informed of the transport because one member of the group tried to divulge the operation at the Swiss Embassy in Prague with the view of getting into Western Europe. After disclosing their intentions, the person was arrested and deported by the Cubans via Moscow back to Damascus.[59] In fact, while Latin American operations accounted for the majority of revolutionaries that the Cubans trained during the 1960s, the Prague connection shows they had far more extended global links and networks.

Operation Manuel's Limitations and Participants

It is clear that Czechoslovak intelligence services knew the real identity of the vast majority of the people passing through Prague. However, Havana's leaders did not provide information about their past or future activities to the Czechoslovaks. According to them, the head of the Soviet station in Cuba was also not informed about individual cases because he "did not intervene in the operational matters of Cubans in any way."[60] However, it seems that even the Cubans did not often have this information. Manuel Piñeiro himself, during his visit to Prague in May 1964, admitted that the Cubans lacked sufficient control of the "political and moral qualities" of the people passing through.[61] This illustrates Cuba's relations with, and support for, revolutionary movements. As an analysis of Manuelistas shows, it was local revolutionary movements who were in charge.

While it is beyond the scope of this chapter to detail all names, it is worth examining the experiences of some of the central participants in Operation Manuel and what these reveal with regards to the extra-regional dimensions of Latin America's Revolutionary Left. It is also worth underlining those who were not formally "Manuelistas" as evidence of the limited trust between the Cubans and the Soviet Bloc at the time and the lack of control that Czechoslovak intelligence services had on all those who passed through Prague. For example, on the latter point, as is well known, the very symbol of the armed struggle, Ernesto Che Guevara, spent time in Czechoslovakia between March and July 1966, after his unsuccessful internationalist mission to Africa. However, the Cubans organized his stay without consulting the Czechoslovak party, meaning that Czechoslovakian sources do not reveal any details of this trip.[62] Cuban agent José Gómez Abad states in his memoirs that Che Guevara insisted the Czechoslovaks should not know about his stay because, as with all states under Moscow's influence, he did not trust them. Indeed, Guevara was relentless in his distrust, despite substantial evidence at the time and since that local authorities were actively helping the Cubans. His fear of wiretaps also meant that he only discussed important matters outside.[63] In this sense, he was remarkably successful: Prague did not learn about Che Guevara's stay until a meeting with a Czechoslovak intelligence officer took place in Havana in 1968. As Gómez Abad notes: "During a meal offered to him the day before his return, Commander Piñeiro revealed that Che had been in the house in Ládví for four months prior to his return to Cuba and subsequent departure for Bolivia. He apologized for not having informed the service because of the discretion that was required of him."[64] This example is another demonstration of Czechoslovakia's engagement in these matters, the goals and implications of which its leaders were unaware of, and the process of which was completely under the direction of Cuba.

Meanwhile, Manuelistas passing through Prague were generally intellectually and politically quite diverse. In addition to a number of high-ranking Communist functionaries with close relations to Moscow who traveled mainly in the first half of the 1960s, members of the Trotskyist and pro-Chinese groups, which the Cubans supported, also passed through Czechoslovakia. The people selected for training in Cuba were chosen by their home organizations. In any given country, there could be even more organizations of this kind. In the case of Venezuela, the Communist Party and the Armed Forces of National Liberation (FALN) were in charge. In Argentina, the Communist Party worked in conjunction with the revolutionary Peronists, who had a representative in Cuba.[65]

The diversity of people in transit clearly shows Cuban efforts to support as many left-wing groups as possible for revolutionary operations, which soon led to numerous problems. For one, these were organizations that opposed each other at the national level. It is therefore not surprising that during their stays on the island considerable disagreement and distrust prevailed among them.[66] Second, pro-Soviet parties, which turned away from Cuban revolutionary ventures in the mid-1960s, were more rational and disciplined in comparison with other leftist organizations. Pro-Cuban organizations, on the contrary, were mostly unstable and internally dispersed, which made their coordination more difficult.

These differences and problems notwithstanding, the Czechoslovaks discerned certain similarities and patterns among the "Manuelistas" who passed through Prague. According to an analysis carried out by intelligence analysts in the spring of 1964, for example, the major proportion of the Operation's participants consisted of young people, and mostly students. Only a small number of people had little or no education at all. About one-sixth were functionaries of parties or national liberation organizations. With regards to the discipline of those passing through, the Czechoslovak intelligence services assessed the Venezuelans and Guatemalans to be the best. In contrast, the travelers from Colombia and Peru were perceived to be by far the worst. As one Czechoslovak report noted, the Colombians often "blamed the Communist Parties of the socialist camp of revisionism and viewed the Chinese as fighters for saving the purity of Marxism-Leninism." Members of the Peruvian MIR, "whether they were students or young highlanders," were meanwhile described as "undisciplined," with "no political orientation," and "[unwilling] to do what they were told to do."[67]

As mentioned above, in the second half of the 1960s, it was almost exclusively left-wing radicals who traveled through Prague. If we look at their later trajectory, we will find that many of them, after returning to Latin America, would die in insurgency struggles or be murdered in captivity. As a report from 1967 shows, Czechoslovak intelligence leaders were fiercely critical of the people passing through. "While in the first years the people that were passing through had good qualities and abilities and were devoted to the revolutionary movement, it is becoming more and more evident that the people are now of a lower intelligence and, to a large extent, those for whom a paid journey to Cuba via Europe is probably a significantly stronger motive than their interest in the revolutionary struggle. Further arrests of participants can therefore be expected."[68] However, Czechoslovakia did not decide on a concrete response to the issue of the transfers and chose not to interfere in Cuban activities. Although a more detailed analysis of the political and intellectual profile of passengers trained in Cuba is not possible here, the tendencies outlined above nevertheless show a progressive fragmentation and radicalization of the Latin Americas' Revolutionary Left. This process led Cuba to lose control over those traveling. And, of course, this situation soon began to expose Czechoslovakia to serious problems.

The Course of Operation Manuel: Cuban Inconsistency and Disclosures

Czechoslovakia did not profit directly from its participation in Operation Manuel. Quite the contrary. Western intelligence services showed an increasing interest in the fact that trained guerrillas were being transported from Cuba via Prague to Latin American countries, which undoubtedly posed a serious threat to Czechoslovakia. Accusations against Prague on the international stage can be found throughout the whole of the 1960s and, as is set out below, in the last years of Operation Manuel, Latin American countries proceeded to impose sanctions accordingly. In spite of the hope that the Prague route would not risk the same surveillance as Mexico City or Madrid, it is clear that transfers from Cuba and back were strictly monitored. As Ciro Bustos, a member of the Masetti group who traveled to Prague in November 1962, recalls: "When you got off the plane to refuel in Gander, you had to walk to the airport departure lounge in single file down a narrow stairway against a wall to the end of a huge hall. The cameras did not miss a single passenger detail, not only their faces, but also their walk, physique, tics and even socks."[69] Bustos also suggests the Cubans were not always careful when it came to issuing false documentation for the very delicate operation of sending people to Prague for transit onto Latin America: "The Cubana plane was leaving in half an hour. Wanting, and needing, to know who I was, I opened my new (Uruguayan) passport only to find that the photograph was of a tall man of about twenty, with blond hair and blue eyes. Although I was bald on top, I actually had a mass of black hair encircling my baldpate, and dark brown eyes. I would also be thirty-one in four months. Only a joke . . . or premeditated sabotage, could explain this stupidity."[70]

When he voiced concerns, Masetti and Piñeiro reassured Bustos that he could depart because Czechoslovakia was an allied country.[71] It is therefore no wonder that from the very beginning Operation Manuel was accompanied by tensions between the Cubans and Czechoslovakians, and by serious issues that threatened its secrecy and therefore that of the participants themselves. In addition to the permanent problems with the adjustment of passports, unannounced arrivals of groups or individuals, for whom the denotation "*paracaidista*" (paratrooper) came to be used, were typical. Another major weakness, as underlined in a 1963 report, was the frequent lack of preparedness of the people passing through. In winter, few participants in the Operation were equipped with warm clothing. And, although their stay on the island should have been strictly confidential, they often brought promotional materials (leaflets, flags, photographs, books) with them, as well as Cuban spirits and cigars.[72]

At check-in, some participants would take out both their false and correct passports, or bank notes they had been given, which they "fastened with a safety-pin to the inside of their breast pockets, sometimes loose, sometimes tied with a piece of string or a rubber band." As a Czechoslovak intelligence official quipped, "It would be appropriate to equip them with wallets."[73] At the same time, it was not uncommon for "Manuelistas" arriving in Prague to demand money for the purchase of the air tickets from the Czechoslovak side even though they had already received funds for this from the Cubans. Sometimes they would even have the contact phone number and passwords written on pieces of paper. The head of the secret service station in Havana, Zdeněk Vrána, talked many times to the Cuban representatives with regards to the ongoing problems. Despite Cuban assurances that the Czechoslovak instructions would be implemented and followed in the future, Vrána remained skeptical: "With their system of work, there will surely be further confusion."[74]

The Czechoslovak leadership was aware that "the only possible connection Cuba [had] with the world [was] via Prague and that the enemy [was] therefore driven to assume, even if they did not have an ounce of evidence, that Prague [was] a gateway for guerrillas."[75] In April 1963, the headquarters therefore informed the station in Havana that the Interior Minister, Štrougal, was insistent that greater care be taken. "The conditions for transport are getting harder because Czechoslovakia is beginning to be spoken about as a central gateway for guerrillas."[76]

During the first six months of Operation Manuel, groups of ten people would arrive in Prague. From 1963 onward, for reasons of clarity and greater confidentiality, only smaller groups of two or three people of different nationalities would be sent. The command to Havana was clear: "Groups with more than five members cannot pass through."[77] For a better understanding of Czechoslovak intelligence workers who operated at the airport in Prague, from the end of 1964 the "Manuelistas" were divided into the following three categories: A—leading functionaries of Communist Parties and people who commanded full confidence; B—ordinary screened participants who could be trusted; and C—ordinary participants who were not entirely screened and trustworthy.

However, according to the Czechoslovakians, the situation did not improve. Instead, as a result of the changing composition of "Manuelistas" outlined above, the reality was the opposite. Intelligence officials in Prague speculated that what they viewed as the low morality and lack of respect for the principles of security by the Latin American travelers could have been because these people came from inferior social conditions and had no experience traveling. According to this Czechoslovak analysis, we can assume that these "Manuelistas" were very unsure during the journey and, in some cases, cultural shock could also occur. Last but not least, distrust toward the Czechoslovak authorities played a significant role. As Helman remembers, "The Soviet Union and the Socialist countries looked at the Latin American partisans and Cuba with discontent. We were therefore afraid of travelling through Prague. We were afraid they would find out why we were in Cuba. Until recently, I had no idea that they knew everything about us. We did not know about the cooperation between the Czechoslovak and Cuban secret services."[78]

Indeed, as a closer look at Operation Manuel demonstrates, Cuba and Czechoslovakia had tremendous distrust of one another despite having the same enemy. From this point of view, it is surprising that such an extremely important operation was carried out for more than seven years. The reason was probably that Czechoslovak leadership considered the operation an ordinary task they need not pay much attention to. As we shall see, the Czechoslovak side became fully aware of the consequences of Prague being a key transit hub of revolutionaries only in the final phase of the operation.

The West's intelligence services were extremely interested in Cuban guerrilla politics, which resulted in a special OAS security committee being established. According to verified reports by the Czechoslovak intelligence service, during the first year and a half of the operation alone, a Venezuelan, Dominican, and Peruvian who had participated in the transits were murdered. During the same period, two people in Venezuela and one person in Ecuador were arrested.[79] Perhaps more revealing of the tensions in the relationship between Havana and Prague was that the Cubans concealed this information from the Czechoslovaks, who learned of the disclosures only in reports from their own stations, people passing through, or the foreign press.[80]

It was also only with delay and by accident that Prague discovered that people who had been fully informed about the operation had defected to the West. In the spring of 1964, for example, Cuban officer Vladimir Rodríguez Lahera emigrated to the United States. There he started working for the CIA and provided them much information. In addition, in April 1965, a Dominican national passing through Prague in April 1964 gave the Americans a list of his compatriots who participated in Operation Manuel.[81] Such cases were numerous.

So why did the operation continue? In the second half of the 1960s, Latin American Communists often questioned why Czechoslovakia helped the Cubans in their actions, which were viewed as inconsistent with the interests of the communist parties in the given countries. That the "Manuelistas" were often former Communists who, after their expulsion, established an alternative radical left-wing party added to their disquiet about the operation. The PCV's Jerónimo Carrera, who had previously been involved in the operation, subsequently engaged in a public dispute with Cuba over the question of armed struggle.[82] In this context, he spoke to Czechoslovak officials about the matter of collaborating with the Cubans in Prague in the autumn of 1966. "Actions that harm the interests of both individual parties and our common cause are practically financed with money from the USSR and socialist countries. The Cubans are, by offering their support to different groups, contributing to the fragmentation of the national liberation movement instead of focusing their efforts on bringing together the forces of unity."[83]

The Czechoslovaks took notice of these comments but chose to maintain a certain amount of benevolence toward Cuban policies. For the Soviet Bloc, it was far more important not to lose Castro's favor than to satisfy the wishes of the local Communist Parties with their very limited political influence. As a statement by the Czechoslovak Ministry of the Interior issued in January 1967 noted, "the Czechoslovak intelligence service has no right or option to judge the objections of the communist parties with regards to the operation. The leadership of some communist parties has reservations about the selection of participants, nevertheless, many of their members and functionaries, who are turning to Fortuny, Carrera or Otero, have already passed through and are still passing through as part of the operation."[84]

The same report reveals that the Czechoslovaks felt trapped when it came to the ending of Operation Manuel. Were they to stop it, they would have left the Cubans relying on Mexicana de Aviación or Iberia, both considered unsafe, or Moscow, which was logistically more difficult. In addition, the only way to prevent transfers would have been to cancel the air link, which was not possible for political reasons. As one report concluded: "Completely stopping the operation is not feasible because it would only be possible if all direct air links between Czechoslovakia and Cuba are cancelled, and if the work of the members of Cuban intelligence at the local embassy is not permitted. This will be seen as a hostile action against the Republic of Cuba. Even simply refusing to provide further assistance for Operation Manuel would lead to a sharp cooling of relations with Cuba, not only in terms of the Ministry of the Interior, but overall, because it would be interpreted as a refusal to assist the national liberation movement in Latin America."[85]

Czechoslovakia was aware that support for the Latin American national liberation movements was a crucial topic for Cuba, and therefore did not want to put the question of revolutionary credibility at stake through its potentially negative approach. Under these circumstances, the Czechoslovak secret service judged it better to dispatch people with the help of its intelligence service to at least partially reduce security risks. "If we stop our participation in the Operation," one report noted, "the participants will then fly through Prague as normal passengers and will be instructed by the Cuban station in Prague which cannot handle the dispatches as well as the Czechoslovak intelligence service with its expertise and technical capabilities. The fact that the dispatches will be carried out by the Cubans will not diminish the responsibility and the vulnerability of Czechoslovakia as a transfer gateway for those travelling under Operation Manuel to Latin America. The lack of expertise will, in fact, substantially increase our vulnerability."[86]

Just a few months later, the Czechoslovak leadership was forced to confront the possibility of terminating the operation again. In March 1967, the brother of the Venezuelan foreign minister was abducted and murdered. The action was sharply criticized by leaders of the Venezuelan Communist Party. Castro responded with a public speech in which he lumped all Soviet-backed parties in Latin America together with a litany of other undesirable counter-revolutionaries.[87] In May, guerrilla troops landed at Machurucuto with the aim of deposing President Raúl Leoni. The guerrilla troops, who were bloodily suppressed, had been armed with AK 47 weapons that, according to the investigation that followed, Czechoslovakia had provided Cuba. Venezuela subsequently tightened the issuance of visas for Czechoslovak citizens.[88]

The Soviets were meanwhile already running out of patience with unsuccessful guerrilla operations. With reason, they felt that this policy was weakening the political and economic positions of the socialist states. In the summer of 1967, Cuban subversive activities in Latin America became one of the topics at a meeting of Foreign Affairs Ministers of the member states of the OAS and the theme of discussion was also the involvement of the Soviet Bloc. There was a possibility of tightening visa requirements in other countries, which would markedly affect trade, and in extreme cases, Latin American states also expelled Communist diplomats. In this respect, in June during a visit to Cuba, Soviet Prime Minister Aleksei Kosygin criticized the policy of armed struggle that threatened Soviet interests in the region. Kosygin told Cubans they had to make a clear choice between support for guerrillas or support from the Soviet Union.[89]

Criticism of the Cuban line of the armed struggle also grew louder in Czechoslovakia in connection with the possible deterioration of relations with Brazil, the country's most important Latin American business partner. By the late 1960s, the Brazilian dictatorship had received credible information that the guerrillas operating in Caparaó, as well as some prominent representatives of the military opposition, were traveling through Prague. In July 1967, the Soviets notified their Czechoslovak colleagues that the Brazilian agent Mauro Santayana, who was working in the Portuguese section of Radio Praga, had provided this information.[90]

The first official complaint concerning the assistance given by the Czechoslovak authorities to Brazilian subversive elements was communicated to the ambassador in Rio de Janeiro on October 17, 1967. The Czechoslovak side responded by saying that Prague was an international transport hub that could be freely used by any passenger. It went on to say that the actual statements of the captured people did not prove the involvement of the Czechoslovak authorities in the said transits.[91] Although Itamaraty (Ministry of Foreign Affairs of Brazil) seriously considered the expulsion of Czechoslovak diplomats, it did not happen. The Prague Ministry of the Interior ordered the diplomats to reduce their movement. Brazil, on the other hand, was interested in maintaining trade with the countries of Eastern Europe. In the months to come, at the time of the reform processes of the Prague Spring, Czechoslovakia also gained some sympathy in the Brazilian government circles, which manifested itself in a certain degree of benevolence.

In reality, the Czechoslovak side was well aware that some of the captured guerrillas in Caparaó had passed through Prague with its help. As a report of the Czechoslovak intelligence indicated:

The guerrillas were trained in Cuba and Uruguay where they arrived through Paris and Prague. However, it is not possible to determine how many of the people passing through returned to Brazil and engaged in any form of opposition actions, and how many of them remained in Uruguay and other Latin American countries. During the course of Operation Manuel, 40 Brazilians passed through Prague. In addition, many others were taken care of by the Cuban station, the World Federation of Trade Unions, the International Union of Students, etc. Neither the Central Committee of the the the Czechoslovak Communist Party nor the First Directorate of the Ministry of the Interior was informed about them.[92]

Termination of Operation Manuel

All the disclosures and security breaches the Czechoslovak intelligence service noted generated increasing pessimism about the operation's overall purpose. As a 1967 intelligence report concluded:

The Cuban line of the armed struggle does not fully take into account the objective situation in Latin American countries and, instead of prudent policy work, focuses on adventurous armed actions that do not have broader political support. They gamble with human and material resources, often compromise and isolate progressive forces, and cause considerable moral and political damage. On this basis, their line is almost equivalent to that of the Chinese with regards to the understanding of tasks and forms of work of the international communist movement and is therefore only supported by some factional elements in Latin American countries. The assistance provided by the Czechoslovak intelligence service under Operation Manuel does not imply an acceptance of its political content and it forms only a minor and insignificant part of their intelligence work. As a result, some workers were allocated to its execution and we thoroughly isolate this activity from the other work of the First Directorate of the Ministry of the Interior.[93]

However, even in this situation, the Czechoslovak government still regarded maintaining good relations with Cuba a priority. As the Chief of the First Directorate of the Ministry of the Interior stated in November 1967, "It must be expected that withholding our help will have a very negative impact on our Cuban friends. The problem will not be solved because our relatively skilled assistance will certainly then be replaced by a series of less-skilled measures implemented by our Cuban friends and, moreover, we will no longer be able to keep track of the operation."[94]

At a meeting of representatives of the First Directorate of the Ministry of the Interior and the KGB, held in Moscow in June 1967, the Czechoslovakians also discovered that the Soviet Union had taken part in the transfers from Cuba. Its attitude was similar. "The Soviets, according to the interviews, participate in the operation because it is inevitable and, on principle, they do not want to cause complications."[95]

However, the negative consequences of the Cuban revolutionary policy on the Soviet Bloc's Latin American interests—namely, the expansion of diplomatic relations and increased trade exchanges—increasingly went beyond verbal criticism. And by the late 1960s, the need to protect Cuban interests was receding. As we have seen, this was not simply to do with ideological differences with regards to the best route ahead for revolutionary change in Latin America or on a global scale, but also a result of practical and logistical concerns with the way the Cubans ran their operation. The declining support Eastern European intelligence services offered Cuba and Latin America's Revolutionary Left also presumably had an impact when it came to sharing information on U.S. and local governments' measures.

On the Cuban side, the reform process in Czechoslovakia—or "Prague Spring"—led to the curtailment of cooperation with Czechoslovak intelligence services. Archival documents show that the Cubans did not trust the reform government in Prague and feared top secret information might be handed to the West.[96] In the period from April 12 to May 17, 1968, therefore, it was only the Cuban intelligence service that was involved in dispatches of Latin Americans back home. The Czechoslovak side, which until then had been in charge of handling passengers arriving from Cuba, was left aside.[97] After the August invasion by Warsaw Pact troops, transfers via Prague were, due to a lack of clarity with regards to further political developments, stopped completely for security reasons.[98]

At the same time, the death of Guevara in Bolivia in October 1967 began convincing several Cuban leaders that armed struggle was not a viable means of building revolutionary alliances in Latin America.[99] By 1966, the Cuban economy was in a critical state and a major rift had opened up with China. These factors, combined with Che's death and the growing tensions with the Soviet Bloc, compelled Cuba's leadership to rethink and move toward a rapprochement with the Soviet Union. It is for this reason that, in

August 1968, while left-wing Parties in many countries roundly criticized the Soviet Union, Cuba refused to condemn the Warsaw Pact invasion of Czechoslovakia.[100]

By expressing his support for the Soviet Union in August 1968, pragmatist Castro achieved a renewed improvement in relations with Moscow. In 1969, Soviet trade with Cuba began to increase dramatically and, within four years, Cuba became a member of the Council of Mutual Economic Assistance (Comecon), the Soviet-dominated trading bloc of socialist countries. Castro, on the other hand, annoyed and disappointed many of those around the world who thought Cuban political developments could be a viable alternative to the two systems that existed during the Cold War. Following the invasion of Czechoslovakia, Cuban transfers gradually picked up in number. However, under the new circumstances it was clear that Operation Manuel would not last for long. Havana, having chosen a more pro-Soviet stance, began to direct its attention to establishing business and diplomatic relations with Latin American countries rather than supporting revolutionary movements. The successes of Latin American guerrilla insurgencies had also been minimal, and the situation worsened in 1969. Havana cut off relations with the Venezuelan guerrillas led by Douglas Bravo and withdrew its fourteen officers from the country. Developments in Colombia, for which Havana had high hopes at the beginning of the year, were also not promising. After the elimination of Inti Peredo, the leader of the Bolivian Ejército de Liberación Nacional, the revolutionary activity in that country was also paralyzed.[101]

Meanwhile, between 1968 and 1969 in Latin America, a significant increase occurred in the number of arrests of people who had passed through Prague. This was partly because foreign intelligence services were already very familiar with the operation. Indeed, Czechoslovak intelligence officials informed Piñeiro during his visit to Prague in October 1969 that, over the two preceding years, CIA agents had started to investigate the details of travelers from Cuba directly at the Ruzyně Airport.[102]

In August 1969 an anti-Czechoslovak campaign was then triggered in Brazil in relation to the testimony of José Duarte dos Santos, a member of the guerrilla group MR-26. He was, according to his testimony, returning from Cuba via Prague, where a Czechoslovak citizen gave him counterfeit documents with a false name.[103] In response to this support for revolutionaries, the Brazilian government in the second half of 1969 severely curtailed all Czechoslovak activities. It did not allow the Czechoslovak Commercial Bank to open its branch in Rio de Janeiro or the Czechoslovak Airlines to open its office in Sao Paulo. The Czechoslovak cultural performance was also limited, and Itamaraty refused to take part in the celebrations of the fiftieth anniversary of the establishment of diplomatic relations. In the atmosphere of anti-Czechoslovak campaigns, a bomb was even found in front of the Czechoslovak Embassy in Rio in October.[104] These events led to the Czechoslovak government sending its first official protest to Havana in October 1969 arguing against Prague being used as a transfer point for "elements" trained in Cuba and sent to Brazil to carry out subversive activities there.

Czechoslovakia's secret service also outlined a plan for the operation's reorganization to Manuel Piñeiro during his visit in October 1969. Piñeiro subsequently proclaimed that Cuba had rethought its forms of assistance to Latin American national liberation movements and expressed his government's desire for the number of transfers via Prague to be minimized or completely stopped. The final decision by Havana to terminate Operation Manuel was made on March 6, 1970. The official reason given was the reorganization of the Ministry of the Interior and the workers' burden of harvesting sugar cane. The real reasons, however, were growing criticisms of Cuba, the island's isolation within the socialist camp when it came to supporting revolution abroad and successive, costly failures of the Revolutionary Left that it had been helping to train.

Conclusion

The Soviet Bloc's indirect support for the Latin American Revolutionary Left's armed struggle was one of the consequences of the missile crisis. Supporting transfers of people from Cuba was born out of the wish to maintain strong political and economic ties with the island at a moment of tension and distrust. Because the transfers were likely to happen anyway given the air link between Havana and Prague, it was also thought that by cooperating with the Cubans, the Soviet Bloc—and the cause of revolution—would be safer.

Czechoslovakia, because of its air links with Havana, was the ideal choice. Due to its geographical location and the presence of many international institutions, Prague had become one of the most important centers of the international leftist movement since the beginning of the Cold War, as well as an important hub with connections to major cities in Western Europe and the Soviet Union. With the establishment of the line to Cuba, however, Prague became the second capital after Havana of the Latin

American revolutionary venture in the 1960s. Thousands of people, including a significant number of experienced guerrilla commanders and organizers, were flowing through it, traveling between Cuba and Latin America.

Even though more than a thousand people were dispatched on the return journey from Cuba within the Operation Manuel with the assistance of the Czechoslovak Intelligence, the Czechoslovak leadership did not realize for a long time how privileged a role Prague played. They did not have detailed information about past passengers and did not even know what their plans would be in their home countries. It was only on the basis of interviews conducted with the people passing through that Prague was able to generate a picture of the tasks being undertaken by the revolutionary organizations.

In fact, from the beginning, the approach of the Czechoslovak leadership to the whole issue was rather passive. The transfers were not considered very important. This approach changed when some states officially complained about the Czechoslovak support for Cuban politics and there was a threat of disrupting foreign trade. The Czechoslovak involvement in Operation Manuel significantly influenced the perception of the country in non-socialist countries. With reason, Czechoslovakia was perceived as a center for Communist organizations, a supplier of arms to subversive groups, and a gateway for the transit of guerrillas.

What is striking is that even the rising number of disclosures and complaints from Latin American governments did not lead Prague to withdraw from the operation. Despite the fact that Czechoslovak intelligence reports repeated statements disagreeing with the Cuban aims and methods, the efforts of the Soviet Bloc not to lose Cuba did not allow Czechoslovakia to refuse Cuban requests. Czechoslovakia was not sufficiently autonomous to be able to counter the higher interests of Moscow. The operation was eventually terminated by Havana itself as a result of the collapse of the Cuban economy and broader policy realignment when it came to divesting of armed revolution and seeking peaceful economic ties and state-to-state relations with Latin America.

Neither Czechoslovakia, nor, it can also be assumed, Moscow, had detailed information on the scope of Operation Manuel and the importance of Prague for Latin America's guerrilla insurgencies. The Cubans kept more detailed information secret for tactical reasons. Conscious of their position on this issue, they never openly admitted to the Czechoslovak leadership that the import of the revolution was largely dependent on the existence of the Havana-Prague line. The extraordinary global significance of Operation

Manuel would come to light many years later when Czechoslovak archival documents were made available.

This study shows that recently declassified documents in the secret police archives in Eastern Europe are excellent sources for the analysis of Latin America's Revolutionary Left during the global Cold War. We find answers to questions about Cuban and Soviet approaches to a number of delicate issues that explain the mechanisms of transnational interaction between these states and revolutionary groups. The Czechoslovak documents on Operation Manuel reveal a considerable amount about the evolution of Latin America's Revolutionary Left and help us understand its global dimension. As this chapter has shown, what is striking is how the Cubans used the missile crisis and its aftermath to its advantage: that their displeasure about how it was resolved played into their needs and allowed them to operate in Latin America—and beyond—in ways it might not have otherwise been able to. That the Cubans themselves were not always in control of operations and personnel involved but merely facilitating Latin American revolutionary movements through training and transfers is also telling. It suggests a far more ad hoc revolutionary threat than was feared by many at the time and a far less potent potential for revolutionary change than adherents of this cause suggested. Rather than a powerful Soviet orchestrated subversive threat, the 1960s guerrilla insurgencies were made possible thanks to precarious agreements underpinned by the need to uphold fragile alliances and give substance to them. In this study, our primary focus has been to analyze the nationalities of "Manuelistas" and reveal the importance of individual states in Cuban revolutionary policy. This is but a first step toward a more detailed analysis of the political affiliation of "Manuelistas" as a means of further understanding the fragmentation and radicalization of Latin America's Revolutionary Left in the latter half of the 1960s and its global history.

Notes

1. Fursenko and Naftali, *One Hell of a Gamble*, 21.

2. Many important documents from the National Archives in Prague concerning the cooperation of Czechoslovakia and Cuba in 1959–1963 are now published in English. See Hershberg and Osterman, "The Global Cuban Missile Crisis at 50."

3. Národní Archiv (NA), KSČ-ÚV-100/3, 107, 344, Záznam rozhovoru soudruha Hendrycha se s. Severo Aguirre, členem PB ÚV LSSK, March 10, 1959.

4. In terms of the context of cooperation between Czechoslovakia and Cuba, Hana Bortlová's book *Czechoslovakia and Cuba in 1959–1962* is of great importance. Through

documents in Czech archives, she analyzes in detail the transformation of Castro's regime into a political and social system of the Soviet type, and at the same time shows the extraordinary significance of Prague in this process. See Bortlová, *Československo a Kuba v letech 1959–1962*.

5. See Opatrný, Zourek, Majlátová, and Pelant, *Las relaciones entre Checoslovaquia y América Latina*; Zourek, *Checoslovaquia y el Cono Sur*.

6. The wider foreign policy context of the Czechoslovak-Cuban relationship is dealt with in Fiala's book *How to Get Rid of Castro (Jak se zbavit Castra)*.

7. Muehlenbeck, *Czechoslovakia in Africa*.

8. Archiv Ministerstva zahraničních věcí (AMZV), Teritoriální odbory–tajné, USA 1960–1964, Úhrada nákladů za zastupování kubánských zájmů v USA, undated.

9. See Spenser, "The Caribbean Crisis," 77–111; Blight and Brenner, *Sad and Luminous Days*, 27–28.

10. The institution was founded by the Czech government in 2007 with the aim of analyzing and making accessible documents from the Nazi and Communist totalitarian regimes.

11. Tomek, "Akce Manuel," 326–333.

12. Spenser, "The Caribbean Crisis."

13. Spenser, "Operation Manuel."

14. Bautista Yofre, *Fue Cuba*.

15. Juan Bautista Yofre, interview with the author, Buenos Aires, April 28, 2016.

16. Bortlová and Sieber, "Plují pesos do Havany," 24–27.

17. ABS, 80589, Zpráva o návštěvě generálního ředitele tiskové agentury Pensa Latina v ČSR, May 20, 1960.

18. Žáček, "Náš soudruh v Havaně," 18–32.

19. NA, KSČ-ÚV-AN II, 278, 260, 32, Vyslání čs. pracovníků na Kubu, September 27, 1960.

20. ABS, Zápis z jednání mezi KGB při Radě ministrů SSSR a ministerstva vnitra ČSSR o výsledcích a dalším rozšíření spolupráce při koordinování rozvědných a kontrarozvědných opatření a o společném provádění těchto opatření, June 26–30, 1961.

21. ABS, 11380/000, Úkoly 2. odboru I. správy MV, vyplívající z jednání s představiteli sovětské rozvědky, konaného v Praze, July 15, 1961.

22. A clear example of the importance that Czechoslovak intelligence had for the Soviet Union's policy of promoting the Cuban régime in Latin America is Operation Družba. See James G. Hershberg's chapter 3 in this volume for more information.

23. ABS, 80723/012, Imon, January 10, 1964.

24. According to the archives of the Czechoslovak Secret Service, its most effective coworker was a leading representative of the Uruguay Socialist Party, Vivian Trías, who was listed as its agent between 1964 and 1977. Another Czechoslovak agent was, for example, Enrique Corominas from Argentina, ex-Minister of Foreign Affairs of Peron's government and former president of the Organization of American States (OAS). ABS, 43943/000.

25. ABS, Směrnice pro agenturně operativní práci v zahraničí, August 1964. ABS, 43943/000, AO Družba, October 1964.

26. ABS, 80589, Letecká linka Praha-Havana, informace, October 19, 1960.

27. Connected with the introduction of the line to Prague, the company Cubana de Aviación canceled its line between Havana and Madrid in the period from December 1961 to December 1963. Moralès, "Les communications aériennes."

28. "New CSA service to Havana," in FLIGHT International, 81, 2753, November 11, 1962, 73.

29. Moralès, "Les communications aériennes," 75–91.

30. Goméz Abad, Cómo el Che burló a la CIA.

31. ABS, 80723/011, Zpráva o jednání s kubánskými představiteli o některých otázkách pomoci protiimperialistickému a národně osvobozeneckému hnutí v Latinské Americe, undated.

32. ABS, 80629/014, April 1961. ABS, 80629/100, Pokračování ke zprávě Prensa Latina, August 10, 1961.

33. Bustos, Che wants to see you, 90–96; Rot, Los orígenes perdidos de la guerrilla en la Argentina, 158–161.

34. ABS, 80723/011, Zpráva z Havany č. 262 ze dne 20. prosince 1962, January 3, 1963.

35. ABS, 80723/100, Záznam pro soudruha poradce, June 14, 1963.

36. Stanislav Svoboda, interview with the author, Prague, October 30, 2013.

37. ABS, 80723/100, Akce Manuel, Stručné zhodnocení dosavadního průběhu a rozbor základních nedostatků a jejich řešení, March 26, 1964.

38. ABS, 80723/100.

39. ABS, 80723/100, September 15, 1966.

40. Alfredo Helman, interview with the author, Viareggio, September 9, 2016.

41. ABS, 80723/100, Zpráva centrály "K vysílání skupin z Havany přes Prahu do Latinské Ameriky," December 27, 1962.

42. Helman interview.

43. ABS, 80723/100, Rozbor a návrhy pro další obsahové a organizační řízení akce Manuel, undated (May 1964).

44. Isidoro Gilbert, interview with the author, Buenos Aires, April 6, 2016.

45. ABS, 80723/100, Rozbor a návrhy pro další obsahové a organizační řízení akce Manuel, undated.

46. ABS, 80723/012, Záznam o druhém dnu pobytu náčelníka kubánské rozvědky v Praze, September 28, 1964. ABS, 80723/019, Ordoňez–záznam o styku za období od 26. 8. do 2. 10., October 3, 1964.

47. Helman interview.

48. Spenser, "The Caribbean Crisis," 99.

49. ABS, 80723/012, Záznam o názorech Justa, které sdělil k různým otázkám během svého pobytu v ČSSR, September 28, 1964.

50. ABS, 80723/012, Imon, January 10, 1964.

51. Spenser, "The Caribbean Crisis," 99–100.

52. Piñeiro, Che Guevara y la Revolución Latinoamericana, 98.

53. ABS, 80723/012, Záznam o pobytu delegace kubánského MV v ČSSR ve dnech 6.–11. května 1964, May 29, 1964.

54. The complex relations between Cuba and the Brazilian Left, as well as with the Soviet Bloc, are analyzed in detail in James Hershberg's chapter 3 in this volume.

55. From this point, until 1986, Czechoslovakia represented Cuba's interests in Brazil. Opatrný, Zourek, Majlátová, and Pelant, *Las relaciones*, 83.

56. There is a question mark even today as to whether these arms were actually Cuban or if they were CIA plants, as the former case officer claimed. See Philip Agee, *Inside the Company: CIA Diary*.

57. Blasier, *The Giant's Rival*, 87–88.

58. ABS, 80723/100, Návrh na zařazení do svodky, February 23, 1967.

59. ABS, 80723/112, Zaškolování Eritrejců na Kubě, 6 December 1968. Žádost o pomoc při zajištění rezervace u letecké společnosti Aeroflot v Praze, December 16, 1968.

60. ABS, 80723/011, JUSTO, January 28, 1963.

61. ABS, 80723/100, Rozbor a návrhy pro další obsahové a organizační řízení akce Manuel, undated.

62. Unfortunately, Cuban archives remain mostly closed.

63. Goméz Abad, *Cómo el Che*.

64. Goméz Abad, *Cómo el Che*.

65. ABS, 80723/100, Rozbor a návrhy pro další obsahové a organizační řízení akce Manuel, undated.

66. Helman interview.

67. ABS, 80723/100, Rozbor a návrhy pro další obsahové a organizační řízení akce Manuel, undated.

68. ABS, 80723/100, Spolupráce československé a kubánské rozvědky–aktualizace zprávy ke dni 1 November 1967, undated.

69. Bustos, *Che Wants to See You,* 87.

70. Bustos, *Che Wants to See You,* 89.

71. Bustos, *Che Wants to See You,* 89.

72. ABS, 80723/100, Výpis ze zprávy do Havany č. 135 ze dne 29. 5. 1963, June 3, 1963.

73. ABS, 80723/100, Akce Manuel, December 22, 1963.

74. ABS, 80723/011, Justo, January 9, 1963.

75. ABS, 80723/100, Telegram do Havany č. 111 ze dne 4. dubna 1963, undated.

76. ABS, 80723/100, Telegram do Havany č. 111 ze dne 4. dubna 1963, undated.

77. ABS, 80723/100, Výpis ze zprávy do Havany č. 144 ze dne 4. 6. 1963, undated.

78. Helman interview.

79. ABS, 80723/100, Rozbor a návrhy pro další obsahové a organizační řízení akce Manuel, undated.

80. ABS, 80723/100, Akce Manuel, Stručné zhodnocení dosavadního průběhu, March 26, 1964.

81. ABS, 80723/100, Záznam, May 12, 1965.

82. Disagreements over the use of armed struggle within the PCV Central Committee began in 1965. In mid-1966 these disagreements resulted in the expulsion of the faction led by Douglas Bravo and the founding of the Party of Venezuelan Revolution (PRV) led by Bravo himself and supported by Cuba.

83. ABS, 80723/100, Záznam, December 6, 1966.

84. ABS, 80723/100, Spolupráce československé a kubánské rozvědky, January 11, 1967.

85. ABS, 80723/100, Spolupráce československé a kubánské rozvědky, January 11, 1967.

86. ABS, 80723/100, Spolupráce československé a kubánské rozvědky, January 11, 1967.

87. Blight and Brenner, *Sad and Luminous Days*, 104.

88. ABS, 80723/100, Stížnost Brazílie na čs. vměšování při dopravě partyzánů z Kuby do LA, November 7, 1967.

89. Blight and Brenner, *Sad and Luminous Days*, 121–131.

90. ABS, 11778/321, Rozpracování typa ve spolupráci s čs. kontrarozvědkou (Mauro Santanaya), July 27, 1967.

91. ABS, 80723/100, Stížnost Brazílie na čs. vměšování při dopravě partyzánů z Kuby do LA, November 7, 1967.

92. ABS, 80723/100, Stížnost Brazílie na čs. vměšování při dopravě partyzánů z Kuby do LA, November 7, 1967.

93. ABS, 80723/100, Spolupráce československé a kubánské rozvědky–aktualizace zprávy ke dni 1. 11. 1967, undated.

94. NA, KSČ-ÚV-05/11, 92, Akce Manuel. Informace o akci Manuel, November 17, 1967.

95. NA, KSČ-ÚV-05/11, 92, Akce Manuel. Informace o akci Manuel, November 17, 1967.

96. ABS, 80723/113, Praha, October 8, 1969.

97. ABS, 80723/100, Příspěvek do denní svodky, May 6, 1968.

98. ABS, 80723/108.

99. Guevara's death was a great political failure and is sometimes interpreted as the end of a cycle and the reduction of expectations in regards to the idea of continental revolution that had followed the Cuban Revolution. In subsequent years, the Cuban government changed its priorites, and armed revolution lost its primary importance. However, Guevara's death paradoxically became an emblem of future struggles, above all in the Southern Cone, where it had an influence in the establishment of armed groups such as the Tupamaros in Uruguay, the evolution of the MIR in Chile, and the ERP in Argentina. See Marchesi, "El llanto en tu nombre es una gran traición," 123–135.

100. Fidel Castro, "Castro Comments on the Czechoslovak Crisis," August 24, 1968, lanic.utexas.edu/project/castro/db/1968/19680824.html

101. ABS, 80723/113, Havana, September 15, 1969. In 1970, a group of youngsters started a hundred-day insurgency in Teoponte. However, following Che Guevara's legacy for this guerrilla action, there was no hope of success and it was suppressed bloodily.

102. ABS, 80723/113, Zpráva o průběhu akce Manuel a provedených opatřeních k odstranění nedostatků, June 1, 1970.

103. ABS, 80723/113, Využití případu José Duarte dos Santos k protičeskoslovenské kampani v Brazílii, August 28, 1969.

104. Opatrný, Zourek, Majlátová, and Pelant, *Las relaciones*, 87–88.

Bibliography

Archiv bezpečnostních složek, ABS (Security Services Archives, Prague)
Fonds: I. správa STB
Archiv Ministerstva zahraničních věcí, AMZV (Archive of the Ministery of Foreign Affairs, Prague)
Fonds: Teritoriální odbory–tajné
Národní Archiv, NA (National Archives, Prague)
Fonds: KSČ-ÚV-100/3, KSČ-ÚV-AN II, KSČ-ÚV-05/11
Gilbert, Isidoro. Interview with the author, Buenos Aires, April 6, 2016.
Helman, Alfredo. Interview with the author, Viareggio, September 9, 2016.
Svoboda, Stanislav. Interview with the author, Prague, October 30, 2013.
Yofre, Juan Bautista. Interview with the author, Buenos Aires, April 28, 2016.

Agee, Philip. *Inside the Company: CIA Diary*. New York: Stonehill, 1975.
Blasier, Cole. *The Giant's Rival: The USSR and Latin America*. Pittsburgh, PA: University of Pittsburgh Press, 1989.
Blight, James G., and Brenner, Philip. *Sad and Luminous Days: Cuba's Struggle with the Superpowers after the Missile Crisis*. Lanham and Oxford: Rowman & Littlefield, 2002.
Bortlová, Hana. *Československo a Kuba v letech 1959–1962*. Praha: Univerzita Karlova v Praze, Filozofická fakulta, 2011.
Bortlová, Hana, and Sieber, Karel. "Plují pesos do Havany". *Dějiny a současnost*, 33, no. 11 (2011): 24–27.
Bustos, Ciro. *Che Wants to See You: The Untold Story of Che Guevara*. London & New York: Verso, 2013.
Castro, Fidel. "Castro Comments on the Czechoslovak Crisis," August 24, 1968, lanic. utexas.edu/project/castro/db/1968/19680824.html
Fiala, Jaroslav. *Jak se zbavit Castra*. Praha: Rybka Publishers, 2016.
Fursenko, Aleksandr, and Naftali, Timothy. *One Hell of a Gamble: Khrushchev, Castro and Kennedy, 1958–1964*. New York & London: Norton, 1997.
Goméz Abad, José. *Cómo el Che burló a la CIA*. Unpublished manuscript.
Hershberg, James G., and Osterman Christian F. "The Global Cuban Missile Crisis at 50." *CWIHP Bulletin*, 17–18 (2012): 349–409. www.wilsoncenter.org/sites/default/files/CWHIP_Bulletin_17–18_Cuban_Missile_Crisis_v2_COMPLETE.pdf
Marchesi, Aldo. "El llanto en tu nombre es una gran traición. Lecturas políticas y emocionales de la muerte de Ernesto Che Guevara en el Cono Sur (1967–1968)." *Políticas de la Memoria*, 18 (2018, 2019): 123–135.
Moralès, Étienne. "Les communications aériennes entre l'Espagne et Cuba à l'épreuve de la crise des missiles (Octobre 1962–Février 1963)." *Relations Internationales*, 3, no. 158 (2014): 75–91.
Muehlenbeck, Philip. *Czechoslovakia in Africa, 1945–1968*. New York: Palgrave Macmillan, 2015.
"New CSA Service to Havana." *FLIGHT International*, 81: 2753 (November 11, 1962): 73.
Opatrný, Josef, Michal Zourek, Lucia Majlátová, and Matyáš Pelant. *Las relaciones entre*

Checoslovaquia y América Latina 1945–1989 en los archivos de la República Checa. Praha: Karolinum, 2015.

Piñeiro, Manuel "Barbarroja." *Che Guevara y la Revolución Latinoamericana.* Colombia: Ocean Sur, 2006.

Rot, Gabriel. *Los orígenes perdidos de la guerrilla en la Argentina: la historia de Jorge Ricardo Masetti y el ejercito guerrillero del pueblo.* Buenos Aires: Waldhuter Editores, 2010.

Spenser, Daniela. "The Caribbean Crisis: Catalyst for Soviet Projection in Latin America." In *In from the Cold: Latin American's new encounter with the Cold War,* edited by Joseph M. Gilbert, Daniela Spenser, 77–111. Durham, NC: Duke University Press, 2008.

Spenser, Daniela. "Operation Manuel: Czechoslovakia and Cuba." *CWIHP, e-Dossier,* 7 (2003), www.wilsoncenter.org/publication/operation-manuel-czechoslovakia-and-cuba

Tomek, Prokop. "Akce Manuel." In *Securitas Imperii: sborník k problematice bezpečnostních služeb,* edited by Jan Táborský, 326–333, Praha: Themis, 2002.

Yofre, Juan Bautista. *Fue Cuba. La infiltración cubano-soviética que dio origen a la violencia subversiva en América Latina.* Buenos Aires: Sudamericana, 2014.

Zourek, Michal. *Checoslovaquia y el Cono Sur: relaciones políticas, económicas y culturales durante la Guerra Fría.* Praha: Karolinum, 2014.

Žáček, Pavel. "Náš soudruh v Havaně, Vznik čs. rezidentury a spolupráce s kubánskou bezpečností." *Paměť a dějiny,* 6, no. 3 (2012): 18–32.

2

Revolutionary Diplomacy and the Third World

Historicizing the Tricontinental Conference
from the Cuban Ministry of Foreign Affairs

BLANCA MAR LEÓN

Albert Paul Lentin dedicated his work *La lutte tricontinentale*, published in 1966 by François Maspero, to his friend, the Moroccan leader and militant Mehdi Ben Barka, who was recognized for his decisive role in the unification of African, Asian, and Latin American anticolonial struggles.[1] In its initial chapters, the French journalist devoted considerable space to describing sociopolitical changes that had taken place after World War II. He put special emphasis on the great anticolonial movement that permanently transformed the international political context.[2] In the postcolonial world, many countries that won their independence acknowledged and vindicated each other, not only through the shared anticolonial character of the movements that had led to their independence, but also because they embraced the Third World cause. This in turn was considered a means by which countries could adhere to the principle of "positive neutrality" or nonalignment with regards to the military blocs configured by the Cold War.[3]

Thus, a new group of countries, aware of their growing influence on the international scene, entered the universal community of sovereign states as members of the United Nations, thereby modifying the world's correlation of forces. Because of its number and its outlook, traditional diplomacy was inevitably transformed into group diplomacy, coalitions, and multilateral conferences, where African and Asian countries played a fundamental role, acknowledging the anticolonial and cause as common ground. This cause had a powerful precedent, for instance, in the Pan-African movements between both world wars, led by prominent intellectual figures such as W.E.B. Du Bois. However, it also had clear limitations. In more than a few cases, the leaders of this community had their own agendas as well as economic and political interests, often determined by geographic proximity. Yet, although these countries' leaders had the ambition of exercising unified international prominence, time and again their extremely complex domestic realities also imposed strong limits on cooperation and made it impossible to attain a lasting common leadership.[4] This was especially the case in a historical context in which growing tensions developed between the member countries of Afro-Asian solidarity organizations toward the USSR and China. As Julius Nyerere said, as early as 1963: "I believe that the Socialist countries themselves, considered as 'individuals' in the larger society of nations, are now committing the same crime as was committed by the Capitalists before. On the international level, they are now beginning to use Wealth for capitalist purposes—that is, for the acquisition of power and prestige."[5]

Acknowledging these realities while refusing to take sides was a delicate political balancing act for the government of any country, especially during Cold War times. Nevertheless, within Latin America, defending and identifying with the anticolonialist and anti-imperialist cause became for many a natural, unavoidable gesture. This was especially the case for Cuba, from January 1959 on, which just like many other revolutions and movements for independence, claimed its right to rebel and to protect itself against external aggression. This included the regional, political, and economic isolation to which it became progressively subjected to in the Americas after successive ruptures of diplomatic relations with almost all Latin American countries except Mexico took place between 1959 and 1964.

In this context, Cuba undoubtedly sought to relate to, and even lead, the Third World. It did so through at least two different channels, which also represented two mutually competing visions.[6] In the first place, it did so through the Afro-Asian People's Solidarity Organization (AAPSO in English, OSPAA in Spanish). This organization had emerged formally at the Afro-Asian Conference in 1958. And it was within this framework that four successive Afro-Asian Conferences took place: the first in Nasser's Egypt (Cairo, December 1957–January 1958); the second in Sekou Touré's Guinea (Conakry, April 1960), the third in Nyerere's Tanganyika (Moshi, February 1963), and the fourth in Nkrumah's Ghana (Winneba, May 1965).[7] Ernesto "Che" Guevara's Afro-Asian tour in June 1959, starting with Egypt, signified the beginning of relations between the Cuban Revolution and some of the national liberation movements represented in Cairo, and the idea, still very much incipient at this stage, of expanding the OSPAA to the three continents.[8]

The other channel of communication between the Cuban revolutionaries and the so-called Third World was the Non-Aligned Movement, formally instituted in 1961. In the middle of the Cold War, the Cubans were entirely aware of the importance of this movement, both because of the platform it represented for supplementing the Afro-Asian Solidarity Conferences, and because of its undeniable symbolic value. Cuba's presence at international meetings of both the AAPSO and the Non-Aligned Movement, together with visits to the island by some Asian but mostly African presidents, who had also participated in these meetings, proved decisive for building and cultivating political networks and relationships. Both of these channels, in turn, allowed for the promotion of what would be the fifth Afro-Asian Conference, also known as the Tricontinental Conference. Cuba, for the first time in the long tradition of Afro-Asian international meetings, would be the first Latin American host.

The global scope of the Tricontinental makes it possible to chronicle it from various conceptual angles and historiographical perspectives: as part of the international history of the Cold War, as transnational history, from the perspective of network theory or oral history.[9] However, no history of the Tricontinental Conference has yet been written using Cuban diplomatic sources. Partial histories are available, thanks to the testimonies of some of the meeting's eyewitnesses and participants; but they are inserted within biographies and within broader studies of the impacts of the Cuban Revolution, the core of which are not focused histories of the Tricontinental. Indeed, since Lentin's attempt fifty years ago, the best story written about this transcendental meeting is the result of the praiseworthy effort of Roger Faligot.[10] The French author, a great journalist, knew how to thread documents, numerous interviews, and memories together not only from meeting eyewitnesses, but also from people who, somehow, were connected materially and emotionally with one of the most globally widespread rebellious moments in history. But this well-documented history did not draw on documents from the Cuban diplomatic archives, meaning that it missed a key part of the story of the Cuban state's official, institutional behind-the-scenes perspective on the conference.

To piece together the history of the Tricontinental Conference preparations from such a Cuban state perspective, research in at least three types of Cuban archives is indispensable: the Foreign Affairs Ministry Archives (hereinafter, MINREX), which houses documents concerning the preparations and activities carried out before the Conference; OSPAAAL's Archives, which have preserved numerous reports and encrypted cables sent after the Havana meeting by Cuban officials and diplomats in cities like Cairo, Algiers, Conakry, Brazzaville, and Dar es Salaam, between 1966 and 1967; and Cuban intelligence archives, which are unfortunately still classified.

Drawing on documents consulted at the Cuban Foreign Affairs Ministry Archives, this chapter contributes a fresh new perspective on a different scale to the usual narratives of this event.[11] It tries to give greater visibility to little-known details and people involved in the preparations for the conference, while simultaneously challenging the Cuban authorities' and archivists' interests in resisting declassification of state documents. MINREX's archive on the Tricontinental Conference includes about five hundred documents, most of them dating to 1965 and 1967. Most sources refer to the preparations for the conference, especially the activities carried out during the second half of 1965 to ensure the greatest participation possible by representatives of all three continents. In this respect, the collection includes records of exchanges between Cuban diplomats and Cuba's Foreign Ministry, between officers from various Cuban political organizations and MINREX, and between OSPAA and MINREX; memoranda concerning international meetings such as a September 1965 Cairo meeting, where the Tricontinental program documents and summons were prepared; and comments made shortly before the conference took place by news agencies such as the AP and UPI.[12] Although researchers are not allowed access to the entire MINREX archive for reasons of "national security," documents they can consult are already revealing and significant, demonstrating the value of Cuban archival research. In the case of the Tricontinental, for example, they show the detailed distinctions and observations made by Cuban officials regarding an innovative conference that sought to chart a new Third World course in global politics, in which Cuba aspired to having a leading role. At the same time, documents also illustrate some of the difficulties that the Cubans had to overcome to bring their initiative of gathering together representatives from three continents on the island to fruition. Among these challenges was the need to include those the Cubans had taken to be their closest supporters: members of Latin America's revolutionary forces.

Finally, MINREX's Tricontinental Conference archive, used in conjunction with other sources, makes it possible to follow the path of the Cuban initiative, its achievements, accidents, and setbacks. Even though explanations for these setbacks are not present in the consulted documents, there is enough information to allow us to make some conjectures. Documents also reveal the Cubans ascribed enormous importance to the delicate task of publicly legitimizing the reasons for Cuba's appointment as host of the event. Finally, we also try to read between the lines to determine not only what was going on between Cuba and the Afro-Asian group and some other members of the international community, but also how the Tricontinental Conference was taken advantage of by the Cuban leadership for reasons related to domestic politics in the sixties.

The Tricontinental Conference in Cuba's Foreign Affairs Ministry Archives

For early Cuban diplomacy after the revolution, formed "on the go," as some of its protagonists remember, the Tricontinental Conference was one of the highpoints.[13] The then recently constituted Foreign Affairs Ministry had been founded based on a pre-1959 structure, the Ministry of State. Its first minister, Roberto Agramonte Pichardo, was quickly replaced by a person who would subsequently become one of the emblematic figures of Cuban revolutionary diplomacy, Raúl Roa García, known in Cuba as "the Chancellor of Dignity."[14] At the end of 1959, the denomination of the agency in charge of the island's international affairs was changed from "Ministry of State" to simply "Ministry," while its chancellor acquired full powers as the main representative and head of protocol. After various changes in structure and internal organization due to a variety of reasons—a new government finding its way; the ideological radicalization of the Cuban government; the breaking of diplomatic relations with some Latin American countries—MINREX established several bureaus, departments, sections, and offices which, during the first half of the sixties, were reshuffled in number and corresponding responsibilities.[15]

MINREX was not the only official Cuban entity in charge of preparations for the meeting—the Communist Party, freshly created in October 1965, and the General Intelligence Office also took part—and it also had few material resources to carry out its task. However, the relative lack of resources and inexperience of the Cuban revolutionary regime's fledgling diplomacy was partially balanced by the Cubans' ability when it came to promoting a successful image of the revolutionary process. Revolutionary Havana's convening power had been consolidated through announcements, conferences, contests, and prizes, and by a wide range of international solidarity actions and networks, to which the United States had unwittingly contributed through successive aggression against the island. Perhaps the best example of this convening power is found at institutions that the Revolution specifically created, such as Casa de las Americas (April 1959) and the Cuban Institute for Friendship Among Peoples (ICAP, December 1960), the latter remembered as a "true machine for making friends" by its first chairman and future Cuban diplomat, Giraldo Mazola.[16]

Meanwhile, MINREX's preparation for the Tricontinental Conference was distributed among various Regional Policy Offices (PR, by its Spanish initials) into which the MINREX had been organized between 1962 and 1964: the Americas (PR-I); Socialist Countries (PR-II); Asia and Oceania (PR-III); Black Africa and the Middle East (PR-IV), and Western Europe (PR-V).[17] Yet another office, the Office for International Agencies, was responsible for writing a paper on the OAS, which was to be edited as a brochure and published in Spanish, English, and French, probably because the OAS was a regional organization with which the Cuban revolutionary government had had serious frictions and it was likely these were not known to most non–Latin American foreign delegates. Another one, the Office for Information, coordinated the work of putting together a list of reporters, editors, envoys, and agencies to be invited as observers to give the conference journalistic coverage in accordance with Cuba's interests. Each office had to prepare specific reports concerning subjects of interest in the immediate context before the conference: the office for Regional Policy in the Americas paid special attention to U.S. intervention in the Dominican Republic; the one dealing with socialist countries concerned itself with the situation in Vietnam, as well as with the differences between the Soviet, Chinese, and North Korean stances regarding the items in the agenda; the office for Asia and Oceania approached the situation in Timor, the movement against nuclear weapons, as well as problems with borders, religion, and national minorities. They had to share this last task with the Office for Africa and the Middle East, which also had to prepare reports on the situation in the Congo, Southern Rhodesia, Palestine, and South Arabia, as well as Portugal's African colonies. One of the few tasks that the four offices shared was the preparation of reports on national liberation movements arranged by area. Some of these topics were explicitly considered as "hot" in the conference's agenda, such as the case of the wars in Vietnam and the Congo.[18]

Putting together the histories of these movements and writing them using a diplomatic language that justified the efforts needed to bring together minds at the conference was a delicate task for Cuban diplomats. Building narratives was deemed indispensable for constructing a consensus that could legitimize the constitution of a new organization (the future OSPAAAL), without implicit ideological conditionings that would mean having to take a side in the context of Sino-Soviet differences. Indeed, transcending this dispute was one of the main political aims underpinning the Cubans' *hidden agenda* for the conference, as they rightly believed it had led to the inaction of the old AAPSO. In order to effectively support national liberation movements, including those that were already under way and those that would emerge in the future, the conference's hosts also believed it was necessary to balance the organization, incorporating other representatives from Latin America. This explains the resources granted to preparing and discussing specific subjects, given the risk they posed for bringing Sino-Soviet tensions to the fore, derailing the meeting, and potentially taking the initiative away from the Cubans when it came to creating a future organization.

Historical research on the international situation was not the only task that the MINREX carried out shortly before the three-continent meeting. Documents reveal how the Ministry deployed its officers to all its embassies where the island had diplomatic representation for the purpose of disseminating the conference's program and combating propaganda against it. Among these destinations, envoys regularly visited embassies in African, Asian, and European countries to further revolutionary Cuba's goals with regards to the conference (the same was not possible in Latin America, which remained diplomatically cut off from Cuba with the exception of Mexico).[19] Travel was often complex, having to be routed through Moscow, Prague, Paris, Madrid, and Rome, or, in the case of Latin America, sometimes through Mexico. However, the trips were regarded as highly useful, despite these various layovers. They helped establish or consolidate contacts and build alliances in line with the goals of the conference. They were also fact-finding operations for establishing information about like-minded political organizations and personalities. Finally, envoys were able to ensure necessary support and cooperation in terms of dissemination and circulation of Cuba's request to hold the conference.

A significant issue that needed addressing, but that did not generate important problems, was that of trying to determine and confirm traveling and lodging costs, and possible travel routes for delegates. In this respect, financing and resourcing for the Tricontinental Conference were ensured through the decisive intervention of Mehdi Ben Barka. He oversaw OSPAA's Solidarity Fund and was therefore one of the great facilitators of the meeting. For now, however, the origin of this solidarity fund constitutes a blind spot of this investigation, although good tracks are available.[20] Even so, as Faligot wrote, Ben Barka's position as facilitator of the meeting is unquestionable: "The jolly Ben Barka had been for a year Vice President in charge of the very strategic Solidarity Fund, for which his elephant's memory held a key role: he had to remember the numbers of the bank accounts, in Switzerland and elsewhere, for funding the world's liberation."[21]

This was truly important and, to a certain extent, paradoxical: while Cuba was able to put into practice an external policy associated with greater nations of summoning the Tricontinental meeting, it could only logistically do so because the revolutionary government had the support of certain international actors who, acting from key positions, provided access to the economic resources of organizations such as the OSPAA/AAPSO. At the same time, political ties had been secured through closeness to the Egyptian writer Youssef El Sebai, appointed by Nasser as Secretary General of the Afro-Asian Peoples Solidarity, since 1957, when the first organization's conference took place in Cairo.[22] Without these support channels, in fact, Latin America's greatest global revolutionary meeting would have never taken place. That is to say, the worldwide relations and interactions that Cuba created and cultivated from 1959—especially in the case of Africa— became essential in bringing the conference to fruition.

Given the size of the summons and the enormous international scope of the conference, coordination among all the participants was also needed to ensure the event's success, not only from abroad, but within the very Cuban political organizations involved in the preparation of the meeting. This was not a minor affair. As in any other revolution, disputes over political power were inevitable. And, in Cuba's case, a fight took place among the various political forces that had been at the root of the January 1959 victory: the July 26 Movement (M-26–7), the March 13 Students' Directorate (MR-13-M), and the Popular Socialist Party (PSP), which were ultimately dissolved and absorbed into the Cuban Communist Party, when it was re-founded in October 1965. It must be noted that these forces held opposing views in connection with the main goal of the conference: resorting to and promoting armed violence in Latin America and the rest of the world. The first two were in favor of armed struggle, while the third favored the Soviet line of peaceful coexistence.

In this sense, MINREX documents refer to the outstanding participation of members of the March 13 Directory and the July 26 Movement, two of the three political forces that made the 1959 revolutionary victory possible. Only a few who did not belong to either of the above were former Popular Socialist Party (PSP) members. For instance, one of Roa's two Vice Ministers, Pelegrín Torras de la Luz, was a man with "an old and outstanding membership in the PSP."[23] Meanwhile, his other Vice Minister, Arnold Rodríguez Camps, had been a conspirator and clandestine fighter in the struggle against Batista, and a member of the July 26 Movement, famous for having kidnapped Juan Manuel Fangio in 1958. Another diplomat, Carlos Alfaras Varela (Head of Regional Policy for Africa and the Middle East), was a member of the July 26 Movement and played a significant role in preparations. Among others involved were Eduardo Delgado Bermúdez (Head of Regional Policy for Southeast Asia and Oceania), also a member of the July 26 Movement. Former members of the March 13 Directorate working at MINREX were Enrique Rodríguez Loeches, also a former member of the Caribbean Legion, Jesús Barreiro González (Head of Socialist Countries), and Armando Entralgo González, (Cuban Ambassador to Ghana and Dahomey). Antonio Carrillo (Cuban Ambassador to France) and Ricardo Alarcón de Quesada (Head of Regional Policy for Latin America) were both members of the July 26 Movement. In the case of Luis García Guitart (Cuban Representative to the UAR) and Jorge Serguera Riverí and Óscar Oramas Oliva (respectively, Ambassador and Person in Charge of Affairs), the former had fought in the Rebel Army and was trusted by Che Guevara, while the latter was a full-fledged partisan of Fidel Castro, and both proved to be fundamental participants, given the connection they helped establish with the other "mecca" of world revolution: Algeria.[24] Other Ministry officials were equally decisive in connection with the organization activities needed for the Tricontinental Conference and were repeatedly mentioned in the minutes of several internal meetings: for example, Fernando Álvarez Tabío, who had a deep knowledge of Marxism and headed the Institute for International Policy, and who was Cuba's Permanent Representative before the United Nations in the years 1964–1965, but who had never been a formal militant of any political party before 1959. Overall, then, at first sight, the Cuban ambassadors and diplomats at the root of the success of the Tricontinental appeared to be those who could best represent the idea, in line with revolutionary ideology, that it was both necessary and also possible to try to subvert the entire world.[25]

But the logistics and organization of a project such as the Tricontinental would be incomplete without alluding to the role played by the Foreign Affairs Commission of the Central Committee of Cuban Communist Party. Indeed, the "CRE," as it was known by its initials in Spanish, was led by Osmany Cienfuegos Gorriarán, who would be one of Cuba's delegates and, of course, Secretary General of the future OSPAAAL.[26] "[The] Foreign Affairs Commission was made up by Osmany, Roa and Piñeiro," recalls a member of Cuban diplomacy in those years.[27] In fact, despite having found no mention to the legendary commander Manuel Piñeiro Losada (*Barbarroja*) in the documents consulted, it was possible to ascertain a very fluid communication between Minister Roa, the various Regional Policy Offices of the MINREX, and the CRE: copies of instructions sent to the various Cuban diplomatic representations abroad as well as detailed reports of the preparatory meetings held between representatives of the Cuban Communist Party and members of the Permanent Secretariat of Afro-Asian Solidarity Peoples' Organization are examples of the documents addressed to Osmany himself or to his closest collaborators. And, of course, most of these instructions were destined to Cuban diplomatic representations in Europe and Africa rather than Latin America as a result of regional sanctions imposed against the island. Apart from the case of Mexico, Cuba's relations with the region were thus conducted with non-state revolutionary groups rather than governments. But the focus on Africa was also because revolutionaries in the region were also generally much more favorable to the Cuban idea, subsequently articulated by Che Guevara in a message to the Tricontinental, of "creating two or three . . . many Vietnams."[28]

Roots and Destination of an Initiative: The Cuban Meeting Request to World Revolution

Cuban chances of becoming the hosts of such a significant encounter were more remote than is assumed. Raúl Roa had imagined a possible Tricontinental Conference as "a conference of hunger" and had suggested it as such to Ahmed Sekou Touré, the first African leader who traveled to Cuba, in October 1960.[29] The idea was not unfamiliar to the Guinean President, for his half-brother Ismael had organized the second Afro-Asian Conference, which took place in Conakry, in April of that same year. And while the Cuban chancellor's proposal was not immediately well received, it at least showed what possibilities were open to the island's revolutionary government for carrying out lobbying activities.[30] It became clear that to "win the nomination as seat" of the imagined conference it was indispensable to dream big and conspire big. For the time being, Belgrade, where the first Non-Aligned Conference took place in September 1961, would be one of the next stopovers toward this end.[31]

At Belgrade, however, the Cuban initiative of a meeting of the three continents with Havana as host was not well received: mutual mistrust between the Cubans and the Yugoslavs had continued to grow since Josip Broz Tito, one of the most important socialist leaders in the world and Secretary General of the Non-Aligned Movement for the 1961–1964 period, refused to sell arms to Cuba in his conversation with Che Guevara during one of the first tours he made of Afro-Asian countries and Yugoslavia in 1959.[32] Cuba's progressively closer ties to the USSR, once the island defined itself publicly as a socialist regime, added to the problem. Finally, Yugoslavia's stance with respect to the Sino-Soviet conflict did not help efforts by Tito to become the leader of the Third World. However, perhaps the greatest obstacle to his aspirations was his position concerning the South Vietnam conflict. According to the Cuban Foreign Ministry, Yugoslavia's position on South Vietnam made it an untrustworthy partner. As a confidential Cuban document written on the event of the Tricontinental Conference at the end of 1965 would note: "Yugoslavia is excluded as a participant in the Conference because, at the Cairo Conference, Vietnam proposed to exclude Yugoslavia from the Conference due to its refusal to back the Geneva agreements concerning Vietnam and its support for the American position in connection with this problem."[33]

As the Cuban documents show, just before the Belgrade meeting, the Fourth Solidarity Council session of AAPSO had also taken place in Bandung (April 10–14, 1961).[34] Subsequently, AAPSO's Executive Committee met in Gaza (December 9–11, 1961).[35] In the same year, Cuba had just emerged victorious from the Bay of Pigs invasion on April 19, 1961, and, wanting to take advantage of the transcendental material and symbolic triumph against the United States, suggested convening a three-continent assembly through the Cuban observer, Pedro Azze Bezil, who attended the Bandung meeting.[36] Because of this proposal and thanks to Cuba's new post–Bay of Pigs prestige, the possibility of Latin America being included as an observer and, perhaps, future host for Afro-Asian Conferences was recommended and considered for the first time. Between April and December of the same year, 1961, other new decisions underpinned the initiative: Osende Afana, the Cameroonian representative in the Afro-Asian Solidarity Secretariat, together with Masao Kitasawa of Japan, led a new impetus to "create a Afro-Asian-Latin American Solidarity Association."[37] With these antecedents and by considering the possibility of hosting such a conference, the Cubans aimed to strengthen the solidarity and collaboration between three continents while intensifying an anticolonial and anti-imperialistic struggle on as many fronts as possible. As Che Guevara, one of the conference's most formidable proponents and a vocal ambassador for the commonality between Latin America's revolutionary cause and the Afro-Asian struggle argued in late 1963, this was inevitably and increasingly an *intercontinental* task that could build on a multiplying effect of existing revolutions: "Avec un Cuba révolutionnaire aux Amériques, un second, un troisième Cuba suivra sûrement en Amérique latine. De méme, avec une Algérie révolutionnaire en Afrique, une seconde, une troisième Algérie suivra." [With a revolutionary Cuba in the Americas, surely a second and a third Cuba may emerge in Latin America. For the same reasons, with a revolutionary Algeria in Africa, a second and a third Algeria will follow.][38]

When Ambassador José Carrillo attended the third Afro-Asian Solidarity Conference in Moshi, Tanganyika, in February 1963, he carried a proposal from the Cuban Prime Minister and was able to raise the case for a meeting of three continents in Havana once again. Unlike previous Cuban proposals, however, this intervention was greeted positively, with the decision made to formally consider the Cuban initiative.[39] What had changed? First, in the wake of the October 1962 missile crisis, relations between the Soviet Union and Cuba were severely damaged. This circumstance was exploited by the Chinese, in open competition for the leadership of the international communist movement at international meetings such as the Moshi Afro-Asian Conference. This forum also made clear the Soviets' interest in preventing the Tricontinental Conference from taking place in Havana. In this respect, a little-known anecdote recently brought to light by Jeremy Friedman that doesn't appear in the records available at the Cuban chancellery is revealing: after a speech by Ambassador Carrillo, the Brazilian, Valerio Konder,[40] a prominent member of the Soviet-sponsored World Peace Council, threatened him, arguing, "Your speech cannot represent the Cuban government. If you speak like this, you will be condemned when you return home." Lying behind his public attack was the USSR's desire to hold a future conference in Brazil through representatives of Latin American Communist Parties and members of the World Peace Council, rather than Cuba. The move was quickly foiled by the Chinese, who managed to make their position prevail.[41] Second, it does not seem a minor coincidence that, by this date, Yugoslavia was on its way out as president of the Non-Aligned Movement. The next leader of the Non-Aligned Movement, the Egyptian Gamal Abdel Nasser, had meanwhile spoken with Che Guevara during the latter's tour of Europe and the Middle East in 1962. Even though witnesses to this first encounter between Nasser and Guevara suggest that the meeting was a clash of the titans, a real "ego duel," a friendship between revolutionary Cuba and Egypt began at this encounter that was undoubtedly a positive step in the competition to "win the chance to become host."[42] Everything seems to indicate that when the Chinese leadership of the Afro-Asian Solidarity Peoples' Organization was strengthened and the Non-Aligned Movement fell into Egyptian hands, respectively, the Cuban proposal finally materialized.

The Moshi conference produced no immediate or definitive decision to accept the Cuban proposal. But it created the conditions for the beginning of discussions of the most efficient mechanisms to organize and formally integrate a preparation committee.[43] This committee was to incorporate six representatives from each continent, and the Asian and African delegates were elected immediately. Africa was to send representatives from Algeria, Ghana, Guinea, South Africa, the UAR, and Tanzania; Asia would send representatives from China, India, Indonesia, Japan, South Vietnam, and the Soviet Union. Thereafter, the first twelve had to choose the six representatives from Latin America, and it was agreed that the preparation committee should travel to Havana and to Mexico City in order to do so. As a MINREX document noted, "In compliance with the resolution adopted at the Third Afro-Asian Conference held in Moshi (February 4–11, 1963), concerning the proposed Preparatory Committee for the Tri-Continental Conference, we enclose herewith a copy of the two letters already we have sent General Lazaro Cárdenas in Mexico and the President of the Integrated Revolutionary Organizations in Cuba as members of this proposed Preparatory Committee."[44]

To achieve this, Algerian President Ben Bella's support for the idea during the inaugural speech of the sixth session of the Solidarity Council of Afro-Asian Peoples was invaluable. Although there is no explicit clue that the Cubans asked Ben Bella to intervene in this way, the Algerian president was regarded by the Cubans as a great friend and ally, and vice versa.[45] Then, Ben Bella made an appeal for attending countries to put together the preparation committee and to expedite the steps for appointing Latin American representatives.[46] At the meeting held in Algeria, the exhaustion that the bitter discussions between the Soviets and the Chinese had generated within the AAPSO was evident. In fact, a kind of third "neutral" bloc was created, composed mainly of representatives of African countries, with Morocco (Mehdi Ben Barka) and Algeria (Mohamed Yazid) leading this group. It then gave the two powers an ultimatum, "threatening to break up the meeting, and presumably the AAPSO itself, unless the polemics were shut off." The maneuvers had the desired effect, and the steps accelerated.[47] The next Afro-Asian Conference held in Winneba ruled in favor of Havana as the seat for the three-continent conference. As the official Cuban invitation to the Tricontinental Conference stated, "You are fully aware that the Fourth Afro-Asian Solidarity Conference that took place at Winneba, Ghana, between May 9 and 16 [1965] has taken a decisive and positive step to widen the solidarity movement between the peoples of Asia, Africa, and Latin America, by way of the decision to celebrate the First Solidarity Conference of the Peoples from all Three Continents at Havana, Cuba."[48] As well as formally announcing the Tricontinental Conference, the Winneba conference also issued an invitation to take part in its detailed preparatory ("plenary") session in September 1965.[49]

Having finally secured the acceptance for a Tricontinental Conference, it was not easy to bring together the wills of all participants and to convince them to accept the Cuban initiative. This was certainly the case when it came to non-state revolutionary Latin American allies. While MINREX documents show little evidence of discrepancies, it must have been a delicate task to conciliate these allies. Like the Cubans, different Latin American groups had their own political agendas and historical leaderships: Latin America had a long tradition of revolutionary struggle, with the Cuban revolution being neither alone nor the first in the twentieth century. As with other subjects that the Cuban Revolution put up for debate in the sixties, the Tricontinental Conference also inevitably became a space for competition.

An example of the contentious nature of the conference, similar to the aforementioned incident that took place at the Moshi Conference, can be gleaned from a report written by Ricardo Alarcón de Quesada, the envoy on behalf of the Cuban chancellery to the World Congress for Peace, National Independence, and General Disarmament that took place at Helsinki on July 10–15, 1965. In a memorandum addressed to Cuba's Ministry for Foreign Affairs, Alarcón confirmed and summarized the existence of two positions among the Latin American liberation movements:

one of them, clearly revolutionary, that places the anti-imperialist struggle at the center of its activity and is generally represented by the Cuban Revolution and the movements that espouse armed struggle; the other line, which is more clearly exemplified by Chile and Argentina [which] has a "Europeanizing" vision of the struggle for national emancipation, seeks to mobilize the masses for the purpose of attaining democratic, reformist or pacifist goals . . . ; this idea, which has here been summarily expressed, leads them to shun placing a clearly anti-imperialist definition at the center of its activities, given that it is understood that this would restrict the breadth of the struggle.[50]

Alarcón based his observations partly on the reservations made by some delegates from South America—for example, Olga Poblete, who presided Chile's Movement for Peace and who was also the Latin American secretary of the World Council for Peace—regarding the way in which the six Latin American representatives were to be elected to the conference's preparation committee. Their misgivings about celebrating the Tricontinental Conference in Havana was also based on logistical problems of reaching Cuba, according to Alarcón's report, "given the difficulties encountered in travelling to our country or returning from Cuba." Among these South American delegates was also the writer Alfredo Varela, a member of the Argentinian Council for Peace. As the Cuban delegate suggested in his report, reservations expressed by these South American delegates generated "a deep displeasure" among Cuban officials. In a personal conversation with Uruguay's representative to the Council, who was more sympathetic with Cuba's revolutionary line and who had an enormous influence among South America's communist parties, Alarcón acknowledged that "if there is a formal discussion about the Tricontinental Conference, we would have no choice but to openly clash with Ms. Poblete and, in general, against all who hold a position like hers." At the same time, the Mexican delegates to Helsinki insisted on the possibility of "creating an environment favorable to carrying out a Second Latin American Conference for National Sovereignty, Economic Emancipation and Peace, like the one carried out on March 1961 under the patronage of General Lázaro Cárdenas del Río; this Latin American Conference would take place in Mexico before the Tricontinental." In any case, Alarcón expected that the lukewarm response from some Latin American delegates to the Tricontinental Conference would be compensated by the presence of representatives from the Afro-Asian world. "Bringing together all three continents should have a positive result, as it may and should act as a catalyst for the national liberation movements in our America," he wrote to the Cuban Foreign Affairs Minister.[51]

The situation Alarcón described after the 1965 Helsinki meeting illustrates the differences of opinion concerning Cuba's designation as the headquarters of the future meeting. However, Alarcón also provided insight into some Mexican political groups' interest not only in organizing a second Latin American Conference, such as the one they had supported some years back, but also in creating a permanent entity—the seat of which is not mentioned—before the budding Tricontinental Conference. Confirming this evidently political interest through other means is easy. For instance, Lázaro Cárdenas very early on expressed the convenience of holding an "Afro-Asian-Latin American meeting." This opinion of the former Mexican president can be traced in an exchange of letters between June 1961 and December 1962 with Olga Poblete, which was copied to John D. Bernal and Valerio Konder, and to Alberto T. Casella, Víctor Chijik-vadse, Wanda Wasilewskaia, and Nicolai Tijonov. All these figures were linked with the World Movement for Peace, as well as Ghanaian President Kwame Nkrumah and the representative of the Chinese Committee for Peace, Kuo Mo-Jo. Indeed, General Cárdenas had exchanged extensive correspondence with them concerning the holding of a conference between three continents. As the former Mexican President had explained in a letter to Poblete in 1961, "I was opportunely informed by the members of the Mexican delegation who attended the New Delhi meeting, of the interest that arose in promoting an Afro-Asian-Latin American meeting. As you yourself say, I think that holding such a meeting would be of significant importance; at such a meeting, similar purposes to those expressed in our Latin American Conference, which met with a warm welcome, should be put forward."[52]

Indeed, Cárdenas's envoys to the Indian capital, his own son Cuauhtémoc Cárdenas Solórzano and Alonso Aguilar Monteverde, a founding member of the Mexican National Liberation Movement (MLN, by its Spanish initials), remember the differences that had to be negotiated with Chinese and African delegates, who apparently held a more radical discourse than other attendants to the New Delhi meeting. Afro-Asians emphatically insisted on national problems, "which had to be called by their proper names" and suggested that ambiguity and eclecticism were to be avoided, since these involuntarily tended to soften the political discourse.[53]

Even so, the Mexican variant of a three-continent conference never took place: the Cubans appear to have won the game against their most important Latin American ally. Several hypotheses can be advanced toward explaining this. For one, the tone that the former Mexican president wanted for a possible conference in which all three continents would take part was different from the tone that the Cubans wanted for "their" three-continent conference. Cárdenas's pacifistic vocation is widely known, as is the emphasis that he placed especially on subjects such as economic independence as pre-requirements for achieving a stable peace and sovereignty. On these issues, as well as on rejecting all kinds of colonialism and racism, the proliferation of nuclear weapons, and being in favor of eliminating military bases, the former president of Mexico and the Cubans agreed, at least in terms of their discourse.[54] Where no agreement was clear was on who the Latin American representatives should be who would take part in the preparatory committee, or on how they should be appointed. It seems obvious that, at the root of the differences between the Cuban and the Mexican projects, lay the idea that Cárdenas had concerning the content and the way in which the conference ought to be prepared. As he had written to Youssef El Sebai, Secretary General of the Organization for Afro-Asian Solidarity in 1963:

We insist before Latin America's agencies and among various individuals regarding the need to begin working towards the Second Latin American Conference for National Sovereignty, Economic Emancipation and Peace within this year's final two months, thus complying with the agreement established at the first Conference and laying out a permanent representative structure for Latin American anti-imperialist forces, which should coordinate and stimulate the common struggle in the hemisphere . . . We also believe it to be advisable that the second Latin American Conference should be held ahead of the Three-Continent Conference, for this would lend more strength and unity to emancipation ideas and purposes, which in turn will develop a permanent continental organization capable of coordinating and consolidating its actions and would thus be represented at the Three-Continent Conference.[55]

It is no coincidence that the Mexicans became aloof from the "Cuban variant" of a three-continent conference, as illustrated by the Mexican delegation's absence from the first meeting of the preparation committee that took place in Cairo at the beginning of September 1965.[56] The meeting's coordination fell to Mehdi Ben Barka and Youssef El-Sebai, respectively Chairman and Secretary General, and who, at the same time, represented Morocco and the United Arab Republic at the preparation committee. Designating the writing committee was not too difficult; it would be made up of representatives from the United Arab Republic, Algeria, Vietnam, and Venezuela (at Cuba's request, who yielded its post to the Venezuelan delegation). Joaquín Más Martínez, Giraldo Mazola Collazo, and Silvio Rivera Pérez attended as Cuban representatives. Also present were Waldo Attias (Frente de Acción Popular, Chile), Gregorio Sapin (Frente de Izquierda de Liberación, Uruguay), and Héctor Pérez Marcano (Frente Armado de Liberación Nacional, Venezuela) as Latin American representatives to the Tricontinental Conference's preparation committee. The meeting's main focus was the conference's agenda, the calendar for its sessions, and the drafting of the general summons.[57]

Yet, the hardest issue to deal with continued to be the integration of the Latin American delegations. The Cubans posited the criteria that, in their opinion, groups should be truly *representative of the people, against imperialism and unitary*. It is hardly a coincidence that these terms were used: around midyear 1965, just before the preparatory meeting in Cairo, the Cubans themselves had to acknowledge an inconvenient situation when the Guatemalan representation to the meeting of the preparation committee, which had originally fallen on Yon Sosa, leader of the November 13 Movement, had to be replaced by a representative of the Revolutionary Armed Forces (FAR). As the Preparatory Committee noted, "the November 13 Movement has been split and has undergone a change in its position. Because of this, we ask the Preparation Committee to please accept this modification."[58] This was far from the only time that factional problems became evident, not only for the Tricontinental Conference as an event, but for the idea of a coherent Latin American regional participation in a three-continent organization. Ultimately these problems rested on disunity in criteria regarding the forms and direction the struggle against the common enemy of "imperialism" should adopt. The Cubans' preference for assuming the offensive and their position in favor of armed struggle clashed with other less radical or "reformist" Latin American positions. And these differences took shape in the way the future hosts of the Tricontinental considered and dealt with those who agreed (or not) with their positions.

Indeed, designating Latin American Conference delegates became the source of serious disputes. Officially, the USSR chose not to take sides, arguing "the representation of Latin America's countries is a matter of their own choosing . . . and that it supported the criteria quoted by the Latin American delegations." The Guinean delegate, supported by Tanzania's, stated "it was not fair for us to accept the organizations proposed by the delegations of Africa and Asia, while rejecting the proposals put forward by the Latin American delegations." The Venezuelan representative thanked the president and the secretary general for the opportunity to take part and supported the Cuban proposal. The representative from Indonesia expressed his inclination for "the Communist Parties from all three continents not to directly take part in this Conference because they raise numerous problems and inviting them creates a kind of instability." Finally, there was an attempt by Ben Barka to find a solution, by explicitly asking Latin American representatives to "produce a definitive list for the committee's president." Indonesian and Japanese delegates then coincided in suggesting another meeting before the three-continent conference itself, for reviewing the invitation proposals. According to a MINREX report of the meeting, "The Chinese delegate supported Ben Barka's proposal but asked that the following paragraph be added: 'this list shall form the basis for discussions, but it should not be the only one and this should not be construed in any way as meddling in the affairs of Latin America.'" In the final vote, the delegates from the USSR, Guinea, India, and Tanzania ended up tipping the balance in favor of the Moroccans' proposal, which was in the end the Cuban proposal. A similar argument took place also for choosing the observers.[59]

Despite the frictions described above, the Cuban revolutionary government's efforts ended up yielding satisfactory results, when it was finally granted the seat of the Tricontinental Conference. The coincidence of the Cuban political "agenda," which openly confronted the United States, with that of other Third World countries ended up being extremely beneficial for the decision. This was the case, for example, with Vietnam, for whom the Havana Conference represented an unparalleled platform from which to denounce the intervention of U.S. troops in the country just a year before. Although the war to secure South Vietnam against communist forces had found other formidable sympathetic tribunes in Western Europe and even inside the United States, as well as in Afro-Asian Conferences, especially the one held at Moshi, the denunciation promoted from Havana and the general call made from the island to promote wide-ranging campaigns and acts of solidarity with Vietnam throughout Latin America and around the entire world sought to provoke a much more powerful and effective reaction.

The negotiations and agreements that led to deciding that 1966 would be the year for holding the Tricontinental Conference probably could not have anticipated a costlier set of circumstances for the meeting to take place: the year 1965 had seen the U.S. invasion of the Dominican Republic in the Caribbean, together with President Lyndon Johnson's ramping up of the U.S. presence and its military activity in Vietnam, respectively during the months of April and July; coups in Algeria (against the government of Ahmed Ben Bella) and in the Congo (against Joseph Kasavubu) in June and November, respectively, while Ben Barka, who had been one of the main organizers and a paramount ally of the Cubans in ensuring that the Tricontinental Conference took place in Havana, was kidnapped and later murdered at the end of October. And yet, while costly, these events also provided a useful context for a politically charged and explicitly anti-imperialist meeting to take place.[60]

Moreover, in the context of such complex political circumstances and with the support of African and Asian countries as co-sponsors, the Cubans hoped that by hosting the Tricontinental Conference, they might protect themselves against a new external attack. True, after the 1962 Missile Crisis, the United States had agreed with the USSR not to invade Cuba. But the growing counter-revolutionary current in international affairs reinforced the Cuban perception of being threatened from the outside and of being isolated: "We were convinced that the United States was planning to attack Cuba," one senior Cuban official noted.[61] Meanwhile, the Tricontinental Conference provided an unparalleled domestic opportunity for making a call for unity and for recapturing political control. Although internal goals could not be handled publicly, celebrating the conference was a way for the regime to consolidate itself against old, renewed threats and betrayals.[62] Finally, almost at the same time that the last preparations for the conference were taking place, the Cuban public's attention could be drawn away while a rescue and withdrawal operation was being carried out to save Che Guevara, the island's best soldier, from the failure of his African adventure in the Congo. When revolutionaries from Africa, Asia, and Latin America gathered in Havana to espouse a new *Tricontinentalism*, Che, defeated, was forced to renounce the possibility of waging a revolutionary war in the Congo.[63] In this difficult context, impossible to anticipate or foresee, the island tried to reshape its political leadership before the world, incorporating into its "natural" rebellious spirit a reiterated belligerence, clothed in global solidarity, to try to force its historical enemy to fight on many fronts at the same time, and thus contribute to hastening its defeat.

Putting the Finishing Touches to Begin the "Year of Solidarity" in Grand Style

The last few months of 1965 had been especially intense for Cuba's Foreign Ministry in trying to ensure the Tricontinental Conference's success. Indeed, between the months of October and December 1965, multiple instructions were sent from the Minister's office to unify Cuban diplomats' efforts regarding the promotion of the meeting. MINREX distributed information and documentation about it in several languages, held press conferences, cocktail parties, and talks, while obtaining public statements of support from outstanding leaders and politicians. Using cable, invitations addressed to the various participants, including members of liberation movements and other social and mass organizations, such as solidarity committees, were formalized. The Cubans, acting as hosts, sent the invitations, although they were also sent on behalf of the Preparatory Committee's president and secretary general, Ben Barka and El Sebai. When the addressees were Afro-Asian countries, contacting the Afro-Asian solidarity organizations in each country was considered important, as was trying to gauge reactions to the inclusion of Latin America as part of the community and as the future headquarters of the three-continent meeting.[64]

As in the case of other sources cited here, the content of these exchanges contributes to illustrating the problems that preparatory committee and, of course, Cuba encountered in deciding which countries to invite and the way to integrate the attending delegations. In countries like Indonesia, where a coup had taken place, the internal political situation made it difficult to put a delegation together. Nevertheless, given the place that the country held in the Afro-Asian community and in the Non-Aligned Movement, it was impossible not to try and ensure the presence of Indonesian representatives at the conference. In Ceylon, meanwhile, political leaderships were clearly divided because of the Sino-Soviet conflict. Cuba also found itself in an embarrassing situation when representatives from Israel expressed their interest in attending the conference, a petition that was declined. Indeed, the Cubans had to prepare themselves against the angry reaction that the news generated among Arab potential delegates, who had embraced the Palestinian cause. And, as already noted, the case of Yugoslavia became especially problematic when the Vietnam representation that participated in the preparation committee vetoed its invitation, given that it had expressed its preference for a negotiated solution to the Vietnam conflict. These are just some examples of a convulsed international situation that, far from favoring the unification of the world's revolutionary forces, seemed to test all efforts to put together the Tricontinental Conference.[65]

Meanwhile, between September 26 and 30, just before his subsequent death, Ben Barka had visited Cuba to meet with Osmany Cienfuegos and his staff. The two greatest facilitators of the future meeting had discussed political preoccupations that both apparently shared. Ben Barka had seemed most worried about the Latin American participants, which had not yet been chosen. It was in this context that the decision was made to directly invite representatives from the British and Dutch Guianas, as well as from Puerto Rico. It was also decided that Latin American countries should put together national committees to attend the conference as representatives/guests. The Moroccan used the opportunity to again put forward the need to create a new entity that should encompass all three continents. As a Cuban record of the conversation noted, "such a new organization would solve the current problems confronting the Afro-Asian organization. This proposal by Ben Barka was favorably received by us, as it coincides with our aspirations."[66]

After Ben Barka's visit to Havana in late September 1965, a team of Cuban diplomats and officials met for several days at the beginning of November with their foreign affairs minister to fine-tune the details of what would be the penultimate preparation meeting before the conference took place. During these working sessions, they discussed various texts in detail, some of which were to be published as extended journalistic essays in the domestic press.[67] It could not have been otherwise: each text was a fundamental part of the great political performance that the Tricontinental Conference was to be. The encounter, which was decisive for Third World diplomatic propaganda, was not only given a great stage (the Free Havana Hotel, formerly the Hilton), consecrated with images of Lumumba, Sandino, and Van Troi, but also had a carefully crafted script, in which words were chosen with the greatest care, so as to anticipate any unforeseen political troubles with the best possible reply, *suaviter in modo, fortiter in re* (gently in manner, firmly in action). The final result was a general framework in which every symbolic and interpretative "raw material" was developed, to be shared later during the event as master narratives for the purpose of creating awareness, loyalty, and political urgency.[68]

Well known for the deep imprint that his interventions left in international forums, where delegates from every part of the world listened to him with special interest and attention, Cuban Foreign Minister Raúl Roa knew well the importance of dramatization as a support for ideas. It thus came as no surprise that, during the work sessions he held with his MINREX colleagues, the minister insisted, explicitly and on more than one occasion, on the need to "dramatize" through language: the world situation was to be exploited for maximum benefit by preparing the public on various subjects with polarizing approaches, using a language that was openly confrontational. For example, speaking about imperialism, the head of Cuban diplomacy suggested:

It is fundamental to take the international situation and the existing tensions as the starting point to underline that its great culprit is imperialism, which does not want peace. Therefore, . . . imperialism must be broken. This must be stated from the beginning, making a concrete reference to war and peace in a revolutionary sense. Talking about the attempts to attain peace and mentioning their failure. Referring to a world disarmament conference, since everything else has been a failure. A clear statement must be made concerning this issue, to put forward the world disarmament conference without excluding any country, referring to the limited and useless role that the UN have played . . . the peoples of the world want peace, imperialism wants war. This is a revolutionary criterion. In conclusion, [the minister said]: "Imperialism must be screw . . . [*descoj*], in clear and unadulterated Spanish." And all of this is a high priority for Cuba, given its international position.[69]

Similar examples occurred during the four workdays held by the Minister's disciples and collaborators, some of which went on into the late hours of the night. In them, the Cuban Minister proposed eliminating excesses from the text drafts (for example, following his indication, all discussion of military blocs was eliminated) that might cause undesired incidents with the conference's delegates; he stated the need to clearly identify central concepts (such as colonialism and imperialism); and made a call to carefully specify the historical realities of the countries invited to the conference. Through these observations, Roa sought to display the complexities of the Afro-Asian situation and give an interpretation of the possible impact that these contexts inevitably had on liberation movements. His interventions are revealing when it came to his view (at times derogatory) of Cuba's partners within the Tricontinental. More broadly, they show how the Cuban revolutionary government conceived the world, global politics, regional configurations, and the most pressing issues of the day. As the minutes of the preparatory meetings noted Roa as saying:

> These factors must be considered in preparing the document; questions must be ordered according to their hierarchy, taking into account the international reality conditioning all work. Africans like to "paint themselves in distinct colors," they are "a loose, rare people." He quoted cases from his personal experience at international conferences. Additionally, he states that there is false information about what goes on in Africa, what is really happening is not what is being reported. A deceitful image has been created. But our government knows well what is happening . . . He exemplifies with the case of the UAR's position at the conferences. It is a singular position, one conceived to gain room to maneuver. And, because of that—he states—imperialism acts and takes advantage of it . . . it knows very well how to exploit that . . . The UAR also plays with those factors and takes advantage from them in their own way, by maneuvering . . . To conclude, the Arab-African world is complicated and, in reality, the true struggle is happening in Congo; everything else is "landscape, propaganda" and these realities needs to be taken into account in preparing the document.[70]

This passage allows several interpretations. For Roa, the important battle was being waged in the Congo: "everything else is landscape" is a very Cuban way of pointing out where the true struggles were taking place.[71] Was Roa aware of the Cuban presence in the Congo? A certain mistrust in his words toward some African countries—"a rare people"—is worth noticing, countries that the Minister further defined as "maneuvering," which in a Cuban framework had negative connotations of being "pragmatic." It is true that some African leaders were not convinced of the pertinence of Cuban participation in local struggles and, consequently, adopted a more cautious stance. Such is the case of Gamal Abdel Nasser, for example.[72] And yet today it is known that the nerve center of the struggle that the Cubans were trying to develop in Africa was, precisely, Cairo. And while this is known today, fifty years ago those who knew were encompassed in a phrase in the passage that we have just quoted: "the government."

Perhaps what was being discussed involved not only Africa's situation. In the last work session held for the preparation of these papers, a small debate took place between the officers and the Foreign Minister, when one of them alluded, as part of his presentation, to the intervention by Ernesto Guevara at the encounter held during the Afro-Asian Seminar, in February 1965 where Che had basically said that the socialist countries were "to a certain extent, accomplices to the imperial exploitation."[73] There followed a discussion about what Che had said and whether it should be mentioned or not as an argument. The terms of the debate deserve to be cited *in extens*:

> . . . FC. [Fernández Cossío] argues that with regard to investment or aid he has limited himself to consigning what Che said in the Afro-Asian Seminar. Roa supports the objections made by Pelegrín [Pelegrín Torras]. FC. mentions a Party meeting. Roa says to him: "If Osmany [Osmany Cienfuegos] sees that, he removes it immediately." Pelegrín explains why this should not be included. And there is a small debate about what Che said and whether or not to say now. Roa points out that nothing of what Che said in Algiers was later discussed with him. "And it was not discussed before," says Arnold [Arnold Rodriguez]. In truth his words there created a "problem" according to Roa, because the government estimated that what he said was not correct, but nothing was said about it to the comp. Guevara for reasons of delicacy; he added that he sent a cable to Che, but that he was the only one to do so. Arnold says the comp. Minister should write his memoirs, which would be very interesting, and Roa smiles. Barreiro [Jesús Barreiro González] points out that Che's work was published in authorized journals. Roa points out that the issue was clarified without affecting Che and closes the issue by expressing: "Che has left Cuba to continue to screw imperialism, do not believe otherwise. Che's withdrawal had nothing to do with what we discussed."[74]

This short exchange illustrates other concerns shared in confronting the absence of the person who best incarnated the three-continental spirit. In brief, it proves how much Roa and how much his staff knew about Che's fate, the latest news of whom had come from his famous farewell letter, read in public by Fidel Castro at the beginning of October 1965, during the re-foundation of the Cuban Communist Party. It seems, judging by the words as recorded in the minutes of the meeting, that the "official" explanation about Che's departure from Cuba had not been enough and that indeed there were significant differences of opinion stemming from Guevara's intervention at the Algiers conference, as well as his participation in this event with his definitive departure from Cuba. Given the existing doubts, Roa uttered a phrase that sought to calm them: "Che has left Cuba to continue to screw imperialism, do not believe otherwise." In the meantime, the three-continent conference was in the bag.[75]

Conclusions

The place occupied by "the South" in the Cold War's conceptualization has been the subject of numerous arguments and histories. The 1959 Cuban Revolution holds a special place within these historiographies, given the role it tried to play within the bipolar logic imposed by the Cold War. In the context of the sixties, a decade characterized as the heyday of great heroic leaderships in the world and in which the correlation of forces appeared to favor the left and international communism, Cuba needed to fight against the effects of the aggressive U.S. policy toward its young revolution. Despite having initially established itself as a nationalistic alternative, in the end the island accepted the aid offered to it by the Soviet Union and the socialist camp. Nevertheless, this did not bring about a complete ideological correspondence on the part of Cuba. In fact, and up to a certain point, the Cuban revolutionary project was considered by Soviet leaders to be a heresy: in the context of its foreign policy, Cuba aspired to extend the revolution to Latin America and around the middle of the decade it began to explore the African continent. The Cuban leadership regarded the development of a guerrilla movement at a continental—and global—scale as a major imperative, and in practice it opposed the Soviet foreign policy of peaceful coexistence. The Tricontinental was born as an essential part of that rebellious foreign policy, which aspired to build an anticolonial, anti-imperial, and revolutionary alliance. The Cuban position vis-à-vis the so-called Third World and Latin America was summarized in Fidel Castro's famous phrase within his "Second Declaration of Havana" (1962) that "the duty of every revolutionary is to carry out the revolution" and was strengthened by the motto for which the conference and its subsequent organization would be identified from early 1967 onward: "To create two, three, many Vietnams."

In this context, Cuba was immersed in two important international circumstances: not only the division of the international communist movement, verified especially in the Sino-Soviet conflict, but also the enormous sociohistorical complexity that made unity around a single third-world project impossible. The Tricontinental Conference was, then, an extraordinary gamble, a unique opportunity for Cubans taking advantage of numerous factors in the international arena to strengthen its political position: African decolonization, the war in Vietnam, the invasion of the Dominican Republic. Given its ability to convene, the conference was considered to have posed an enormous danger not only for the United States, but also for those countries who sought to establish other orders based on political subordination, as displayed by Moscow and Beijing in those times. The disputes around it were extremely negative for the unity of several movements, such as the Non-Aligned Movement and the Afro-Asian People's Solidarity Organization, which sought to transcend ideological positions. In these complex conditions, Cuba attempted to act as a political mediator, avoiding taking sides with the USSR or China, while seeking to capitalize on its enormous international prestige to influence these organizations through certain African leaders with whom the island cultivated a deep relationship. In this effort, figures such as Algerian President Ahmed Ben Bella and Moroccan Mehdi Ben Barka were indispensable facilitators for Cuban purposes.

Telling the story of the Tricontinental thus becomes a challenge, to the extent that "official" narratives seek to ignore or minimize the conflicts that existed in those years in the face of Cuba's goal. The most controversial story about the preparations for the meeting has been little looked at. But by incorporating new angles of analysis and multiple actors, and by considering their relationships and interactions, as well as the means and resources available to them, the researcher is in a better position to do justice to the complexity of the historical moment—indeed global moment—and also to the path chosen by the Cuban revolution. In this sense, and with the information available from the diplomatic documents consulted, it is possible to infer, for example, that some representatives of Latin American forces of those years, like Mexico, attempted to hinder the Cuban purpose of winning the conference venue. In other words, the positions of Latin America's revolutionary forces were far from automatic or unavoidable. Most likely, other behaviors, to be considered in future works, allowed the Latin American forces to be balanced against the Cuban initiative. In any case, to understand the roles of all these actors in the making of the Tricontinental Conference, the original documents of Cuban archives are invaluable to help establish an increasingly accurate history.

Notes

1. See *Mehdi Ben Barka 50 ans après*, / ouvrage coordonné par l'association Sortir du colonialism, Paris, Les Petits Matins, 2015.

2. See chapters "1. De Bandoung a La Havane" and "2. La tricontinentale," Lentin, *La lutte tricontinentale*, 19–67.

3. There is, of course, a vast literature about the Third World in the context of the Cold War. See, for example, McMahon, *The Cold War in the Third World*.

4. See Laron, "Semi-Peripheral Countries and the Invention of the 'Third World.'"

5. "Address of President Julius Nyerere at the Inaugural Session of the Conference." In *The Third Afro-Asian peoples' Solidarity Conference*, 9–14.

6. See Vitalis, "The Midnight Ride of Kwame Nkrumah."

7. See Jansen, *Nonalignment and the Afro-Asian States*; Kimche, *The Afro-Asian Movement*.

8. See itinerary and chronology of Guevara's first trip in Fernández Cañizares, *Un viaje histórico con el Che*, 194–198.

9. As illustrative examples of the various historiographical approaches published on the Tricontinental and its aftermath, see, for example, Barcia, "'Locking horns with the Northern Empire'"; Harmer, "Two, Three, Many revolutions?"; Anne Garland Mahler, "The Global South in the Belly of the Beast"; Erik Zolov, "La tricontinental y el mensaje del Che Guevara." I am grateful for access to additional nonpublished academic work thanks to the infinite generosity of friends and interlocutors, for instance, Alexis Anagnan's research, "L'événement tricontinental: genèse, réalités et enjeux d'une Conférence tiers-mondiste," Mémoire de maîtrise sous la direction d'Annick Lempérière, Université de Paris I, 2006.

10. Faligot, *Tricontinentale*.

11. This research at the Cuban Foreign Affairs Ministry Archives was made possible with support from Reinier Hernández and Manuel Normando Agramonte Sánchez, who, in 2016, attended investigators at the offices of the Archives of the Ministry of Cuban Foreign Affairs. No one could imagine that today's octogenarian Agramonte is the same person who was a former officer of the Cuban Military Mission and Cuban ambassador to the Congo, between 1965 and 1967. See, for example, the very interesting photo and its corresponding caption in Gleijeses, *Conflicting Missions*, 167.

12. The Tricontinental Conference archive at MINREX is not specifically catalogued. Therefore, the documents examined here will be quoted by their full title, author, date, and page number whenever possible. In order to avoid unnecessary repetitions, unless otherwise specified, all documents from the aforementioned archive share the same origin: Fondo Archivo Central, Centro de Gestión Documental, MINREX-Cuba, Tricontinental, 1965–1981, ordn. [Hereafter MINREX-Cuba, Tricontinental, 1965–1981, ordn.]

13. "On the go" ["a la carrera"] is an expression that living Cuban diplomats from that era like to use in order to refer to the way in which they were trained to become ambassadors and representatives of the revolutionary government despite their inexperience in the foreign service. See, for example, Martínez Salsamendi, *Las carreras para ser diplomático*.

14. Raúl Roa García (1907–1982) was one of the most comprehensive Cuban intellectuals. A grandson of mambí, he carried rebellion in his blood naturally. Member of the "Generation of the 30s," lawyer and diplomat, university teacher, prolific writer, founder of cultural institutions and several journals, Cuban ambassador and Foreign Minister for more than a decade since the first months of the revolution, great reader, polemicist, and caustic orator, knowledgeable like few of his language, he was indefatigable to the bone and a key piece in the history of the Tricontinental. For more on the life of Foreign Minister Raúl Roa, see Ramos Ruiz, *Ni juramentos ni milagros*.

15. For a Cuban institutional history of the MINREX, see Céspedes Carrillo, *Las relaciones exteriores de Cuba*. For a contrasting ideological position, see Braña, *El aparato*.

16. See interview to Giraldo Mazola, first president of ICAP, "La defensa de la Revolución cubana es un deber internacionalista del pueblo cubano" in Suárez Salazar and Kruijt, *La Revolución cubana en nuestra América*.

17. See, for example, "Relación de actividades realizadas para la Conferencia Tri-continental," Dirección de Política Regional V, Europa Occidental. MINREX-Cuba, Tricontinental, 1965–1981, ordn., 2 p.

18. "Trabajos a realizar por las distintas Direcciones del Ministerio para la Conferencia Tri-continental," Havana, October 20, 1965, 2 p., MINREX-Cuba, Tricontinental, 1965–1981, ordn.

19. On Cuban diplomatic relations after 1959, Alzugaray Treto explained: "If in 1958 these were extended to 49 countries—21 of them in America—, in 1965 the figure was 65—but only 2 in America and the rest in Asia, Africa and Europe. Over the course of those years, 21 states broke or suspended their official ties with our country, and Cuba, in turn, cut them with two: Nationalist China (Taiwan) and the Dominican Republic. In return, relations were established with 10 countries in Asia, 13 in Africa and 11 in Europe." See Alzugaray Treto, "Raúl Roa García y la creación de una cancillería revolucionaria."

20. In a small and rare monograph, Charles Neuhauser stated: "The Conakry Conference has authorized the establishment of an AAPSO Fund Committee, whose primary purpose would be to help finance the 'struggle' of the various liberation movements affiliated with the AAPSO . . . the chairman of this fund was the Guinean Ismail Touré, and one deputy chairman was to the Moroccan leader Mehdi Ben Barka. Both these men at this time were cooperating quite closely with the other deputy chairman, Chu Tzu-chi: these three men were further authorized to disburse fund in exceptional cases without consulting with other members of the Fund Committee," 35. David A. Crain shares this position when he states sharply: "AAPSO, founded in 1957–1958 as a non-governmental organization, maintained its headquarters in Cairo and was financed by Moscow, Peking and the United Arab Republic." Crain, "The Course of the Cuban Heresy," 130.

21. Faligot, *Tricontinentale*, 16, 60–61.

22. See *Youssef El-Sebai, in memoriam*. Cairo, Egypt: Permanent Secretariat of AAPSO, 1978.

23. See Martínez Pérez, *Los hijos de Saturno*, 100.

24. Jeffrey James Byrne has published a wonderful investigation on the role played by Algeria in relation to the Third World and the Cold War, from its independence until 1965. While Algeria did not take part in the Tricontinental Conference, Ahmed Ben Bella

was fundamental because of his support for the young Cuban revolutionaries in connection with the project for the three-continent meeting. See Byrne, *Mecca of Revolution*.

25. To consult data from some of these diplomats, it is useful to visit www.ecured.cu/EcuRed:Enciclopedia_cubana. Some recent historical investigations contribute to rounding the biographical information pertaining to these officers. See, for example, Kruijt, *Cuba and Revolutionary Latin America*; Suárez Salazar Dirk Kruijt, *La Revolución cubana en nuestra América*; López Blanch, *Historias secretas de médicos cubanos*.

26. Osmany Cienfuegos Gorriarán (1931–)—brother of one of the emblematic heroes of the Revolution, Commander Camilo Cienfuegos—had militated in the Socialist Youth, along with Raúl Castro, prior to the revolutionary triumph of January 1959. Trained as an architect, Osmany was exiled in México during the fights in the Sierra Maestra. He was appointed Minister of Public Works at the revolutionary movement's victory. In 1965, he was appointed head of the Foreign Affairs Commission of the recently founded Cuban Communist Party. When the Tricontinental Conference took place, he was designated OSPAAAL's General Secretary. Tad Szulc described him as a man "not very dear in Cuba, Osmany rarely appears in public; he is the classic 'man in the shade,' calm and gray, and an example that it is no longer necessary to be a faithful gentleman to exercise power on the island." Carlos Rafael Rodríguez, Raúl Castro, and Osmany Cienfuegos, said Szulc, "form the first line of the power structure directly under Fidel." Tad Szulc, *Fidel, un retrato crítico*, Barcelona: Grijalbo, 1987, 61, 64. Osmany Cienfuegos was one of the key individuals in ensuring Cuba's presence in Africa. Gleijeses, *Conflicting Missions*, 91.

27. See Suárez Salazar and Kruijt, *La Revolución cubana en nuestra América*, 409.

28. "Crear dos, tres . . . muchos Vietnams. Mensaje a los pueblos del mundo a través de la *Tricontinental*," Havana, Cuba, April 16, 1967. www.marxists.org/espanol/guevara/04_67.htm

29. See Roa Kourí, *En el torrente*, 151–153; DuBois, *The Conakry Conference*; Weinstein, "The Second Asian-African Conference."

30. "Índice de los documentos especiales de la Conferencia Tri-continental," no date, 1 p. MINREX-Cuba, Tricontinental, 1965–1981, ordn., 28 p.

31. Concerning the Belgrade Conference, see Pettinà, "Global Horizons."

32. The anecdote, recovered by one of Che's inseparable witnesses on that tour, is remembered in these terms: "At the beginning of the conversation was the press, but Marshal Tito told them, "Well you can go, I WANT TO TALK TO THE REVOLUTIONARIES OF AMERICA." There was a time when Che was able to talk to him alone. Then on the plane, Che said to me, "Look Omar how these people are, I asked for help to buy armaments and he told me that he did not have that in existence however, the newspaper of that day talked about a weapons sale of Yugoslavia to Africa.' Che told me, 'I told him to buy no giveaway.'" Fernández Cañizares, *Un viaje histórico con el Che*, 136. (Capital letters in original text.)

33. "Instrucciones enviadas/Tareas asignadas, República Federativa Socialista de Yugoslavia," Confidencial 4/65, page 2, MINREX-Cuba, Tricontinental, 1965–1981, ordn.

34. "The Council RECOMMENDS THAT a detailed study of the possibilities of summoning to a Solidarity Conference of Afro-Asian and Latin American Peoples be

conducted." "Decisión adoptada en la IV Sesión del Consejo de la Organización de Solidaridad de los Pueblos Afro-asiáticos (Decision adopted at the IV Session of the Council of the Solidarity Organization of Afro-Asian Peoples)," Bandung, April 1961, Doc. No. PAAL/1, MINREX-Cuba, Tricontinental, 1965–1981, ordn. (Capital letters in original text.)

35. "Decisión adoptada en la sesión ejecutiva, con relación a la Convocatoria de una conferencia de solidaridad de los pueblos latinoamericanos y afro-asiáticos (Decision adopted at the executive session regarding the Summons to a conference of solidarity of the Latin American and Afro-Asian Peoples), Gaza, December 9–11, 1961." doc. No. PAAL/2. MINREX-Cuba, Tricontinental, 1965–1981, ordn.

36. Armando Entralgo, "Reunión Tri-continental, De Bandung a Moshi," *Política Internacional*, Habana, Instituto de Política Internacional del MINREX, año 1, no. 2, Segundo Trimestre, 1963, 39–52.

37. "In a letter to the Cuban leaders, Cameroonian Osende Afana expressed: 'It is our duty to mobilize the peoples of the entire world to the fullest and particularly those of Latin America, Asia and Africa. *We already have an important common base: it is the Solidarity movement of Afro-Asian peoples. It is enough to extend it to the anti-imperialist organizations of Latin America, in accordance with the decision of the last meeting of Bandung*'" Entralgo, "Reunión Tri-continental, De Bandung a Moshi," 42–43. (Italics in original).

38. Faligot, *Tricontinentale*, 73.

39. "Decision adopted at the meeting of the 12 members countries elected by the Third Solidarity Conference of Afro-Asian Peoples," Moshi, February 1963, and "Special Resolution concerning the Three-Continent Conference," Doc. No. PAAL/3 and 4. MINREX-Cuba, Tricontinental, 1965–1981, ordn.

40. Verified among attendees as conference observer. *The Third Afro-Asian Peoples' Solidarity Conference*, 142.

41. Friedman, *Shadow Cold War*, 98.

42. See Heikal, *The Cairo Documents*, 343–357.

43. "Special Resolution on the Three Continent Conference." In: *The Third Afro-Asian peoples' Solidarity Conference*, 110–111.

44. "Decision of the 12-Member Committee (Cairo, Junio 8, 1963)," Doc. No. PAAL/8. MINREX-Cuba, Tricontinental, 1965–1981, ordn.

45. Piero Gleijeses claimed that the Cuban adventure in Africa began in Algeria. By this he referred to the early assistance that the Cubans had given to the Algerians: "in January 1962, a Cuban ship unloaded weapons at Casablanca for the Algerians and returned to Havana with seventy-six wounded guerrillas and twenty children from refugee camps." Gleijeses, *Conflicting Missions*, 7. According to Roger Faligot, the Algerian-Cuban friendship was sealed when the Cuban ambassador to Algeria, Jorge Serguera Riverí, served as a facilitator for Cuban military and material aid to arrive in Algeria, amid the imminent danger of the outbreak of war with Morocco, in October 1963. On the other hand, also in Faligot's account is the trip by Guevara to Algeria in July 1963, where Che met with several advisers of the Algerian president, who offered to support the project of the Tricontinental. See "Le trio Ben Bella, Guevara, Ben Barka," Faligot, *Tricontinentale*,

15–23. This information can be confirmed in Serguera's reports. See Serguera, *Caminos del Che*, 149–161.

46. "Decision of the Sixth Session of the Solidarity Council of Afro-Asian peoples (Algeria, March 1964)," Doc. No. PAAL/9, MINREX-Cuba, Tricontinental, 1965–1981, ordn.

47. For instance: "At the conclusion of the meeting, Yazid and Ben Barka flew to Cairo, where they were able to get the AAPSO Permanent Secretariat to 'agree' that ideological debates should not be conducted at organization meetings. At the same time new consultations were held on the issue of the Afro-Asian-Latin American meeting, and it was again agreed that a special delegation be sent to Castro to explore the possibilities of such a meeting." See Neuhauser, *Third World Politics*, 50.

48. "Carta de invitación al Comité Preparatorio de la Conferencia Tricontinental (Letter of Invitation to the Preparation Committee of the Three-Continent Conference)," Cairo, June 26, 1965 (Signed) El Mahdi Ben Barka, President of the Preparation Committee; Youssef El Sebai, Secretary General of the Permanent Afro-Asian Secretariat. Doc. No. PAAL/15, MINREX-Cuba, Tricontinental, 1965–1981, ordn.

49. "Decisión de la IV Conferencia de solidaridad de los pueblos afro-asiáticos (Decision of the IV Solidarity Conference of Afro-Asian Peoples)," Winneba, May 1965. Doc. No. PAAL/14, MINREX-Cuba, Tricontinental, 1965–1981, ordn.

50. "Memorándum de Ricardo Alarcón de Quesada a Señor ministro [Raúl Roa]. Asunto: Conferencia Tricontinental, La Habana, 30 de julio de 1965, 'Año de la Agricultura,'" 6 p., MINREX-Cuba, Tricontinental, 1965–1981, ordn.

51. "Memorándum de Ricardo Alarcón de Quesada a Señor ministro [Raúl Roa]. Asunto: Conferencia Tricontinental, La Habana, 30 de julio de 1965, 'Año de la Agricultura,'" 6 p., MINREX-Cuba, Tricontinental, 1965–1981, ordn.

52. "Letter from Lázaro Cárdenas to Olga Poblete," June 14, 1961, *Epistolario de Lázaro Cárdenas*, México, Siglo XXI Editores, 1974, v. 2, III, *Temas Internacionales*, 218–219.

53. See *Alonso Aguilar Monteverde. Por un México libre y menos injusto*, México, Grupo Editorial Cenzontle, 2007, pp.72–73.

54. See Keller, "Heated Rhetoric, Cold Warfare and the 1961 Latin American Peace Conference," 93–104.

55. Letter, Mr. Lázaro Cárdenas to Mr. Youssef El Sebai, Secretary General of the Organization for Afro-Asian Solidarity, Mexico, Abril 23, 1963, Doc. No. PAAL/7, MINREX-Cuba, Tricontinental, 1965–1981, ordn.

56. "Compendio del Proceso Verbal de la Primera Reunión del Comité Preparatorio (Compendium of the Verbal Process of the First Meeting of the Preparation Committee," Wednesday, September 1, 1964 (morning), (tape n. 1, track 1). Doc. No. PAAL/30, MINREX-Cuba, Tricontinental, 1965–1981, ordn., 3 p.

57. "Llamamiento para la Primera Conferencia de la Solidaridad de los Pueblos de África, de Asia y de América Latina." Doc. No. PAAL/25, MINREX-Cuba, Tricontinental, 1965–1981, ordn. [3 p.]

58. Letter, Waldo Attias (FRAP, Chile), Gregorio Sapin (FIDEL, Uruguay), Giraldo Mazola (PURS, Cuba), Héctor Pérez Marcano (FLN, Venezuela) to the Preparatory

Committee of the Tricontinental Conference, Doc. No. PAAL/27, MINREX-Cuba, Tricontinental, 1965–1981, ordn. 1 p.

59. "Compendio del Proceso Verbal de la Tercera Reunión del Comité Preparatorio (Compendium of the Verbal Process of the Third Meeting of the Preparation Committee)," Thursday, September 2, 1965 (morning), (band no.1, tracks 3 and 4), Doc. No. PAAL/36, MINREX-Cuba, Tricontinental, 1965–1981, ordn., 4 p.

60. In connection with Ben Barka's murder, see Boukhari, *Raisons d'États, tout sur l'affaire Ben Barka et d'autre crimes politiques au Maroc*.

61. See conversation between Jorge Risquet and Nikita Krushev as quoted in Gleijeses, *Conflicting Missions*, 93.

62. See "Proces Cubela: échec de la CIA gace à la Tricontinentale," Faligot, *Tricontinentale*, 483.

63. According to Piero Gleijeses, "at 3:00 A.M. on November 21 [1965], Che's column left the Zairean shore aboard the two new motorboats manned by a Cuban crew . . . On November 27, Tanzanian army trucks drove them [the cubans] to Dar-es-Salaam. On December 6, they boarded two Aeroflot IL-18s, which had been sent for them, flew to Moscow and from there to Cuba. Che Guevara was not among them . . . Che lived in a small apartment in the embassy in Dar-es-Salaam for more than three months, and due to security concerns, he never went out. In this apartment, he wrote two documents for Fidel: 'Pasajes de la guerra revolucionaria (Congo)' and 'Evaluación del personal a mis órdenes.'" Gleijeses, *Conflicting Missions*, 147–149.

64. Instructions consulted had a single heading: "Intercambio de correspondencia e información para la [nombre de la misión] con relación a la Conferencia Tricontinental durante la semana que termina el [día] de [mes] de 1965." They were issued to the Cuban embassies in Austria, Finland, Denmark, Mali, Algeria, Guinea, Ghana, UAR, Morocco, Canada, Jamaica, Mexico, Ceylon, Indonesia, Japan, Pakistan, India, Great Britain, France, Italy, Spain, Greece, Netherlands, Norway, Sweden, Belgium, Switzerland, Lebanon, GDR, Democratic Korea, Democratic Republic of Vietnam, Czechoslovakia, Rumania, China, Yugoslavia, Mongolia, USSR, Albania, and Hungary.

65. "Informes sobre los problemas conflictivos del Área Asiática no-socialista que pueden presentarse en la Conferencia Tri-Continental (Reports about the problems in the non-socialist Asian area that could arise at the Three-Continent Conference," no date, 64 p., MINREX-Cuba, Tricontinental, 1965–1981, ordn.

66. "Breve resumen para informar a los embajadores de Cuba en el extranjero de los asuntos tratados con el Sr. Ben Barka durante la visita a Cuba que realizó del 26 al 30 de septiembre de 1965." MINREX-Cuba, Tricontinental, 1965–1981, ordn. [2 p].

67. Fernando Álvarez Tabío, Jesús Barreiro González, Fernando Flores Ibarra, José Fernández Cossío, Pelegrín Torras, Arnold Rodríguez, Carlos Alfaras, and Eduardo Delgado Bermúdez were present at the meetings.

68. Meetings were held on November 1, 1965 (9 am to 12:30 pm); November 2 (9 am to 11:30 am); November 4 (9 am to 9:30 am); and November 5 (4 am to 7:45 am).

69. "Conferencia Tricontinental. Reunión sobre ponencia, Noviembre 2 de 1965, de 9 am. a 11:30 am," November 2, 1965, MINREX-Cuba, Tricontinental, 1965–1981, ordn. p. 2.

70. "Noviembre 4 de 1965, de 9 am. a 9:30 am." November 4, 1965, MINREX-Cuba, Tricontinental, 1965–1981, ordn. pp. 4–5.

71. The Cuban presence in Congo lasted approximately seven months. It began in April 1965 and concluded in November of the same year. It was led by Ernesto Guevara himself, who commanded Column One, and the reservation of Column Two. In his *Passages of the Revolutionary War (Congo)*, Guevara described the Cuban experience in that country as "a failure" due to the "decomposition of combative morality," not only of the Congolese, but of the Cubans, in a phenomenon that Guevara called Cubans' "congolization." In a derogatory tone, he referred to this as a "set of habits and attitudes towards the Revolution that characterized the Congolese soldier in those times of struggle." See "Preliminary Warning," Guevara, *Pasajes de la Guerra Revolucionaria (Congo)* 27–29.

72. Nasser's advisor will remember the verbal exchange between Che and Nasser as follows: "You must forget all about this idea of going to the Congo. It won't succeed. You will be easily detected being a white man, and if we got other white men to go with you, you would be giving the imperialists the chance to say that there is no difference between you and the mercenaries . . . If you go into Congo with two Cuban battalions and I send and Egyptian battalion with you, it will be called foreign interference and it will do more harm than good." See Heikal, *The Cairo Documents*, 316–319.

73. See Gleijeses, *Conflicting Missions*, 79. In the original version of the speech, Che uses the word "imperial," not "imperialist," as Gleijeses quotes in his book.

74. "Noviembre 5 de 1965, de 4 am. a 7:45," November 5, 1965, MINREX-Cuba, Tricontinental, 1965–1981, ordn., 12.

75. Several authors, from different ideological positions, have speculated on the "real" causes that led Ernesto Guevara de la Serna to leave the island: See, for example, Anderson, *Che Guevara*; Castañeda, *La vida en rojo*; Taibo II, *Ernesto Guevara también conocido como El Che*, to mention some of the most important examples. The CIA speculated as follows in one of its reports: "4. Cuba. The Castro regime's ideological mentor, Che Guevara, is apparently in trouble. Guevara hast not been seen in public since last March. Rumors abound on his present status and whereabouts, but nothing solid has been reported. The most likely explanation is that Guevara's hard-line Marxism has at some point come into conflict with Castro's less orthodox approach to policy matter. There is no evidence, however, that a dispute has assumed such fundamental proportions as to shake the stability of the regime." CIA FOIA, "The president's daily brief, May 29, 1965," www.cia.gov/library/readingroom/docs/DOC_0005967704.pdf. Piero Gleijeses provides the most compelling version of this history. See Gleijeses, *Conflicting Missions*, 101–107.

Bibliography

Alzugaray Treto, Carlos. "Raúl Roa García y la creación de una cancillería revolucionaria: los primeros años (1959–1965)." In *Raúl Roa: Imaginarios* compiled by Ana Cairo Ballester. La Habana: Ciencias Sociales, 2008.

Anderson, John Lee. *Che Guevara: una vida revolucionaria*. Barcelona: Emecé Editores, 2nd ed., 1997.

Anagnan, Alexis. "L'événement tricontinental: genèse, réalités et enjeux d'une Conférence tiers-mondiste." Mémoire de maîtrise sous la direction d'Annick Lempérière, Université de Paris I, 2006.

Barcia, Manuel. "'Locking Horns with the Northern Empire': Anti-American Imperialism at the Tricontinental Conference of 1966 in Havana." *Journal of Transatlantic Studies* 7, no. 3, (2009): 208–217.

Boukhari, Ahmed. *Raisons d'États, tout sur l'affaire Ben Barka et d'autre crimes politiques au Maroc.* Aïn-Sebaâ-Casablanca: Editions maghrébines, 2005.

Braña, Manuel. *El aparato.* Coral Gables, FL: Service Offset Printers, 1964.

Byrne, See Jeffrey James. *Mecca of Revolution. Algeria, Decolonization & the Third World Order.* New York: Oxford University Press, 2016.

Castañeda, Jorge G. *La vida en rojo: una biografía del Che Guevara.* Mexico: Alfaguara, 1997.

Céspedes Carrillo, Alicia. *Las relaciones exteriores de Cuba. Cambios estructurales (1868–2006).* Habana: Ministerio de Relaciones Exteriores, Editorial José Martí, 2008.

Crain, David Allan. "The Course of the Cuban Heresy: The Rise and Decline of Castroism's Challenge to the Soviet line in the Latin America Marxist Revolutionary Movement, 1963–1970." Doctoral thesis, Indiana University, Bloomington, Indiana,1972.

DuBois, Víctor. *The Conakry Conference: Its Implications for American Foreign Policy.* Pittsburgh, PA: Duquesne University Press, 1960.

Epistolario de Lázaro Cárdenas. Mexico: Siglo XXI Editores, 1974, 2 vols.

Faligot, Roger. *Tricontinentale, Quand Che Guevara, Ben Barka, Cabral, Castro et Hô Chi Minh préparaient la revolution mondiale (1964–1968).* Paris: Éditions La Découverte, 2013.

Fernández Cañizares, Omar. *Un viaje histórico con el Che.* La Habana: Ciencias Sociales, 2nd ed., 2008.

Friedman, Jeremy Scott. *Shadow Cold War. The Sino-Soviet Competition for the Third World.* Chapel Hill: University of North Carolina Press, 2015.

Garland Mahler, Anne. "The Global South in the Belly of the Beast: Viewing African American Civil Rights through a Tricontinental Lens." *Latin American Research Review* 50, no. 1 (2015): 95–116.

Gleijeses, Piero. *Conflicting Missions: Havana, Washington, and Africa, 1959–1976.* Chapel Hill: University of North Carolina Press, 2002.

Guevara, Ernesto Che. *Pasajes de la Guerra Revolucionaria (Congo).* Mexico: Ocean Sur, 2009.

Harmer, Tanya. "Two, Three, Many revolutions? Cuba and the Prospects for Revolutionary Change in Latin America, 1967–1975." *Journal of Latin American Studies* 45, no. 2013: 61–89

Heikal, Mohammed Hassanein. *The Cairo Documents: The Inside Story of Nasser and his Relationship with World Leaders, Rebels, and Statesmen.* Albany, NY: Doubleday, 1973.

Jansen, G.H. *Nonalignment and the Afro-Asian States.* New York: Frederick A. Praeger, 1966.

Keller, Renata. "Heated Rhetoric, Cold Warfare and the 1961 Latin American Peace Conference." In *Beyond the Eagle's Shadow: A Few Histories of Latin America's Cold War,* edited by Virginia Garrard-Burnett, Mark Atwood Lawrence, and Julio E. Moreno. Albuquerque: University of New Mexico Press, 2013.

Kimche, David. *The Afro-Asian Movement: Ideology and Foreign Policy of the Third World.* New Brunswick, NJ: Transaction, 1973.

Kruijt, Dirk. *Cuba and Revolutionary Latin America. An Oral History.* Zed Books Ltd., 2017.

Laron, Guy. "Semi-Peripheral Countries and the Invention of the 'Third World,' 1955–1965." *Third World Quarterly* 35, no. 9 (2014): 1547–1565.

Lentin, Albert Paul. *La lute tricontinentale. Impérialisme et revolution après la Conference de la Havane.* Paris: François Maspero, Coll., 86–87, 1966.

López Blanch, Hedelberto. *Historias secretas de médicos cubanos.* La Habana: Ediciones *La Memoria*, Centro Cultural Pablo de la Torriente Brau, 2005.

Martínez Pérez, Liliana. *Los hijos de Saturno: intelectuales y Revolución en Cuba.* Mexico: FLACSO-Mexico—Miguel Ángel Porrúa, 2006.

Martínez Salsamendi, Carlos. *Las carreras para ser diplomático.* Barcelona: Ruth Casa Editorial, 2013.

McMahon, Robert. *The Cold War in the Third World.* Oxford & New York: Oxford University Press, 2013.

Monteverde, Alonso Aguilar. *Por un México libre y menos injusto.* Mexico: Grupo Editorial Cenzontle, 2007.

Neuhauser, Charles. *Third World Politics: China and the Afro-Asian People's Solidarity Organization, 1957–1967.* Cambridge, MA: Harvard University Press, 1968.

Pettinà, Vanni. "Global Horizons: Mexico, the Third World, and the Non-Aligned Movement at the time of the 1961 Belgrade Conference." *The International History Review* 38, no. 4 (2016): 741–764

Ramos Ruiz, Danay. *Ni juramentos ni milagros. Raúl Roa en la cultura cubana.* La Habana: Editorial UH, 2016.

Roa Kourí, Raúl. *En el torrente.* La Habana: Fondo Editorial Casa de las Américas, 2004.

Serguera Riverí, Jorge. *Caminos del Che. Datos inéditos de su vida.* Mexico: Plaza y Valdés, 1997.

Suárez Salazar, Luis, and Dirk Kruijt. *La revolución cubana en nuestra América: el internacionalismo anónimo.* Barcelona: Ruth Casa Editorial, 2015.

Szulc, Tad. *Fidel, un retrato crítico.* Barcelona: Grijalbo, 1987.

Taibo II, Paco Ignacio. *Ernesto Guevara también conocido como El Che.* 3rd ed. Mexico: Planeta, 1996.

The Third Afro-Asian Peoples' Solidarity Conference. Moshi: Tanganyika, February 4–11, 1963. Published by the Permanent Secretariat of the Afro-Asian People's Solidarity Organization, Cairo UAR.

Vitalis, Robert. "The Midnight Ride of Kwame Nkrumah and Other Fables of Bandung (Bon-Doong)," *Humanity* 4, no. 2 (2013): 261–288.

Weinstein, Franklin B. "The Second Asian-African Conference: Preliminary Bouts." *Asian Survey* 5, no. 7 (1965): 359–373.

Zolov, Erik. "La tricontinental y el mensaje del Che Guevara. Encrucijadas de una nueva izquierda" *Palimpsesto* 6, no. 9 (2016): 1–13.

3

The Brazilian Far Left, Cuba, and the Sino-Soviet Split, 1963

New International Evidence on a Discordant "Struggle for Ascendancy"

JAMES G. HERSHBERG

In early 1963, Brazil's far Left was riven by division, competition, and complex maneuvering. The convoluted, murky, at times acrimonious jockeying for power among revolutionary, communist, and "ultra-nationalist" figures and factions was firmly rooted in Brazilian domestic politics, characterized by plotting against or with—or, in some cases, both—the center-left government of President João Goulart of the Brazilian Labor Party (PTB).

This chapter focuses on the story's international dimensions. In the aftermath of the Cuban Missile Crisis, against the backdrop of residual Soviet-Cuban tension, a sharpening Sino-Soviet schism, and the ongoing U.S.-Cuban battle (and the specter of "Castroism" in Latin America, particularly in Brazil), the internal Brazilian struggle inevitably entwined with both the East-West Cold War and deepening divisions in the communist world.

As the CIA observed, the first half of 1963 was marked "by a continuation of the struggle for ascendancy in obtaining Cuban recognition and assistance among several Brazilian Communist and pro-Communist groups."[1] Most important among these groups were the pro-Moscow, orthodox Brazilian Communist Party (Partido Comunista Brasileiro, PCB), led by Luís Carlos Prestes; and two rivals favoring armed struggle in Brazil: a dissident, pro-Beijing faction, the Communist Party of Brazil (Partido Comunista do Brasil, PCdoB), and in the country's destitute northeast, the Peasant

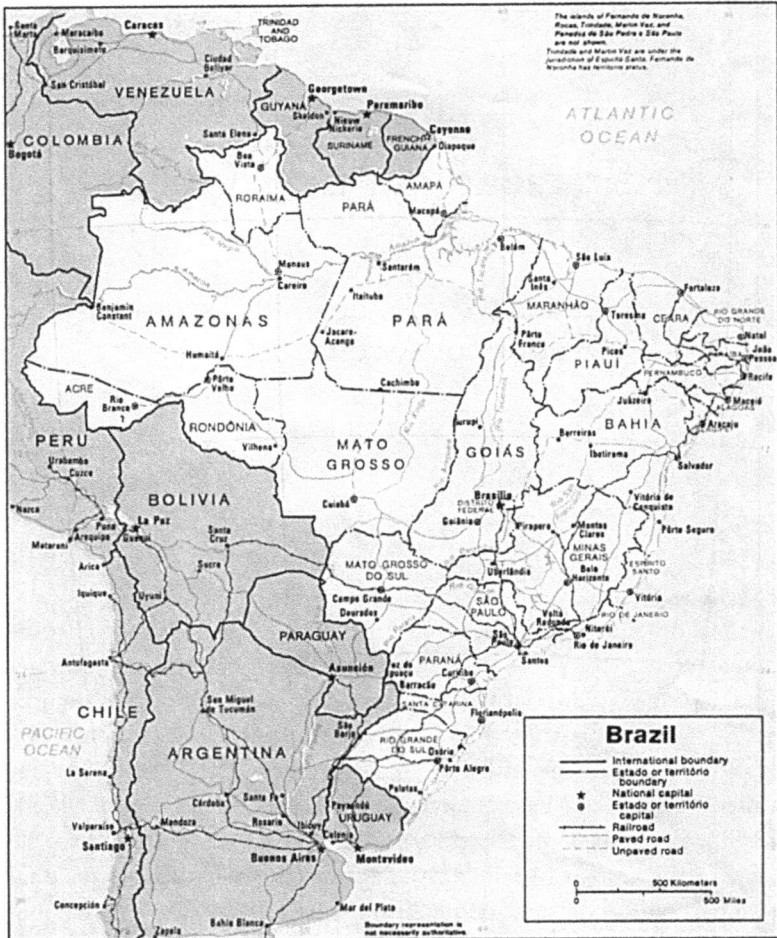

Figure 3.1. Map of Brazil. Courtesy University of Texas Libraries.

Leagues (Ligas Camponesas), led by Francisco Julião, whose role models included Fidel Castro and Mao Zedong.

Much of the context is well known in the literature. Scholars have long noted strains in U.S.-Brazilian relations in early 1963.[2] Terming the situation "extremely critical," with Brazil in "much more danger of turning to [communist] bloc than any other large Latin American country," U.S. Ambassador to Brazil Lincoln Gordon warned Washington the country's "loss"—evoking the ghost of China!—"would represent [a] blow to security interests of United States of historic proportions."[3]

Studies of Brazil's turbid domestic politics during this period, including standard works on the nation's Communists, have also noted, in passing, the internecine strains on the country's far Left, though none explores in depth the international linkages regarding Cuba, China, the USSR, and the Sino-Soviet split in the early 1960s.[4] The most serious examination of Brazilian-Cuban relations, Moniz Bandeira's *De Martí a Fidel*, briefly mentions a key episode examined here—concurrent, competing missions to Havana to seek Castro's support in February–March 1963 by Prestes and Julião—but cites only a single Brazilian document.[5] So, too, does Elio Gaspari's study of leftist resistance to the military dictatorship, which also covers the Goulart years.[6] Biographers of Prestes and Julião also fail to probe the matter.[7] Recent Brazilian scholarly investigations delve into such pertinent topics as the Brazilian Communist split into pro-Soviet and pro-Chinese factions and Cuba's support for armed revolution in Brazil and impact on Brazilian Communists, but mostly rely on Brazilian sources.[8]

By contrast, the present inquiry taps not only Brazilian sources, particularly cables from the Itamaraty (foreign office) archives in Brasília, and the usual potpourri of declassified Western records (from U.S., British, Canadian, and French archives), but also recently opened materials from the Soviet bloc, including archives in Moscow, Prague, Warsaw, Berlin, Budapest, Sofia, and—to a very limited extent—Havana.[9]

Moreover, this chapter examines another intersection between Brazil's far Left and the international communist realm concerning the Sino-Soviet split and Cuba: the Brazilian Communist fissure between the PCB, which endorsed Khrushchev's "peaceful coexistence" line, and the PCdoB, which favored armed struggle, claimed to be Brazil's only "legitimate" Communist party, and sought (and got) Chinese and Cuban support. Beijing archives illuminate Mao's reception, in early 1963, of rival Brazilian communist delegations—new evidence that sheds light both on Brazilian far-leftist competition and on Mao's perceptions, expectations, and tactics regarding revolution in Brazil and Latin America.

The early 1963 drama involving the Brazilian far Left and key international communist actors—Moscow, Beijing, and Havana—reflected, at a crucial juncture, the wider Sino-Soviet battle for influence in the Third World. Central to this dispute was the issue of whether to support armed violent revolution against imperialism (and U.S. "neo-colonialism") or to back leftist political and social reforms, economic development, and the gradual rise of communism, even in collaboration with nationalist and bourgeois political forces.[10] Similarly, the rift between Brazilians who favored peaceful versus violent roads to power—the Soviet versus the Chinese line—mirrored comparable quarrels elsewhere in the Third World, both within communist parties and between those parties and revolutionary movements.[11]

In sum, this story penetrates and illuminates global far-Left struggles in the early 1960s between fervent revolutionaries and comparative pragmatists. Exploring it requires first introducing the key Brazilian actors.

Luís Carlos Prestes and the Brazilian Communists

Some said his power and authority were ebbing as he reached his sixties, but the figure still towering over Brazilian communism in the early 1960s remained Luís Carlos Prestes. Though he had made his name through armed exploits four decades earlier, the leader of the pro-Moscow PCB had since World War II focused on making political progress (and regaining legal status, lost in 1947) through nonviolent means.[12] After Castro took power in Havana in 1959, Prestes gave him tepid rhetorical support, but "still condemned radical revolutionary and terrorist activities in Brazil and advised Marxists there to proceed with caution," citing different conditions from Cuba's.[13]

In the early 1960s, under Jânio Quadros and then Goulart, Prestes acted warily, pressing for leftist economic steps, reduced U.S. clout, and expanded Brazilian ties with communist nations, alternately cooperating with and contesting presidents and other leftists in search of greater legal status and political sway. By 1963, his caution had inspired resentment on Brazil's far Left, including from Stalinist hard-liners within his own party and others eager to take arms. His main fear—well-founded, foreshadowing the 1964 *golpe*—was that Castroist or Maoist violence would not only fail but provoke a harsh military crackdown that would evict Goulart, who at least sought social justice, a modicum of independence from excessive U.S. influence, and closer communist links. Recalling past disasters, Prestes feared that "the reckless tactics of the amateurs on the left might provoke a premature test of force that the left was bound to lose." (His concerns mirrored Khrushchev's; the Soviet hoped Brazil might enter a revolutionary phase by the end of JFK's expected second term,[14] but for now concentrated on improving ties with, rather than overthrowing, Quadros and Goulart, shying away from Castro's ardor for armed struggle.[15]) Young Brazilian radicals, eager to emulate the Cubans and Chinese, scorned Prestes as "the tired bureaucratic manipulator of an obsolete apparatus, comparable in mentality to the 'bankrupt' elite of the center and right."[16] In March 1963, Brazilian finance minister Santiago Dantas told U.S. secretary of state Dean Rusk that Prestes "still enjoys some prestige, but he no longer appears to be the [Communists'] effective leader."[17]

Violent Revolution versus "Peaceful Coexistence": Brazil's Communists, Cuba, and the Sino-Soviet Split

Disputes among Brazilian communists between militants and relative moderates predated the (visible) Sino-Soviet schism. In August 1957, after a bitter year-long internal spat, four senior party figures were ejected for objecting to Prestes's "revisionist" endorsement of Khrushchev's "peaceful coexistence" strategy, adopted during the CPSU 20th Congress the year before, and waging what Prestes termed an "undercover factional fight."[18] A deeper fissure opened four years later, in synch with the increasingly public Sino-Soviet rift, the Cuban Revolution, and the rise of more radical contenders within Brazil, especially Julião in the northeast. In late 1961— after Prestes, seeking legalization, changed the PCB's name from Partido Comunista do Brasil (Communist Party of Brazil) to Partido Comunista Brasileiro (Brazilian Communist Party)—the orthodox party expelled, "for fractional activities," "opposing Prestes and demanding a more militant line," João Amazonas, Pedro Pomar, Mauricio Grabois, Calil Chadde, and other China- and Cuba-inspired "factionalists."[19]

In early 1962, the expelled dissidents formed their own faction. Calling for "a people's government and revolutionary struggle using armed as well as legal means," they reclaimed the discarded party name Partido Comunista do Brasil and revived the old party organ (*A Classe Operária* [*The Working Class*]) as their own. Though much smaller than Prestes's PCB, the dissident faction claimed to be the "legitimate" communist party, and, breaking angrily with Prestes's support for the October 1961 22nd CPSU Congress and Khrushchev's ongoing criticism of Albania, backed China in the Sino-Soviet split and violent revolution in Brazil.[20]

The PCdoB's rise coincided with Castro's louder militancy. In December 1961, the Cuban had openly embraced Marxism-Leninism; and in early February 1962, in a retort to the Organization of American States (OAS) conference in Punta del Este, which had blasted Cuba's extra-hemispheric communist ties, he issued the "Second Declaration of Havana"—a clarion call for hemispheric, Cuban-style revolution. "The duty of every revolutionary," he asserted, "is to make revolution"—and, by implication, to disregard Moscow's and Khrushchev's advice to patiently pursue political reform and await riper conditions before launching "adventurist" actions.[21]

Castro's fiery statements emboldened pro-Chinese Brazilian communists (and Julião and his followers), but rankled Prestes.[22] After touring South America, Yugoslavia's ambassador to Cuba told a colleague that the PCB head, and other pro-Moscow communists he spoke to, disdained Fidel's 2nd Havana Declaration. "In Brazil," he reported, "the party criticizes it strongly and Prestes threatened the Cuban party with public action if they did not give up propagating views . . . contrary to the position of the Brazilian party."[23] Privately, Prestes assured the Soviets that his PCB would "not hesitate to call on the people to take decisive violent actions" when the time was right, but for now, trying to replicate the Sierra Maestra in Brazil would "only harm the [country's] democratic movement."[24]

Dissatisfied by Prestes's "soft" line—which may have evoked sour memories of the pro-Moscow Cuban Popular Socialist Party (PSP), which had only belatedly supported Castro's revolt after denouncing it as adventurist—Fidel clearly preferred more militant Brazilian leftists. In April 1962, the CIA learned, "Havana informed the PCB that it approved the [PCdoB's] 'revolutionary character'" and invited two dissident party leaders (Amazonas and Grabois) to Cuba, where they met Cuban leaders and PRC representatives, securing an invitation to China to seek Mao's support—a voyage Amazonas and a PCdoB comrade would undertake almost a year later.[25] In Havana, the militant Brazilian communists also first contacted the Albanian and North Korean parties, who shared their yen for violent revolution, tilt toward Beijing in the Sino-Soviet rift, and disdain for Khrushchev.[26]

Their trip climaxed when they met Fidel. According to CIA reports, during a talk in late May, "Castro expressed identity of feeling with the dissident Brazilian Communists and criticized the regular Communist party for its failure 'to take a strong revolutionary line'" in deference to Khrushchev's wary posture toward local "wars of national liberation" at the 22nd CPSU congress. Castro reportedly urged the PCdoB to launch a revolt in Brazil "as soon as possible." State reprisals provoked by guerrilla attacks and massive urban protests—the Venezuelan model—would spur discontent and attract new recruits, causing the "revolutionary movement to gain strength until the government . . . [could not] contain it." Foreshadowing Mao's later advice, Castro counseled the militants to widen their base beyond the cities, "among agricultural workers and the inhabitants of rural areas."[27]

Castro's warm reception of the PCdoB communists irked Prestes. Meeting the newly arrived Soviet ambassador in Rio, he criticized Cuba's support for revolutionary violence in Latin America—in Venezuela this "led in fact to a weakening of the democratic forces"—and voiced "bewilderment" at Castro's embrace of the "anti-Party group." Havana welcomed Amazonas and Grabois to May Day festivities, he griped, while not inviting any PCB leaders. Moreover, Castro had given far more personal attention to Clodomir Santos de Morais—evicted from the PCB, now organizing, with Cuban help, guerrilla activities for Julião's Ligas—than the last senior PCB official to visit Cuba (Manuel Jover Teles). Prestes considered going to Cuba "to discuss with Fidel personally the situation."[28]

Julião, Castro, Mao, and the PCB

Among Brazilian peasants, especially in the poor, volatile northeast, the chief agitator for revolutionary change in the early 1960s, if necessary by armed force, was Francisco Julião, the Peasant Leagues head, admirer of Fidel and Mao (among others), periodic visitor to Cuba and China, and lead source of alarm to Americans fearing "another Fidel Castro" in the hemisphere. A charismatic Recife lawyer, Socialist state legislator from Pernambuco, Julião had since the mid-1950s defended and organized peasants who faced harsh conditions, persecution, and reprisals from landowners for whom they worked, mostly growing sugar cane. He burst into American consciousness in late 1960 when a *New York Times* series spotlighted the peril of a Castroist/Maoist revolt in Brazil's northeast led by this "little Fidel" whose Ligas were the "purest" *fidelista* movement outside Cuba.[29] He was said to work closely with, but had not joined, Prestes's PCB, which, operating quasi-legally, helped organize peasant unions.[30]

Julião's radicalization had accelerated in March-April 1960 when he visited Cuba in the delegation of Brazilian presidential candidate Jânio Quadros—even though he, like Prestes, endorsed Quadros's rival, War Minister Henrique Lott. (Another key Peasant Leagues figure, de Morais, who later liaised between the Ligas and Havana, accompanied Julião; this first direct exposure to Cuba's revolution and agrarian reform excited both.[31]) While short, Joseph A. Page wrote, the trip was "long enough, however, to whet Julião's appetite," and shortly afterward he returned for a long visit" becoming "an ardent *fidelista*."[32] In Fidel, writes one scholar, Julião found his "guru."[33]

The affection proved mutual. As de Morais recalls, the Bay of Pigs further radicalized Ligas leaders, spurring preparations for guerrilla resistance, lest Brazil, too, as Castro's friend, be victimized by U.S. aggression.[34] (Like

Clodomir, Julião was on the island right after the failed invasion, seeking "Cuban support for the armed struggle"—against the advice of a PCB visitor, Manuel Jover Teles; Cuban military training for Ligas militants and other would-be Brazilian revolutionaries ensued.[35]) After Quadros's sudden resignation in August 1961 sparked fears of civil war, de Morais secretly tried to build a "military arm" to resist military or *latifundist* terror. While de Morais prepared guerrilla camps and hid arms caches, it was alleged, Julião focused on the Ligas' political radicalization.[36] In December, shortly after he (fearing a loss of independence) rebuffed an effort by Goulart and Prestes, at a national peasant's congress in Belo Horizonte, to incorporate his Ligas into a national rural workers' union, Julião hailed Castro's public oath to Marxist-Leninism, swearing his own, and extolled Cuba's revolution as a model.[37]

Links between Julião and Castro tightened in 1962. Ligas publications fawned over Cuba; Julião again visited the island (e.g., to attend a "Peoples Assembly" in Havana in January whose participants included Mexico's Lázaro Cárdenas and Chile's Salvador Allende, and witness Fidel's Second Declaration of Havana) and sent his children to school there; his wife, a revolutionary herself, met Fidel and received Cuban guerrilla training.[38] Supporters went to Cuba for "agricultural" and "guerrilla" tutoring; and rumors circulated in Brazil that Havana gave Julião's group money and perhaps weapons, squirreled away in hidden caches in the northeast and elsewhere.[39] "Despite Julião's insistence that Cuba was merely a symbol and Castro merely another hero in his wonderfully eclectic revolutionary pantheon (along with Moses, Jesus, Saint Francis of Assisi, Mao Tse-tung, Ben Bella, Thomas Jefferson, Abraham Lincoln, and others), his words often carried thinly veiled implications that Cuba was to be more than just an inspiration," Page recounted.[40] To enhance the armed option, in April 1962 Julião created the Movimento Revolucionário Tiradentes (MRT), with the slogan "Agrarian reform in law or by force." Intended to unite various extreme leftist groups (including the Ligas and PCdoB), linking rural and urban revolutionaries, the Cuba-inspired MRT was seen as the "embryo" of a rural guerrilla movement.[41]

Cuban leaders made their preference clear to the Soviets. In April 1962, Interior Minister Ramiro Valdés told the KGB that Fidel had secretly decided to arm Latin American guerrillas, even if that contradicted Khrushchev's "peaceful coexistence" doctrine. "We have no intention of unleashing either a local war or a world war," he said, "but we have to help brother nations."[42] Castro explained that a careful survey showed that several Central

American nations (besides Mexico) and five in South America (Argentina, Brazil, Peru, Paraguay, Venezuela), were ripe for revolution, but needed a push to ignite an armed uprising. Since most communist parties were passive, he said, Cuba had to back militant groups such as Brazil's Peasant Leagues; Venezuela's Revolutionary Left Movement (MIR); Argentina's Peronists; leftist student groups in Columbia; and Guatemala's 13 November Revolutionary Movement. Cuban financial aid to Julião's group, he conceded, had caused a "significant deterioration" in Havana's relations with the PCB.[43]

While Communist leaders in Latin America and especially Brazil were "timid," captive to "old dogmas," just "grow[ing] old and unable to think in a revolutionary way" or appeal to youth, Castro declared, Julião was "working to attract the broad masses of the Brazilian peasantry to his side."[44] Carlos Rafael Rodríguez, director of the National Institute of Agrarian Reform (INRA) and Fidel's top Communist, rapped Prestes for various sins—from neglecting to visit revolutionary Cuba despite repeated invitations, to failing to organize a warm popular reception for Cuban President Osvaldo Dorticós when he transited Brazil on his way to Punta del Este, to working too hard to cultivate political allies rather than with Julião (who needed "proper management"); Prestes's attitude, in sum, confused Cubans and "[damaged] their common cause."[45]

By spring 1962, the Julião-Prestes split sharpened. At a secret summit in Rio between them, Prestes criticized Julião's "adventurist and untimely actions," which the PCB felt could yield pointless bloodshed, strengthen "reaction," split "democratic forces," and hurt Brazil-Cuba relations. Defiantly, Julião vowed to continue preparing an "armed uprising" that, once launched, the Communists would have to back—"as . . . in Cuba."[46] Publicly, the PCB censured Julião for his readiness to use force, expelled de Morais (an ex-"party stalwart") for "adventurism," and—along with the radical Catholic *Ação Popular*—contested the Ligas for control of rural peasant unions in the northeast. "Julião's break with the Communists resulted from a profound divergence in their attitudes toward the style and substance of what both sides saw as the coming revolution in Brazil," observed Page. Julião, "relying on the authentic traditions of the region, felt that the peasant's religious faith and innate mysticism could be well-springs of revolutionary consciousness." He considered Brazil "essentially a rural nation," susceptible to a Maoist revolt in the countryside, while PCB Communists clung to the dogma that revolution must originate in the urban working class, and "wanted to convert the peasants into orthodox Communists without regard for the cultural forces that for centuries had shaped life in the Northeastern countryside; they sought to compromise with the middle class in an attempt to manipulate the revolution from above, rather than to encourage an awakening peasantry to make their own revolution from below." As Page wrote, the PCB increasingly saw Julião as "overwhelmed by success and taken in by his own charisma, an egotist who thought he could personally orchestrate the Brazilian revolution"; feared his militancy might provoke a broad crackdown; and accused him of "leftist extremism, the childhood disease of communism."[47] Distrusting Julião's autonomy and extremism, the PCB sought gradual progress in the northeast on "labor legislation" and "legal aid, schools, medicines, and burial funds rather than with making an appeal for radical agrarian reform."[48] Irritated at Julião's lavish Cuban financing, Prestes told the Soviets he was not really a Marxist but "a petit-bourgeois ideologue."[49]

In June 1962 the CIA judged rising PCB-Peasant Leagues friction still short of an outright break: Brazilian Communists criticized Julião yet "have nevertheless tended to cooperate with him." Keeping his options open, the Ligas head had not openly "admitted [PCB] membership" and was said to be improving ties with the PCdoB faction that, like Castro, backed "violence and a revolutionary line." "Juliao and dissident Communist leaders have apparently agreed to join forces to advocate revolutionary activity," the CIA reported, noting Amazonas and Grabois's visit to Cuba in early May "at Juliao's instigation to receive instructions in revolutionary techniques."[50]

When in Cuba, Julião often huddled with Che, whom Castro gave special responsibility for promoting Latin American revolution, and whose ardor for radical agrarian reform and hemispheric upheaval resonated with the Brazilian. In a secret May 1962 speech, Guevara highlighted northeastern Brazil's poverty and large, "particularly combative" peasantry, and termed the region "ideal for insurrection" (echoing Castro, who, while flying over northern Brazil in 1959, praised the terrain's suitability for revolution[51]). Implying sympathy for Julião's Ligas, Che said Brazil's left was "represented, above all, by the peasant masses of the northeast [that] are clearly willing to seize power despite the opposition of the bourgeoisie (the bourgeoisie puts up little opposition; imperialism is the real enemy)." Though Brazil was now in a "strange situation of unstable equilibrium," he foresaw future clashes there, inspired by Cuba's example and the 2nd Declaration of Havana.[52] Yugoslavia's ambassador in Havana reported in mid-June 1962 that in a recent conversation, Che had "persistently argued that in Brazil there is no other exit but revolution, and that very soon."[53]

Some analysts considered U.S. fears of Julião to be exaggerated.[54] Yet, by late 1962, his fortunes, and those of the northeastern Left, seemed to be rising. That summer, concerned U.S. security officials doubted the wisdom of a JFK stop in Recife (whose mayor was communist-leaning Miguel Arraes) during a planned visit to Brazil (delayed and ultimately canceled). A report that Julião's followers in Rio planned to hurl a "red paint bomb" at Jacqueline Kennedy sparked more worry; arms caches of uncertain provenance were "frequently reported" to be in the Ligas' possession in Pernambuco and neighboring Paraíba.[55] In October 7 parliamentary elections, Julião (running on the Socialist Party ticket) easily won a seat as a federal deputy, giving him a national rather than a regional platform, and Arraes was elected Pernambuco governor. By then, Ligas/MRT farms for guerrilla training, bought and supervised by de Morais, were said to exist in six Brazilian states: Goiás, Maranhão, Mato Grosso, Bahia, Rio, and Rio Grande do Sul.[56]

In mid-October 1962, on the eve of the missile crisis, Fidel's enthusiasm for Julião and his Ligas as opposed to Prestes and the PCB continued. Discussing Brazil with Czechoslovak visitors, Castro said Cuba was "turning exclusively toward JULIAO, to whom they provide every support," derided the PCB's failure to back Julião in recent elections, complained that the PCB had expelled supporters of Cuba (presumably alluding to PCdoB activists), and carped that Prestes had failed to visit Cuba despite seven invitations, though there was "hope" he might soon come.[57] Moscow's ambassador, meanwhile, scoffed that Fidel had fallen "in love" with Julião, because he considered him the "most revolutionary" and able Brazilian leader, deserving full Cuban support despite his spat with Prestes's PCB.[58] Around this time, the PCB in Brazil's northeast complained to Czech intelligence agents that Julião and Clodomir Morais had lavish funds ("millions" of Brazilian Cruzeiros "of foreign origin") at their disposal for "printing presses, weapons, etc.," and were training "guerrillas" for a farmer-led "socialist revolution." Prague, alarmed, instructed its agents to scale back their work with Julião as it was growing "too broad and threatens unpleasant consequences."[59]

Then Julião and his movement sustained sharp setbacks. On November 27, a Brazilian *Varig* B-707 airliner carrying a Cuban delegation (headed by national bank president Raúl Cepero Bonilla) homeward from a UN Food and Agriculture Organization meeting in Rio crashed in the Andes near Lima, killing all aboard. In the wreckage, Peruvian authorities found Bonilla's briefcase containing documents exposing links between Havana and Julião's guerrilla training camps, including data on money and arms transfers and de Morais's role as a go-between, plus "possible logistic support" for an upcoming pro-Cuba solidarity congress in Brazil by elements in Goulart's government.[60] The Peruvians (or CIA, some Brazilians allege[61]) leaked the Cuban records to the Lima press, and shared at least some with Brazil's resident ambassador.[62] Within weeks, authorities raided several Peasant Leagues camps that had received Cuban help, including a farm in Dianópolis, in Goiás province east of Brasília.[63]

Dealing a blow to the Ligas' armed struggle scheme, in Rio de Janeiro, Guanabara police in mid-December arrested de Morais while he allegedly transported arms (in a vehicle belonging to Julião) to Goiás, where he was "in charge" of the Dianópolis training camp; police also found an inscribed calling card to Julião from a Soviet diplomat, "an indoctrination program for members of the Peasant League, a plan for training guerrillas and an outline for projected subversive activities in the area around Dianopolis." Clodomir's confiscated arsenal was paltry (six rifles, two pistols, a machine gun, and ammunition) but he, far more than Julião, who at times seemed "ambiguous or contradictory" toward armed struggle, had robustly backed and overseen efforts to prepare for guerrilla war.[64] (Described as a "megalomaniac" by one ex-militant, de Morais, recalled another, "wanted to be the Brazilian Fidel Castro, using Julião as a front."[65])

By early 1963, these reverses—plus Julião's refusal to back Goulart's January 6 plebiscite to strengthen presidential rule, which the PCB strongly supported—had crippled the Peasant League's (and MRT's) sketchy preparations for armed struggle, dented Julião's standing, and deepened his isolation on the left.[66]

Deflecting pressure on its foreign policy, Goulart's administration discounted the seized arsenal and arrested militants, downplaying the Cuba link. Claiming authorities already knew of the training camps before seeing the recovered Cuban records, prime minister Hermes Lima termed the captured arms "ridiculous in their quantity and quality" and the Cuban documents "insignificant and only proving . . . Brazilian communists [were] poorly organized"; in a "terrible state."[67]

American officials gathered conflicting data on Havana's involvement. One raided camp seemed to treat Che's *Guerrilla Warfare* as gospel (125 copies found), and a confidential Brazilian report asserted that the hundred or so Ligas militants there "want to be the Brazilian equivalent of those who fought in the Sierra Maestra and so bring the hard Chinese-Cuban type revolution to Brazil," but U.S. embassy and CIA officials initially believed, contrary to local press reports, that the site's arms cache was of Brazilian rather than Cuban origin.[68] By early January, however, the CIA station in Rio reported pressure on Goulart to penalize Cuba for aiding Julião's fighters and quoted a Brazilian source calling the documents "explosive," proving Cuban sponsorship of revolution.[69] According to the CIA, the Cuban records revealed "shortcomings" in Julião's group, regarding both the upcoming pro-Cuba solidarity congress and the training of "subversive guerrilla units."[70] By March, U.S. officials concluded that at least some of the "illegal arms caches have been attributable to the Cubans," an effort that seemed "significant" though "not on a very large scale."[71]

The disarray evidently chagrined Havana, which the CIA reported ended support for Julião and his movement "abruptly" in December 1962, though it quoted no sources. Other evidence (see below) suggests that Castro's aid to Julião persisted.[72]

Toward the Trips to Havana—and the Pro-Cuba "Solidarity" Congress in Brazil

The CIA attributed Julião's and Prestes's overlapping visits to Cuba in February–March 1963 to "a Soviet-inspired attempt to coordinate policy."[73] U.K. diplomats in Havana surmised that Castro "was attempting some kind of reconciliation in keeping with his self-appointed role as a peacemaker in the communist world."[74] Yet, Soviet records suggest Prestes acted on his own initiative to prod Castro to stop backing Julião and the PCdoB. Meeting Moscow's envoy in Rio, Andrei A. Fomin, on November 15, 1962, Prestes criticized Havana and indicated he would visit Cuba in early 1963 to hash out these disputes with Fidel.[75]

Learning of Prestes's planned trip, the CIA in Brazil gleaned that in Havana he would seek to moderate Cuba's activities in Latin America and "divisive influence on Brazilian Communist affairs." The PCB hoped "not only to improve relations but to protest a report that Castro is supporting Juliao" and complain that Cuba gave the PCdoB "considerably more support" than the orthodox party.[76] In January, Prestes also told the Soviets he wished to visit Havana *and* Moscow to harmonize policy.[77]

One factor that drove Julião and Prestes to Havana in late February 1963 was the looming pro-Cuba congress in Brazil that both had been promoting. Delayed for months, the "Continental Congress of Solidarity with Cuba"—a sequel to a well-publicized pro-Cuba hemispheric peace conference two years earlier in Mexico City "widely credited with bringing about violent efforts to subvert the governments of Venezuela and Peru and with organizing leftist agitation in Panama and Puerto Rico"[78]—was set for Rio in late March, immediately after a national (Brazilian) pro-Cuba congress there.

According to the CIA's communist sources in Brazil, the impetus for the gathering came from Cuba in September 1962, acting through Julião (without consulting the PCB). In a manifesto to Brazil's national student union, the "rabble-rousing president of the Brazilian Peasants League" (the CIA's term of endearment) said Cuba remained threatened by armed aggression and called for the convening of a "Latin American Congress for the Defense of the Cuban People." Linking this cause to the broader aim of a hemispheric revolt, he declared that such a meeting would bring all revolutionaries in the region together in "a solid union for the defense of Cuba, for the Latin American Revolution may be forged."[79] However, distracted by his electoral bid, Julião let the matter slide, PCB "friends" told Poland's ambassador. On learning of the planned congress, PCB communists were said to be lukewarm—"rather tepid," evidently fearing that Julião would exploit the event for his own personal and political gain, U.S. analysts thought[80]—yet, "to avoid any scandal, decided to join the action." Still, the PCB pushed to delay the congress, feeling the time wasn't right due to organizational problems and, likely, the blow to Havana's standing in Brazilian public opinion inflicted by the missile crisis (which bolstered U.S. charges that Cuba had let the Soviets use the island as a military base). Hence, the event was deferred to a more "realistic" date, initially the end of December, then January, and finally late March. Countering Julião's organizational committee, backed by what a Bulgarian diplomat in Rio termed the PCdoB's "Trotskyite elements," the PCB "with great effort" expanded the congress' political platform beyond its original more radical, narrow base.[81]

By mid-February, signs of serious discord between rival sponsors of the congress reached U.S. ears. In Mexico City, the CIA heard that Vicente Lombardo Toledano, the labor activist, Marxist-Leninist, and leftist Popular Socialist Party head, had been recruited by unnamed European "comrades" to go to Brazil to mediate. "Something went wrong in Brazil," Lombardo had told an aide to Mexican president Lopez Mateos, "because, apart from the committee which convoked the congress [Julião's group], a second separate committee had sprung up whose aims are the same, and that a sort of rivalry has developed between the two groups." His own mission, he said, was to forge a single, united group to plan the congress "and ensure its success." If he failed, and "the prima donnas and ornamental figures" took over, he said, he would not attend.[82]

Behind the scenes, likely unknown to U.S. intelligence, other communist intrigue concerning the pro-Cuba congress in Brazil was afoot: For months, a joint Soviet-Czechoslovak intelligence operation in Latin America code-named AO "DRUŽBA" [Active Operation "Friendship"] had sought "to create a permanent organization that would support the Cuban revolution and protect her against US imperialism."[83] The Soviets designed the overall program, but Czech foreign intelligence operatives carried out initial work in Brazil; in mid-operation, Prague transferred control to the KGB after the USSR and Brazil restored diplomatic ties following a fourteen-year hiatus and, in mid-1962, Moscow reopened its embassy in Rio, putting Soviet assets on the ground (just as Washington had forewarned Brasília).[84]

AO Družba's efforts to promote the conference took various forms. Not surprisingly, a Czech post-mortem emphasized that, even after they handed over operational control to Soviet comrades, their own agents were "decisive for the success of the operation . . . connecting members of the preparatory committee with their supporters in Brazil and abroad, they were also active members of the preparatory committee and they participated in activities of a weekly magazine financed by us that was essential for the *propaganda* of the Congress."[85]

AO Družba's operatives hoped to minimize the Brazilian communists' role in organizing the congress and emphasize instead "nationalist" personalities and movements, especially student and labor forces, but could not conceal the PCB's increasingly dominant role as it vied to wrest control from Julião. In mid-February, security police of the anti-communist governor of Guanabara, Carlos Lacerda, seized two different lists of "purported sponsors" of the pro-Cuba conference from Prestes's luggage at the airport before he left for Moscow. The promptly leaked lists overlapped but also diverged on who the congress' top sponsor was: Julião or Prestes. Julião's list included a strong proposed declaration backing Cuba; the other list's documents were "much milder in tone."[86]

While in Havana, Julião said he came to Cuba to organize the upcoming congress and hoped participants would include such high-profile international figures as Algerian revolutionary Ben Bella, British philosopher Bertrand Russell, and Mexican ex-president Lázaro Cárdenas, the "producer, director, and star" of the 1961 pro-Cuba congress.[87] It was widely assumed, a communist diplomat reported from Rio, that Julião's main aim in going to Havana was to obtain Cuban funds to support the event.[88] During his own visit, Prestes also promoted the conference—for example, soliciting GDR participation from East Berlin's envoy, and touting it in a *Revolución* interview.[89] However, Prestes's top priority was to ascertain the Cuban leadership's attitude toward his and Julião's divergent paths to power in Brazil, and if possible to push Castro toward his own (and Moscow's) emphasis on evolutionary, not revolutionary, change.[90]

U.S. intelligence presumed, wrongly, that Julião and Prestes met in Havana, and that this would influence the congress. The CIA, only hazily informed on what was occurring in Cuba's capital, also speculated that "Soviet pressure may be exerted to postpone the meeting"—which didn't happen—though it acknowledged that, given recent loud Soviet-bloc defenses of Cuba, the congress would likely convene in some form.[91]

*   *   *

While usually tight-lipped in public about internecine leftist tensions, before leaving for Moscow and Havana, Prestes groused to communist envoys in Rio about various rivals: "ultra-nationalist" Leonel Brizola, Goulart's brother-in-law and governor of Rio Grande do Sul, and especially Julião and the PCdoB, with its Chinese and Cuban backers. To Poland's ambassador, he carped that Beijing treated the PCdoB "as the 'Communist Party of Brazil.'"[92] Reflecting "ultra-nationalism's" ideological ambiguity (stressing anti-U.S. views, not leftist economic doctrines), he dismissed Brizola as "a leader of the Nasser-like type, who does not believe in the masses, but in a military coup carried out by nationalistic groups."[93]

He reserved his sharpest criticism for Julião, and Fidel, for misjudging the prospects for armed struggle in Brazil and South America. In January 1963, Warsaw's envoy reported that "political tension" between Julião and the PCB had "increased significantly." The Peasant Leagues, he cabled, was "outright accused of carrying out provocative activities" and cooperating with Lacerda's police. Moreover, Julião and Prestes had split on Goulart's crucial recent political move, the January 6, 1963, constitutional referendum to give him full presidential powers, eliminating limits imposed in the deal that let him succeed Quadros. Signaling his approval of the president's foreign policy and willingness to work with him, Prestes and the PCB backed Goulart's plebiscite, but Julião urged followers to abstain.[94] (Goulart won overwhelmingly.)

Prestes told communist diplomats that the Ligas lacked "any real influence on the peasant masses, because such leagues are artificial creations made possible with . . . money . . . generously forked out by Julião," whom he termed "a political bully and a dreamer." Since the PCB and Julião had cut ties, Prestes said that the party's "only real influence" in the northeast was through its own farmer unions and peasant groups. Julião and his people, he said, had been "discredited" due to the authorities' success in dismantling guerrilla camps and arresting "Julião's confidants."[95]

Foreshadowing his message in Havana, Prestes told Poland's envoy he would discuss such matters with Castro, whom he stressed had exaggerated prospects for revolts in Brazil and Latin America. Unhappy with a recent Castro speech that favorably rated the odds of a Cuban-style revolution in South America, Prestes declared that "at the moment there are no conditions to conduct any armed struggle in Brazil. The all-too premature occurrences in Venezuela and Peru only ended in many losses within the ranks of comrades. Fidel is isolating Cuba from the entire continent. And, he could give us all a big favor by building socialism well in Cuba and transforming his country so it could serve as an attractive example for the rest of Latin America."[96]

Rumors of these intra-leftist quarrels spread. On February 21, Goulart told Gordon he had "fresh evidence from Brazilian left-wing sources . . . of increasingly bitter schism between orthodox communists and Chinese-Castro followers." Prestes, he said, "had gone to Cuba to try to patch up these differences but without success." (The PCB boss had left for Moscow but not yet reached Havana.) So worried were "some orthodox communists," Goulart reported, they now sought his "help" to "fight Julião Chinese-support group," the Peasant Leagues. "Goulart foresaw a period of intensifying strife which would greatly weaken both these groups," Gordon cabled.[97]

Prestes and Julião in Cuba: February–March 1963

Before venturing to Cuba, Prestes had gone to Moscow. Even before he arrived, the Soviets and their loyal Brazilian communist allies had recently cooperated to try to limit Cuban and Chinese influence. Earlier in February, this coordination had surfaced at the third conference of the Afro-Asian Peoples' Solidarity Organization (AAPSO), a radical, Cairo-based group formed in 1957 to support anticolonial liberation struggles. At the Moshi, Tanganyika, meeting in 1963 the Soviets had sought to thwart a Chinese-Cuban effort to have the gathering vote to stage a "Tricontinental" (Africa-Asia-Latin America) conference in Havana; as an alternative, they "flew in uninvited representatives" of loyal Latin American parties (including the PCB) who proposed instead to confer in Brazil "under the auspices" of the Moscow-run World Peace Council. After Cuba's delegate delivered a rousing speech, "the Soviets sent the Brazilian delegate to threaten him," claiming his remarks were so extreme that Havana would "condemn" him on his return. The efforts were futile: AAPSO ultimately endorsed the Chinese-Cuban proposal, for reasons that Blanca Mar León's chapter in this volume explains, and the Tricontinental conclave of the Afro-Asian-Latin American Peoples' Solidarity Organization (AALAPSO) would convene in Havana in January 1966.[98]

When, on February 23, 1963, Prestes met Khrushchev at the Kremlin, they plotted a higher-level CPSU-PCB collaboration to curb the Cubans. According to a statement released afterward, clearly alluding to Sino-Soviet strains, the conversation revealed "the identity of views of the two parties with respect to international issues and those of the communist movement." Diplomats observed that Prestes, unsurprisingly, given his history of obeisance to Moscow, fully endorsed the Soviet "rules of procedure" for handling the internecine conflict, which foresaw a Marxist-Leninist party conference with a clear anti-Chinese tilt.[99]

Though unmentioned in the communiqué, Prestes and Khrushchev also charted the Brazilian's impending visit to Havana. Sharing Prestes's opposition to Cuban-Chinese promotion of violent revolution in Brazil, the Soviet endorsed his intent to prod Castro to end Cuba's backing of Julião and the PCdoB. Neither Soviet nor Brazilian records of those talks have emerged, but a revealing account was given soon afterward by a Prestes associate to Yugoslavia's envoy in Rio. According to PCB Central Committee executive commission member Marco Antônio Coêlho, Khrushchev derided Castro's handling of both domestic and foreign policy. He complained that Cuba "costs the USSR, on average, one million dollars [about $8.45 million in 2020] per day, that the economic situation in Cuba worsened, particularly supply; that Fidel makes mistakes in the domain of foreign policy, that the difficult internal situation is the result of hasty and extreme measures such as, for example, nationalization of the most important companies." Khrushchev asked Prestes to push Castro toward a "more realistic" approach to Latin America—an effort the Soviet indicated he would resume himself when the Cuban visited the USSR in the spring for "serious conversations."[100]

Despite recent fiery rhetoric promoting revolution in Latin America, Fidel gave the Soviets hope he might moderate his position. A few days before, he had assured Moscow's envoy in Havana that he grasped the need to maintain decent ties with leading hemispheric nations such as Brazil, Mexico, and Canada, to encourage "contradictions" between them and Washington and frustrate U.S. efforts to rally Latin America behind an anti-Cuba "adventure." Earlier in February, Castro had cooperated with a special emissary Goulart sent to resolve a longstanding bilateral dispute over asylum-seekers crowding Brazil's embassy in Havana.[101] "Cuba is doing everything possible to support Goulart and strengthen his foreign policy," Castro told Soviet ambassador Alexander Alexeev, promising to urge Julião, whom he would see in a few days, "to conduct a more cautious policy" and target "reactionary elements that can seize power." Alexeev complimented the Cuban leader's more "realistic" approach: "Fidel began to understand correctly the contradictions of imperialism, allowing the possibility of maneuvering and exploiting these."[102]

After seeing Khrushchev, Prestes finally flew to Havana, for his first visit to the island since the revolution's triumph more than four years earlier ("the major old-time Latin American Communist leaders did not hurry to make the pilgrimage," observed Theodore Draper).[103] His visit, the Brazilians learned, followed another by a pro-Moscow Latin American communist boss, also with Soviet foreknowledge and approval. Like Prestes, Ecuador's Pedro Saad explained that Latin America's—and Ecuador's—conditions were not those that "Fidel desires."[104]

By the time Prestes reached Havana, on February 25, Julião had already been in Cuba for several days, prompting speculation that one of his aims was to influence Prestes's reception ("pre-negotiating" his visit), hoping to harden Castro's support for his Peasant Leagues.[105] As the Soviet embassy noted, Prestes received a cool welcome at José Martí International Airport, with no senior members of the leadership (i.e., the ORI, or Integrated Revolutionary Organization) greeting him, although Cuban radio announced his arrival.[106] In what Prestes considered more evidence of his "very cold" reception, after escorting him to his hotel the low-level Cubans departed, and no Cubans visited him for two days. This "indifference" ended only after several "fraternal" diplomats, including (North) Vietnam's ambassador, called, having learned of his presence from a short newspaper article. After this "precedent," a Prestes comrade told a Hungarian diplomat, "the Cuban leaders could no longer afford to stay away."[107]

The first Cuban official Prestes met in Havana was Blas Roca, the veteran communist leader of the PSP—now superseded by the Castro-led ORI. As the Soviets noticed, the Cuban press ignored the meeting, though it lavishly covered Julião's visit.[108] During their talk, Prestes later said, Roca complained that Cuban communists were "relegated to [an] inferior position" in the ORI, and Castro, relying on "bourgeois socialists" rather than communists, "had committed one blunder after another."[109] Later, after he saw various senior figures, such as Fidel Castro and Carlos Rafael Rodríguez, Prestes told Czech communists "that the meeting with Blas Roca had been the coldest of all the meetings with Cuban comrades that he had had."[110] After visiting Cuba, a PCB comrade reported, Prestes viewed the island's CP as "largely liquidated," with Roca in the "very strange position" of impotently "tag[ging] along behind F[idel]."[111]

The next morning, February 27, Prestes saw the Soviet ambassador. Alexeev's brief account of the meeting illuminates both Soviet-Cuban and Prestes-Julião-Cuba relations. During his "visit of respect," Alexeev noted, Prestes was accompanied by "a staff member of the Cuban security organs." Mostly, Prestes spoke of the Brazilian scene, and said he had only seen Blas Roca but expected to meet Fidel Castro and Dorticós. Wary of the Cuban minder, Alexeev praised "the development of the Cuban Revolution" and the current situation on the island—a topic on which candor would have produced a far dimmer appraisal. "We have the impression that the Cuban leaders were not greatly enthused by Prestes' visit, and they prefer Julião," added Alexeev, noting the contrast between the Cubans' treatment of the two.[112]

On March 2, Prestes met Castro. The intergenerational encounter between the *barbudo*, thirty-six, who had seized power in a violent revolution, and orthodox communist, sixty-five, who had vainly led an armed rebellion in Brazil nearly three decades earlier but now followed Khrushchev's line, was marked by sharp disagreement. Publicly, Prestes held his tongue. Afterward, to a reporter, he praised Castro, "undoubtedly the most distinguished personality in Latin America," and blandly explained that he had finally come to Havana "to learn about the Cuban Revolution first hand."[113]

Such anodyne statements failed to sate the curiosity of journalists, spies, or diplomats. American officials examining Cuban influence in Brazil were particularly intrigued. The day before Prestes and Castro met, the U.S. embassy in Rio reported that at least four hundred Brazilians had gone to Cuba in 1962, some "receiving training in subversive activities," and noted the PCB had "strenuously objected to independent Cuban ventures being organized outside orthodox party channels through Brazilians like Francisco Juliao." However, it wondered whether Prestes's recent Moscow visit, and talks in Havana "with both Juliao and Castro," might yield "any sort of agreement blocking independent Cuba-based ventures of more or less Maoist sort and perhaps also in reopening possibility of coordination bloc use of Cuba as base for activities elsewhere in Latin America including Brazil." The analysis doubted Goulart "and much of [his] entourage" would like "subversive training" of Brazilians "even if run by most orthodox Moscow-oriented commies," but suspected Brazilian "objections to Cuban-connected ventures in Brazil might diminish if Prestes-Juliao-Castro agreement [were] reached and resulted in changed attitude PCB toward them."[114]

The U.S. embassy laid most of the onus for "arms caches in Brazil" recently seized by authorities on "Cubans working through the paramilitary groups" linked to Julião's Ligas, and suspected that orthodox communists sought "to get control of paramilitary units originally organized by Juliao. We are inclined to think, moreover, that primary reason for coincident presence of Juliao and Prestes in Cuba represents an effort by the PCB, which has apparently sought Moscow's help on the matter, to prevent independent Cuban ventures, as well as, possibly, to reopen use of Cuba for coordinated bloc efforts of one sort or another aimed at Brazil."[115]

We lack Cuban sources on Castro's talks with Prestes and Julião, but Soviet records suggest Havana gave Moscow a positive gloss on its handling of the two visitors. After Prestes saw Cuba's leader, Carlos Rafael Rodríguez told Alexeev that Castro was "satisfied" by the conversation, regretted not meeting Prestes earlier, and most important, "agrees completely with the policies of the Brazilian communists aimed at supporting Goulart." Moreover, after seeing Prestes, Fidel had "tr[ied] to impress upon [Julião] the need for a more flexible policy" toward Brazil's government. Such comments signaled a shift from a year before, when Havana had clearly preferred the Ligas leader to Prestes. Despite Julião's enthusiastic reception in Cuba, Rodriguez said, he suffered from "anarcho-rebellious disease," and his militant stance apparently lacked "wide support" in Brazil.[116] After the PCB boss left Havana, Dorticós told Alexeev he was "very pleased" by his talk with Prestes, who made a "positive impression" and illuminated the Brazilian situation and its communist party.[117]

Yet, the CIA, via a midlevel Brazilian communist source, later obtained a less positive account of the Castro-Prestes encounter from a PCB delegation member. During the three-hour talk, David Capistrano da Costa related, "Prestes tried in vain to convince Castro that the PCB and not Juliao was following the correct communist line," but Castro, due to his "lack of understanding" of Brazil, firmly defended Julião's advocacy of armed revolt. "When Prestes pointed out that Juliao had little prestige and was barely elected federal deputy, Castro replied that this proved his point. Communism could not be achieved through elections."[118]

If Castro had aspired to be a "peacemaker" between Prestes and Julião, a British diplomat wrote, "he does not appear to have had much success."[119] Comparing their "public behavior" in Havana, Brazil's embassy noticed that, in contrast to Prestes's caution, Julião "openly" supported the need for revolution in Latin America.[120] Even before arriving in the Cuban capital, during a stopover in Chile, Julião had declared that "social and economic reforms in Brazil could only be achieved by armed revolution, and he boasted that elements of the armed forces were secretly supporting his cause."[121] In Havana, his militant message continued. Castro's 2nd Declaration of Havana should "guide the struggles of the Latin American peoples for their liberation from *yanquí* imperialism and from internal underdevelopment that slows progress," and was a "manifesto of our time for the subjugated peoples of [Latin] America," he told *Bohemia*.[122] To the AP, he rapped Goulart's government ("weak, contradictory, and lacking in popular support") and party (in the PTB, "one finds holders of large tracts of land . . . At the moment there is no Brazilian political party capable of attracting the masses"), and, most provocatively, endorsed violence as necessary for the peasants to obtain justice. "I wish there were ways other than force," he said, "but against the landowner and the imperialists, it is only force." He also did not deny that this Sino-Cuban-aligned view put him at odds with the PCB.[123]

Prestes, conversely, criticized Julião's sympathy for armed struggle in Brazil to comradely publications.[124] Disputing the applicability to Brazil of Castro's 2nd Havana Declaration, he stopped short of publicly denouncing Fidel. Yet, attacking Julião implied his rift with Cuba's leader, much as Soviet censure of alleged Albanian extremism had substituted for explicitly blasting Mao's China. "The 'old guard,'" Draper observed," had "painful memories of the heavy price paid years ago for the misuse of force, and considers the stakes too high to be risked lightly. Soviet Russia and not Communist China has, after all, given Castro the material assistance and military equipment that have made his belligerence possible."[125]

Prestes told *Hoy* that initiating a violent revolt in Brazil in present conditions would be "completely wrong," but privately he used far stronger language to condemn Julião's (and the Cuban and Chinese) stand. The respective positions of Prestes and Julião, in separate meetings with Fidel, had "diverged totally," Brazil's embassy in Havana reported, and due to this "irreparable" difference they had studiously avoided any joint interviews. While Julião considered Brazil ripe for revolution, Prestes told the Cubans it would be "criminal" to take that path. "Despite some contradictions, in Brazil one breathes democracy, there are no imprisoned politicians and it is possible to attract the bourgeoisie to the formation of a united front that can win power by an evolutionary pathway," he argued, explaining the PCB "lacks reasons to be hostile" toward Goulart, especially as, in foreign policy, he followed (within limits) Khrushchev's line of "peaceful coexistence." As for their meetings with Castro, the Brazilians reported Julião's was focused on the pro-Cuba congress in Brazil, while Prestes complained the 2nd Havana Declaration's "principles and methods" damaged the PCB's work, especially proselytizing among the young; Fidel's response was not ascertained.[126]

Communist sources, mostly compatible, reveal Prestes's views of talks in Havana. As East Berlin's envoy reported, Prestes "assessed that Fidel Castro had become more personally understanding than before" (Rodriguez was "the most understanding"), yet the Cubans still "greatly overestimated" Julião and "greatly exaggerated" his influence. Prestes complained the "very sectarian" Julião, though frequently attacked "and partially discredited" in Brazil, still had "large financial resources . . . [from] Cuba or possibly a different power"—China?[127] After Prestes returned to Brazil in mid-March, an associate gave Belgrade's envoy in Rio an account of the PCB chief's "long and difficult discussions" with Castro. The Cuban had "immediately accused the PCB of passivity" and stressed that he, Fidel, was obliged to lead the Latin American revolution—but, eventually, Prestes had convinced him that Julião was an "adventurer" and Goulart's foreign policy was "very beneficial for the preservation of Cuba's independence." Ultimately, Prestes had found talking with Castro "very useful, at least for the PCB, because now the Cubans have a real picture of Brazil, and he knows that Fidel later told his associates that Julião is an adventurer."[128] According to an account reaching Hungarian ears, Prestes told the Cubans that Julião's "so-called revolutionary path" was "false" and "harmful," and it was "inappropriate to incessantly talk about 'exporting' the Cuban Revolution to Brazil."[129]

While in Havana, both Julião and Prestes—separately—also saw China's ambassador, for very different reasons. CIA sources said Julião sought to arrange a trip to the PRC and "an alliance" with the pro-Beijing PCdoB.[130] Prestes, by contrast, "expressed outrage" (a GDR diplomat reported) that China's radio and news agency supported the splinter group, spreading

Portuguese-language propaganda—repeating a complaint his delegates had made to the Chinese at the East German SED party congress in Berlin in mid-January. Even as PCdoB figures ejected from the PCB visited Beijing in early March to seek additional Chinese support, Prestes wished to send a PCB Central Committee member to China to plead the orthodox party's case.[131] The PCB's aim, Prestes's comrade told a communist envoy, would be to explain to the Chinese their "mistakes" in Latin America, "concretely in Brazil," by favoring the PCdoB.[132] Much as Fidel heard out competing assessments of the prospects for revolution in Brazil from Julião and Prestes, Mao would hold lengthy meetings with delegations from the rival Brazilian communist factions, both seeking his support.

Prestes in Prague

Prestes left Cuba on March 7 (Julião a night later) and was said to be heading back to Moscow.[133] Before reaching the Soviet capital, the PCB head stopped in Prague. In secret talks with Czechoslovak Communist Party (CPCz) leaders, first international department head Bohuslav Laštovička, then General Secretary Antonin Novotný, Prestes related impressions of his encounters in Havana, the Sino-Soviet split's impact in Cuba, and more radical Brazilians.[134] The exchanges, in the absence of contemporary or detailed records of Prestes's discussions with Khrushchev, expose Soviet-bloc skepticism toward Castro and his support for violent revolution in Brazil and Latin America.[135]

On the plus side, Prestes told Laštovička, the general Cuban situation was "improving," especially Havana's view of the Soviets (e.g., appreciating recent speeches by Khrushchev and Defense Minister Rodion Malinovsky vowing to defend Cuba), and China's influence, having peaked during the missile crisis, had waned. Still, Cuban opinion on Moscow remained mixed.

On their own neighborhood, Prestes repeated his view that "Cuban comrades had false impressions of the situation in other Latin American countries." Prestes had "very openly told Fidel Castro that his support of various extremist elements in Latin America, often without any knowledge of central committees of respective Communist or workers' parties, could not bring any benefit to Cuba or to Latin American nations." Regarding Cuba's "wrong" backing for Julião, Prestes said Castro seemed "rather surprised" at criticisms, which only showed that Cuba's information on

Latin America was "much distorted." Not only had Cuba's example failed to spark guerrilla wars or undermine U.S.-owned enterprises in the hemisphere, but (he had told Fidel) Havana's policies (and Castro's statements, he might have added) were counterproductive, vexing those countries who wanted, despite U.S. pressure, to preserve decent ties with revolutionary Cuba. "Brazil's position is particularly hard," he noted, "as Brazil is striving to maintain diplomatic relations with Cuba, and Cuba's foreign policy is not helping Brazil's efforts at all."

Prestes said he had also bluntly critiqued Cuba's internal policy including steps with disastrous domestic results that boomeranged abroad, discrediting the revolution. In particular, "the rapid nationalization of even small businesses and shops had had negative political consequences in other Latin American countries and, moreover, had not had good results even in Cuba," hurting production. Yet, the Cubans had held firm. Rafael Rodriguez, with whom Prestes had his best meeting, had apparently said there was no way back.

On inter-communist discord, Prestes blamed China for backing "various adventurist groups in different Latin American countries" including expelled members of "communist or workers' parties"—obviously alluding to PCB dissidents in the PCdoB. Echoing Khrushchev, Prestes stressed "peaceful coexistence" and preserving good links between Cuba and the rest of the hemisphere. Rather than its violent revolution, he said, Cuba's freedom and elevation of working people, "so different from other Latin American countries," could serve as "a good example for other countries of the continent." The next day, Prestes expressed similar complaints about Cuban "meddling" and Julião to Novotný. Why hadn't Julião been arrested? Because, Prestes said, "reactionary forces want to keep the provocateur." The real question was "where Julião gets so much money from"—and again he answered his own query: Cuba.

Prestes had told the Cubans that, rather than aid an insurgent like Julião, they should protect their relations with Brazil, "which is now the only Latin American country backing Cuba, like the apple of their eye." Goulart, after all, had resisted acute anti-Havana pressure from both Washington and internal critics—for example, "reactionary media" that cited Peru plane crash documents to claim that Cuba aided subversives in Brazil. "For the time being, Goulart is still a strong advocate of Cuba's self-determination, and was also the strongest [Latin American leader] during the Cuban missile crisis," conducting a popular foreign policy despite a "reactionary" domestic approach. Actually, he added, Cuba could have normal ties "with every Latin American government, but [its] way of addressing them had so far been thwarting any efforts."

Prestes's complaints found a receptive audience. Like Khrushchev, Novotný hoped to advance communist aims by supporting, not toppling, Brazil's president. Goulart, he said, "was playing a significant role for our foreign policy. It is not that he likes Communists, but he knows he can put Brazil's strength into effect only if he makes use of the hatred of Brazil's people against Americans to strengthen his position as the president and the position of Brazil as a counterweight of the United States in Latin America."[136]

Prestes had a more jaundiced view. Goulart, he said, faced rising internal pressure from "reactionary forces" but was "afraid" to "lean on the masses." In foreign policy, Goulart had continued Quadros's opening to the Soviet bloc, yet "turns to socialist countries only to achieve more from imperialists." (U.S. officials agreed that this was Quadros's and Goulart's strategy.) Confidently—overly so—Prestes foresaw "no big risk of a right-wing coup" against Goulart, who was "stronger today than he was when he assumed his office." Though in the armed forces "nationalist officers prevail," they were balanced by "Communist influences in high places" and "democratic traditions." Warily—presciently—Novotný called Goulart's position "very unstable and unlikely to be tenable for more than just a few years" (only one, it turned out).

When Prestes noted finance minister Dantas's concurrent mission to Washington and likely U.S. arm-twisting to get Brazil to alter its foreign policy in exchange for aid, Novotný seemed confident Brazil would stand firm. Otherwise, "Goulart would no longer be Goulart and Brazil would be just another Latin American country, which Goulart knows very well." Prestes agreed, recalling—after Novotný said Goulart could resist the Americans since they knew too much pressure could backfire, pushing the Brazilian leftward—that Goulart had vowed he "would not sell Brazil's independence."

Prestes continued to dwell on disputes with Cuban comrades: on domestic matters, for example, the Cubans blamed Washington, but "have been reducing their economic base themselves." Their nationalization policy went too far, too fast, and they "should slow down a bit and perhaps take a few steps back." Agreeing, Novotný said the Cubans had ignored repeated Czech warnings against extremist errors, insisting that their situations differed. For instance, they built "luxury houses while we, a developed country, proceeded very cautiously," and radically insisted on rent "equalization" while Prague charged higher rents to those with higher incomes. "The material incentive principle should be adhered to at all times," Novotný reasoned, sounding like a capitalist. Prague gave Cuba huge loans, but Havana kept deferring repayment even while seeking more credits, he complained: the Cubans "should be told that they have to implement a sound economic policy; we cannot afford to finance experiments." The prospect of ultimately having to write off the loans especially annoyed him because, unlike some other developing nations Prague aided, Cuba was "rich both in raw materials and in agricultural products."[137]

After Prague, the Czechs expected Prestes to return to Brazil via Moscow, but details of any conversations he may have had in the Soviet capital remain obscure. He told the Czechs he did not want to transit Havana again on his way home[138]—another hint that his first trip to revolutionary Cuba had not been so pleasant or productive.

Julião, rather than heading straight home from Cuba, stopped in Peru, where he warned the Lima press that if a possibly "imminent" U.S. attack on Cuba happened, he had "already prepared a vast plan of sabotage and destruction of North American property in Brazil" and hoped other Latin American countries would follow suit. To Brazil's envoy (who noted that Julião was under close police watch), he speculated that a Brazilian break with Cuba could spark "civil war," and boasted that the Peasant Leagues counted, on the continent, some forty million supporters.[139]

Julião's bellicosity during his travels did not go unnoticed at home. As Poland's envoy cabled from Rio, the views he expressed in Cuba "were very negatively received by Goulart"—who, to Moscow's ambassador, said "with undisguised irritation" that Julião's policies harm the "the nationalist forces in the country, undermining their unity." Brazil's president had allegedly placed a "highly damning article about Julião" in the national press. Moreover, a Soviet-bloc diplomat surmised, Goulart "was sure to make it clear to Havana that if Julião's views corresponded with those of Castro, then he would be forced to change his attitude towards the Cuban government."[140] In Brazil, as elsewhere in the global south, far-leftist movements' promotion of armed struggle, in the Cuban or Chinese mode, roiled relationships in both domestic and international spheres.

The February–March 1963 Prestes/Julião Visits to Cuba: Consequences?

What consequences did Julião's and Prestes's visits to Cuba in February–March 1963 have in terms of Fidel Castro's views and actions regarding the rival Brazilian leftist factions? Assessments varied. U.S. intelligence collected reports that, while sketchy and inconsistent, suggested that Castro had, as Prestes and Moscow hoped, somewhat moderated his course. In late March, an official Cuban source indicated that, in February, Fidel "attempt[ed] to insure" that Julião became "less aggressive" toward Goulart. Castro had curbed his usual yen for violence because Julião "has no real chance of coming to power in Brazil at this time, but might be able to bring about the downfall of Goulart, which would be undesirable." (The CIA source, contacted in Mexico City, speculated that "Castro apparently is either personally friendly to Goulart or regards the Goulart government with favor, at least from a pragmatic standpoint.")[141] The CIA linked this gossip to Prestes's recent trip, receiving a note quoting Julião as saying that "Prestes had brought back to Cuba from Moscow the line that terrorism should be discarded in Brazil."[142]

In July 1963, admitting that Castro had muted his calls for hemispheric revolution since February (if not altering his ultimate aim), the CIA noted that, after returning to Brazil from Havana, "both Juliao and Prestes claimed to have won Castro's support—Prestes for a 'peaceful' approach and Juliao for continued violence"—and suspected that any compromise reached had "favored Prestes and his Moscow-oriented party."[143] Another CIA assessment acknowledged an ambiguous outcome to both trips, adding: "Reportedly Juliao will continue to get moral and material aid from Cuba but will be unable to send trainees there."[144]

A more detailed CIA study reached a similarly mixed verdict, ascribing Julião's and Prestes's Cuban trips to a likely "Soviet-inspired attempt to coordinate policy." While Prestes and the CPSU had obtained promises Castro would publicly moderate his views on revolution in Brazil, Julião reportedly had "quoted Castro as expressing renewed conviction of the necessity for armed revolution in Brazil," and "promised continued moral and material support." The Cuban allegedly "was convinced that Julião's armed revolutionary plans, rather than the united-front line of the PCB, represented the most practical method of securing a revolution in Brazil." Meanwhile, Prestes said Castro had "refused to discuss the matter" of support for Julião, interpreting this as evidence of continued Cuban support for him. CIA sources also noted Prestes "probably remonstrated against Castro's contacts with the [PCdoB]."[145] In late 1963, the CIA then heard from an "excellent" source that the Cubans felt "considerable disgust" toward Prestes and the PCB, which they "considered too 'soft,'" and had promised Julião more arms and money "when . . . the moment [was] opportune to start an armed revolt."[146]

Communist sources also suggest strains between Prestes and Castro subsequently persisted, despite a seeming uptick in relations after the Cuban's spring 1963 trip to the USSR. Though records of Castro's talks with Khrushchev remain spotty, analysts suspect the Soviet pushed him to moderate his policies toward Latin America and its pro-Soviet communist parties.[147] In late July, a Prestes associate told a Hungarian diplomat that PCB relations with Cuba had "greatly improved, particularly after Fidel Castro's visit in the Soviet Union."[148] Yet, in September, Prestes told Moscow's envoy in Rio that Fidel's "intransigence," his "open calls for revolutionary uprisings" in Latin America and "direct attacks" on their leaders, deepened Havana's hemispheric isolation and hindered campaigns against interference in *Cuba's* internal affairs.[149] Prestes's continued displeasure with Castro in late 1963 was clear when he recounted his Cuba visit to a GDR visitor. Contrary to what he had told the Czechs in March, the PCB boss now judged that "the Chinese influence in Cuba is extremely strong and is even increasing" (prompting the East German to quote another Brazilian comrade as stating, "the Cubans show their stomachs to the Soviet Union, but they give their hearts to China"). Not only did Cuban media echo the CCP's "dogmatic and ultra-left views," but Fidel's advice to Latin American communists was "very much in the spirit of the Chinese ultra-radical line." Prestes scorned the "ultra-radical Cuban economic policy as especially dangerous," noting that even workshops with as few as three employees had been nationalized. Prestes had raised such questions "very openly and critically," but Castro failed to respond "in any way." Deriding Havana's incompetence "as a major deficiency," Prestes noted that Cuba's new unity party (merging communists and *fidelistas*), the Partido Unido de la Revolucion Socialista (PURS), "barely functions organizationally."[150] Prestes's private criticisms of Castro sharply contradicted the public image of solidarity he purveyed, which anti-Castro activists swallowed.[151]

Indeed, Brazil's embassy in Havana in mid-April 1963 reported that Prestes, during his visit the month before, had cut a deal with Castro. According to a "trustworthy" source,[152] Prestes "felt satisfied" with Castro, who vowed to stop supporting the PCdoB in exchange for Prestes's vow "to honor the Cuban revolution."[153] Rejecting Fidel's "insinuations," Prestes clarified that his pro-Moscow party had published Castro's 2nd Havana Declaration (while viewing it "as a merely Cuban document" rather than authoritative throughout the hemisphere). After listening to him, Prestes told the Brazilian's East European informant, Fidel "comprehended for the first time the peculiarities of the Brazilian situation." Another source told the Brazilians that Julião also left Cuba in early March "disposed to seek in Brazil a base of understanding with Prestes, 'conserving, however, the originality of his own position.'" Julião had reportedly said that the missile crisis changed the situation on the continent, "and one should evaluate henceforth 'the new responsibilities of the Soviet Union.'" The seemingly milder stand toward Moscow surprised Brazil's acting ambassador in Havana, who doubted his hosts could have pressed this line: "I don't know who could have influenced Julião, but I doubt they have been the Cubans."[154]

Fidel's own utterances after seeing Khrushchev implied that, despite his dalliance with Julião, he no longer backed an armed revolt in Brazil. The shift apparently reflected, besides Soviet pressure, Castro's pragmatic recognition that maintaining decent relations with at least a few key countries in the hemisphere was an important tactic to resist Washington. In Moscow, he openly cited Cuba's relations with Brazil, Mexico, and Canada as models for the "normal" ties he wanted with the United States.[155] After returning to Cuba, Castro reverted to a more militant tone, but exempted Brazil (where "reaction has not been able to defeat the Goulart government"), along with Mexico, Chile, Uruguay, and Bolivia, the other countries that still kept embassies in Havana, from Latin American nations he thought ripe for revolution, noting that their governments "respect the sovereignty of Cuba" and "have not been instruments of Yankee imperialism in its aggressions."[156] Castro's changed outlook was evident in Brazil; his new ambassador, Raúl Roa Kouri, insisted that Cuba's embassy in Rio would not "act as aggressively as in the past and will support more a policy of peaceful coexistence."[157]

The Pro-Cuba Solidarity Congress, March 1963

The Continental Congress for Solidarity with Cuba, set for Rio in late March, focused the far Left's intramural battle between militant and moderate wings, complicated Brazil's foreign relations, and nearly triggered a showdown between Goulart and a domestic adversary. The timing discomfited Brazil's president, coinciding with finance minister Dantas's talks in

Washington. "The image of Brazil hospitably hosting a pro-Castro gathering while seeking more American aid did not sit well with the American Congress or public," one scholar wrote.[158]

To avoid this awkward juxtaposition, Goulart pleaded with the PCB to further delay the conference, but Prestes's party—"usually so anxious to curry favor with the Goulart regime," State Department analysts noted—"refused to budge." Noting the PCB's "unusual boldness," U.S. observers sensed it desired "to test the limits of President Goulart's 'independent' foreign policy, perhaps to force a show-down with anticommunists in domestic politics, and to avoid being flanked by extremists in the communist movement itself."[159] Similarly, Brazil begged Havana to oppose the congress, saying it would be "inopportune and prejudicial," not only for Brazil-Cuban relations but for Cuba's standing in the hemisphere, since it would "radicalize" public opinion (thereby exacerbating Cuba's isolation).[160] But Havana refused to discourage this "spontaneous" show of solidarity, especially at the time of a "hostile" gathering in Costa Rica (where JFK met that month with Central American leaders), and rejected the claim that the congress was ill-timed; after all, "for Cuba all times were exactly alike," since U.S. hostility was "a constant."[161]

Hoping to blunt the damage, Goulart's government assured U.S. officials that, while unable to bar the meeting, it would try to limit its size and impact. Publicly, it vacillated, vying to satisfy Washington yet not unduly alienate domestic leftists.[162] After some flip-flopping, annoying both sides—and arousing suspicions of a tussle between Itamaraty (eager to reassure Washington) and Planalto (the presidential palace[163])—Goulart and Foreign Minister Hermes Lima implemented a strategy of not opposing the congress outright, but refusing visas to potential "Iron Curtain" participants, even if Latin American citizens (other than residents of European colonies such as British Guyana) could freely visit Brazil as "tourists."[164]

While in Washington, Dantas assured Rusk that Brazil opposed the congress, explained the restrictive visa policy, and (like Goulart at home) tried to calm U.S. nerves by minimizing the peril to Brazil's stability posed by domestic communists or foreign (i.e., Cuban) subversives. The finance (and ex-foreign) minister insisted that communists were "not very important on the domestic scene," busy clinging to "positions of leadership in the labor unions, where they are being challenged by non-communist labor leaders." As to Brazil's divided far Left, Dantas told Rusk that "communist contacts with Moscow were made mainly through Czechoslovakia, although the pro-Peking faction had a closer contact with Cuba," and "the orthodox communists were now denouncing those who had close ties with Cuba, such as Francisco Julião." Itamaraty aide Carlos Bernardes also soothed Rusk: Havana trained Latin American guerrillas, he admitted, but Brazilians did not seem to be among them. Rather than Southern Cone targets, such as Brazil, Argentina, or Uruguay, Castro concentrated on Venezuela and the Caribbean.[165]

As for the Soviets, Goulart avoided a direct "no" but, to Moscow's ambassador in Rio, rued the meeting's "very bad timing" and wrung his hands so strongly that the Soviets easily inferred his preference that they *not* send delegates.[166] The day before the national congress began, Brazil's foreign minister not only reiterated to Fomin the refusal to give foreign participants visas but said two cosmonauts touring Brazil shouldn't show up (they didn't).[167]

Amid the visa wrangle, the Brazilian Left's disunity as the congress neared was evident. To a U.S. reporter, the spat between Prestes's PCB, on the one hand, and Julião and the PCdoB, on the other, reflected the Sino-Soviet rift's sharpness in Brazil. "The young Castro-Communist actionists have come to look upon Julião as something of a hero and the aging Prestes as a conservative fuddy-duddy who ought to become an elder statesman and leave the day-to-day management of party affairs in the hands of someone like Juliao, if not Juliao himself."[168]

A flashpoint between the PCB and more militant Brazilian factions, the pro-Cuba congress also precipitated an internal Brazilian standoff between Goulart and Lacerda. The anti-communist Guanabara state governor blocked the congress from meeting in Rio, "on pain of prison and court action." Harassed by police, who arrested more than fifty, the Cuba supporters fled across Guanabara Bay to the city of Niteroi.[169] There, in a neighboring state jurisdiction safe from Lacerda's police, they staged the national (26–28 March) and continental (28–30 March) pro-Cuba solidarity congresses in a seamen's trade union building, albeit (U.S. officials gleefully noted) "with greatly reduced attendance." Few foreigners made it, mostly Latin American, none prominent, with a Xinhua news agency rep pressed into service as a Chinese "delegate-guest," and no Soviet delegation due to visa restrictions, *Pravda* sadly acknowledged.[170]

At both two-day congresses, militants clamored for armed struggle. At the national congress on March 27, "violent" arguments split the group drafting resolutions between "those advocating the peaceful path to revolution and those in favor of the Cuban path," urging the creation of a "United Revolutionary Anti-Imperialist Front." Moderates ultimately prevailed, endorsing Brazil's noninterventionist line in Cuba. The continental congress opened the next day, with greetings from Castro and Soviet and Chinese leaders (a Bulgarian report loyally said delegates received Khrushchev's with "great enthusiasm" but applauded Mao's "less enthusiastically"). According to a communist account based on PCB "friends" who attended the closed sessions, "a serious ideological struggle" erupted between relatively moderate Brazilians (the PCB and "the nationalist honest, progressive community") and "the representatives of Trotskyist and ultra-leftist elements of another country": the Peruvians, led by Movement of the Revolutionary Left (MIR) head Luis de la Puente Uceda. The Cuban-trained, pro-Chinese militant "proposed revolution by announcing a general strike throughout Latin America starting immediately in all Latin American countries," featuring "attacks on U.S. persons and property" and forging a "Union of Soviet Socialist Latino Republics." However, PCB communists opposed de la Puente's "ultra-leftist thesis," and his "extremist" stand was soundly defeated.[171]

Notably absent from the detailed U.S. account—based on reports in *Novos Rumos* (the PCB newspaper) and CIA sources—was any sign that Julião had advocated this more militant course or promoted armed force to advance the revolutionary struggle. Had Castro counseled him to pull his punches, as the CIA had heard from one source purportedly close to Cuba's leader?[172] (Another figure Cuba liked, Brizola—Havana's new ambassador called him Brazil's "greatest leftist leader" "with the greatest revolutionary potential"[173]—did not even attend.)

Eventually, Prestes's (and Khrushchev's) line triumphed. Passed resolutions championed Cuba and vowed more meetings, committees, and "days of solidarity," but did not endorse violent revolution, Castroist or otherwise, in the hemisphere. While ruing the congress' "vicious efforts" to "picture the United States as the primary enemy of the peoples of Latin America," U.S. analysts noted the split over "the best strategy for combating that enemy."

Extremist elements favored immediate effort toward a Castro-type revolution throughout Latin America, aimed at the sudden and complete destruction of the social, economic, and political structure of the bourgeoisie, to be preceded by a general strike and attacks on U.S. persons and property. The orthodox communists, led by the Brazilian Communist Party, advocated a peaceful pathway to revolution with level-headedness and patience and apparently won out, as evidenced by the relatively mild exhortations contained in the final drafts of the Niteroi declarations and resolutions. Those documents suggest that the Kremlin may not be ready to encourage or to underwrite a Castro-type revolution throughout the whole of Latin America—at least for the present.[174]

Before it met, the State Department feared a "successful well-attended" congress could "1) provide effective vehicle promote Castro/Communist subversive efforts in hemisphere 2) help Castro regain some of lost prestige and 3) suggest break in solid front against Castro which hemisphere has maintained since October crisis."[175] More worried about potential peril to fragile U.S.-Brazilian economic and political relations, the U.S. embassy in Rio warned that "excess publicity in US may build up congress—as it built up Julião—way beyond intrinsic importance" and urged Washington against publicly condemning the meeting, which was, "so far at least, receiving very little public attention outside commie circles."[176]

U.S. verdicts, both public and classified, mostly considered the conference a flop, citing low attendance; absence of international luminaries (Russell, Bella, Sartre, Cárdenas, etc.) and few notable Brazilians; chaotic arrangements, disrupted by Lacerda; and bland resolutions that failed to draw much international notice. "An almost total fiasco," judged the Rio embassy, even if it fed international communist propaganda.[177] The State Department's Bureau of Intelligence and Research (INR) concurred but conceded that—largely thanks to the "rough-and-tumble" clash with Lacerda—it achieved "wide publicity" and communists viewed the "mere holding of it in Brazil" "a worthwhile accomplishment."[178]

Indeed, international communist propaganda hailed the congress even if private views were mixed. Bulgaria's envoy in Rio felt it "played a positive role in this stage of the struggle" for Latin American "national and economic independence and the strengthening of the Cuban Revolution," and praised Prestes's closing speech as a high point.[179] He even saw a silver lining in Lacerda's actions, which provoked "unexpected spontaneous manifestations of agitation, outrage, and determination of resistance in defense of legality and democratic freedom," swiftly accomplishing "what the organizers had been unable to promote." Similarly, Poland's ambassador reported the PCB believed Lacerda's heavy-handed expulsion of the gathering from Rio to Niteroi "made the congress even more popular at the time when the prospects for it were bleak."[180] However, the Bulgarian wrote, the results would have been "much more positive" had the congress met a month later, allowing more preparation and larger, more prestigious attendance.[181]

In their own post-mortem, the Czechs found serious deficiencies: *AO Družhba* "succeeded in launching several campaigns" culminating with the congress, "but it did not reach its final objective: establishment of stable structures" to support Cuba. The congress had a "significant" political impact in Latin America and drew global interest, yet could have yielded more results but for organizational "shortcomings." Most important, the original idea was to confine the PCB to a backstage role, "so that the Congress would be organized primarily by uncompromised democratic forces in Latin America and that would enhance the prestige and impact of the Congress." Instead, preparations were dominated by communists, who "had a rather reserved stance towards people out of their circles, including . . . so-called nationalist forces and this led to loss of some valuable contacts that were made through our endeavour." Other faults included "unrealistic time planning—postponing and changes of dates created a lot of confusion and misunderstanding"—and contradictory information from Moscow compared to from "our people in Brazil" (suggesting the need for more frequent personal contact between headquarters and *rezidentura*).[182]

Perhaps the most provocative interpretation came from Brazil's embassy in Havana, which suspected Prestes's participation in the "Congress of Niteroi" and the relative moderation of the resolutions ultimately passed stemmed from his deal with Fidel Castro to get him to stop financially backing the PCdoB.[183]

China, Mao, and the Inter-Communist Brazilian Struggle, 1963

Ever since February 1956, when Khrushchev's de-Stalinization speech at the 20th CPSU congress discombobulated the communist world, Mao Zedong and his associates had courted Brazilian communists and tried to wean them from Moscow. Attending the 8th Chinese Communist Party congress that September, a top Prestes aide, Diógenes Arruda, was among Latin American communists who warmly welcomed Liu Shaoqi's prediction that the "anti-colonial struggle" would spread from Africa and Asia to their hemisphere. He was even more impressed when Liu and Mao met with the Latins for substantial talks—compared to his trips to the Soviet Union, where, "he had never had the honor of being received by the most obscure member of the [CPSU] Central Committee." Signaling warming relations, the Brazilians followed up by sending cadres to China for "six months of indoctrination."[184]

Three years later, in October 1959, Prestes himself was among communist bigwigs who gathered in Beijing to celebrate the PRC founding's 10th anniversary. He spent almost a month touring Chinese cities, but his visit climaxed when he met the CCP chairman. After initial hesitation, the PCB boss had swung firmly behind Khrushchev's "peaceful coexistence" line, alienating some senior party hardliners who opposed denouncing Stalin. By the time he welcomed Prestes to lunch on October 25 in Jinan, Mao had already had a stormy secret conversation with Khrushchev, but the intensity and hostility of their rift, and the Sino-Soviet schism it portended, remained hidden to the outside world behind the façade of communist solidarity.[185]

To Prestes, however, China's leader apparently did not hide his displeasure with Moscow. According to a CIA report based on the Brazilian's recounting of his foreign travels to PCB insiders, in their talk Mao rapped Khrushchev for "denigrati[ng]" Stalin "in a very negative and abrupt manner, which dismissed all the merits which Stalin had"; praised Soviet ex-foreign minister Vyacheslav Molotov (whom Khrushchev had purged, making him ambassador to Mongolia); and "asserted that peaceful disentanglement is a theory which had no historical precedent and that all Communist parties throughout the world should be ready to fight." Echoing other CCP figures Prestes had seen, and implying doubts about the Brazilian's purge within the PCB Central Committee, Mao urged him to adopt a more militant posture. On "internal party dissension," Mao observed, "many Communist Parties had had to fight leftist deviation for so long that they had lost sight of the necessity for curbing rightist deviation." (Even the Soviets hinted that the Brazilian communists had veered too far right. In Moscow, Prestes was told by CPSU ideological watchdog Mikhail Suslov that the PCB needed to stiffen its working class and labor support—even Castro had recognized the need to "strive for the hegemony of the working class," he noted—and do more to penetrate various organizations. "We believe that it is possible the Brazilian revolution can be carried out peacefully," Suslov warned him, "but you must be prepared for the other possibility.")[186]

According to the Chinese record of their talk—which, mysteriously, lacks the anti-Soviet comments the CIA reported Mao making—Prestes confessed leftist "dogmatism" in 1950 for opposing Vargas (he was "progressive and anti-imperialist but we boycotted the elections") and explained the party's current strategy of collaborating with Kubitschek's vice president, Goulart, and his PTB. Mao expressed understanding, likening this tactic to his periodic cooperation with Jiang Jieshi (Chiang Kai-shek). Still, he cautioned Prestes that, while the PCB's emphasis on a peaceful transition to communism and the proletarian class' pacific desires might make political sense, the party also must prepare for an armed struggle, suggesting the slogan: "If the enemies resort to violence to oppose the people, the people should use weapons." Too many Latin American communist parties—including by implication the Brazilian—failed to adequately consider this second path, he felt. Mao had also, in what would be a frequent refrain to Brazilian communists, urged Prestes to focus on winning countryside support and creating a worker-peasant alliance, citing the CCP's quest to cultivate Chinese peasants.[187]

Prestes left this smoky encounter convinced that Mao had a shaky grasp of Brazilian realities, but on returning home penned articles praising "People's China" for the party press. As Sino-Soviet strains emerged, he remained stoutly loyal to Moscow but avoided openly rapping Beijing, calling only for the "unity of the international communist movement."[188]

As Castro's revolution turned toward the communist world—and moved to establish relations with the PRC to replace Batista's ties with Taiwan— Cuba zoomed to the forefront of Mao's thinking about Latin America.[189] Brazil represented China's second most important priority in the hemisphere, both in terms of encouraging eventual revolution—through ongoing contacts with Brazilian communists and other radicals, such as Julião— and developing interstate relations.

Those latter efforts intensified after Quadros, on becoming Brazil's president in January 1961, expanded relations (both economic and political) with communist nations and diverged from U.S. hardline anti-Beijing policies (e.g., at the UN). While not immediately normalizing relations with the PRC (i.e., jettisoning ties to Taiwan and alienating Washington), Quadros avidly pursued Sino-Brazilian trade: in May 1961 he welcomed an economic mission from the mainland,[190] and in August he sent Goulart on a reciprocal trip to China (after visiting the USSR). The Brazilian vice president received a lavish airport welcome, and banquets and meetings with Zhou and Mao, and Goulart responded accordingly, publicly praising the "great leader" Mao for raising his country from "the yoke of their exploiters," commending the "people's communes" at the heart of the (disastrous) "Great Leap Forward," and voicing shared animus to "imperialists."[191] In private meetings with Mao in Hangzhou, Chinese records show, Goulart was even more explicitly anti-Washington (and anti-Jiang), condemning the "oppression of American capital," affirming that Jiang "does not represent the Chinese people," and echoing Mao's analysis of the U.S. role in oppressing not only socialist but nationalist, independence-seeking peoples.[192] Impressed, Mao later endorsed Goulart's maneuvering to succeed to Brazil's presidency over conservative opposition, especially in the military, after Quadros's sudden exit in late August.[193]

Mao also, separately, received Brazilian communists. On August 19—as Prestes, in Brazil, purged pro-Beijing militants who would form the PCdoB—a PCB delegation saw the Chinese leader in Hangzhou between his meetings with Goulart. As the Chinese record shows, Mao remained somewhat hazy about Brazil—uncertain of its proximity to Cuba, whose struggle, he emphasized, mutually supported the revolutionary fight for Brazil and all Latin America—and about the Brazilian communist party's leader. Asked by Mao whether the party was behind the "guerrilla war led by Prestes" (in the '20s), the PCB reps sheepishly admitted that at the time "Comrade Prestes was an idealist," against feudal oligarchy and for democracy, and only later "studied Marxism hard" and became a communist theorist. Informing the Chinese leader on the PCB's background, they acknowledged shortcomings and delays in mobilizing peasant support, which Mao emphasized as essential, citing CCP history. Mao also warned the PCB not to trust the national bourgeoisie, which would "contend for leadership," whether in opposing imperialism or promoting land reform, in contrast to the "exploited poor peasants" and "non-exploiting middle peasants," who were a "reliable ally." Again, Mao warned the Brazilian communists to be ready for a violent showdown with imperialism; the visitors vowed they were "preparing the party and the people to take the military road should American imperialism and its agents require that."[194]

Mao's alternating receptions for Goulart and PCB comrades reflected his double game: cultivating Marxist-Leninists he hoped might lead a Brazilian revolution, and at the same time enhancing relations with Brazil's government to undermine U.S. influence. He soon embarked on a "double-double game": besides promoting both interparty and interstate Sino-Brazilian ties, he would simultaneously maintain fraternal relations with the PCB and expand exchanges with the dissident PCdoB.

Indeed, after militants expelled from the PCB formed their own faction, Mao shared the upstarts' yen for armed struggle, but hesitated before burning bridges to Prestes's party. "It seems," suggests Cecil Johnson, "that the

Chinese were unwilling to place their stamp of approval on the newly established party until they had satisfied themselves regarding the orthodoxy of the pro-Chinese group." Not only did China's press ignore the breakaway party's founding in February 1962, but a month later the CCP Central Committee sent fraternal greetings to its PCB counterpart.[195] In late 1962, Mao received two Prestes comrades; though he later told PCdoB emissaries that the couple said they "agree with the new party" despite still belonging to the old one, a brief *Peking Review* notice gave no hint of the internecine Brazilian communist rivalry.[196]

That competition intensified in early 1963. As Prestes, with Khrushchev's support, tried to convince Castro to end Cuba's backing for more militant Brazilian leftists, the PCB and PCdoB also sent delegations to China to compete for Mao's endorsement.

Historiographical confusion over this episode exists due to the mistaken identification in key works of the Brazilian delegation that met Mao in April 1963 as belonging to the pro-Beijing dissident party—it was actually sent by Prestes—and consequent misanalysis of China's handling of the visit.[197] The confusion may stem from the fact that PCB delegation head Manuel Jover Teles *subsequently* broke with Prestes. After the 1964 *golpe*, Teles, unlike Prestes, backed Mao's favored option of armed struggle against Brazil's military dictatorship, was expelled from the PCB executive committee in 1967, and then, along with other PCB figures seeking a tougher stand, founded the "revolutionary" Brazilian communist party (PCBR) in 1968 (he later joined the PCdoB).[198] Even before his 1963 visit, Teles had displayed a more militant posture than Prestes, as shown by his warmth toward Cuba. Teles had visited the island in May 1961, shortly after the Bay of Pigs, and imbibed the revolutionary spirit (likely enhanced by a briefing from Che), feelings evident in a *Novos Rumos* trip report.[199] Some associates later said he was already acting in a "dual role" when he went to China, carrying out his official mission for Prestes, which included contesting the PCdoB, yet already pursuing the more militant ideas he and other PCB stalwarts dissatisfied with "peaceful coexistence" preferred; said one ex-PCdoB member, Teles had "one eye on the priest [i.e., Prestes] and another on the mass."[200]

Though absent from standard accounts, the PCdoB *had* recently sent a delegation to China which met Mao but received no Chinese press coverage. As the CIA reported, correctly distinguishing the rival missions,[201] the dissident duo that visited China in February–March 1963 consisted of João Amazonas and Lincoln Oest, following up on the invite Amazonas and Grabois received from China's embassy in Havana during their spring 1962 visit. In "extensive discussions," the CIA learned, "high CCP officials" told Oest and Amazonas that "Peking supported the [PCdoB] but could not then break publicly with the PCB because such official Chinese recognition of the [PCdoB] would add fuel to CPSU charges that the CCP was sowing disunity within the world Communist movement."[202] Justifying to the PCdoB this half-hearted support, and citing their own historical experience (as Mao often did), the Chinese elaborated that "all political bodies have a right, a left, and a center, the majority . . . always gravitating to the center." They urged their guests "never to lose sight of this fact, and to work continuously to win over the central majority of Brazilian Communists who, while then aligned with the 'rightist' Brazilian Communist Party (PCB), could be persuaded eventually to join forces with the [PCdoB]."[203] The CIA summarized Mao's message as having cautioned "dissident Brazilian Communists not to expect an easy revolution in Brazil, and to bear in mind that the Chinese revolution had taken thirty years." Cuba's revolution, according to the Chinese, had been "rapid because the Batista government was clearly reactionary and oppressive." In Brazil, "Goulart's nationalist demagoguery . . . deceived the masses into believing he was not obeying the imperialists" and because the PCB collaborated with Goulart, this was "delaying the revolution." The Chinese reportedly therefore "advised the [PCdoB] to concentrate its efforts on winning over the bulk of the Brazilian Communists from the PCB."[204] As for the "official" PCB delegation that a month later visited China, the CIA heard only that it had a "'friendly'" audience with Mao.[205] "Peiping accorded red-carpet tours of the mainland to Amazonas as well as orthodox party leaders it hopes to influence," it noted.[206]

However, new Chinese evidence reveals in far more detail Mao's handling of the two delegations. When Mao received Amazonas and Oest in Zhongnanhai on March 6,[207] he praised their faction as the true Brazilian communist revolutionaries and scorned Prestes's PCB: "You are a Marxist-Leninist party, determined to pursue revolution. There are some parties now that are Communist in name but are determined not to pursue revolution. A Marxist-Leninist must pursue revolution," he said, echoing Castro's 2nd Havana Declaration. "What sort of Communist Party is it if it does not [pursue] revolution? If one does not [pursue] revolution, from the people's perspective, there is no great difference with the political parties of the capitalist class." As an example of this sort of "Communist-in-name-only," Mao named India's Shripad Amrit Dange—"he doesn't have the slightest difference from the big national parties of the big bourgeoisie and the landlords"—but said this category also included the PCB's leader. Praising Castro's recent claim that "objectively Latin America has a revolutionary situation, but it lacks in subjective conditions," Mao inferred the Cuban meant that "many countries' communist parties are opportunist, including Prestes's party" as well as the Mexican, Argentine, Chilean, Uruguayan, Ecuadorian, and Peruvian.[208]

Hearing from Amazonas that his party enjoyed "semi-legal" status, Mao grudgingly conceded that this situation had advantages (activists could openly publish, meet, organize, rally), but rued that the lack of harsh repression was "not very good for a revolutionary's toughening," which was needed to harden the party's capabilities, even, perhaps, at the cost of cadres' lives. Predictably, Mao cited the "always illegal" CCP experience—losing many activists to the "white terror" of "imperialism and its running dog Jiang Jieshi" before triumphing—and also Castro's loss of *compañeros* who had traveled aboard the *Granma* to Batista's forces before he fled to the Sierra Maestra. Brazil's communists, he implied, needed to endure comparable adversity before they, too, could wage a victorious revolutionary campaign, and he urged them to "prepare themselves mentally and organizationally, and also, if possible, prepare themselves militarily." One lesson Mao tried to impart was to focus on the countryside, their likely eventual guerrilla base; peasants were easily put off by urban intellectuals and professionals. Julião, he said, was an urban revolutionary who failed to gain their trust.

For now, Mao concluded, Brazil lacked a "real revolutionary situation and a real revolutionary movement," with capitalists not yet fearful enough to unleash a "white terror," and hardly concerned by Prestes's "old party" that "has already become a tool of the capitalist class." Once the communists whipped up revolutionary fervor, inspiring a mass movement, he predicted, the imperialists, the big landlords, the "comprador capitalist class" would hammer down hard—as they had in Cuba—and the militant communists must be ready to take arms, for "You are the revolutionary faction of Brazil." Mao vowed continued support for Amazonas's party—"China's help is your right and our obligation"—which took on extra import since Castro was simultaneously, it appears, as noted above, in response to Prestes's (and Khrushchev's) pressure, cutting Cuban aid to the militants.

There is (disputed) evidence that at this juncture China covertly backed the PCdoB. In a March 20, 1963, letter, a "Comrade Cheng" in Bern, Switzerland, urged a "Comrade Wang" (one of nine Chinese in Brazil, sent to promote Sino-Brazilian economic and cultural ties, arrested after the April

1964 military coup), as part of his "subterranean work," to "continue to maintain relations with the leaders of the true Communist Party of Brazil." In the letter, "Comrade Cheng" said the two recent PCdoB visitors, Amazonas and Oest, plus Grabois, were "important for the REVOLUTION" and "willing to be guided by us," and named other alleged military and political sympathizers. The letter was seized from the Rio flat of the nine Chinese by Guanabara police and later introduced as evidence in their trial for subversion; their lawyer called it "an obvious forgery."[209]

If authentic, the letter fits the CIA-favored view that Beijing inclined toward the PCdoB yet were reluctant for tactical reasons to recognize it yet as the legitimate Brazilian party and break openly with Prestes's PCB. The Chinese record of Mao's talk with Amazonas/Oest includes no explicit statements to this effect, but (as noted above) the CIA reported that "high CCP" officials told the visitors that China "supported" the PCdoB "but could not then break publicly with the PCB because such official Chinese recognition of the [PCdoB] would add fuel to CPSU charges that the CCP was sowing disunity within the world Communist movement." However, the Chinese thought it just a matter of time before the PCB broke with Beijing; then they could openly back the PCdoB.[210]

In line with this wary strategy, the Chinese ignored the PCdoB pair in the press, but, in March, publicly welcomed the PCB delegation, and during their three-week visit, amid tours of "people's communes, factories, schools and other places of interest," announced their meetings with high-level figures such as Politburo member Peng Zhen, leading to the ultimate honor: an audience and dinner with Mao.[211] These open references blithely concealed any hint of discord between China and Prestes's party, even though the visit's top aim was to protest the PRC's de facto support for the dissident faction—as reflected in Xinhua news agency and Beijing radio use (in Portuguese-language broadcasts) of *A Classe Operária* items, and financial aid for PCdoB publications—and Julião's "'revolutionary' appeals."[212] Despite the warm welcome, the Chinese played dumb, ignoring complaints, a Prestes comrade later told a communist diplomat. "The Chinese leaders listened to all these comments, but in most cases they pretended to be wholly unaware of the whole issue," PCB Central Committee member Apolónio Carvalho groused. "As if they had nothing to do with the aforesaid matters." The trip accomplished little, he said, save to expose the Brazilians to the Chinese rulers' "dogmatic, inflexible attitude."[213]

Viewed alongside his earlier talk with Amazonas and Oest, Mao's talks with the PCB delegation on April 17–18 in Hangzhou[214] reveal his double game: privately disdaining Prestes's party, yet cordial to his delegates (and sending greetings and health inquiries to Prestes). At the outset, Teles described his mission as "to come and report on our situation and to understand the views of the Chinese comrades concerning the split in the international communist movement" and mentioned their prior talks with CCP Central Committee comrades: they had reported on the Brazilian situation to foreign affairs department head Wu Xiuquan and functionary Li Qixin (both present at the conversation with Mao), and, with Peng Zhen and alternate politburo member Kang Sheng, they had discussed "the problems of the split of the international communist movement," the Sino-Indian dispute, Cuban crisis, Yugoslavia, "revolutionary strategy and tactics, and so on." Teles left unsaid, however, part of those talks' likely content: PCB complaints that China had promoted the dissident PCdoB, and the CCP comrades' negative response. By the time they saw Mao, the Brazilians apparently had got the message: they had run into a brick wall, and politely refrained from complaining directly to China's leader.

Accordingly, Mao spent much of the conversation grilling Teles on Brazil's economic, political, and social scene (and geography, comparing the Amazon and Yangtze rivers). Asked about "nationalist" and "bourgeoisie" politicians the PCB sometimes worked with, Teles assessed "capitalist" figures from Vargas to Kubitschek to Quadros to the vexing Goulart, who "says that he belongs to the nationalist parliamentary front but in reality he has contradictions with this front" and failed to implement his party's labor, land reform, and nationalization programs. Mao professed to find Brazil's political prognosis puzzling, with the national bourgeoisie containing both "sell-out" and "people's" ("patriotic" was Teles's term) factions—the latter including Goulart's PTB, which made it more difficult to oppose—and seemed intrigued by Brizola and the PCB's relations with him (Teles: "We used to struggle together with him," but "we have no illusions" since he is "Goulart's left arm"). Citing his own history of dealing with Jiang, as was his habit, "just for reference," Mao recounted the pros and cons of cooperating with the national bourgeoisie, the dangers of both rightist and leftist deviation, the need to prepare for armed struggle. Yet, he avoided the topic of the Brazilian communist split, and did not mention the PCdoB delegation he had recently seen. Near the end of their second talk, Teles remarked that, though it might not be "appropriate" to raise the international communist schism, he was "very willing to hear" Mao's comments on the topic; Mao had none.

In the months after the rival Brazilian communist delegations visited

Mao, the Sino-Soviet split intensified. For the first time, the polemics between the Soviet and Chinese parties directly entangled the Brazilian communist split and featured Beijing's backing of the PCdoB. The dissident party mouthpiece, *A Classe Operária*, reprinted and endorsed the CCP's anti-Soviet barrages as correct guidance for Brazilian communists. On July 14, 1963, a CPSU "open letter" accused the CCP of attacking established (pro-Moscow) communist parties and supporting "anti-party breakaway groups" in various countries, including Australia, Italy, and Brazil, where it specifically mentioned the Chinese party's support of "the Amazonas-Grabois group." Prestes's party, naturally, echoed Moscow. On July 27, in an open "Reply to Khrushchev," the PCdoB angrily rejected as "outright slander" the charge that China had instigated the break from the PCB, reviewing the Brazilian communist internal struggles since the 20th CPSU congress and stressing that their dissent from Prestes's endorsement of Khrushchev's "peaceful coexistence" line predated the Sino-Soviet rift. Signaling their now-open preference among the Brazilian communists, the Chinese reprinted this message, carried in *A Classe Operária*, in the *Peking Review*, for the first time referring to the faction as the Communist Party of Brazil.[215] The Chinese also clarified their choice in the ongoing polemics with Moscow. In early 1964, the CCP rebutted the CPSU charge of dividing communist parties—the Soviets themselves were "the greatest splitters of our times"—and praised "the Brazilian Communists represented by Joâo Amazonas, Mauricio Grabois and other comrades" as heroic, true Marxist-Leninists "embodying the great revolutionary spirit of communist fighters."[216] On March 29, 1964, ten PCdoB militants left Brazil for Beijing to receive political-military training, but as Gaspari observes, they embarked "thinking of overthrowing Jango," but by the time they reached China they were "facing a much harder nut to crack, a military dictatorship."[217]

On April 1, a military coup ousted Goulart. As part of his swerve to the left in early 1964, he had moved to improve ties with the PRC, approving, after a delay, the staging of a Chinese industrial and cultural exhibition in Brazil.[218] The military dictatorship quashed this tenuous Sino-Brazilian rapprochement, arresting the nine Chinese who came to Brazil to arrange the exhibition and charging them with espionage and subversion. (Brazil, still under military dictatorship, would not normalize relations with Beijing until 1974.[219]) Cracking down on domestic communists, the *ditatura* satisfied Mao's wish that, like his own party, the Brazilians build character and toughen their revolutionary mettle by enduring repression and terror.

As Halperin notes, when confronted by the *golpe*, "the pro-Chinese Communist party failed as miserably as [Prestes's] official pro-Soviet party," so it had much to learn.[220]

Prestes, for his part, fled into exile in Uruguay (leaving behind reams of documents for police to seize). Though bitterly denouncing the *junta* and calling for the restoration of democracy, he still adhered to Moscow's reluctance to endorse armed revolution in Latin America, and pursued a "united front" policy of collaboration with opponents of the dictatorship, communist or not. To the Chinese, the coup proved the "bankruptcy" of Prestes's "revisionist line," and they continued to support the PCdoB and its invocation of violent struggle.[221]

PCdoB remnants who escaped arrest (in exile or Brazil) called, predictably, loudly for armed resistance to the new military rule. When party head Carlos Danielli saw him in July 1965, Mao openly scorned Prestes: "From a leftist he has become a rightist," the CCP chairman said, appalled that the PCB boss had failed to take military precautions before the coup or arouse the peasantry (he "basically does not understand the countryside"), and had let party files fall into state hands. Mao heartily encouraged more radical communists to work methodically for armed struggle and not be discouraged by inevitable setbacks. In line with his earlier view, that Brazil's rebels needed to endure a "white terror" as the CCP had, Mao seemed pleased to hear that the new regime had suppressed *A Classe Operária*: "This is a good thing. I was worried about this open paper of yours. Because this [its open publication under Goulart] meant that the conditions were not revolutionary."[222]

Mao no longer had to worry that Brazilian communists weren't enduring the toughening "terror" the CCP had: the *ditadura* ruthlessly suppressed the PCdoB and other militant groups, in Brazil and in exile. (In 1972, his visitor, Danielli, was tortured and murdered by the regime's secret police.) Mao got his wish for a severe test, but without the ending he scripted. Brazilian military rule finally ended after two decades, but not as the result of the glorious violent revolution that Mao or Fidel imagined and, for a time, promoted.[223] Brazil never became a revolutionary *foco*, let alone one of the "two, three, many Vietnams" Che hoped would mire Washington in Latin America and the Third World. When an amnesty was declared and civilian rule returned, some surviving leftists, communists, and revolutionaries— including, *inter alia*, Prestes, Julião, and Brizola—returned from exile and resumed political activity, with mixed results.[224] In 1990, with Moscow's empire in ruins and China abandoning communism, Fidel Castro paid a friendly visit to Brazil, having long dropped his support (both rhetorical and clandestine) of violent revolution in the country.

The splintering of Brazil's radical left, and its competing international alignments against the background of the Sino-Soviet split, weakened the revolutionary and communist movements in the final phases of the Goulart government leading up the 1964 military coup, and likewise undermined their efforts to fight the U.S.-backed military regime that prevailed until 1985—not that a more robust violent struggle would have achieved a materially different outcome, besides provoking even harsher reprisals and crackdowns (and human rights abuses) by the Brazilian *ditadura*. The story told here, excavating the Brazilian far-Left's relations with Cuba, the Soviet Union, and China, aims at deepening our understanding both of the country's domestic actors during this traumatic period and of the key communist powers as they jostled for influence among themselves and promoted revolutionary aims in Latin America at the height of the Cold War and the Sino-Soviet schism.

Notes

1. "Cuban Subversion in Latin America since February 1963," July 25, 1963, CIA FOIA website.

2. See, for example, Skidmore, *Politics in Brazil*, 234–243; Dulles, *Unrest in Brazil*, 199–202; Parker, *Brazil and the Quiet Intervention*, 32–43; Leacock, *Requiem for Revolution*, 133 ff; Weis, *Cold Warriors and Coups D'Etat*, 158–161; Smith, *Brazil and the United States*, 157–158.

3. U.S. Embassy, Rio de Janeiro (Gordon) [hereafter USE/RdJ], tel. 1499, February 8, 1963, Brazil, General 2/63, box 13, National Security Files (NSF), John F. Kennedy Presidential Library (JFKL), Boston, MA.

4. See Skidmore, *Politics in Brazil*, 276–284, 414n43; Dulles, *Unrest in Brazil*, 161, 188, 368–374; Chilcote, *The Brazilian Communist Party*, 207–211.

5. Moniz Bandeira, *De Martí a Fidel*, 535–536. An Itamaraty study of Brazil-Cuba relations—Marques Bezerra, *Brasil-Cuba*—ignores Prestes's trip to Cuba.

6. Gaspari, *A Ditadura Envergonhada*, 178.

7. There is brief mention of Prestes's 1963 visit to Cuba in Aarão Reis, *Luís Carlos Prestes*, 310; but no mention in Leocadia Prestes, *Luiz Carlos Prestes*; or Jorge Ferreira, "The Brazilian Communist Party and João Goulart's Administration." The overlapping Prestes/Julião trips are ignored in Andrade Porfirio, *De Pétalas e Pedras* and cited briefly in Aguiar, *Francisco Julião*, 440.

8. Silva Silveira, *Dissidência comunista*, 291–322; Rodrigues Sales, "O impacto da revolução" and "A revolução cubana, as esquerdas brasileiras e a luta contra a ditadura militar"; Rollemberg, *O apoio de Cuba à luta armada no Brasil*.

9. Brown, *Cuba's Revolutionary World*, chap. 10, uses limited documents from Cuba's Ministry of External Relations (MINREX) archive in Havana.

10. Friedman, *Shadow Cold War*.

11. See, for example, Asselin, *Hanoi's Road*, esp. chap. 6.

12. On Prestes's long journey leading rebellious forces in the 1920s through the Brazilian countryside before going into exile, see Macaulay, *The Prestes Column*; Castro said Prestes's "heroic" march was "almost like" Mao's "Long March" in China a decade later: Fidel Castro and Ignacio Ramonet, *Fidel Castro*, 532.

13. Liss, *Marxist Thought*, 107–112; Skidmore, *Politics in Brazil*, 21–23, 61–62; Chilcote, *Brazilian Communist Party*.

14. Khrushchev-Carlos Rafael Rodriguez memcon, Moscow, December 11, 1962, *Cold War International History Project Bulletin* [*CWIHPB*] 17/18 (Fall 2012): 152.

15. On Soviet-Brazilian relations under Khrushchev, see Caterina, "Um grande oceano"; Hershberg, "Soviet-Brazilian Relations and the Cuban Missile Crisis."

16. Skidmore, *Politics in Brazil*, 278–279.

17. Dantas-Rusk memcon, March 12, 1963, in *FRUS, 1961–1963*, Vol. XII: *American Republics*, doc. 159; Dantas-JFK, draft memcon, March 25, 1963, Brazil 3/22/63–3/31/63, box 13A, NSF, JFKL. In April 1962, Prestes estimated the PCB had more than 40,000 members. V.V. Stolyarov, memcon with Prestes, RdJ, April 3, 1962, f. 5, op. 50, d. 412, ll. 80–89, Russian State Archive of Contemporary History (RGANI), Moscow; trans. M. Baranova. The CIA put PCB membership at about 30,000 and the PCdoB's far lower. Deputy Director, Plans, to Chief, U.S. Secret Service, "Subject: Visit of President Kennedy to Brazil," July 12, 1962, NARA record no. 119-10003-10076, John F. Kennedy Assassination records (JFKA).

18. CIA Intelligence Report, ESAU XXVIII, "The Sino-Soviet Dispute within the Communist Movement in Latin America," June 15, 1967, CIA FOIA; Tad Szulc, "Prestes Effects Red Purge in Rio," *New York Times (NYT)*, September 7, 1957; Johnson, *Communist China and Latin America*, 183; Chilcote, *Brazilian Communist Party*, 64–73; Pomar, *Pedro Pomar*, 234; Prestes remarks to U.S. and Canadian communists, Moscow, November 12, 1961, at vault.fbi.gov/solo/solo-part-39-of-44; Devlin, "Boring from Within," 27–39; "Partido Comunista do Brasil (PCdoB)" at atlas.fgv.br/verbete/6071.

19. Amazonas and Grabois were among those expelled from the party's executive commission in Aug 1957. CIA/RSS DDI/Staff Study, ESAU XXIII-63, "The Sino-Soviet Struggle in Cuba and the Latin American Communist Movement," November 1, 1963, 148; Dulles, *Unrest in Brazil*, 161, 373–374; Johnson, *Communist China and Latin America*, 184; Skidmore, *Politics in Brazil*, 279; Prestes to U.S. and Canadian communists, Moscow, November 12, 1961.

20. CIA Intelligence Report, "The Sino-Soviet Dispute within the Communist Movement in Latin America," June 15, 1967, CIA FOIA; Dulles, *Unrest in Brazil*, 161, 373–374; Johnson, *Communist China and Latin America*, 184; Chilcote, *Brazilian Communist Party*, 207–209; Rodrigues Sales, "O Partido Comunista do Brasil nos anos sessenta"; Pomar, *Pedro Pomar*, 233, 262.

21. Goodsell, ed., *Fidel Castro's Personal Revolution*, 264–268.

22. www.pcdob.org.br/documento.php?id_documento_arquivo=298. On philosoph-

ical disputes between Castro and pro-Moscow Latin American communists over armed revolution, see Tismaneanu, "Castroism and Marxist-Leninist Orthodoxy," 756–779.

23. Hungarian Embassy, Havana (Beck), "Subject: Conversation with Yugoslavian ambassador to Havana, Boško Vidaković," March 19, 1962, *CWIHPB* 17–18 (Fall 2012): 422.

24. Stolyarov, memcon with Prestes, April 3, 1962.

25. CIA Intelligence Report, "The Sino-Soviet Dispute within the Communist Movement in Latin America," June 15, 1967, CIA FOIA.

26. In May 1963, two months after two leaders of the dissident party met Mao in Beijing, a PCdoB delegation (Pedro Pomar and Consueto Calado) visited Tirana and spoke with Enver Hoxha and other Albanian communist leaders. "It was through these travels," the party's website comments, "that the PCdoB leadership became aware of the scale of the crisis that affected the unity of the international communist movement." www.pcdob. org.br/documento.php?id_documento_arquivo=298

27. [CIA] "Memorandum: Cuban Subversion in Other Latin American Countries," October 4, 1962, folder 30, box 6, Joseph A. Califano papers, Lyndon B. Johnson Presidential Library (LBJL), NARA record no. 198–10005–10018, p. 64, JFKA; CIA/RSS DDI/ Staff Study, "The Sino-Soviet Struggle in Cuba and the Latin American Communist Movement," November 1, 1963, 150.

28. Soviet Ambassador in Brazil I. S. Chernyshev, memcons with Prestes, May 16 and June 20, 1962, f. 076. op. 25. pap. 109. d. 2. ll. 30–35, 63–67, Archive of Foreign Policy, Russian Federation (AVPRF), Moscow; also Stolyarov, memcon with Prestes, April 3, 1962.

29. Tad Szulc, "Northeast Brazil Poverty Breeds Threat of a Revolt," *NYT*, October 31, 1960; Szulc, "Marxists Are Organizing Peasants in Brazil," *NYT*, November 1, 1960; Szulc, "Castro Tries to Export 'Fidelismo,'" *NYT*, November 27, 1960.

30. Page, *The Revolution That Never Was*, chap. 3; de Morais, "História das Ligas Camponesas do Brasil," 11–69; Aguiar, *Francisco Julião*; and Sarzynski, *Revolution in the Terra do Sol*.

31. de Morais, "História das Ligas Camponesas do Brasil," 35–36. According to one report of uncertain provenance, Julião and de Morais, in Havana, were personally received by Fidel, whom they asked for financial aid for the Leagues; allegedly, Castro declined to offer financial support due to concerns regarding organization. The report said Julião obtained a commitment of financial aid from China when he visited in late 1960, to be "channeled" through Cuba, and sent League members to Cuba for guerrilla training beginning in 1961. "History of the Development of the Communist Peasants' Leagues in Brazil—Proof of Subversion in Brazil," quoted by Rep. William C. Cramer (R-FL), 88th Congress, 1st session, Cong. Rec. 109 (March 25, 1963), 4867.

32. Page, *Revolution That Never Was*, 49; de Morais, "História das Ligas Camponesas do Brasil," 35–37. On Julião's relations with Castro, Sales, *O impacto da revolução cubana*, 130ff, and Brown, *Cuba's Revolutionary World*, 288–292.

33. de Moraes, *A Esquerda e o Golpe*, 30.

34. de Morais, "História das Ligas Camponesas do Brasil," 41; de Moraes, *A Esquerda e o Golpe*, 83.

35. Brilhante Ustra, *A verdade sufocada*, 69–70, in Silva Silveira, "Além da Traição,"

146; Jover Teles, "Report to the [PCB] Executive Committee on my activities in Cuba," May 1961, in Mario Magalhães, "Cuba apoiou guerrilha já no governo Jânio," *Folha de S. Paulo*, April 8, 2001. In his report, Teles said he urged the Cubans to reject Julião's request for arms, since it could lead to a crackdown by Quadros and a rupture between Brazil and Cuba, and to discuss the matter with Prestes.

36. de Moraes, *A Esquerda e o Golpe*, 83–85.

37. "Brazilian Follows Lead of Castro," *Miami Herald*, December 7, 1961; Brown, *Cuba's Revolutionary World*.

38. Re Alexina Lins Crêspo de Paula: Flávio José Gomes Cabral, Maria da Glória Dias Medeiros, and Antônio Henrique da Silva Araújo, "Lugar de mulher é na revolução: Confissões de uma clandestina," U Colóquio de História: Perspectivas Históricas: historiografia, pesquisa e patrimônio, November 16–18, 2011, www.unicap.br/coloquiodehistoria/wp-content/uploads/2013/11/5Col-p.1205–1218.pdf; also Crispo interview, *Diário de Pernambuco*, March 31, 2004, in Ustra, *A Verdade Sufocada*, 71–72.

39. Cuban support to Peasant League: Rollemberg, *O apoio de Cuba* à *luta armada no Brasil*, 14–26; [CIA] "Memorandum: Cuban Subversion in Other Latin American Countries," October 4, 1962, 63–64. Julião later acknowledged Cuban financial support, while insisting the money never went through him personally and de Morais denied receiving financial aid from Cuba, stressing contributions from inside Brazil, particularly wealthy "bourgeoisie" against U.S. imperialism concerned by the prospect of a military coup. Moraes, *A Esquerda e o Golpe*, 85–86.

40. Page, *Revolution That Never Was*, 92–93.

41. Ridenti, *O Fantasma da Revolução Brasileira*, 28–29; de Moraes, *A Esquerda e o Golpe*, 86–87. This MRT should not be confused with a militant group established in the late 1960s to oppose Brazil's military dictatorship.

42. Memo re KGB-Valdes conversation, April 14, 1962, in Yofre, *Fue Cuba*, 214–216.

43. Memo re Fidel Castro-Soviet [deleted] conversation, June 9, 1962, in Yofre, *Fue Cuba*, 216–218.

44. Sergey Kudryavtsev memcon with Fidel Castro, February 10, 1962, f. 0104, op. 18, 121, d. 3, ll. 71–77, AVPRF.

45. Kudryavtsev memcon with Rodriguez, February 15, 1962, f. 0104, op. 18, 121, d. 3, ll. 97–100, AVPRF.

46. PCB CC executive committee member Giacondo Dias described the April 25, 1962 summit to a Soviet diplomat. V. Stolyarov, memcon with Dias, RdJ, April 28, 1962, f. 5, op. 50, d. 412, ll. 90–94, RGANI; trans. M. Baranova.

47. Page, *Revolution That Never Was*, 85–86, 95.

48. Forman, "Disunity and Discontent, 183–205.

49. Stolyarov-Dias memcon, April 28, 1962, Chernyshev-Prestes memcons, May 16 and June 20, 1962.

50. CIA, Office of Current Intelligence, Current Intelligence Weekly Summary, OCI no. 0419/62, June 1, 1962, "Peasant Leagues in Northeastern Brazil," CIA FOIA; also memo, "Northeast Brazil," June 28, 1962, President's trip: proposed Brazil trip (1 of 2 folders), box 242, NSF, JFKL.

51. Leitão da Cunha, *Diplomacia em Alto-Mar*, 208.

52. Piñeiro, *Che Guevara and the Latin American Revolution*, 45–46; Guevara May 18, 1962, speech to Cuban Department of State Security (DSE), in Guevara, *The Awakening of Latin America*, 394–395. In embracing Julião, Che had discounted the advice of Celso Furtado, head of the Superintendency for the Development of the Northeast (Sudene), the Brazilian government agency. At Punta del Este in August 1961, the leftist economist recalled, Guevara wishfully imagined the Ligas as "vigorous mass organizations" ready to rebel and overrated Julião's capacity to run an armed struggle. Furtado's view of Julião differed sharply: "a sensitive man, a poet, subject to periodic psychosomatic crises," a "cunning and brilliant lawyer." Furtado, *Obra autobiográfica*, 312–313.

53. Yugoslav Embassy [YugE], Havana (Vidaković), tel. 166, June 18, 1962, Archive, Ministry for Foreign Affairs, Belgrade, Confidential Archive (Series), Cuba (folder), 1962, file no. 68; translated by Milorad Lazic.

54. Leeds, "Brazil and the Myth of Francisco Julião," 190–204. Sarzynski also suggests the "likely exaggeration of Cuba's connection with the Ligas." Sarzynski, *Revolution in the Terra do Sol*, 226

55. CIA, Office of Current Intelligence, Current Intelligence Weekly Summary, OCI no. 0419/62, June 1, 1962, "Peasant Leagues in Northeastern Brazil," CIA FOIA; also memo, "Northeast Brazil," June 28, 1962, President's trip: proposed Brazil trip (1 of 2 folders), box 242, NSF, JFKL; CIA, Office of Current Intelligence, Current Intelligence Weekly Review, October 5, 1962, CIA FOIA, and "Brazil Reds Plan Outbreaks During Visit by Kennedy," *Miami Herald*, October 21, 1962.

56. "History of the Development of the Communist Peasants' Leagues in Brazil—Proof of Subversion in Brazil," in *Congressional Record—House*, March 25, 1963, pp. 4867–4868.

57. Czechoslovak intelligence record, October 15, 1962, conversation with Fidel Castro, Havana, svazek 80721/000, začátek 6/6, Security Services Archives (ABS), Prague, Czech Republic.

58. Report on October 18, 1962, conversation with Soviet ambassador Alexander Alexeev, in Havana, svazek 80721/000, začátek 6/6, ABS. (Khrushchev had told Raúl Castro, during the Cuban defense minister's visit to Moscow in July, that Havana should try to repair relations with Prestes, Alexeev said.)

59. Report from Rio de Janeiro no. 139/URAN/3 November 1, 1962 [*sic*], svazek 80723_014, začátek 3_6, ABS.

60. Documents were from a guerrilla code-named "Gerardo"—likely Cuban guerrilla, intelligence agent, journalist, and later diplomat Miguel Brugueras del Valle, then under diplomatic cover as a cultural counselor at Havana's Rio embassy, Gaspari speculates—to "Petronius" in Havana. They denounced the camp's disorder, strategic futility, waste of Cuban money, saying the scheme harmed the Brazilian revolutionary cause and Cuba's reputation. Gaspari, *A Ditadura Envergonhada*, 179. On Brugueras, see also "Cuban Role Demands More Scrutiny As Brazil Investigates Military Dictatorship's Abuses," August 6, 2012, "Cuba Confidential" blog; and "History of the Development of the Communist Peasants' Leagues in Brazil—Proof of Subversion in Brazil," 4869. The recovered documents also allegedly included reports from Carlos Franklin Paixão

de Araújo, son of communist lawyer Afrânio Araújo, who was "responsible for buying arms for the Peasant Leagues." Del Nero, *A Grande Mentira* (RdJ: Biblioteca do Exercito Editora, 2001), 84, 92, in Ustra, *A Verdade Sufocada*, 71.

61. Rollemberg, *O apoio de Cuba*, 20; Gaspari, *A Ditadura Envergonhada*, 179; Ferreira, *João Goulart*, 311; Porfirio, *De Pétalas e Pedras*, 61.

62. The story broke on December 4 in *La Tribuna* (Lima); Havana's reaction, U.S. officials noted, "tends [to] confirm authenticity of document." USE/RdJ (Bond), tel. 1180, December 4, 1962, Brazil cables, box 13, NSF, JFKL. Brazil's ambassador in Lima complained the Cuban documents published in *La Tribuna* were not among those Peruvian officials gave him. USE/Lima (Henderson), tel. 723, February 1, 1963, Cuba POL 17 Diplomatic + Consular Representation 2/1/63, box 3877, CFPF, 1963, Record Group (RG) 59, National Archives (NA).

63. Plane crash and "Dianópolis caper": Page, *Revolution That Never Was*, 94–99; Dulles, *Unrest in Brazil*, 219; Leacock, *Requiem for Revolution*, 132; Sales, *O impacto da revolução cubana*, 141–151; Rollemberg, *O apoio de Cuba*, 19–21; Gaspari, *A Ditadura Envergonhada*, 179; Ferreira, *Goulart*, 310–311; USE/RdJ (Bond), tel. 1180, December 4, 1962, Brazil, General, 12/1/62–12/15/62, box 13, NSF, JFKL; and USE/RdJ (Keppel), Airgram A-986, "Subject: Arms Caches in Brazil," March 4, 1963, Brazil, General, 3/1/63–3/11–63, box 13A, NSF, JFKL.

64. Rollemberg, *O apoio de Cuba*, 17–18; de Moraes, *A Esquerda e o Golpe*, 83–84; Page, *Revolution That Never Was*, 96 ("in charge"); de Morais arsenal: USE/RdJ (Keppel), airgram A-986, "Subject: Arms Caches in Brazil," March 4, 1963, cited above; Canadian Embassy, Rio de Janeiro [CanE/RdJ] (Chapdelaine), n.l. 829, "Peasants League and Subversive Activities," December 20, 1962, file 2348-40, pt. 8, vol. 5047, RG 25, Library and Archives Canada, Ottawa (LAC). Noting that Guanabara's "political and social police" (DPPS) tended to "exaggerate considerably the Communist menace in Brazil," Canada's ambassador observed that de Morais' activities suggested the Peasant Leagues were trying to "keep active" in the context of government surveillance.

65. de Moraes, *A Esquerda e o Golpe*, 89, 90.

66. Page, *Revolution That Never Was*, 98–99.

67. USE/RdJ (Gordon), tel. 1437, January 30, 1963, and other documents in CSM-Communism (Brazil) folder, CSM 9.6 Subversion & Propaganda, box 33, Bureau of Inter-American Affairs, Office of Coordinator of Cuban Affairs (ARA/CCA), Subject Files, 1960–1963; and USE/RdJ, Airgram A-912, February 8, 1963, POL 15–1 BRAZ 2/1/63, CFPF, 1963, box 3837; both RG 59, NA. Hermes Lima spoke after a former Kubitschek justice minister read the Cuban documents on TV and "accused the government of not taking precautions in repelling Castrist subversion." CanE/RdJ (Chapdelaine), n.l. 100, "Cuba," February 12, 1963, file 12797-40 pt. 3, vol. 8561, RG 25, LAC.

68. USE/RdJ, tel. 1122, December 10, 1962, and CIA, Brasília, IN 33026, December 11, 1962, summarized in note, n.d., folder 30, box 6, Califano papers, LBJL, in NARA record no. 198-10005–10018, p. 9, JFKA.

69. CIA, RdJ, IN 43586, January 2, 1963, summarized in note, n.d., folder 30, box 6, Califano papers, LBJL, in NARA record no. 198-10005–10018, p. 39, JFKA.

70. CIA, "Brazil's Congress of Solidarity with Cuba," March 11, 1963, CREST.

71. USE/RdJ (Keppel), airgram A-986, "Subject: Arms Caches in Brazil," March 4, 1963.

72. "Cuban Subversion in Latin America since Feb 1963," July 25, 1963, CIA FOIA; also CIA, Office of Current Intelligence, Special Report, "Cuban Subversion in Latin America," August 9, 1963, Cuba 1/63–12/63, box WH-31, Arthur M. Schlesinger, Jr. papers, JFKL; and CIA/RSS DDI/Staff Study, "The Sino-Soviet Struggle in Cuba and the Latin American Communist Movement," November 1, 1963, 148–149.

73. CIA/RSS DDI/Staff Study, "The Sino-Soviet Struggle in Cuba and the Latin American Communist Movement," November 1, 1963, 149.

74. P.H. Scott, British Embassy [BritE], Havana, to A.D. Parsons, American Dept., FO, March 13, 1963, FO 371/168139, The [U.K.] National Archives, Kew Gardens, England (TNA).

75. Soviet (Acting) Ambassador to Brazil A.A. Fomin, Record of Meeting with Prestes, November 15, 1962, f. 076, op. 25, p. 109, d. 2, ll. 142–145, AVPRF, trans. S. Radchenko.

76. CIA, RdJ, IN 42868, December 31 [1962], and file CIA, São Paulo, TDCS-3533404, January 9 [1963], both box 6, folder 30, Califano papers, LBJL, NARA record no. 198–10005–10018, pp. 98–99, JFKA.

77. Fomin, record of meeting with Prestes, January 9, 1963, f. 076, op. 26, p. 110, d. 3, ll. 10–16, AVPRF.

78. Julian Hartt, "Sino-Soviet Rift Casts Shadow on Latin Talks," Los Angeles Times, March 10, 1963; Keller, "Don Lázaro Rises Again," 129–149; Keller, Mexico's Cold War, 87–98; Brands, Latin America's Cold War, 29–30.

79. Julião manifesto to UNE, O Seminario (Rio de Janeiro), September 20, 1962, in "Brazil—Juliao Calls for Defense of Cuba," CREST; his appeal was also published in the Cuban party newspaper Hoy (Havana) on September 22, 1962; CIA, "Brazil's Congress of Solidarity with Cuba," March 11, 1963, CREST.

80. Thomas L. Hughes, INR, to Secretary of State Rusk, Research Memorandum RAR-23, "Subject: Pro-Castro 'Congress of Hatred' in Brazil," May 13, 1963, Cuba, Subjects, Intelligence-INR Materials, 1/15/63–11/30/63 (folder 2 of 3), box 50A, NSF, JFKL.

81. Polish Embassy [PolE], RdJ (Chabasinski), nr. 106, March 29, 1963, AMSZ, trans. M. Gnoinska; Bulgarian minister, RdJ (Stefanov), memo, April 15, 1963, in Foreign Affairs and International Relations Department, Bulgarian Communist Party CC, Report on First Continental Congress for Solidarity with Cuba (in Brazil, March 28–30, 1963), May 7, 1963, Central State Archive, Sofia, Bulgaria, courtesy Jordan Baev, trans. Alex Fisher; Hungarian Legation, RdJ (Drappe), "Subject: Brazil and Cuba," February 22, 1963, Hungarian National Archives (MNL; formerly MOL), Budapest; obt. Balazs Szalontai, trans. Sabine Topolansky.

82. CIA Information Report TDCS-3/537, 187, February 14, 1963, box 6, folder 30, Califano papers, LBJL, NARA record no. 198–10005–10018, 100–101, 104, JFKA. U.S. analysts called him the "main coordinator, fund supplier, and trouble shooter for the organizers"—Hughes to Rusk, "Subject: Pro-Castro 'Congress of Hatred' in Brazil," May 13, 1963—but it's unclear whether Toledano, who reportedly left for Brazil on February

13, conducted mediation before Prestes and Julião left, separately, on their own travels less than a week later, or if his mediation efforts went anywhere.

83. Descriptions of this joint Czech-Soviet intelligence operation rely on the report on AO "DRUŽBA," n.d. [late 1963?], at cepol24.pl/stb/ao_druzba.html; translation from Czech by Matyáš Pelant. See also Kraenski and Petrilák, *1964: O Elo Perdido*, chap. 16.

84. Brazil broke relations with Moscow in 1947, but Czechoslovak-Brazilian diplomatic relations continued. On the 1961 restoration of Soviet-Brazilian ties (and the U.S. warnings), see Caterina, "Um grande oceano;" Hershberg, "Soviet-Brazilian Relations"; Hershberg papers presented to the Asociación de Historiadores Latinoamericanistas Europeos (AHILA), Berlin, Germany, September 10, 2014, and the Society for Historians of American Foreign Relations (SHAFR) annual meeting, Arlington, VA, June 27, 2015.

85. Mid-operation the Czechs gave the Soviets control over the agent running this unnamed "nationalist weekly magazine."

86. Gen. Leite was prominent on both lists. Hartt, "Sino-Soviet Rift Casts Shadow on Latin Talks," *LAT*, March 10, 1963; USE/RdJ (Keppel), Joint Weeka 8, February 20, 1963, POL 2–1 BRAZ 2/1/63, box 3833, CFPF, 1963, RG 59, NA; also Hungarian Legation, RdJ, "Subject: Brazil and Cuba," February 22, 1963.

87. George Arfeld, "Force Only Way, Says Leader of Peasant Struggle in Brazil" (AP dispatch from Havana), *Washington Post* (*WP*), March 3, 1963; Keller, "Don Lázaro Rises Again," 130.

88. Hungarian Legation, RdJ, "Subject: Brazil and Cuba," February 22, 1963.

89. GDR Embassy, Havana (Lösch), report to Ulbricht, March 9, 1963, NL 182/1290. Bestand: Ulbricht, Walter, Stiftung Archiv der Parteien und Massenorganisationen der DDR im Bundesarchiv (SAPMO), Berlin, trans. for CWIHP by Sean O'Grady; *Revolución* (Havana), March 2, 1963, in "Pro-Cuban Continental Congress to Be Held in Rio de Janeiro in March," n.d. [March 1963], CREST.

90. On Prestes's support of the congress and PCB views of Cuba, Julião and PCdoB, see S. Clissold, March 29, 1963 comment on AK 1015/22, FO 371/168139, TNA.

91. CIA, "Brazil's Congress of Solidarity with Cuba," March 11, 1963, CREST.

92. PolE/RdJ (Chabasinski), nr. 25, January 29, 1963, AMSZ, trans. M. Gnoinska.

93. PolE/RdJ (Chabasinski), nr. 36, February 8, 1963, AMSZ, trans. M. Gnoinska.

94. PolE/RdJ (Chabasinski), January 5, 1963, AMSZ, trans. M. Gnoinska.

95. PolE/RdJ (Chabasinski), nr. 36, February 8, 1963, AMSZ, trans. M. Gnoinska.

96. PolE/RdJ (Chabasinski), nr. 36, February 8, 1963, AMSZ, trans. M. Gnoinska.

97. USE/RdJ (Gordon), tel. 1594, February 22, 1963, Brazil, General 2/63, box 14, NSF, JFKL.

98. Friedman, *Shadow Cold War*, 97–98, 241n188, citing Liu Ningyi report to CCP CC on Third AAPSO Conference, February 8, 1963, doc. 108–00320–02, Chinese Foreign Ministry Archives (CFMA), Beijing; Thomas, *Diplomacy of Liberation*, 164.

99. French Embassy, Moscow (Maurice Dejean), tel. 1000/1001, February 24, 1963, folder 48, Amérique: BRÉSIL: 1952–1963, MAE, Centre des Archives Diplomatiques, La Courneuve (Paris). Joining Prestes and Khrushchev were PCB CC members Batista and Capistrano, and Boris Ponomarev, head of the CPSU CC international department.

100. YugE, RdJ (Barišić), tel. 118, March 18, 1963, Politicka arhiva, 1963 Brazil, fascikla 13, dosije 7, signatura 49690, Diplomatski arhiv, Ministarstvo spoljnih poslova Republike Srbije (MSP RS), Belgrade; obt./trans. M. Lazic.

101. See Hershberg, "An Embassy or an Asylum? Brazil-Cuba Relations and the *Asilado* Crisis in Havana, 1957–1964," paper for the 56th International Congress of Americanists (ICA), Salamanca, Spain, July 16, 2018.

102. Alexeev memcon with Castro, Havana, February 20, 1963, f. 0104, op. 19. por. 124, d. 3, ll. 72–76, AVPRF.

103. Theodore Draper, "Castroism," in Drachkovitch, ed., *Marxism in the Modern World*, 191–224 (quotation on 215). A biographer writes that Prestes made his "first trip" to Cuba "soon after attending" the October 1961 22nd CPSU congress in Moscow but supplies no contemporary evidence and cites a later Prestes interview that may, instead, have referenced the 1963 visit. Reis, *Prestes*, 297.

104. Brazilian Embassy [BrazE], Havana (Gamboa), tel. 112, 20 April 1963, Archives of the Ministry of External Relations (AMRE), Brasília, Moniz Bandeira collection, National Security Archive (MB/NSA).

105. Hungarian Legation, RdJ, "Subject: Brazil and Cuba," February 22, 1963. Exactly when Julião arrived in Havana is unclear; *Prensa Latina* reported on February 18, 1963, that he had left Brazil for Cuba. "Havana's Revolutionary Program for Latin America," February 19, 1963, CREST.

106. "Brazil Red in Cuba," WP, February 27, 1963, A4; Alexeev memcon with Prestes, Havana, February 27, 1963, f. 0104, op. 19. por. 124, d. 3, l. 95, AVPRF, trans. S. Radchenko.

107. PCB CC member Apolónio Carvalho to Hungarian chargé d'affaires a.i. Lőrinc Soós, in Hungarian Legation, RdJ, "Subject: The situation of the Brazilian Communist Party," August 10, 1963, MNL, XIX-J-1-j Brazil 1945–1964, 001492/1/1963; obt./trans. B. Szalontai. Prestes *caderneta* 8, Arquivo Geral-fichas temáticas, 30-Z-9, São Paulo State Public Archive (APESP), obt. Gianfranco Caterina; trans. Thomas Andre-Alves de Lima.

108. Alexeev memcon with Prestes, Havana, February 27, 1963.

109. CIA information report, TDCS-3/553,579, "Subject: Plans of Fidel Castro to establish dictatorship of proletariat in Cuba," distr. July 16, 1963, Cuba, Subjects, Intelligence-TDCS 6/63–11/63 (folder 2 of 4), box 53, NSF, JFKL. The report cited Prestes's comments to Heros Trench, head of the rural commission of the PCB national directorate.

110. Memcon between Prestes and Bohuslav Laštovička, Head of International Department, CPCz CC, Prague, March 11, 1963, CPCz papers, National Archives, Prague; obt. Oldrich Tuma, trans. Jiři Mareš.

111. Marco Antônio Coêlho in YugE, RdJ (Barišić), tel. 118, March 18, 1963.

112. Alexeev memcon with Prestes, Havana, February 27, 1963. Other Havana-based diplomats agreed. After both men left town, a U.K. aide observed "Julião was clearly feted more than Prestes": the hosts enabled both to address "revolutionary organizations, the CTC-R [Workers' Central Union-Revolutionary] and the press," but Julião was also a "main" speaker at a pro-Venezuela solidarity rally broadcast on radio/TV on February 28 "and he remained in the public eye on subsequent days, addressing the Federation of University Students, tobacco workers and fishery workers in Batabanó." Scott to Parsons, March 13, 1963.

113. Arfeld, "Force Only Way, Says Leader of Peasant Struggle in Brazil," *WP*, March 3, 1963, A14.

114. USE/RdJ (Mein), tel. 1635, March 1, 1963, Cuba Cables, 1/1/63–3/14/63 folder 3 of 4, box 43, NSF, JFKL.

115. USE/RdJ (Keppel), Airgram A-986, March 4, 1963, cited above. Tad Szulc wondered if the simultaneous Havana visit was a way to mend splits between them. "Soviet Indicates 10,000 Will Stay on Duty in Cuba," *NYT*, February 28, 1963, 1, 3.

116. Alexeev memcon with Carlos Rafael Rodriguez, Havana, March 4, 1963, f. 0104, op. 19, p. 124, d. 3, ll. 100–103, AVPRF.

117. Alexeev memcon with Dorticós, March 10, 1963. f. 0104, op. 19, p. 124, d. 3, ll. 108–109, AVPRF.

118. CIA Information Report, TDCS-3/541,669, "Subject: Continued Support of Leader of Brazilian Peasant League by Cuban Government," March 26, 1963, "Cuba-Subjects: Intelligence-TDCS & CSDB, 3/63–5/63" (folder 2 of 4), box 52, NSF, JFKL. Capistrano said Julião attended the Castro-Prestes talk, according to the CIA's informant, but other evidence (cited below) suggests Prestes and Julião only met separately with Castro. A senior Cuban guerrilla and intelligence chief later hinted at their divergent approaches when he recounted Prestes had come "to get to know the Cuban process at close hand and establish contacts with Che and other leaders. He talked a lot about the Brazilian situation, defending the principle of an alliance with sectors of the nationalist bourgeoisie and expressing optimism about the conditions for the development of socialism in Brazil." Piñeiro, *Che Guevara and the Latin American Revolution*, 45.

119. Scott to Parsons, March 13, 1963.

120. BrazE/Havana (Ruiz de Gamboa), tel. 78, March 6, 1963, 500.1 Comunismo—1960–1966, AMRE.

121. Gerry Robichaud, "Major Red Rift Is Brewing in Brazil," *WP*, March 25, 1963, A10.

122. Julião interview, *Bohemia*, March 8, 1963, in Bezerra, *Brasil-Cuba*, 44.

123. Arfeld, "Force Only Way, Says Leader of Peasant Struggle in Brazil," *WP*, March 3, 1963.

124. Prestes comments to Chilean CP newspaper, in CIA, *Bi-Weekly Propaganda Guidance* 115, May 6, 1963, CREST; and Prestes interview, *Hoy*, March 9, 1963, in "Brazil Communist Says Revolt Would Be Unwise," *WP*, March 10, 1963.

125. Draper, "Castroism," 223.

126. BrazE/Havana (Gamboa), tel. 78, March 6, 1963, 500.1 Comunismo—1960–1966, AMRE.

127. Lösch, report to Ulbricht, March 9, 1963.

128. Talk with Marco Antônio Coêlho, YugE, RdJ (Barišić), tel. 118, March 18, 1963.

129. Carvalho to Soós, in Hungarian Legation, RdJ, "Subject: The situation of the Brazilian Communist Party," August 10, 1963.

130. CIA/RSS DDI/Staff Study, "The Sino-Soviet Struggle in Cuba and the Latin American Communist Movement," November 1, 1963, 149.

131. Lösch report to Ulbricht, March 9, 1963, cited above; PCB complaints at SED congress: CIA/RSS DDI/Staff Study, "The Sino-Soviet Struggle in Cuba and the Latin American Communist Movement," November 1, 1963, 150.

132. YugE, RdJ, tel. 118, March 18, 1963.

133. Lösch report to Ulbricht, March 9, 1963; "Brazil Communist Says Revolt Would Be Unwise," *WP*, March 10, 1963, D26.

134. Prestes-Laštovička memcon, March 11, 1963, and Prestes-Novotný memcon, March 12, 1963, both CPCz papers, National Archives, Prague; obt. Oldrich Tuma, trans. Jiři Mareš. Accounts of both talks rely on these documents.

135. Novotný's views did not stray far from Khrushchev's. A loyal Moscow ally, he had recently heard the Soviet sharply criticize Castro's conduct during the missile crisis. See *CWIHPB* 17/18 (Fall 2012): 400–403.

136. Novotný recalled when he met Goulart, who visited Prague shortly before taking office as Quadros's vice president, the Brazilian "harbored progressive opinions and would not yield to Americans." According to the CPCz record, Goulart slipped away from local Brazilian embassy aides to assure his communist hosts—beyond the ears of Itamaraty, "the most reactionary institution in the political life of Brazil"—that once in office he would fight "against reactionary circles" and for Brazil's improved relations with, and eventual inclusion in, the socialist bloc: the aim of his post-election travels to the communist world, including Moscow and Beijing. Czechoslovakia, he suggested, might serve as a "beachhead through which such support of the socialist bloc countries would flow to Brazil," and he advised setting up a backchannel, perhaps via Prague's embassy in Rio. "Report on Goulart's Visit to Czechoslovakia, 2–5 December 1960," CPCz papers, National Archives, Prague; obt. O. Tuma, trans. J. Mareš.

137. Only implying private criticism of the Cubans and Chinese, a communiqué declared Novotný and Prestes had achieved a "complete agreement of opinions . . . on questions of [the] unity of [the] international Communist movement and on [the] present international political situation." USE/Prague (Horsy), tel. 488, March 14, 1963, POL 7 BRAZ 2/1/63, box 3835, CFPF, 1963, RG 59, NA.

138. Note on Prestes-Novotný memcon, March 12, 1963. The PCB's Marco Antônio Coêlho told Belgrade's ambassador in Rio Prestes had returned to Brazil on March 14, casting doubt on his transiting Moscow; he met Novotný in Prague on March 12, and two days hardly seem sufficient to connect in Moscow, fly home, and brief PCB associates. YugE, RdJ (Barišić), tel. 118, March 18, 1963.

139. BrazE/Lima (Bopp), tel. 49, March 10, 1963, AMRE, MB/NSA.

140. PolE/RdJ (Chabasinski), nr. 71, March 12, 1963, AMSZ, trans. M. Gnoinska; Fomin memcon with Goulart, March 21, 1963, f. 076, op. 26, por. 3, pap. 110, ll. 93–94, AVPRF.

141. CIA information report TDCSDB-3/653,942, "Subject: Desire of Fidel Castro to ensure that activity of Francisco Juliao's Peasant Leagues does not topple government of President Goulart," distr. March 29, 1963, Brazil, 3/22/63–3/31/63 file, box 13A, NSF, CO, JFKL (sanitized); also "Cuba, Subjects, Intelligence—TDCS & CSDB 3/63–5/63, subfolder: Reports from Cuban Ambassador Raul Roa Kouri 3/63, box 52A, NSF, JFKL.

142. Headquarters comment citing information report TDCS-3/540,309 in ibid.

143. "Cuban Subversion in Latin America since February 1963," July 25, 1963, CIA FOIA /CREST.

144. CIA Directorate of Intelligence, Intelligence Memorandum, "Subject: A Review

of Reporting on Cuba, 1 April–20 June 1963," July 15, 1963, Cuba, Subjects, Intelligence Materials, 7/14/63–11/22/63, box 52, NSF, JFKL.

145. CIA/RSS DDI/Staff Study, "The Sino-Soviet Struggle in Cuba and the Latin American Communist Movement," November 1, 1963, 148–150.

146. CIA report TDCS DS-3/658,572, "Cuban Government's Effort to Promote Revolution in Latin America," December 18, 1963, box 32, NSF, CO, LBJL; Bromley K. Smith to McGeorge Bundy, n.d., box 32, NSF, CO, LBJL. Ibid.

147. BrazE/Havana (Gamboa), tel. 112, 20 April 1963, AMRE; e.g., Draper, "Castroism," 215.

148. Apolónio Carvalho (PCB CC member, veteran of the Spanish Civil War and French resistance) July 29, 1963 remarks, Hungarian Legation, RdJ, "Subject: The situation of the Brazilian Communist Party," Augusy 10, 1963. According to a Cuban source of unclear reliability, Havana invited Prestes to return to the island to attend July 26 celebrations, and during his visit he and Cuban defense minister Raúl Castro conducted interparty talks. [July 12, 1963 entry, "Cronología de las relaciones bilaterales Cuba-Brasil, 1959–2000," Fondo Brasil, MINREX archives, Havana, courtesy Jonathan C. Brown.] However, I found no corroboration of a Prestes visit to Cuba in July 1963, and Soviet records indicate that the PCB leader, in Rio, saw Moscow's envoy on July 25 and did not mention any Cuba journey. Fomin, memcon with Prestes, July 25, 1963, f. 076, op. 26, p. 110, d. 4, ll. 46–47, AVPRF. Prestes's next reported trip to Cuba after February/March 1963 was in early 1964. Prestes, *Meu companheiro*, 158.

149. Fomin memcon with Prestes, September 18, 1963, f. 5, op. 50, d. 501, ll. 110–112, RGANI, trans. M. Baranova.

150. Johann Lorenz Schmidt to Walter Ulbricht, October 28, 1963, NY 4182–1290, Bestand: Ulbricht, Walter, Stiftung, SAPMO, Berlin; trans. Sean O'Grady.

151. See, e.g., *Free Cuba News*, December 14, 1963, 5–7.

152. BrazE/Havana (Gamboa), ofício 175, "Attitude of Cuban Government in Relation to Brazil," July 12, 1963, MDB—HAVANA OFÍCIOS REC—1962/1964 (Cx 49), AMRE.

153. BrazE/Havana (Gamboa), tel. 111, April 19, 1963, AMRE. This account fits information a scholar obtained from "an East European diplomatic source" in Havana that Prestes had persuaded the Cubans "to stop their subsidies, thus making the dissident Party dependent on Chinese aid alone." Halperin, "Peking and the Latin American Communists," 140.

154. BrazE/Havana (Gamboa), tel. 111, April 19, 1963, AMRE.

155. Castro speech to Soviet-Cuban friendship rally, Moscow, May 23, 1963; BrazE/Moscow (da Cunha), tel. 126, May 24, 1963, AMRE.

156. Halperin, *Rise and Decline of Fidel Castro*, 270; CIA, "Cuban Subversion in Latin America," August 9, 1963; Castro speech, Havana, July 26, 1963.

157. Other alleged failings of ex-ambassador Joaquín Hernández Armas were "wrong contacts," "bad information from the Brazilian leftists," and "lack of experience during the Oct crisis." CIA information report, TDCS-3/549,875, "Subject: Views and opinions of Raul Roa Kouri, Cuban ambassador to Brazil," distr. June 8, 1963, Cuba, Subjects, Intelligence-TDCS-6/63–11/63 (1 of 4), box 53, NSF, JFKL.

158. Leacock, *Requiem for Revolution*, 141; see, e.g., "Communist Inspired Continen-

tal Congress of Solidarity with Cuba Meets in Rio While United States Gives More Aid to Brazil—To Build Trade with Russia," *Congressional Record—House*, March 25, 1963, 4864 ff.

159. Hughes to Rusk, "Subject: Pro-Castro 'Congress of Hatred' in Brazil," May 13, 1963, cited above; PolE/RdJ (Chabasinski), nr. 106, March 29, 1963, AMSZ, trans. M. Gnoinska.

160. Brazilian Foreign Ministry to BrazE/Havana, March 13, 1963, AMRE, MB/NSA.

161. BrazE/Havana (Gamboa), tel. 91, March 20, 1963, AMRE, MB/NSA.

162. U.S. pressure: deptel 1651 to USE/RdJ, March 8, 1963, CSM Communism BRAZ (RI) 2/1/63, box 3687, CFPF, 1963, RG 59, NA; also David Kraslow, "Surprise! Reds Get A 'No' In Brazil," *Miami Herald*, March 4, 1963, 7.

163. Washington especially disliked the influence of Goulart's press secretary, Raul Ryff a veteran PCB communist. See, e.g., CIA Current Intelligence memo, OCI No. 1259/62, March 30, 1962, box 12A, NSF, JFKL; USE/RdJ, Aigram A-990, "Subject: Key Brazilian Sub-Cabinet Positions and Their Incumbents," March 4, 1963, POL 15–1 BRAZ, CFPF, 1963, RG 59; CIA, *Bi-Weekly Propaganda Guidance* 115, May 6, 1963, CREST.

164. Itamaraty to embassies in Washington, Moscow, and Havana, March 13, 1963, AMRE. On US-Brazil exchanges on the congress, see esp. documents in CSM Communism BRAZ (RI) 2/1/63, box 3687, CFPF, 1963, RG 59, NA.

165. Memcon, Washington, DC, March 12, 1963, *FRUS, 1961–1963*, Vol. XII, doc. 159.

166. Fomin, record of meeting with Goulart, March 21, 1963.

167. Fomin, record of meeting with Hermes Lima, March 25, 1963, f. 076, op. 26, por. 3, pap. 110, d. 3, ll. 95–96, AVPRF. The cosmonauts were Vostok 3's Andriyan Nikolayev and Vostok 4's Pavel Popovich.

168. Robichaud, "Major Red Rift Is Brewing in Brazil," *Chicago Daily News* dispatch in *WP*, March 25, 1963, p. A10.

169. See, e.g., USE/RdJ (Mein), tel. 1821, March 26, 1963, and (Gordon), tel. 1839, 27 March 1963, both CSM-Communism BRAZ (RI) 2/1/63, box 3687, CFPF, 1963, RG 59, NA; Juan de Onis, "Red Rally Barred By Rio's Governor," *NYT*, March 27, 1963, p. 1, and "Banned Red Rally Eludes Rio Police," *NYT*, March 28, 1963, 3. Lacerda's opposition to the Cuba congress and confrontation with Goulart: John W.F. Dulles, *Carlos Lacerda, Brazilian Crusader*, 131–135.

170. Hughes to Rusk, "Subject: Pro-Castro 'Congress of Hatred' in Brazil," May 13, 1963, cited above; Bulgarian minister, RdJ (Stefanov), memo, April 15, 1963, cited above; USE/Moscow (Kohler), tel. 2446, March 30, 1963, CSM-Communism BRAZ (RI) 2/1/63, box 3687, CFPF, 1963, RG 59, NA.

171. Bulgarian minister, RdJ (Stefanov), memo, April 15, 1963, cited above; USE/RdJ, Airgram A-1266, May 6, 1963, Cuba Cables, 5/1/63–5/15/63, box 44, NSF, JFKL. Luis de la Puente Uceda: Klarén, *Peru: Society and Nationhood*, 318, 329–330.

172. Though Goulart still considered him a "major threat," Julião's influence had peaked and would decline sharply in coming months. USE/RdJ (Gordon), tel. 1964, April 9, 1963, POL BRAZ, box 3832, RG 59, NA.

173. CIA information report, TDCS-3/549,875, "Subject: Views and opinions of Raul Roa Kouri, Cuban ambassador to Brazil," distr. June 8, 1963, Cuba, Subjects, Intelligence-

TDCS-6/63–11/63 (1 of 4), box 53, NSF, JFKL; CIA Special Report: Weekly Review, "Cuban Subversive Activities in Latin America: 1959–1968," February 16, 1968, CIA FOIA.

174. USE/RdJ (Keppel), Airgram A-1266, May 6, 1963, Cuba Cables, 5/1/63–5/15/63, box 44, NSF, JFKL.

175. Deptel 1626 for all ARA diplomatic posts, March 21, 1963, CSM Communism BRAZ (RI) 2/1/63, box 3687, CFPF, 1963, RG 59, NA.

176. USE/RdJ (Mein), tel. 1807, March 23, 1963, CSM-Communism BRAZ (RI) 2/1/63, box 3687, CFPF 1963, RG 59, NA.

177. USE/RdJ (Keppel), airgram A-1266, May 6, 1963, Cuba Cables, 5/1/63–5/15/63, box 44, NSF, JFKL. See also CIA Directorate of Intelligence, Intelligence Memorandum, "Subject: A Review of Reporting on Cuba, 1 April–20 June 1963," July 15, 1963, Cuba, Subjects, Intelligence Materials, 7/14/63–11/22/63, box 52, NSF, JFKL; CIA, "Cuban Subversion in Latin America," August 9, 1963.

178. Hughes to Rusk, "Subject: Pro-Castro 'Congress of Hatred' in Brazil," May 13, 1963, cited above. Western observers echoed the U.S. assessment. See CanE/RdJ (Chapdelaine), n.l. 245, "Continental Congress of Solidarity with Cuba," April 8, 1963, file 12797–40 pt. 3, vol. 8561, RG 25, LAC; I.J.M. Sutherland, BritE/Washington, to A.D. Parsons, American Dept., FO, June 11, 1963 (enc. INR Research Memorandum RAR-23, May 13, 1963), and R.A. Burroughs, BritE/RdJ, to Sutherland, June 27, 1963; both FO 371/168152, TNA.

179. As Brown notes, Prestes's long speech praising the Cuban Revolution's achievements did not mention Fidel Castro. *Cuba's Revolutionary World*, 293.

180. PolE/RdJ (Chabasinski), nr. 106, March 29, 1963, AMSZ, trans. M. Gnoinska.

181. Bulgarian minister, RdJ (Stefanov), memo, April 15, 1963.

182. Report on AO "DRUŽBA," n.d. [late 1963?], cepol24.pl/stb/ao_druzba.html; translation from Czech by Matyáš Pelant. The intelligence operatives resolved to draw on these lessons to improve planning for "AO 'DRUZBA II'" which would organize a pro-Cuba solidarity congress in June 1964 (originally in Montevideo but moved to Chile after Uruguayan authorities forbade it). Already, however, they rued that despite the prior experiences some mistakes were being repeated—including the "even larger," even dominant, communist role in organizing the event, that was impossible to conceal, and risked exposure of the secret intelligence support; confusion about dates and locations also hampered organization, preparation, and publicity.

183. BrazE/Havana (Gamboa), tel. 111, April 19, 1963, AMRE.

184. Johnson, *Communist China and Latin America*, 182–183; Peralva, *O Retrato* (Rio de Janeiro: Editora Globo, 1962), in Halperin, "Peking and the Latin American Communists," 110. On Mao's influence on Prestes, see Prestes, *Prestes*, 316.

185. Mao-Khrushchev memcon, October 2, 1959, *CWIHPB* 12/13 (Fall/Winter 2001): 262–270.

186. CIA, "Visit of Brazilian Communist Delegation to China, USSR and Satellites," n.d. [1960], CIA FOIA (sanitized).

187. Mao-Prestes memcon, Jinan, October 25, 1959, *Mao Zedong jiejian waibin tanhua jilu huibian* [Collection of Records of Mao Zedong's Conversations with Foreign Guests] (internal circulation), trans. S. Radchenko.

188. Reis, *Prestes*, 284.

189. On post-revolution Sino-Cuban ties, see, e.g., Johnson, *Communist China and Latin America*; Cheng, "Sino-Cuban Relations," 78–114;. Hershberg and Radchenko, with Qian, "Sino-Cuban Relations and the Cuban Missile Crisis," 21–116; and Fardella, "Mao Zedong and the 1962 Cuban Missile Crisis," 73–88.

190. USE/RdJ (Bash), Foreign Service desp. 58, "Subject: Sino-Soviet Bloc Politico-Economic Relations," July 21, 1961, CDF 621.60/7-2161, box 1328, RG 59, NA; C.J. Small, Canadian Government Trade Commissioner, Foreign Trade Service, Hong Kong, to Under-Secretary of State for External Affairs, Ottawa, May 13, 1961, and CanE/RdJ (Chapedelaine), n.l. 289, "Eastern lights in Brazil," May 5, 1961, both file 5302–40, pt. 1, vol. 3204, RG 25, LAC.

191. Johnson, *Communist China and Latin America*, 27–28; "Goulart Admires Mao of Red China," *NYT*, August 27, 1961, 31; Ferreira, *Goulart*, 224–227.

192. Mao-Goulart memcons, Hangzhou, August 18 and 19, 1961, file 204–01443–02, CFMA.

193. See Mao's favorable comments ("Ah! It seems that Goulart does have a trick up his sleeve. Very good tactics.") to Cuban President Osvaldo Dorticos, Beijing, September 28, 1961, *CWIHPB* 17–18 (October 2012), 73.

194. Record of Mao meeting with Brazilian communists, Hangzhou, August 19, 1961, file 111–00584–01, CFMA, trans. S. Radchenko.

195. Johnson, *Communist China and Latin America*, 189.

196. Mao meeting with Rachel Cossoyn and Amarilio de Oliveira Vasconcelos, Beijing, December 3, 1962, *MZD NP*, vol. 5, pp. 173–174, trans. S. Radchenko; *Peking Review*, December 7, 1962, p. 20; record of Mao meeting with Amazonas/Oest, March 6, 1963, CFMA, file 111–00608–03, trans. S. Radchenko.

197. The standard study of Sino-Latin American relations during this period described Manuel Jover Teles and Jaime Miranda arriving in Beijing on March 31 and seeing Mao on April 19, representing the "new party" and inferring that Chinese references to a "Brazilian Communist Party" delegation masked their guests' true identity and purpose. During their stay, Johnson erroneously speculated, the visitors "explored the possibility for receiving Chinese assistance in their struggle against the Prestes faction" and, to back their request, must have cited *A Classe Operária's* reprinting of many articles from *People's Daily* blasting the Soviets. Johnson ascribed their high-level reception to Beijing prioritizing "winning the[ir] goodwill" but not being ready to formally recognize the PCdoB as the sole Brazilian communist party and break with the PCB. He speculated the Chinese may have provided funds but not recognition. Chilcote, noting correctly the PCB split "occurred . . . when the Chinese were reluctant to support divisions in the Communist parties on an international scale," erroneously wrote "in March 1963 a two-man delegation of the splinter party that visited Peking and was received by Mao Tse-Tung was still described in *Peking Review* as a [PCB] delegation . . . Not until September was there any indication that the PC do B had been officially recognized by Peking." Johnson, *Communist China and Latin America*, 189–190; Chilcote, *Brazilian Communist Party*, 209. Another confused analyst wrote that a delegation representing

the "pro-Chinese [Brazilian] Communist Party" "arrived . . . on April 19." Low, *The Sino-Soviet Dispute*, 148.

198. Silveira, "Além da Traição."

199. Silveira, "Além da Traição, 143–148; Teles report in Prestes notebook (*caderneta*), quoted in Department of Public Safety-Department of Political and Social Order (SSP-DOPS), Report, "Investigation launched against Luiz Carlos Prestes and others during the Revolution of March 1964," São Paulo, September 30, 1964, 40, microfilm 09.01.455, 30-Z-9, São Paulo State Public Archive (APESP), courtesy Gianfranco Caterina.

200. Alberto Santos, in Silveira, "Além da Traição," 155.

201. CIA/RSS DDI/Staff Study, "The Sino-Soviet Struggle in Cuba and the Latin American Communist Movement," November 1, 1963, 149–151, and CIA Intelligence Report, "The Sino-Soviet Dispute within the Communist Movement in Latin America," June 15, 1967, pp. 6, 158–159, CIA FOIA.

202. CIA Intelligence Report, "The Sino-Soviet Dispute within the Communist Movement in Latin America," June 15, 1967, 158–159, CIA FOIA.

203. CIA Intelligence Report, "The Sino-Soviet Dispute within the Communist Movement in Latin America," June 15, 1967, 6, and CIA/RSS DDI/Staff Study, "The Sino-Soviet Struggle in Cuba and the Latin American Communist Movement," November 1, 1963, 151, CIA FOIA; Euler de França Belém, "China de Mao Tsé-tung e Chu En-Lai não deu apoio decisivo à Guerrilha do Araguaia," *Jornal Opção*, February 23–March 1, 2014.

204. CIA/RSS DDI/Staff Study, "The Sino-Soviet Struggle in Cuba and the Latin American Communist Movement," November 1, 1963, 151.

205. CIA/RSS DDI/Staff Study, "The Sino-Soviet Struggle in Cuba and the Latin American Communist Movement," November 1, 1963, 149–150.

206. CIA, Office of Current Intelligence, Special Article, "Chinese Communist Activities in Latin America," May 10, 1963, CIA, Subjects: Intelligence, 4/63–6/63, box 272, NSF, JFKL.

207. All quotations from record of Mao Zedong's meeting with Brazilian communists (Amazonas and Oest), Beijing, March 6, 1963, file 111–00608–03, CFMA, trans. S. Radchenko.

208. In contrast, Mao alluded approvingly to the more militant Venezuelan party and a leftist Colombian CP faction. He referred to Castro's January 16, 1963, speech at the Congress of the Women of the Americas. Castro here echoed Che, who in 1961 had also stated that objective conditions, such as hunger and oppression, existed for a Latin American revolution, but "subjective" conditions, such as the "consciousness of the possibility of victory" through violence, were "lacking." Guevara, "Cuba: Historical Exception or Vanguard of the Anti-Colonialist Struggle?" *Verde Olivo*, April 9, 1961, in James, *Guevara*, 128.

209. Dulles, *Resisting Brazil's Military Regime*, 71–76; also idem, *Unrest in Brazil*, 230–231. After being convicted of espionage, the nine Chinese were later expelled.

210. CIA Intelligence Report, "The Sino-Soviet Dispute within the Communist Movement in Latin America," June 15, 1967, 158–159; CIA/RSS DDI/Staff Study, "The Sino-Soviet Struggle in Cuba and the Latin American Communist Movement," November 1, 1963, 149–151, CIA FOIA.

211. *Peking Review*, April 26, 1963, 5; Johnson, *Communist China and Latin America*, 189–90, citing the Hong Kong-based *South China Morning Post*.

212. CIA/RSS DDI/Staff Study, "The Sino-Soviet Struggle in Cuba and the Latin American Communist Movement," November 1, 1963, 149–150. During the PCB delegation's visit, Chinese media hailed the pro-Cuba solidarity congress in Niteroi, but ignored the orthodox Brazilian communist party's role in organizing the event and approvingly quoted de la Puente's view that to defeat "U.S. imperialist enslavement and control the only road is that of the Cuban revolution, that is, the road of armed struggle." Hsiao Ming, "In Solidarity with Cuba," *Peking Review* 15 (April 12, 1963), 13–14.

213. Hungarian Legation, RdJ, "Subject: The situation of the Brazilian Communist Party," August 10, 1963.

214. Mao Zedong's meetings with Brazilian communists, Hangzhou, April 17–18, 1963, file 111–00608–04, CFMA; trans. S. Radchenko.

215. Johnson, *Communist China and Latin America*, 185–188; "Reply to Khrushchev: Resolution of the Communist Party of Brazil," *Peking Review* 37 (September 13, 1963), 39–43. *Peking Review* had recently reprinted from *A Classe Operária* an article praising Mao. See Grabois, "The World Revolution's Vanguard and Leading Force," *Peking Review* 35 (August 30, 1963), 27–28.

216. "The leaders of the CPSU are the greatest splitters of our times" (comment on CPSU CC "open letter"), February 4, 1964 (Peking: Foreign Languages Press, 1964).

217. Gaspari, *A Ditadura Envergonhada*, 180, citing Jacob Gorender, *Combate nas trevas*, 117.

218. He simultaneously balanced these steps by signing, in February, a long-delayed trade agreement with Taiwan. USE/RdJ (Goldstein), Airgram A-5, "Sino-Soviet Bloc Politico-Economic Relations, Dec 1963–May 1964," July 1, 1964, RG 84, NA.

219. See Becard, *O Brasil e a República Popular da China*.

220. Halperin, *The Peaceful and the Violent Road*, 12–13.

221. "The Domestic Situation in Brazil and the Tasks of the Communist Party of Brazil," *Peking Review* 22 (May 28, 1965), 20–22.

222. Mao-Carlos Nicolau Danielli memcon, July 20, 1965, file 111–00637–01, CFMA, trans. S. Radchenko.

223. By 1966, the PCdoB had grown disillusioned with Cuba. That March, in an open letter to Fidel Castro, the party accused him of siding with Soviet "revisionists," objecting to representatives of Prestes's PCB attending the "Tricontinental" in Havana while the PCdoB was excluded. *Yearbook on International Communist Affairs: 1966* (Stanford, CA: Hoover Institution Publications, 1967), 189–191.

224. Brizola, the most successful, after returning from Uruguay, the United States, and Portugal, founded a new Democratic Labor Party (PDT) and won two terms as governor of Rio de Janeiro state; Julião, back from Mexico after a pardon, allied with Brizola's PDT and ran for parliament, but was defeated and divided his time between Brazil and Mexico until his death in 1999; Prestes, after a decade in Moscow, spent his final years in Brazil, abandoning the PCB but not Marxism, and backing Brizola's 1989 presidential bid, before his death the following March.

Bibliography

Aguiar, Cláudio. *Francisco Julião: Uma biografia*. Rio de Janeiro: Civilização Brasileira, 2014.

Anderson, Jon Lee. *Che Guevara: A Revolutionary Life*. New York: Grove Press, 1997, 2010.

Andrade Porfirio, Pablo Francisco de. *De Pétalas e Pedras: A Trajetória de Francisco Julião*. Universidade Federal do Rio de Janeiro, 2013.

Asselin, Pierre. *Hanoi's Road to the Vietnam War, 1954–1965*. Berkeley: University of California Press, 2013.

Becard, Danielly Silva Ramos. *O Brasil e a República Popular da China: Política Externa Comparada e Relações Bilaterais (1974–2004)*. Rio de Janeiro: Fundação Alexandre de Gusmão [FUNAG], 2008.

Bezerra, Gustavo Henrique Marques. *Brasil-Cuba: Relações Político-Diplomáticas No Contexto da Guerra Fria (1959–1986)*. Brasília: Fundação Alexandre de Gusmao, Ministerio das Relações Exteriores, 2010.

Brands, Hal. *Latin America's Cold War*. Cambridge, MA: Harvard University Press, 2012.

Brilhante Ustra, Carlos Alberto. *A verdade sufocada: a história que a esquerda não quer que o Brasil conheça*. Brasília: Editora Ser, 2007.

Brown, Jonathan C., *Cuba's Revolutionary World*. Cambridge, MA: Harvard University Press, 2017.

Castro, Fidel, and Ignacio Ramonet. *Fidel Castro: My Life: A Spoken Autobiography*. New York: Scribner, 2008.

Caterina, Gianfranco. "Um grande oceano: Brasil e União Soviética atravessando a Guerra Frida (1947–1985)." Doctoral dissertation, Centro de Pesquisa e Documentação de História Contemporânea do Brasil, Fundação Getulio Vargas (CPDOC-FGV), 2019.

Cheng, Yinghong. "Sino-Cuban Relations during the Early Years of the Castro Regime, 1959–1966." *Journal of Cold War Studies* 9, no. 3 (2007).

Chilcote, Ronald H., *The Brazilian Communist Party: Conflict and Integration 1922–1972*. New York: Oxford University Press, 1974.

Chilcote, Ronald H., ed., *Protest and Resistance in Angola and Brazil: Comparatives Studies*. Berkeley: University of California Press, 1972.

Devlin, Kevin. "Boring from Within." *Problems of Communism*, March 1964: 27–39.

Draper, Theodore. "Castroism," in *Marxism in the Modern World*, edited by Milorad M. Drachkovitch. Sanford, CA: Stanford University Press, 1965.

Dulles, John W.F., *Unrest in Brazil: Political-Military Crises 1955–1964*. Austin: University of Texas Press, 1970.

———. *Brazilian Communism, 1935–1945: Repression during World Upheaval*. Austin: University of Texas Press, 1983.

———. *Carlos Lacerda, Brazilian Crusader*, vol. 2: *The Years 1960–1977*. Austin: University of Texas Press, 1996.

———. *Resisting Brazil's Military Regime: An Account of the Battles of Sobral Pinto*. Austin: University of Texas Press, 2010.

Ferreira, Jorge. *João Goulart: Uma biografia*. Rio de Janeiro: Civilização Brasileira, 2011.

Ferreira, Jorge. "The Brazilian Communist Party and João Goulart's Administration." *Revista Brasileira de História* 33, no. 66 (2013).

Forman, Shepard. "Disunity and Discontent: A Study of Peasant Political Movements in Brazil." In *Protest and Resistance in Angola and Brazil: Comparatives Studies*, edited by Ronald L. Chilcote. Berkeley: University of California Press, 1972.

Friedman, Jeremy. *Shadow Cold War: The Sino-Soviet Competition for the Third World.* Chapel Hill: University of North Carolina Press, 2015.

Furtado, Celso. *Obra autobiográfica.* São Paulo: Companhia das Letras, 2014.

Garrard-Burnett, Virginia, Mark Atwood Lawrence, and Julio E. Moreno, eds., *Beyond the Eagle's Shadow: New Histories of Latin America's Cold War.* Albuquerque: University of New Mexico Press, 2013.

Gasperi, Elio. *A Ditadura Envergonhada.* São Paulo: Companhia das Letras, 2002.

Goodsell, James Nelson, ed. *Fidel Castro's Personal Revolution in Cuba 1959–1973.* New York: Knopf, 1975.

Guevara, Ernesto Che. *The Awakening of Latin America.* Melbourne: Ocean Press, 2013.

Halperin, Ernst. *The Peaceful and the Violent Road.* Cambridge, MA: Center for International Studies, MIT, 1965.

———. "Peking and the Latin American Communists," *China Quarterly* (January–March 1967).

Halperin, Maurice. *The Rise and Decline of Fidel Castro.* Berkeley: University of California Press, 1972.

Hershberg, James G. "Soviet-Brazilian Relations and the Cuban Missile Crisis." *Journal of Cold War Studies* 22, no.1 (2020):175–209.

Hershberg, James G., and Sergey Radchenko, with Zhang Qian. "Sino-Cuban Relations and the Cuban Missile Crisis, 1960–62: New Chinese Evidence," *CWIHPB* 17–18 (October 2012).

Horowitz, Irving Louis. *Cuban Communism.* New Brunswick, NJ: Transaction Publishers, 1989.

James, Daniel. *Ché Guevara: A Biography.* New York: Cooper Square Press, 1969/2001.

Johnson, Cecil, *Communist China and Latin America 1959–1967.* New York: Columbia University Press, 1970.

Keller, Renata. *Mexico's Cold War: Cuba, the United States, and the Legacy of the Mexican Revolution* (NY: Cambridge University Press, 2015)

———. "Don Lázaro Rises Again: Heated Rhetoric, Cold Warfare, and the 1961 Latin American Peace Conference," in Virginia Garrard-Burnett, Mark Atwood Lawrence, and Julio E. Moreno, eds. *Beyond the Eagle's Shadow: New Histories of Latin America's Cold War.* Albuquerque: University of New Mexico Press, 2013.

Klarén, Peter Flindell. *Peru: Society and Nationhood in the Andes.* New York: Oxford University Press, 2000.

Kraenski, Mauro. "Abranches" and Vladimír Petrilák. *1964: O Elo Perdido: O Brasil nos arquivos do serviço secreto comunista.* Campinas: VIDE Editorial, 2017.

Leacock, Ruth. *Requiem for Revolution: The United States and Brazil, 1961–1969.* Kent, OH: Kent State University Press, 1990.

Leeds, Anthony. "Brazil and the Myth of Francisco Julião," in Joseph Maier and Richard W. Weatherhead, eds., *Politics of Change in Latin America.* New York: Praeger, 1964.

Leitão da Cunha, Vasco, *Diplomacia em Alto-Mar: Depoimento ao CPDOC*. Rio de Janeiro: Editora da Fundação Getulio Vargas, 1994.
Liss, Sheldon B., *Marxist Thought in Latin America*. Berkeley: University of California Press, 1984.
Low, Alfred D., *The Sino-Soviet Dispute: An Analysis of the Polemics*. Madison, NJ: Fairleigh Dickenson University Press, 1975.
Macaulay, Neill. *The Prestes Column: Revolution in Brazil*. New York: New Viewpoints, 1974.
Marques Bezerra, Gustavo Henrique. *Brasil-Cuba: Relações Político-Diplomáticas No Contexto da Guerra Fria (1959–1986)*. Brasília: Fundação Alexandre de Gusmao, Ministerio das Relações Exteriores, 2010.
Moniz Bandeira, Luiz Alberto. *De Martí a Fidel: A Revolução Cubana e a América Latina.* 2nd ed. Rio de Janeiro: Civilização Brasileira, 2009.
Morais, Clodomir Santos de. "História das Ligas Camponesas do Brasil," in João Pedro Stedile, ed., *História e Natureza das Ligas Camponesas*. São Paulo: Editora Expressão Popular, 2002.
Moraes, Dênis de. *A Esquerda e o Golpe de 64*. Rio de Janeiro: Espaço e Tempo, 1989.
Page, Joseph A., *The Revolution That Never Was: Northeast Brazil 1955–1964* New York: Grossman Publishers, 1972.
Parker, Phyllis R., *Brazil and the Quiet Intervention, 1964*. Austin: University of Texas Press, 1979.
Piñeiro, Manuel. *Che Guevara and the Latin American Revolution*. Melbourne: Ocean Press, 2001/2006.
Pomar, Wladimir. *Pedro Pomar: uma vida em vermelho*. São Paulo: Editora Fundação Perseu Abramo, 2013.
Porfiro, Pablo Francisco de Andrade. *De Pétalas e Pedras: A Trajetória de Francisco Julião*. Universidade Federal do Rio de Janeiro, April 2013.
Prestes, Anita Leocadia. *Luiz Carlos Prestes: Um Comunista Brasileiro*. São Paulo: Boitempo Editorial, 2015.
Prestes, Maria. *Meu companheiro: 40 anos ao lado de Luiz Carlos Prestes*, 3rd ed., trans. Marta Saxlund. Rio de Janeiro: Anita Garibaldi e-papers, 2012.
Reis, Daniel Aarão, *Luís Carlos Prestes: Um revolucionário entre dois mundos*. São Paulo: Companhia Das Letras, 2014.
Ridenti, Marcelo. *O Fantasma da Revolução Brasileira*, 2nd ed. São Paulo: Editora UNESP, 2005.
Rollemberg, Denise. *O apoio de Cuba à luta armada no Brasil: o treinamento guerrilheiro*. Rio de Janeiro: Mauad, 2001.
Sales, Jean Rodrigues. "O impacto da revolução cubana sobre as organizações comunistas brasileiras (1959–1974)." Doctoral thesis, State University of Campinas, December 2005.
———."A revolução cubana, as esquerdas brasileiras e a luta contra a ditadura military nos anos 1960 e 1970," paper for 5th European Congress of Latin Americanists (CEISAL), Brussels, April 2007.
———. "O Partido Comunista do Brasil nos anos sessenta: estruturação orgânica e atuação política," *Cadernos AEL* 8:14/15 (2001).

Sarzynski, Sarah R. *Revolution in the Terra do Sol: The Cold War in Brazil.* Stanford, CA: Stanford University Press, 2018.

Silveira, Éder da Silva. "Além da Traição: Manoel Jover Teles e o comunismo no Brasil do século XX." Doctoral thesis, Universidade do Rio dos Sinos, São Leopoldo, August 2013.

———."Dissidência comunista: da cisão do PCB à formação do PCBR na década de 1960," *Anos 90* (Porto Alegre) 20:37 (July 2013).

Skidmore, Thomas E. *Politics in Brazil, 1930–1964: An Experiment in Democracy.* New York: Oxford University Press, 1967.

Smith, Joseph, *Brazil and the United States: Convergence and Divergence.* Athens: University of Georgia Press, 2010.

Thomas, Scott. *The Diplomacy of Liberation: The Foreign Relations of the ANC Since 1960.* London: I.B. Tauris, 1995.

Tismaneanu, Vladimir. "Castroism and Marxist-Leninist Orthodoxy in Latin America," in Irving Louis Horowitz, *Cuban Communism.* New Brunswick, NJ: Transaction Publishers, 1989.

Weis, W. Michael, *Cold Warriors and Coups D'Etat: Brazilian-American Relations, 1946– 1964.* Albuquerque: University of New Mexico Press, 1993.

Yofre, Juan B. *Fue Cuba: la infiltración cubano-soviética que dio origen a la violencia subversiva en Latinoamérica.* Buenos Aires: Editorial Sudamerica, 2014.

PART II

Latin America's
Revolutionary Left
and Europe

4

The Italian Communist Party between "Old Comrades in Arms" and the Challenges of the New Armed Left

GERARDO LEIBNER

The second half of the 1960s and the 1970s are often described as a period of emergence of a "New Left," a heterogeneous political and cultural current considered as being opposed to the established "Old Left," consisting of Communist, Socialist, or Social Democratic parties. While the Western communist parties' policies and attitudes of the period are usually depicted as part of a rational (and moderate) strategy continually aiming to obtain political legitimation from broad sectors of society, the "New Left" currents are usually understood as representing rebellious impulses of radicalized youth. Some interpretations point, correctly, to the impact of national liberation struggles and revolutionary movements outside Europe in the radicalization processes of European new left currents. In this chapter I question the strict prevalent distinction between "New" and "Old" Lefts, showing how the Italian Communist Party (the biggest and most important communist party in West Europe), a prototype of an "Old Left" party, gave support to Brazilian revolutionaries, supposedly representing a "New" and armed Left, for reasons other than rational political calculations. I also show how the entanglement of Latin American and Italian political violence in 1972 required them to reconsider their attitude.

*   *   *

On May 6, 1971, Renato Sandri, the director with primary responsibility for Latin American policy for the Central Committee of the Communist Party of Italy (PCI)'s Division of Foreign Affairs, delivered a report on the recent arrival in Italy of three exiled Brazilians. The report began: "J. M. Vandervelde (former president of the Student Federation of Brazil) and Rene de Carvalho (son of Apolonio, a combatant of the International Brigades in Spain and hero of the French Resistance), who were released in exchange for the Swiss and German ambassadors (as was Apolonio), are in Italy. Also spending time in Rome is Marighella's companion Carmen, who escaped from the hospital where she was recovering from injuries sustained from torture after her capture."[1] The three exiled Brazilians, the report explained, belonged to underground organizations that were currently engaged in armed struggle against the Brazilian government and had "requested a meeting with Italian Communist Party leaders (as well as the leaders of other parties)." The report also noted that the three Brazilians had held a press conference on Thursday, April 22, 1971, at the bookstore Paesi Nuovi, at which the Christian Democratic Member of Parliament, Carlo Francanzani, was present. The report concluded by highlighting the personal connections between these young Brazilian guerrillas and the leftist old guard of Italy: "Rene Carvalho brings a letter from his father to comrades [Luigi] Longo and Giuliano Pajetta, with whom he fought in Spain."[2]

Although on the surface the report appeared to be a brief communiqué about a new development, it was, in fact, part of an ongoing effort by Sandri to legitimize the Brazilian guerilla organizations in the eyes of the Italian Communist Party leadership. Two weeks earlier, Sandri had participated in the aforementioned press conference with the Brazilian guerrillas. It is also highly likely that Giuliano Pajetta already knew that the son of his former comrade-in-arms had arrived in Italy.[3] However, Sandri had used the report to respond indirectly to criticisms made by General Secretary of the Communist Party of Brazil (PCB) Luís Carlos Prestes of Sandri's policy advocating political, practical, and financial support for the Brazilian guerrillas.

Prestes, an emblematic figure in the international communist movement, was also in Italy at this time. In an interview with his old friend Arturo Colombi, president of the PCI Control Commission, he had expressed harsh criticism of Italian communist press coverage of developments in Brazil. According to Prestes, the stories in *L'Unità* and in the journal *Rinascita* demonstrated a blatant ignorance of the work being done by the PCB to resist the Brazilian dictatorship.[4] The Italian communist press, he asserted, was guilty of "exalting terrorist groups" that were no more than "little groups made up of the children of the bourgeoisie, whose actions posed no threat to the regime that concentrates all its repressive force on the PCB."[5] Prestes also explicitly objected to Sandri's policy of supporting Brazilian guerilla organizations and asked that the secretary general of the PCI intervene to rectify the situation. He explained that because the PCI was held in such high esteem in Brazil, the stance taken by Italian communist publications was undermining the PCB's efforts against the Brazilian dictatorship.

Acutely aware of these objections, Sandri had made sure his official report emphasized that the Brazilian guerilla organizations included esteemed members of the "communist family," namely the son of Apolonio and the companion of Marighella. Once this information was disseminated, Prestes's assertion that the Brazilian guerrillas were from "terrorist groups" and the "sons of the bourgeoisie" simply no longer rang true. Consequently, Prestes's attack strategy quickly backfired. And yet, as this chapter demonstrates, subsequent developments in Italy would turn the tide in his favor.

The stakes in this struggle were high, with each side claiming the authority to represent the legitimate interests of communism and of the Brazilian revolutionary movement.[6] The struggle pitted individuals against one another whose actions from the recent past epitomized communist heroism. Luís Carlos Prestes, an ardent opponent of guerilla warfare in the 1960s and 1970s, was an internationally known hero of communism, celebrated for his military campaigns against the Brazilian government in the 1920s and 1930s. Initially an officer in the Brazilian military, he deserted in the 1920s and became a leading figure in the insurrection against the Brazilian government. Prestes, not yet a member of the Communist Party, had led a group of army mutineers and peasants in an epic march through the interior of Brazil. Across hundreds of kilometers, his military column had engaged in guerilla warfare against the Brazilian army and state police forces. Eventually defeated, he was forced into exile.

In 1931, Prestes had traveled to the Soviet Union where he developed contacts with the Communist Party and joined the Comintern. In early 1935 he returned to Brazil and took a leading role in the communist uprising against the dictatorial regime of Getúlio Vargas. For his part in the uprising, he spent the next ten years in prison, during which time the campaign for his release made him one of the most famous political prisoners on the planet. In 1942, Jorge Amado's biography of the jailed militant leader, *Vida de Luis Carlos Prestes. O cavaleiro da esperança* (The Knight of Hope) was published in Spanish in Argentina, and despite being banned in Brazil, the original text in Portuguese circulated clandestinely. It offered a passionate and romanticized account of the 1920s march of the "Prestes column" and after being translated to many languages became an international bestseller in the 1940s and 1950s, transforming Prestes into a communist legend, whose fame rivaled that of Dolores Ibarruri "Pasionaria," the "Passion Flower," of the Spanish Civil War.[7]

In 1945, Prestes was released from prison and for the next three decades served as secretary general of the Communist Party of Brazil. Starting in the mid-1950s, he pursued policies aimed at supporting the reform efforts of progressive and nationalist elements in the bourgeoisie. This policy was based on the two-stage theory of revolution, according to which the completion of the tasks of the national and democratic bourgeois revolution were seen as an historical prerequisite for approaching the challenges of socialist revolution. Applied to Latin America, it meant that progressive and nationalist sectors of the nation's bourgeoisie must first advance the path of political democracy and industrial development, overcoming American imperialism before the socialist tasks of revolution could be considered. However, a growing number of leftists in Latin America, inspired by the Cuban Revolution example and encouraged by the Argentinian born Ernesto Che Guevara who became a prominent leader in the Cuban Revolution, were challenging this theory of revolution.

Within the Brazilian Communist Party (PCB), this challenge reached a critical stage following the April 1964 military coup, when Prestes refused to involve the party in armed resistance to the regime. What was perceived as PCB's inaction outraged many members, creating factions that were soon expelled or split from the party, influenced by Guevarist and Maoist critiques of the moderation and lack of revolutionary spirit of most Latin American pro-Soviet communist parties. Several ex-PCB leaders and a large percentage of Communist youth left the party and formed more militant organizations that promoted, organized, and carried out armed struggle against the military government. Prestes's impeccable revolutionary credentials, however, limited the types of charges that dissatisfied radicals could make against the PCB leader; no one could accuse Prestes of failing to understand the principles of guerilla warfare or claim that his refusal to support armed struggle was guided by cowardice.[8]

However, this same logic applied to the attacks that Prestes could launch successfully against his opponents, as they too had impressive revolutionary credentials—a fact clearly highlighted in Sandri's report. Apolonio de Carvalho, like Prestes, had served in the Brazilian military before becoming a communist. In 1935, as a young officer, he had taken part in the unsuccessful insurrection against the Vargas dictatorship and had been imprisoned for his involvement. Released in 1937, he had joined the PCB and immediately volunteered to serve in the International Brigades fighting against the Nationalists in Spain.[9] While serving in the brigades, he collaborated closely with the Italian communists, Luigi Longo (chief political commissar of the Twelfth International Brigade organized on the initiative of the Comintern) and his assistant Giuliano Pajetta. After the Republican defeat in Spain, Apolonio fled to France where he was sent to a detention camp for Spanish war combatants. In 1941, he escaped from the detention camp and joined the French resistance. He rose to the rank of colonel in the resistance and after liberation was awarded the Legion of Honor, in recognition of the bold campaigns he led against the Vichy police in Marseilles and against the German army.

After the war, he returned to Brazil and rejoined the PCB.[10] In 1967 Apolonio was one of the members of the party's Central Committee critical of PCB's moderate course that were expelled for factionalist activities. Heading a group of splinters, he founded the Revolutionary Brazilian Communist Party (PCBR), one of the groups that initiated armed struggle against the Brazilian military government. In January 1970, he was arrested, tortured, and imprisoned. The following year, along with dozens of other political prisoners, Apolonio was released and sent into exile in Algeria in exchange for the release of the West German ambassador who had been kidnapped by guerrillas. His son Rene was released shortly thereafter in exchange for the kidnapped Swiss ambassador. The Italian communist press provided sympathetic coverage of the released prisoners' arrival in Algeria.[11]

Carlos Marighella, a guerilla leader also referenced in Sandri's report, had been shot and killed by Brazilian police during an ambush in late 1969. Like Prestes and Apolonio, he had been arrested, imprisoned, and tortured during the Vargas era. In 1966, in the midst of the debate over armed resistance, he had resigned from the PCB Central Committee.[12] In July 1967, he had then attended the first Organization of Latin American Solidarity (OLAS) conference held in Havana, Cuba. The conference, which PCB had boycotted, adopted resolutions affirming the inevitability of armed struggle in Latin America. A year later, Marighella founded the National Liberation Alliance (ALN), another militant Brazilian organization dedicated to armed resistance. And, in 1969, shortly before his death at the hands of the police, he wrote the very influential *Mini-Manual of the Urban Guerilla*.[13] A short time after Guevara's death and the failure of his guerrilla attempt in Bolivia, as well as the failure of many previous "countryside-foco" guerrilla attempts (particularly in Venezuela, Argentina, and Peru), the innovative urban guerrilla seemed to many radicalized leftists a new option to move the revolutionary armed struggle forward, especially suitable for countries with large modern cities.

The early careers of Luigi Longo and Giuliano Pajetta—two important leaders of the PCI in 1971—had followed similar trajectories as those of the exiled Brazilian revolutionaries. In the early 1930s, they had been involved in the Italian antifascist underground. Like many Communists, they had answered the call for volunteers to fight against the Nazi and Fascist supported Nationalists in Spain, and the two men had risen to important politico-military positions in the International Brigades. After the Spanish Republican defeat, Pajetta had fled to France, where he was arrested and interned in various refugee and prison camps operated by the Vichy regime in Southern France. Following his escape, he had then devoted his energies to organizing Communists in hiding. Toward the final stages of World War II, Pajetta had returned to northern Italy to pursue clandestine actions against the fascists and German occupiers. In 1944, he had been captured in Milan, tortured, and sent to the Mauthausen Concentration Camp, where he helped organize resistance inside the camp. He remained there until the camp's liberation in May 1945.[14]

These Communists' experiences of armed struggle during the Spanish Civil War and the Resistance during World War II were international. They created strong transnational links among the fighters that survived and, no less important, they became an important part of Communist identity. During the 1950s and 1960s, West-European and most of the Latin American communist parties were not involved in armed struggle as a political method. Instead, when possible they were trying to integrate themselves into democratic and mostly legal politics through worker-unions' struggle and parliamentary representation and, when confronting dictatorships, they generally opted for mass-civic struggle methods and broad antifascist alliances. They also supported the Soviet thesis of pacific coexistence between antagonistic social systems. However, using songs and commemorations, the Communists still remembered and exalted their own heroism and fighting spirit in the near past.[15] Indeed, the epic of the 1930s and 1940s' armed struggle experiences became an important part of Communists' identity and was transmitted to younger generations of militants.

Having spent their youth engaged in clandestine actions and guerilla warfare, Longo and Pajetta identified strongly with the spirit of exiled Brazilian guerrillas who in their estimation were fighting heroically against a fascist-style dictatorship. It was a sentiment shared by many in the Italian Communist party, no matter how moderate or bureaucratic they had become in their subsequent careers as parliamentary politicians. The fact that some of the young Brazilian revolutionaries were the children of their former comrades-in-arms reinforced this sentimental connection and undoubtedly informed the warm reception given to the Brazilian militants. Although they respected Prestes and knew that their own PCI's official policy did not encourage armed struggle in Latin America, they simply could not bring themselves to disavow the children of their former comrades as "terrorists" or as "radicalized representatives of the petty-bourgeoisie."

An official meeting between representatives of the PCI leadership and the Brazilian guerrillas soon followed the warm reception. According to an internal PCI memorandum, Giuliano Pajetta committed his party to providing practical assistance to the exiled guerrillas, part of which was given immediately and the remainder over the course of the next few months. The PCI leadership pledged: (1) to submit immediately a formal request to the Italian parliament demanding a ban on the sale of military spare parts to the Brazilian government; (2) to mobilize Genoese dockworkers to refuse to load military parts for shipment to Brazil; (3) to utilize *L'Unità* to publicize and denounce the situation in Brazil; (4) to sponsor booths at PCI and *L'Unità* events, whose goal would be to promote solidarity with Brazilian political prisoners and with the struggle of the Brazilian people; and (5) to organize in conjunction with other organizations mass protests against the use of torture in Brazil. PCI leaders also committed to making a political effort to present the Brazilian guerrillas in a positive light to ruling parties in socialist countries.[16] It was a pledge whose outcome was uncertain. The PCI's unequivocal condemnation of the 1968 invasion of Czechoslovakia by Warsaw Pact troops and its search for a democratic way for socialism had already strained its relations with most ruling communist parties.

The Party also provided other financial and logistical assistance to the exiled guerrillas. For example, the PCI paid for medical treatment for the injuries that the Brazilian representatives had sustained during torture. It covered travel costs for a multi-city Italian propaganda campaign and arranged for the Brazilian exiles to have access to a motorcycle during their time in Rome. The Party also offered to stage a painting exhibit at a PCI building in Milan to raise funds for Brazilian organizations and to assist them in obtaining travel documents. In an apparent effort to secure a visa for Apolonio to travel from Algeria to Italy, PCI leaders also cautiously pursued contact with Angelo Salizzoni, undersecretary for Aldo Moro, then the minister of Foreign Affairs and a prominent leader of the ruling Christian Democracy.

However, much of the PCI's financial support of the Brazilian revolutionaries between mid-1971 and early 1972 was directed to Carmen, introduced in Sandri's report as Marighella's companion. Carmen was the alias of Zilda Paula Xavier Pereira. Arrested in January 1970 by Brazilian police, she had been subjected to torture that left her with lifelong medical issues. During her time in Italy, she had received news that the Brazilian police had killed her son, and she feared that her young daughter was in danger of suffering the same fate. Renato Sandri's reports to the PCI Foreign Affairs Committee documented her repeated requests for clandestine and direct assistance for Brazilian militants.[17]

We know from later documents that the support given the exiled Brazilians beginning in 1971 was not the first time that the PCI had assisted a Brazilian activist who had broken with the official PCB party line. Between late 1969 and late 1971, the PCI had provided logistical and financial support to José Maria Crispim, who was organizing Western European solidarity networks in support of the Brazilian revolutionaries. Already in 1952, Crispim had been expelled from PCB; in 1966, he had co-founded the politico-military organization known as the Popular Revolutionary Vanguard (VPR).[18] Still, the PCI's warm welcome and support to the Brazilian guerrillas in 1971 is intriguing, mainly because it appeared to be in contradiction with the PCI's official political line.

The PCI's Latin American Policy

Since the early 1960s, the PCI had developed a foreign policy program that staked out a certain degree of autonomy from Moscow. In the final years of his life, Palmiro Togliatti, a former key figure in the Comintern and the main leader of the Italian Communist Party from 1927 until his death in 1964, had become one of the principal promoters of a decentralized model of the international communist movement. He argued that all the communist parties had a responsibility to respect the historic role of the Communist Party of the Soviet Union as the vanguard of the communist movement. This meant to defend the Soviet Union from imperialistic ideological aggressions, to support its struggle for peaceful development and to learn from its experience. However, each communist party should have full control over its own national policy. Officially this was also the concept advocated by the Soviets themselves since Khrushchev days. At a regional level, considering the common situations of different countries in a same geopolitical area, Togliatti argued, policies should be discussed and elaborated by the communist parties in each region based on "proletarian internationalism"—understood as relations of friendship, cooperation, and solidarity among communist parties, other worker parties, and national liberation movements.[19] According to this view (rejected by the Soviets during the Brezhnev period and by most of the more conservative communist parties), national communist parties needed a certain degree of autonomy to develop bilateral and multilateral relations with leftist parties and national liberation movements and to exchange views and take positions not conditioned by the Soviet policy or interests in a certain region.

This autonomy, PCI leaders clarified, did not mean breaking with Communism as an international movement or abandoning the idea that national parties should function within the framework of a general common policy. Quite the contrary, the political development of each and every party, PCI leaders argued, could proceed only from adherence to general statements, which provided the basis for determining the specific objectives and means of struggle in each country and the correct strategy for certain regions. Practiced in this manner, national autonomy preserved unity, while at the same time recognizing legitimate forms of communist pluralism and the validity of multiple centers of decision making. It was a complex position that endeavored to cultivate diversity in unity and to provide a constructive model for repairing the damage to the international communist movement caused by the 1948 Tito-Stalin conflict (unsolved despite Khrushchev's efforts) and, moreover, by the later Sino-Soviet split.

With respect to Latin America, PCI foreign policy experts first developed a special interest in the strategies of communist parties and revolutionary movements on that continent in 1960. This interest was prompted by the decidedly socialist turn in the Cuban Revolution that year.[20] However, it is important to note that due to cultural proximity and the existence in several Latin American countries of important centers of Italian immigrants and workers (some of them communists), the PCI had always maintained some contacts in Latin America and possessed a certain degree of knowledge about developments in the region. The rapid growth of the Latin American Left and of communist parties in the region in the wake of the Cuban Revolution nevertheless prompted the PCI to take a more active interest in developments there. Considering itself the most powerful communist party having a similar cultural background, the PCI offered itself to act as interlocutor and adviser to interested communist parties in Latin America. Renato Sandri assumed primary responsibility for touring Latin America, informing the PCI about continental developments, and proposing a course of action to be implemented its Central Committee's Division of Foreign Affairs. Between June 16 and July 15, 1964, Sandri conducted his first fact-finding tour of Latin America to learn more about the communist movement there; he visited Uruguay, Argentina, Chile, Peru, and Mexico and met with the principal leaders of the communist parties, activists, Italian diplomats, and some leftist intellectuals.[21]

The metaphor of "uncle," I would suggest, is a useful one for understanding the role that the PCI intended to develop in Latin America, as it picks up on a recurring theme in the international communist movement, that is, the notion of the "great communist family" made up of "brother parties," sometimes of "adult parties" and "not-grown up parties" or, in early versions, with Stalin as the father figure and the Soviet Communist Party playing a paternal guiding role. The uncle is an adult family member who, having greater life experience, acts as mentor and sometime sponsor of his younger nephews. Yet because he is not the parent, he can afford to take a less rigid approach, providing the young nephews with gentler paternal guidance and affectionate counsel and support. In the case of a favorite nephew, the uncle may even become complicit in their "adolescent" activities or at least to show some sympathy and understanding.

The growing tensions in the international communist movement caused by the Sino-Soviet dispute and by the Cuban Revolution strongly influenced the development of the PCI's policy toward communist parties and leftist movements in Latin America.[22] The emergence of radicalized anti-imperialist movements in Latin America posed new political challenges for communist parties in general and for the PCI in particular. The most notorious case of PCI involvement in Latin American affairs, which went beyond symbolic support or public statements, was the extensive support the PCI provided the Communist Party of Venezuela (PCV) throughout the 1960s. From roughly 1963, the PCV had worked with the MIR (Movement of the Revolutionary Left) to form the FALN (Armed Forces of National Liberation). The FALN was the first serious attempt in Latin America to repeat the success of the Cuban rural guerrilla–led revolution. It was based on a leftist united front assuming that armed action could unify different groups despite ideological differences. During its first years this effort had been supported by the PCI, which enthusiastically reported the guerrilla actions and reflected the official FALN positions in its own newspaper.[23]

The support was not just verbal. In April 1965 Dr. Alessandro Beltramini and Josefa Ventosa were arrested at the Caracas airport carrying more than 300 thousand dollars in cash. Beltramini, a known Italian physician member of the PCI, and Ventosa a very young Spanish worker, were accused of carrying money for the Venezuelan communist guerrilla. They were expelled from Venezuela after several weeks in prison.[24] In the second half of the 1960s, when the PCV decided to withdraw from the armed struggle, placing the party at odds with most of the guerilla organization leaders and with Fidel Castro, who had been providing political and military support to the combatants, the PCI continued to be an important source of support for PCV leaders.

The PCI's support for the Venezuelan Communist Party, both during the guerilla phase and afterward, entailed diffuse solidarity with the Venezuela situation.[25] At different points in time, this included political solidarity as well as logistical and financial support for exiled Venezuelans, PCV leaders, and militants traveling in Europe (e.g., travels costs and in some cases clandestine mail services to Venezuela via Italian expatriate). Correspondence and reports from the archives of the PCI's Department of Foreign Affairs reveal that supporting PCV embroiled the PCI in a delicate and volatile situation. The PCV was internally divided on the issue of armed struggle and on other issues, and the varying factions within PCV vied to win PCI's officials support and approval for their proposed course of action.[26] Although the PCI avoided making any public intervention in these internal conflicts, its continued dialogue and frequent contacts with the PCV leadership nonetheless implied the PCI's tacit support for the decision of the PCV leadership to withdraw from the armed struggle and to resume the legal and peaceful battle for democratic reform.

The Latin American party with which the PCI had the most harmonious relationship was the Communist Party of Chile.[27] The Chilean Party had adopted a peaceful strategy, involving alliances, popular mobilization, and electoral and parliamentarian struggles—an approach that closely resembled the PCI's envisioned policy for Italy.[28] Yet despite this affinity, the PCI never endorsed publicly any position in the internal Latin American communist debate on paths to socialism that suggested an openly anti-Cuban or anti-OLAS stance. The PCI also avoided aligning with the more conservative pro-Soviet communist parties that shunned the youthful radicalization of 1960s due to their rigid adherence to the Stalinist two-stage theory of revolution. In fact, certain PCI officials like Renato Sandri or Saverio Tutino (*L'Unità* correspondent in Cuba), specializing in Latin American affairs, were highly critical of many communist parties that towed the Soviet line, such as the Argentinian and Brazilian parties. They viewed these parties as too moderate and too immobile. In their estimation, they lacked the passion and initiative needed to tackle the dramatic events unfolding in their countries; consequently, they were losing relevance.

The PCI's open condemnation of Soviet oppression of the Prague Spring in fall 1968 introduced another modulation in the PCI's international politics, shifting it from autonomous to truly independent. Specifically, the party no longer abstained from intervening in controversial situations involving other communist parties. During a new divisive crisis in the Communist Party of Venezuela in 1969–1970, the PCI had maintained formal relations with both the small group of more conservative and dogmatic leaders who controlled the party and those youngers who had split to form Movement toward Socialism (MAS). However, in practice, the PCI had closer ties with MAS leaders, many of which had visited Italy in the previous years and had been influenced by the PCI's flexible approach to politics.

Understanding PCI Support for Brazilian Guerilla Organizations

As this chapter has shown, the PCI implicitly supported the decision of the Venezuelan Communist Party to withdraw from violent struggle and enthusiastically embraced the peaceful policies pursued by Popular Unity in Chile, while at the same time providing support to Brazilian militants who had split with the PCB and formed movements supporting armed struggle. The decision to support the Brazilian guerrillas, to a large extent, was based on sentimental factors already discussed in this chapter. But aside from sentimental reasons, a certain political logic allowed the Italian Communists to differentiate some of the Brazilian guerilla organizations from other Latin American guerrillas. The decision of Marighella or Apolonio to take up arms in Brazil was a direct response to a military coup and to a cruel repressive dictatorship that had eliminated all possible means of legal struggle. It did not emerge as part of the Guevarist "foco" strategy of revolution, whereby a vanguard of guerilla fighters initiates armed struggle with the purpose of radicalizing the confrontation with government troops, supposedly leading to a general revolution.[29]

This was an important distinction for many Italian communist leaders, who had spent their formative years fighting fascism in Europe. Having also been labeled "terrorists" in their youth, they did not automatically accept

Prestes's description of the Brazilian guerrillas as such. Moreover, based on their earlier contacts with PCB activists and with other leftist groups in Brazil, they had already reached the conclusion that the PCB leadership attitude toward dictatorship was too passive. Having closely followed PCB internal debates in the mid-1960s and the subsequent splits from the party, Renato Sandri was convinced that the PCB had made serious strategic errors.[30] Negative assessments of the PCB attitude by other esteemed Latin American communists, such as the Uruguayan Rodney Arismendi, had solidified this perspective.[31] The Brazilian guerilla organizations, the PCI's leaders concluded, deserved their support, if for no other reason than they were resisting dictatorship. The participation of at least two young Italian PCI members that emigrated to Brazil in the early 1960s in the ALN guerrilla led by Marighella contributed to opening PCI minds to the arguments favoring armed struggle in Brazil.[32]

Leaving aside the strong personal connection that some PCI leaders felt for certain Brazilian guerrillas leaders, this case calls into question the tendency to draw a sharp line of demarcation between two supposed polarized camps: On one side are communist parties reluctant toward the armed struggle and, on the other side, the militant Left, sometimes labeled the "New Left," consisting of groups prepared to launch a revolutionary armed struggle. This overly simplistic demarcation was first advanced by actors of the "revolutionary camp" at the 1967 OLAS conference, led by Fidel Castro, which adopted Guevara's call to fight imperialism by creating "two, three, many Vietnams."[33] Yet, curiously, this division—advanced by certain actors at a particular moment in history, fueled by harsh polemical publications, and aggravated by Guevara's defeat in Bolivia in October 1967 as well as the confrontation between the Soviet Union and Cuba in early 1968—has persisted in the collective imaginary that feeds contemporary historiography. This historiography tends to consider all Latin American communist parties as opposed to armed struggle and even as legalistic, despite the known cases of the guerrilla involvement of the communist parties in Guatemala, El Salvador, and Colombia, the logistical support the Communist Party of Uruguay extended Guevara for his Bolivian venture, and the numerous ways in which different communist parties were evolved in illegal and underground tasks (not necessarily armed) in different countries.

It was no coincidence that Rodney Arismendi, whose negative comments about the PCB's reaction to the 1964 military coup helped to legitimize the Brazilian guerrillas' strategy in the eyes of the PCI, had advanced an intermediary and nuanced position at the OLAS Conference. At the conference, Arismendi, a pro-Soviet leader but also a personal friend of Castro, had acknowledged the likely inevitability of armed struggle in the Latin America revolutionary process; however, he had also advised careful consideration of all means of struggle, including mass, peaceful, and legal avenues. In short, Arismendi had earned the respect of PCI interlocutors by taking a stand against both the inaction of pro-Soviet parties, such as the Brazilian and Argentinian parties, and against the dogmatic, unwavering insistence on armed struggle of the Revolutionary Left.[34] So, while the Italian Communists preferred the peaceful route of the Chilean Communists, they also appreciated the nondogmatic and flexible political attitude of the Communist Party of Uruguay.[35] Like Arismendi, Italian Communists did not rule out the necessity of armed struggle in countries where legal and peaceful avenues had been shut down. Thus, within the Communist "Old Left" camp, even within the main European PC that was asserting a strategy of peaceful and legal democratic road to socialism in their countries, there was a certain room for acceptance of armed struggle in Latin America. In requesting assistance, the Brazilian guerrillas had evoked the heroic communist struggle against fascism in Spain and France; clearly, important sectors of the armed "New Left" had deep political and cultural roots in the communist "Old Left."

PCI support for the Brazilian guerrillas, however, did not last long. Undoubtedly, it was no easy feat to provide substantial financial, logistical, and propagandistic assistance to Brazilian guerilla organizations that did not have the support of their national Communist Party, while at the same time officially endorsing the electoral route of the Popular Unity government in Chile and the Broad Front (Frente Amplio) in Uruguay. But in 1972 (before the military coups in Uruguay and Chile), one could argue for multiple pathways, whereby the criterion for peaceful struggle was the existence of a legal, democratic framework for advancing communism, and the criterion for armed struggle, albeit not the only one, was the existence of a military dictatorship.

Ultimately, the PCI's decision to withdraw support nevertheless had little to do with strategic considerations in Brazil or in Latin America at large. The PCI mainly stopped support because of a challenge from the radical Left at home. By early 1972, a new trend in the Italian far-Left had emerged that was willing to use the same techniques as urban guerrillas in Latin America. This radicalization of young Italian leftists led PCI leaders to rethink their stance on Brazilian guerrilla groups. What had once seemed a valid response to a Latin American dictatorship now appeared as a potential contagion that had infected Italian youth and threatened the PCI's national strategy.

If, since the French Revolution, Latin American radicals were used to adopting European ideas and models regarding political and social change, since the 1960s and the 1970s, radicalized young Europeans were adopting ideas and models created in Latin American reality. As Eurocentric Latin Americans had acted in the past, these transatlantic adoptions were generally acritical, without seriously taking into account the differences of context. For many of the young European leftists in the 1960s and 1970s, Latin America became a source of inspiration. The transnational character of the adoption of simplistic models and symbols of revolutionary violence by young Italians who were radicalized during the 1968 student revolt and by the endless workers conflicts interfered in the national context and created difficulties for the PCI, a very sophisticated political party accustomed to making fine distinctions of context and opportunity in the design of its politics, both international and domestic. What was the meaning, for example, of the image of Che Guevara's face, with its military beret and long hair? The image quickly became a counterculture symbol, but in the early 1970s it also meant for many young revolutionaries, even in Europe, a call to revolutionary violence—to armed struggle.

Indeed, as a result of domestic circumstances, between February and May 1972, the tide quickly turned against PCI officials who favored supporting the Brazilian guerilla organizations. As noted earlier, Renato Sandri had secured additional support for the Brazilian guerrillas in February 1972; Giancarlo Pajetta, a member of the PCI secretariat and brother of the already-mentioned Giuliano Pajetta (head of the PCI's Division of Foreign Affairs), had authorized this assistance. Positive press coverage of the Brazilian guerrillas in *L'Unità* continued through April 1972.[36] But by May 1972 a debate had erupted within the PCI Division of Foreign Affairs. In a written memorandum, Franco Saltarelli denounced support for groups of "Brazilian adventurers" as an anomaly.[37] Most likely this written statement was the culmination of a major, largely undocumented, internal debate. But once the Party leadership accepted Saltarelli's position, all positive references to the Brazilian guerrillas in the Italian communist press and in PCI offices abruptly ended. No more applications for financial, logistical, or political support were approved and, in mid-1972, Prestes returned to

Italy, was received by PCI officials as the legitimate representative of Brazilian communism, and relations between the two communist parties were
normalized.[38]

Given this reaction, it is well worth dwelling on Saltarelli's arguments.
From a policy and procedural point of view, Saltarelli noted that the decision to support Brazilian revolutionary groups contradicted the PCI's 1971
decision to abstain from supporting any communist group in Brazil, because of the deep divides within the Brazilian revolutionary movement. In
fact, he observed, one revolutionary group—the National Liberation Alliance—had received copious support via Carmen. Saltarelli also drew attention to another discrepancy: namely, that the PCI had resolved to issue no
press release on the official meetings with the Brazilian organizations and
asked them for discretion; yet an ALN bulletin had announced PCI support
for armed struggle in Brazil. Finally, Saltarelli objected to irregularities in
how funds had been approved. Instead of going through official institutional channels, all requests for support had been personally managed by
Sandri.[39]

From a substantive point of view, Saltarelli advanced three arguments.
First, he argued that the Brazilian organizations, which the PCI had supported, were isolated extremist groups that had neither the support of the
peasantry, the workers, nor the Brazilian Communist Party. Moreover,
their actions were not based on clear objectives. Realizing that many of
his colleagues held Marighella in high esteem, Saltarelli claimed that the
ALN had changed since his death; it had lost touch with its working-class
base in Sao Paulo.[40] The representatives in exile, he asserted, had an even
more tenuous relationship with the workers of Brazil. By giving a dispro-
portionate amount of aid to ALN, the PCI had undermined its relationship with other Brazilian groups seeking similar support. Moreover, supporting "adventurous" groups while officially endorsing mass mobilization
and protests sowed the seeds of discord and distrust between the PCI and
other communist parties. Second, Saltarelli focused on Carmen's activities
in Rome; he pointed out that she had developed contacts with extremist
Italian groups, including Il Manifesto, a dissident group led by intellectuals
who had split with the PCI and recently entered into a confrontation with
the party. Finally, he pointed out that Brazilian groups had announced their
plans to establish a base of operation in Chile, much closer to Brazil. The
Brazilian exiles had traveled to Chile, but they had returned to Italy, where
they continued to solicit PCI assistance.[41]

Although the first and third arguments were not without merit, the second argument was the critical one. The first argument had been articulated and discussed for years. Yet it had never been a significant impediment to providing support. The third argument also represented no major obstacle to support. Proponents of support could have easily countered this argument by pointing out the need for maintaining a European base of operation. But the second argument had gained salience for PCI leaders due to a series of recent actions involving radicalized Italian leftists. These actions had escalated concerns in the PCI about the possible interconnections between groups of the Italian New Left and Brazilian militant organizations or, at least, a concern about the unwanted inspiration that the Brazilian and other Latin American revolutionaries could have on Italian young radicals.

The first event took place on March 3, 1972. A nascent cell of the Red Brigades had kidnapped Idalgo Macchiarini, an executive for the electronics company Sit-Siemens. The three kidnappers had grabbed Macchiarini as he was leaving his office. Held for only twenty minutes, he had been photographed with a Red Brigades sign around his neck and then released semi-nude at the doorstep of Sit-Siemens at change of shifts. The poster still around his neck tauntingly announced: "Red Brigades—bite and flee!—nothing will go unpunished—strike one to educate one hundred—all power to the armed people." The brief kidnapping was the first armed propaganda action by the Red Brigades; it also was the group's first use of the five-pointed red star, a symbol Red Brigadists borrowed from the Uruguayan Tupamaros National Liberation Movement. For PCI leaders, the kidnapping had been an act of provocation by an unknown group.[42]

An event of greater immediate significance occurred a week and a half later. On March 14, 1972, Giangiacomo Feltrinelli, an influential leftist editor and publisher, died when manipulating explosives during a failed attack on a high-voltage tower on the outskirts of Milan. The attack exposed the existence of the small, armed leftist organization led by Feltrinelli, the Partisan Action Group.[43] From the PCI's point of view, individuals carrying out these armed actions or defending their use in the Italian context were acting from the fascist playbook; that is, they were helping the rightist "high tension" strategy—the attempt to create confusion and fear from political violence in order to stop the advance of PCI and of the Left in general among Italian voters.

The whole Feltrinelli affair had disturbing connections to Latin America revolutionary messages. Feltrinelli had been one of the most important disseminators in Italy of Guevara's foco theory of revolution, in which armed cadres provide an initial focus of revolutionary action to attract popular discontent and to educate the masses for uncompromised struggle. As Eduardo Rey Tristan's chapter in this volume illustrates, Feltrinelli had published various Latin American guerilla texts in Italian translation and served as editor for the Italian edition of *Tricontinental*, a magazine first established in Havana, Cuba, to promote armed struggle in Latin America, Africa, and Asia.[44] Following the failed attack, the police had raided the homes of several members of Feltrinelli's political group whom they suspected of involvement in the attack; the raid yielded documents referencing the Latin America guerrillas. And in its coverage of the incident, the Italian Communist newspaper mentioned this Italian-Latin American connection.[45] PCI leaders now probably feared that the recent embrace of violent action by young Italian leftists was the product, among other sources, of contact between these young Italian radicals and the exiled Brazilian guerrillas living and acting in Italy with the aid of the PCI. This concern, undoubtedly, informed Saltarelli's written intervention,[46] which he made just two months after these incidents. As militant actions continued to unfold, PCI concern about this possible connection developed a heightened sense of urgency.

On March 21, 1972, the Argentinian guerilla organization known as the People's Revolutionary Army (ERP) kidnapped Oberdan Sallustro, deputy director of Italian Fiat in Argentina. Sallustro had played a leading role in a previous crackdown on the Fiat worker's union; hundreds of workers with suspected union sympathies had been fired in the months prior to the kidnapping. Whatever sense of satisfaction the fired workers may have felt for this reprisal made on their behalf, Fiat Union leaders in Italy realized it would have a devastating impact on their cause and endeavored to distance their organization from the ERP action in Argentina. The ERP guerrillas had demanded from the company a ransom of $1 million, the reinstatement of the fired workers, and an agreement that there would be no future layoffs or reprisals against union workers. The ERP also demanded that the ruling military dictatorship release imprisoned ERP members. Fiat agreed to the conditions, but the government refused. On April 10, 1972, the police surrounded the ERP hideout; Sallustro was killed during the ensuing shootout between his ERP captors and the police.

A PCI internal report of the incident revealed that Fernando Aloiso, the leader of the Italian contingent in the Communist Party of Argentina, had tried to act as mediator in the conflict. He had contacted former members of the Communist Party of Argentina that allegedly had ties with ERP. With the support of the Italian ambassador to Argentina, he had tried to negotiate a compromise solution and prevent a fatal outcome. Aloiso believed that such actions could eventually play into the hands of the most conservative faction in the Argentinian ruling army.[47] Although Aloiso had failed to negotiate a peaceful resolution, his effort earned the praise of the Italian Foreign Ministry and the PCI.

Meanwhile, Sallustro's death triggered a series of political reactions from the Italian Left. On April 11, 1972, the PCI-led Federation of Metalworkers released a statement expressing its condolences to the family of the deceased executive. In the same statement, the union also expressed solidarity with Fiat workers in Argentina, condemning the repressive practices of the company and of the military government. It blamed the executive's death on the cynical and intransigent behavior of the Argentinian government, while also condemning the ERP's use of kidnapping as a means of struggle.[48] The next day, Enrico Berlinguer, in one of his first speeches as the new secretary general of PCI, described the situation similarly: "We stand in solidarity with the workers of Fiat Argentina and with all freedom fighters; but we condemn unacceptable methods of struggle as well as concepts which are foreign to us, such as those adopted by the group that kidnapped Sallustro."[49]

The union's declaration evoked a sharp response from the Italian radical Left. *Il Manifesto*, a journal founded by a group of Communist writers who had broken with the PCI, published an article by Rossana Rossanda attacking the metalworkers' union for failing to show solidarity with the Argentinian guerrillas. This article, in turn, triggered a response by Emilio Sereni, who published a lengthy rebuttal in *L'Unità* in which he polemicized against armed struggle on doctrinal grounds. Citing Engels's 1885 condemnation of political assassination as a method of struggle, Sereni emphatically rejected the use of terrorist means of struggle by the labor movement in advancing its cause.[50]

The growing acceptance of such violent tactics by certain sectors of the radicalized Italian Left greatly alarmed PCI leadership. In fact, the alarm was so great that in an effort to counter support for radical Italian groups, such as Lotta Continua and Potere Operario, and win the hearts and minds of left-wing Italian youth, *L'Unità* decided to take an unprecedented step for a communist party newspaper: They published a statement (similar to the PCI statement) by the secretary of the Fourth International (the Trotskyist International), the arch-ideological rival of the communist parties.[51] *L'Unità* also noted that even the Italian branch of the Fourth International had emphatically stated that the ERP, the armed organization of the PRT (Workers Revolutionary Party), had no connection to Trotskyism or to the Fourth International; their Argentinian branch was not PRT but the Worker's Party (Partido Obrero).[52]

The following day in a pre-election debate with a Christian Democratic opponent, Giancarlo Pajetta referenced the Sallustro case to condemn the use of terrorist tactics.[53] Yet, prior to Italian groups showing a penchant for armed struggle, Pajetta supported aid for Brazilian organizations that used the very same tactics he now condemned. The exiled Brazilian revolutionaries, whom Pajetta and other PCI leaders had hailed as heroes the year before, had won their freedom thanks to the kidnapping of the German and Swiss ambassadors by radical militants.

The Sallustro case also influenced the actions of groups on the radical Left, such as Lotta Continua and the Red Brigades. On April 19, 1974, roughly two years after the Sallustro case, the Red Brigades kidnapped Genoa Assistant State Attorney Mario Sossi. During the telephone call in which they announced the kidnapping and their demands, the Red Brigadists warned that if their demands were not met, the judge would experience the same fate as Sallustro.[54]

For their part, from the end of April 1972 onward, PCI leaders were convinced of the strategic necessity of denouncing the risks of armed struggle; it was the only way, they believed, to prevent escalating violence by the radicalized Italian Left that would play into the hands of the Italian reactionary Right. Against the backdrop of growing leftist violence at home, supporting Brazilian urban guerrillas whose tactics included kidnapping and extortion became untenable for the PCI, which was gaining its political power through peaceful means. PCI leaders now took seriously Saltarelli's warning about contacts between exiled Brazilian guerrillas and local extremist groups. Moreover, for this debate the significance of Luigi Longo's replacement as PCI Secretary General by Enrico Berlinguer in mid-March 1972 cannot be ignored. While Longo was strongly attached with the militant past of the 1930s and 1940s, Berlinguer represented a generation of Italian communist leaders who decided in favor of a democratic historical compromise with Christian Democracy. This replacement paved the way for PCI to end its support for the Brazilian guerrillas and to adopt a clearer approach, championing the "peaceful road to socialism."

As this chapter has demonstrated, the communist networks forged during the Spanish Civil War and the antifascist resistance ethos of World War II played a vital role in the warm reception given the Brazilian guerrilla exiles in 1971. Although the transition from Longo to Berlinguer did not introduce an about-face in PCI's foreign policy, we can assume that the younger Berlinguer was much less likely to be swayed by sentimental feelings for "old comrades-in-arms" or nostalgia for the glory days of the armed "Old Left," especially if acting on these sentiments contradicted current domestic and foreign policy interests.

Conclusions and Questions for Further Research

At least four interesting conclusions to this historical episode reach beyond our specific case of study: (1) the affective elements that shaped political decisions in an important communist party; (2) the first influences that Latin American revolutionary policies had among the European Left; (3) the evolution of the PCI's independent international policy; and (4) the need to revise distinctions between "Old" and "New" Lefts, along with the place that communism has in these labels.

With regards to the first point, communist parties, on both sides of the Atlantic, are considered as political forces that developed highly rational, disciplined political lines and conducts over the course of the twentieth century derived from external instructions (the Comintern, the Soviet Union) or the way in which different leaders interpreted doctrine. In this case, however, we see that in in departing from the international communist movement's discipline and developing its own policies, the decision to support the Brazilian guerrillas derived not so much from doctrinal and rational considerations but from leaders' own historical ethos as combatants and their sentimental considerations.

With regard to the second point, Latin American Lefts emerging at the end of the nineteenth and beginning of the twentieth centuries had undeniable Eurocentric aspects, a product of the appropriation of ideas and concepts generated from Europe's own history. Throughout the course of the 1960s, and in direct relationship to the Cuban Revolution, alongside Latin America's literary boom, and a growing European interest in artistic expressions from the region, developments in Latin America began to have a significant impact on European political imagination. And, in this respect, new research on the role of leftist editors such as Feltrinelli or Maspero, who translated and published Latin American political literature in Europe, is very important. Ideas, concepts, styles, images, and symbols now flowed in both directions across the Atlantic. This new process was simultaneous and parallel to the PCI's autonomous international policy and its growing interest in involving itself in Latin American political processes with a view to fulfilling a commitment to communist proletarian internationalism, albeit renovated and brought up to date (*aggiornato*, to use its Italian term). At the start of the 1970s, the combination of both processes was reflected in a phenomenon that had not been anticipated by Italian Communist leaders: radicalized youth in Italy found inspiration in Latin American guerrilla movements and, in particular, in their adoption of urban guerrilla strategies.

Third, while the Cuban Revolution and its leaders' policies questioned the strategies employed by Latin American communist parties and their leaders, inspiring and actively encouraging revolutionary organizations, including splinters of communist parties toward armed struggle, the PCI advocated the democratic and "peaceful road" to socialism questioning the orthodox doctrinaire definitions of the Soviet Communists. However, over the course of a decade, the Italian Communists were able to distinguish between supporting armed struggle in Latin American contexts (for example, the Venezuelan guerrilla at the start of the 1960s) and the practical and doctrinal development of its positions for Europe. In keeping with the PCI's growing independence was the practical support offered to Brazilian guerrillas despite this being contrary to the will of the Brazilian Communist Party. The distinction the PCI made between the Latin American and European contexts allowed it to support armed struggle in some countries in Latin America and discourage political violence in Italy. Even so, the political texts, symbols, aesthetics, and the mere presence of Brazilian guerrilla representatives had the apparent effect of inspiring young radicalized Italians, which the PCI began to fear in the context of urban guerrilla actions in 1972. Although the PCI repaired its relationship with the Brazilian Communist Party shortly after, this did not mean that its international policy necessarily returned to privileging relations with official Communist Party leaders. Instead, the PCI promoted close relations, support, and mutual learning from various left-wing Latin American forces that opted for nonarmed struggle based on broad political alliances.

Last, as we have seen, old transatlantic militant networks, principally Communist, established in the 1930s and the 1940s as a result of Europe's struggle against fascism, served as the basis for creating relations of solidarity and collaboration between Italian communism and the guerrilla struggle against the Brazilian dictatorship in the 1960s and early 1970s. This case defies the usual historiographical distinctions made between the "New Left" and communist parties. Beyond the generally recognized fact that certain sectors of the "New Left," both Latin American and European, emerged in the 1960s from Communist Party splinter movements, we can see here how a large and important Communist Party formed part of a network of support for Brazilian organizations usually considered part of the "New Left." This study therefore invites us to reconsider the categories of "Old" and "New" Left and communist identity within them. From a historical point of view, this case thus highlights the continuities between networks of solidarity established during the Spanish Civil War and solidarity networks in the 1960s and 1970s, inviting those conducting research on the revolutionary Left in these decades to probe the antecedents and continuities with the experiences of the Spanish Civil War and the antifascist struggle in Europe. Another interesting conclusion is that in this case, it was precisely veteran communist leaders (Longo and Pajetta) who felt impelled to support Brazilian guerrillas, while it was a younger generation (Berlinguer) who took the decision to end this support.

These conclusions and the analysis presented in this chapter also raise questions for future research. Principally, these include the perspective of revolutionary Brazilians, as well as the perspective of other sectors of the Italian left regarding the Brazilians' presence and their impact. We also need further examination on the degree and nature to which Latin American revolutionary inspiration shaped the development of the new Italian armed Left.

Notes

1. Renato Sandri, Rome, May 6, 1971, AFG PCI 0162 0151.
2. Renato Sandri, Rome, May 6, 1971, AFG PCI 0162 0151.
3. PCI journalists released two reports on the press conference. See "Tre testimonialize dal Brasile," *L'Unità*, April 19, 1971 and "Il regime brasiliano allestisce basi militari contro la guerriglia," *L'Unità*, April 23, 1971.
4. Sandri, "La resistenza brasiliana: una semina da non disperdere," *Rinascita*, XXXVI, March 12, 1971, 12–13.
5. Arturo Colombi, Rome, May 2, 1971, AFG PCI 0162 0150.
6. As shown by James Hershberg in chapter 3 of this volume, the Brazilian communists and other groups of revolutionaries were divided and competing for international recognition even before the coup against Goulart in 1964. However, the previous split from the PCB was from a pro-Maoist faction, irrelevant from the point of view of the Italian Communist Party, that was considered by them as revisionist. The new factions that arose between 1966 and 1969 were seeking recognition and support from non-Maoist communist parties—that is, competing with the PCB in its own international sphere.
7. See Amado, *Vida de Luiz Carlos Prestes*.

8. See also notes 13 and 14 in Hershberg's chapter in this volume.

9. Paulo Roberto de Almeida, "Brasileiros na guerra civil espanhola."

10. Comissão Estadual da Verdade, "Trajetória do militante Apolonio de Carvalho," https://www.youtube.com/watch?v=KYzaDrqQUFg, accessed October 12, 2017.

11. "40 testimonialize sulle torture: 'Saremo liberi quando il Brasile sara libero,'" *L'Unità*, June 17, 1970.

12. The letter of resignation to the PCB Executive Committee, penned in Rio de Janeiro on December 10, 1966, was published along with other writings just a few days after his death. See Ferreira, *Carlos Marighella* (Havana: Tricontinental, 1969), 33–51.

13. When Marighella died, *L'Unità* published statements describing the fallen guerilla leader as a hero as well as long excerpts from an open letter to European revolutionaries that he had written shortly before his death. See "Ritratto di un combattente per la liberta del Brasile. Carlos Marighella" and "L'ultima lettera dell'eroe," *L'Unità*, November 8, 1969. Shortly thereafter, *L'Unità* published the ALN's account of its leader's assassination. See "Como fu ucciso Carlos Marighella," *L'Unità*, December 17, 1969. References to Marighella in *L'Unità* displayed the unbridled romanticism reserved for the "best sons of the working class" and no signs of the critical tone typically used to describe those who had left communist parties. For example: "Son of an Italian and a black woman. Carlos loved to say that through his veins coursed the blood of revolutionaries such as Garibaldi, as well as that of the slaves who took up arms and formed communities of rebels to confront the landowners of large estates."

14. See Meschiari, *Giuliano Pajetta*, 16, 18, 25–26.

15. For example, "Bella Ciao," "Si me quieres escribir," "Ay Carmela," "Que culpa tiene el tomate."

16. AFG PCI 0162 0153.

17. See, for example, Renato Sandri to Giancarlo Pajetta, February 16, 1972, AFG PCI, 053 1138.

18. On his expulsion from the party, see "Reunio-se o Comité Nacional do Partido Comunista do Brasil: Expulso das fileiras do P.C.B. o traidor José Maria Crispim," *Imprensa Popular*, March 2, 1952. On his Western European campaign, see Jose Maria Crispim to Luigi Longo, Roma December 22, 1971, AFG PCI, 0162 0156.

19. The Yalta Memorandum was first published in *L'Unità* on September 4, 1964. For the text in English translation, see Palmiro Togliatti, "The 'Togliatti' Memorandum," www.marxists.org/archive/togliatti/1964/memorandum.htm. In the memorandum, Togliatti argued for Communist Party meetings organized by shared regional interests. He also responded to the Maoist thesis that threatened to divide the party and argued that communist parties in capitalist countries needed to develop relationships not only with communist parties in colonial and former colonial countries (it is unclear how he classified Latin America), but also with all movements that opposed imperialism.

20. Pappagallo, *Verso il nuovo mondo.*

21. At the time of his death, Togliatti had a copy of Sandri's detailed report in his possession. AFG PCI, Estero 1964, 0520–0232, 0251.

22. Sandri's report emphasized the diverse realities that existed on the ground in Latin America. His report cited Rodney Arismendi, leader of the Uruguayan Commu-

nist Party, who warned Sandri: "In Europe, you have a superficial understanding of Latin America as a uniform whole."

23. For example, see how the PCI newspaper reported on the 1963 Venezuelan elections: "Oggi la frode in Venezuela," *L'Unità*, December 1, 1963. The newspaper considered the elections as an announced fraud. Behind the headlines, it showed a picture of "two patriots of the FALN" accused of an armed action who were arrested by Trinidad police and given to the Venezuelan authorities, "each one of the comrades is at risk of getting thirty years in prison."

24. *L'Unità*, the PCI newspaper, covered the case "believing" the arrested couple's "explanations" that the money was supposed to allow him to divorce his wife and build a new life in South America with his young Spanish lover: "Beltramini trattenuto in torcere illegalmente," April 17, 1965 ; "Josefa Jimenez conferma: i soldi erano per divorziare," April 21, 1965; "Ondata repressiva in Venezuela e in Colombia," April 25, 1965; "Il dottor Beltramini rimesso in e espulso dal Venezuela," May 27, 1965. *L'Unità* continued to cover the story defending the couple from sanctions in Italy after they returned: "Beltramini a Milano. Libero dopo 12 ore di interrogatorio," May 28, 1965; "Josefa Ventosa ancora ricoverata in clínica," May 30, 1965; "Un provvedimento assurdo e ingiustificato. L'Inam sospende il dott. Beltramini," June 2, 1965; "Beltramini riassunto e risarcito dall'INAM," March 28, 1968.

25. In the decisive moments of the decision to stop armed struggle, PCV Secretary General Jesús Faría, recently liberated from Venezuelan prison, visited Rome on his way to Moscow and met the PCI leaders. "A Roma Jesus Faria ton altri dirigenti della sinistra venezolana," *L'Unità*, March 20, 1966.

26. For example, in a letter sent to Berlinguer and signed in Caracas in July 1964, Italian communists living in Venezuela argued that the majority of the then PCV leadership had a "neo-Trotzkyite" deviation and that the core of "real Marxist-leninists" inside PCV did not accept the official line of armed struggle. The writers did not ask PCI to intervene in the inner struggle since "the local battle for the PCV is the privilege and the responsibility of the Venezuelan communists," but they suggested that the PCI should not publish in *L'Unità* the unrealistic reports sent by PCV leadership. AFG PCI 0520/3110.

27. See Santoni, *El comunismo italiano y la vía chilena* and Hobel, "Pci, sinistra cattolica e politica estera (1972–1973)."

28. In close conversations, PCI officials tried to explain to the Cuban leadership that the Chilean democratic way to socialism was not just "an electoral way" but also a means of advancing social struggles, structural reforms, and deepening democracy. Ugo Pecchioli, Secretary of PCI Federation of Torino in a report regarding a meeting with Fidel Castro, August 12, 1963, AFG PCI 0492/2555.

29. As described in Debray, *Revolution in the revolution?*

30. Pappagallo, *Verso il nuovo mondo*, 207–210, 236–238.

31. Arrigo Boldrini, "Note suit due incontri avuti con il Segretario del PCU, Rodney Arismendi," Ag. 1966, AFG PCI 0537/0888.

32. Dario Canale and Urbano Stride arrived in Brazil in 1965, established contact, and acted in support of PCB clandestine activities. Later, in 1967, Canale became one of the closest assitants to the founding group of ALN. Captured and tortured by the Brazilian

political police after a strong international campaign organized by the PCI, they were released and expelled back to Italy. In Italy they became important actors in the denunciation of the Brazilian dictatorship and advocated ALN inside the PCI. Del Roio, "Dario Canale, um revolucionário internacionalista."

33. Guevara, *Mensaje a los pueblos del mundo*; Leibner, *Camaradas y compañeros*, 496–514.

34. Other Latin American Communists endorsed similar positions. For example, the Salvadoran Communist leader Schafik Handal favored the consideration of all methods of resistance in relation to political circumstances. See Handal, "Reflections on Continental Strategy for Latin American Revolutionaries," 24–29.

35. "Incontro con il compagno Arismendi," August 25, 1967, AFG PCI, 0546/0912.

36. See, for example, *L'Unità*'s story on Zilda Paula Xavier Pereira (Carmen), a leader of the ALN, "Il martirio del Brasile: A colloquio con una protagonista della resistenza," *L'Unità*, April 4, 1972.

37. Franco Saltarelli, "Promemoria," Rome, May 19, 1972, AFG PCI, 053/1140.

38. The normalization of relations involved an official public meeting in November 1972 between a PCB delegation and representatives of the PCI; Saltarelli was in attendance, but Sandri was not. "Incontro fra delegazioni del PC brasiliano e del PC italiano," *L'Unità*, November 13, 1972. For the new status accorded Prestes, see "La verita sul Brasile. A coloquio con Luis Carlos Prestes, segretario del Partito Comunista," *L'Unità*, August 24, 1973

39. Franco Saltarelli, "Promemoria," Rome, May 19, 1972, AFG PCI, 053/1140.

40. This argument was based on the self-criticism redacted by a dissident group from ALN that defined itself ALN-Leninist Tendency. The first document of this group, entitled "A necessary self-criticism," was translated into Italian already in August 1971, and it circulated among Italians related to solidarity with Brazilian revolutionaries. Jose dos Santos, "Una autocritica necessaria," CEDEM–ASMOB (UNESP, Sao Paulo) cx13.03.41,1/n. Saltarelli mentions that dissidence inside ALN and considered it closer to the PCI line.

41. See note 40.

42. "Grave provocazione alla Sit-Siemens di Milano," *L'Unità*, March 4, 1972.

43. See, for example, "Conferenza di stampa del sedicente Potere Operario: Aberranti posizioni di un gruppo estremista," *L'Unità*, March 22, 1972, and "Leri sera all'Università di Roma: Assemblea provocatoria di alcuni 'gruppetti,'" *L'Unità*, March 22, 1972.

44. The magazine was published bimonthly in Italy under the title *Tricontinental, Organo teorico della Segreteria Esecutiva dell'Organizzazione di Solidarietà dei Popoli d'Asia, Africa e America Latina*. In the 16–17 issue of 1969, it published an Italian translation of Marighella's *Mini-manual of the Urban Guerilla*. For more on Feltrinelli's role in disseminating the theory and actions of the new Latin American guerilla organizations, see Rey Tristán and Gracia Santos, "The Role of the Left-wing Editors on the Diffusion of the New Left Wave," 89–109.

45. In the home of the fugitive Giuseppe Saba the police found among other things leftist political literature, including a copy of a volume on the Tupamaros published by

Feltrinelli and an issue of *Tricontinental*. For communist reporting on this raid, see "Saba accusato di partecipazione agli attentati ai due tralicci," *L'Unità*, March 27, 1972.

46. Saltarelli used the term "extremist groups" to describe some of the contacts Carmen had in Rome. "Extremist groups" was the negative term the PCI coined to refer to radical left organizations. Franco Saltarelli, "Promemoria," Rome, May 19, 1972, AFG PCI, 053/1140.

47. Pappagallo, 232–233.

48. "Sallustro trovato ucciso a Buenos Aires dopo uno scontro tra soldati e raptori" and "Il comunicato dei metalmeccanici," *L'Unità*, April 11, 1972.

49. "Un'avanzata del PCI necessaria al paese," *L'Unità*, April 12, 1972.

50. "Dopo l'uccisione di Oberdan Sallustro: A chi giovano?," *L'Unità*, April 14, 1972.

51. "Today Argentina, soon Italy" was one of the many expressions of support found in the newspaper of Lotta Continua. On the impact of Sallustro case on this paper, see Gabriele Donato, 'La lotta é armata,' 297–301. For the Italian Communist paper's coverage of the Fourth International statment, see "La Schmidt avrebbe confessato di avere ucciso Sallustro," *L'Unità*, April 14, 1972.

52. The Italian Trotskyites were well informed about the Argentinian orthodox Trotskyites' split from the PRT (the party that created the ERP guerrilla) during the late 1960s, precisely as part of a harsh debate on the issue of initiating the armed struggle. See Mangiantini, Martín, *El trotskismo y el debate en torno a la lucha armada*.

53. "Pajetta: con i comunisti un modo nuovo di governare," *L'Unità*, April 15, 1972.

54. S. Porcù and S. Veccia, "Ore di ansia a Genova per il provocatorio e criminale sequestro del magistrato Sossi," *L'Unità*, April 20, 1974.

Bibliography

Amado, Jorge. *Vida de Luiz Carlos Prestes: El caballero de la esperanza*. Buenos Aires: Editorial Claridad, 1942.

Caso, Antonio, *Los subversivos. Testimonios de guerrilleros brasileros*. La Habana: Casa de las Américas, 1973.

De Almeida, Paulo Roberto. "Brasileiros na guerra civil espanhola: combatentes na luta contra o fascismo." *Revista de Sociologia e Política* no. 12 (June 1999): 35–66.

Debray, Regis. *Revolution in the Revolution?Armed struggle and political struggle in Latin America*. New York: MR Press, 1967.

Del Roio, José Luiz. "Dario Canale, um revolucionário internacionalista." Prefácio a Canale, Dario. *O surgimento da Seçao Brasileira da Internacional Comunista (1917–1928)*. São Paulo: Editorial Anita Garibaldi–Fundaçao Mauricio Grabois, 2013.

Donato, Gabriele.'La lotta é armata': Sinistra rivoluzionaria e violenza política in Italia (1969–1972). Rome: DeriveApprodi, 2014.

Ferreira, Camara J. *Carlos Marighella*. La Habana: Tricontinental, 1969.

Guevara, Ernesto. *Mensaje a los pueblos del mundo a través de la Tricontinental*. La Habana: 1967

Handal, Schafik. "Reflections on Continental Strategy for Latin American Revolutionaries." *World Marxist Review* 2, no. 4 (1968): 24–29.

Hobel, Alexander, "Pci, sinistra cattolica e politica estera (1972–1973)." *Studi Storici* Anno 51, no. 2 (April–June 2010): 403–459.

Leibner, Gerardo. *Camaradas y compañeros: Una historia política y social de los comunistas del Uruguay.* Montevideo: Trilce, 2011.

Mangiantini, Martín, *El trotskismo y el debate en torno a la lucha armada. Moreno, Santucho y la ruptura del PRT*, prólogo de Hernán Camarero, "Un debate de la izquierda revolucionaria de los '60," Buenos Aires: El Topo Blindado, 2014.

Meschiari, Alberto. *Giuliano Pajetta: Un protagonista del'900 nei ricordi dei Reggiani.* Rome: FILEF, 2007.

Neri Serneri, Simone, ed. *Verso la lotta armata. La politica della violenza nella sinistra radicale negli anni Settanta.* Bologna: Società editrice il Mulino, 2012.

Nocera, Raffaele, and Claudio Rolle, eds. *Settantatré. Cile e Italia, destini incrociati.* Napoli: Think Thanks edizioni, 2010.

Pappagallo, Onofrio. *Verso il nuovo mondo: Il PCI e l'America Latina (1945–1973).* Milan: FrancoAngeli, 2017.

Pozzetta, Andrea. "Luigi Longo e la costruzione del "nuovo internazionalismo": 1964–1969." *Storia e futuro. Rivista de storia e storiografia online*, no. 44 (June 2017).

Rey, Tristán Eduardo, and Guillermo Gracia Santos. "The Role of the Left-wing Editors on the Diffusion of the New Left Wave: The Case of Giangiacomo Feltrinelli." In *Revolutionary Violence and the New Left: Transnational Perspectives*, edited by Alberto Martín Álvarez and Eduardo Rey Tristán, 89–109. New York & London: Routledge Studies in Latin American Politics, 2017.

Santoni, Alessandro. *El comunismo italiano y la vía chilena. Los orígenes de un mito.* Santiago de Chile: RIL–USACH, 2011.

5

The Influence of Latin America's Revolutionary Left in Europe

The Role of Left-Wing Editors

EDUARDO REY TRISTÁN

Throughout history, ideas have circulated at different speeds and intensities, in different forms and through different channels, whatever their provenance (religious, political, economic, scientific, etc.), the means that were used to this end or the obstacles that they encountered, and irrespective of whether they were legal or clandestine. Depending on these circumstances, times, forms, and relationships, the actors involved, and indeed the impact of these ideas—an interest in which they themselves awakened—also had their repercussions. There are numerous examples, such as the spread of Protestantism in Europe in the sixteenth century, the Enlightenment of the eighteenth century, and the republican and liberal ideals that, around 1800, fueled the Latin American independence movements, among others. The struggle for the control of knowledge and thinking and their direct effects on organizations and mobilizations is as old as dissent in the history of mankind. Only their forms varied according to the times.[1]

In the context of political violence in the Contemporary Age, the pioneering work of David C. Rapoport[2] on its cyclic nature emphasized the importance of the forms, channels, and systems of dissemination by characterizing the waves of international violence that he himself had defined: from the use of railways, the press, and technical progress in communication by the first wave of anarchists at the end of the nineteenth century, to the Internet employed by Jihadists in the fourth wave, through the diverse forms adopted in the second and third waves.

This chapter will address all these processes in one of those cycles and in relation to one of its modes and actors: the editors of the New Left, specifically the Italian Giangiacomo Feltrinelli, the Frenchman François Maspero, the German Klaus Wagenbach, and the Swiss Nils Andersson. All four represented the political-ideological commitment of their generation deriving from specific traumatic experiences and their subsequent stance on them in the following decades.[3] Moreover, they played a key role in the dissemination of those works and ideas that fueled the thinking and mobilization of the New Left in Europe throughout the 1960s, serving as a nexus between their different components and representing the transition from antifascism and anticolonialism to liberation struggles, Third-Worldism, and revolution.

The specific analytical framework here is the third wave of international political violence, vis-à-vis that cycle of activity taking place between 1960 and 1990 which led to the birth of many political organizations that resorted to violence as a key element in their repertoire of action, in order to bring about a radical transformation of society, and which are generically known as revolutionary organizations of the New Left.[4]

The central ideas that led to the wave emerged as a result of the triumph of the Cuban Revolution in Latin America and—particularly in Europe— were heavily influenced by the Algerian Revolution, before being broadened, qualified, and enriched by events such as the Vietnam War and by different actors in the following decade. This was due to both the wave's intrinsic development and its relationship and dialogue with other key debates in the political Left at the time, such as those relating to liberation, anti-imperialism, anticolonialism, and Third-Worldism. All of which contributed to shape a basic ideological corpus that spread quickly on both sides of the Atlantic during the 1960s and gave rise to many organizations that, first in Latin America and then in Europe, defended those ideals through violence.

The aim here is to ponder the ways in which Latin American revolutionary ideas were disseminated in Europe. The literature on the wave has barely addressed this issue. Only in the past few years have two of the main channels of that process of political-ideological dissemination been defined: the journals of the New Left emerging throughout the decade on both sides of the Atlantic; and the editors to which this chapter is dedicated.

Notwithstanding the differences in their capabilities, activism, involvement, and scope, there were editors who participated, to a greater or lesser degree, in the dissemination of that ideology practically throughout Europe during the 1960s and at the beginning of the following decade. Their interest lies not only in the fact that they published the core texts of Latin American thinking and revolutionary transformation. Their educational and political backgrounds linked them to the Left's main ideas for renovation at the time, starting with the antifascism inherited from World War II, the anticolonialism surfacing as a result of the Algerian War since the 1950s, the Third-Worldism that began to take shape around the same time, anti-imperialism and, last, liberation. Further, they sometimes had personal ties, both among themselves and with the relay station—namely, Cuba—thereby creating networks that are of great interest for the study of dissemination processes of this historical period.

Miscellaneous political-ideological texts circulated through those networks, which thanks to the publishing houses of the four editors analyzed here ended up in the hands of those young people who, at the end of the decade and depending on their particular worldview and their place in it, occasionally undertook sociopolitically important organizational missions whose ultimate purpose was the socialist and revolutionary transformation of their societies through armed struggle.

Approaching these editors involves identifying the actors, channels, and forms of political-ideological dissemination at the time. This helps, in turn, to determine the rationales, importance, and roles played by both the processes *per se* and their leading actors in the study of the dissemination of ideas, in general, and in the waves of political violence, in particular.

The objective here is not to perform a detailed analysis on the endeavors of these editors or their specific roles in the dissemination of Latin American ideas in Europe from the mid-1960s. What interests us is gaining a deeper understanding of their personal and political backgrounds, with the aim of understanding the significance of the influence these had on their editorial work. In doing so, we seek to explain both the circumstances prevailing during the years in which their publishing careers took shape, the networks created and ties forged by and between them, and the essential role these factors played in their position as editors of the Latin American revolution. We thus hope, on the one hand, to gain further insights into the roles played by these "militant" editors from a more long-term perspective, in relation to their personal situations and to the most outstanding sociopolitical conflicts of the previous period; and, on the other, and in light of the former, to explore continuities in cycles of political violence, in general, and in the processes of interwave dissemination, in particular.

Political Violence and Dissemination

The waves of international political violence conceptualized by David C. Rapoport reveal the fundamental role played by dissemination processes in their evolution, namely, as basic variables either in fleshing out their ideological frameworks or in understanding a shared project that gave meaning to all of its constituents. These developed thanks to the collective contributions of the actors and their interactions, providing both crucial knowledge and training in the evolution and dimension of the cycle, such as contacts and ties between diverse groups in different regions of the world, as well as the appearance of new organizations and their links—direct or indirect, due to influence, imitation, or adaptation[5]—to existing ones.

Those relationships were either direct, through personal contacts between organizations, or indirect or mediated by cultural and political products created either by the organizations themselves or by ideologically like-minded groups or individuals. Those highly diverse products—the legal or underground publications fueling the cycle being central—were the vehicles through which ideas were transferred and discussed and evolved. This process took place both within the wave and between waves, insofar as it was accumulated knowledge on which other promoters in new cycles of activity could draw.

The study of the dissemination processes has been partially addressed by the literature on social movements. This has led, first and foremost, to the idea that dissemination is a complex and multidimensional process in which it is essential to analyze both that which is disseminated and the way in which this is achieved;[6] and, second, the identification of some of the process' key elements: that is, the context in which dissemination occurs, the messages that are conveyed, and the messengers.[7]

This chapter focuses on the latter, understanding them as those people with the ability to disseminate ideas, to transmit messages and, eventually, to connect actors in different places who had not been in contact before. My hypothesis is that the four editors of the New Left I deal with played a vital role in the dissemination process of the wave and can be identified with the figure of the political entrepreneur defined in the literature as a "connector"—the key hub in the network in terms of position, financial means, or personal traits, among other factors.[8] These editors were individuals who played a mediating role—proposed by Rebecca Givan, Kenneth Roberts, and Sarah Soule when analyzing the mechanisms through which dissemination occurs—inasmuch as they might have had direct or mediated contacts with both parties and might have partially influenced the process by participating in terms of their personal preferences, beliefs, and interests.

Even though the testimonial literature on the prime movers of that cycle of mobilization has repeatedly stressed the importance that Latin American experiences had in their education and early activism or in the initial stages of their organizations,[9] research on the editors of the European New Left has been hitherto thin on the ground. The topic was addressed by Quinn Slobodian[10] in his day and more recently in a collective work edited by Alberto Martín and Eduardo Rey.[11] This is also the case with analysis of the transnational relations in the third wave and especially the roles of Latin America, in general, and the Cuban Revolution, in particular, in the cycle of radicalization and violence of the European New Left in the wake of 1968.

To date, the only academic work that has elaborated on the role of the European editors on the basis of their political profiles and their links to the New Left has been Julien Hage's doctoral thesis. The author examined the careers of Giangiacomo Feltrinelli, François Maspero, and Klaus Wagenbach, albeit in an eminently descriptive fashion, confining himself to their private lives and to the catalogues of their publishing houses. Although drawing on what was written by and about them, he did so without associating them with the dissemination processes of the period or their role in the construction of the New Left wave.[12] Above and beyond this, only Fiammeta Balestracci[13] has shown an interest in Wagenbach as a left-wing editor and, more recently, I have also published research on the case of Feltrinelli and his role in the wave.[14]

There are indeed biographical or eyewitness accounts. Giangiacomo Feltrinelli has aroused special interest because of his life circumstances (a multimillionaire transformed into a revolutionary), his activism, his time in hiding, and, finally, his death during an act of sabotage performed by his underground group in March 1972. His two biographies were written by Aldo Grandi[15] and his son Carlo Feltrinelli.[16] Thanks to these works, we are familiar with the most important episodes of his life, even though they are more descriptive than interpretive and belong more to the biographical genre, understood either as an account of events and life circumstances or as a characterization and understanding of a unique historical figure.

Although Feltrinelli appears in practically all of the works dealing with the Years of Lead in Italy,[17] more than anything else these offer anecdotal information on his beginnings, are lacking in depth, and do not pinpoint him as a political-ideological catalyst through his publishing career and his subsequent underground activities.[18] This implies not fully recognizing the role that he played in the process of violence in Italy during the first years of the 1970s.

In the case of François Maspero, Klaus Wagenbach, and Nils Andersson there are memoirs and personal accounts relating to their lives and publishing activities.[19] Andersson's career was also analyzed in François Valloton's work on his Swiss publishing house La Cité Éditeur (1958–1967).[20] Besides this, his catalogues and personal archives, whose access is restricted due to their confidential nature, are also interesting sources.

In the following pages we will explore the central topic of this chapter through the four editors and their publishing activities, with an eye to gaining insights into their personal and professional profiles and the networks they established, all central to interpreting their role in the wave's dissemination. The chapter argues that both their initial and later personal pursuits contributed to shape their subsequent political stances and editorial lines; on the basis of which, they played a key role in the thinking of the nascent New Left in Europe, representing the transition from antifascism and anticolonialism to liberation struggles, Third-Worldism, and revolution.

The Editors

The four editors shared what Karl Mannheim called "generational unity"— that is, they were individuals born around the same time: Giangiacomo Feltrinelli in 1927, Klaus Wagenbach in 1930, François Maspero in 1932, and Nils Andersson in 1933. As such, they participated in the social currents of the moment and "agitated together."[21] Since they lived at the same time, they had similar life experiences as regards the major events marking the period, albeit with certain differences. The key is World War II. First, because of the personal experiences and traumas to which the conflict gave rise. Second, because it shaped the antifascist identity of some of them (chiefly Maspero and, to a lesser extent, Feltrinelli), which would later expedite their shift toward anticolonialism through the Algerian conflict.[22] And last, insofar as it was the onset of a different time marked by the conflict between blocs, the Cold War and decolonization processes. All of which would be crucial to shaping their personal stories, to influencing their ideological predispositions, and, of course, to understanding the political stances that they took both personally and professionally, with all the connotations and consequences that this would entail.

The childhood of Giangiacomo Feltrinelli, heir to one of the major fortunes in Italy at the time, was marked (when he was nine) first of all by the early death of his father in 1935 and then by the outbreak of World War II. His mother isolated the family as a way of softening the impact of the war, which led, in turn, to the absence of spaces of socialization and education during his adolescence. Even so, during the last months of the conflict, Feltrinelli managed to join a group of partisans and, once it was over, the Italian Communist Party (PCI), with which he would maintain a stormy relationship during the following decade. The resistance, the insurgent struggles that this represented, and antifascism would be constants in both his personal life and professional career as an editor.[23]

François Maspero, the offspring of a French family of intellectuals, suffered personally during the conflict, due to the changes, journeying, and deprivations, and, above all, to the death of his father and brother at the hands of the Nazis, the former in a concentration camp (where his mother managed to survive) and the latter in the resistance, in which both were active. His memoirs record the trauma experienced and the shadow that it cast over the rest of his life, evinced in his quest for information, understanding and perpetuating the memory of his father, his brother, and the struggle they had represented.[24] His antifascism and sympathy for those nations striving to cast off their colonial yokes (deriving from his experiences in occupied France and inevitable for those who had defended certain principles there) would also be a lifelong stance.

Klaus Wagenbach came from a conspicuously Christian Democratic and anti-Nazi middle-class family.[25] His childhood was also marked by the war, which subsequently altered his life, education, and travels, while generating fear and uncertainty. The vicissitudes in Berlin during the Cold War, the division of Germany, and the direct legacy of the conflict in his country, especially in his hometown, would be key aspects later on in his personal life and publishing career. Although his left-wing inclinations were inseparable from the course that his life took, his political sympathies cannot be attributed in such an unequivocal fashion to harrowing experiences, as was the case with Maspero and Feltrinelli.

Nils Andersson's story is more unusual. Although his family was of Swedish extraction, he was born in Switzerland, a relevant issue since it meant he was not a Swiss national, something that in the 1960s would lead to his being expelled for his publishing and political activities. With respect to World War II, and as indicated in his memoirs,[26] since Switzerland's neutrality isolated him from the rigors of the conflict, his childhood would always be an albeit distant touchstone for him. His political activism, which began in his adolescence, would be associated with communism.

The legacy of these individuals' childhoods, the war, and the ordeals they all experienced as a result, except perhaps in the case of Nils Andersson, was antifascism. Even though this stance was not fully developed during their youth, the conflict undoubtedly marked their lives and is essential for understanding their postwar political positions which, incidentally, were not that exceptional for their generation.

Except for Klaus Wagenbach, the other three editors would take fairly similar political stances, becoming linked in one way or another to communism. This was especially the case with Giangiacomo Feltrinelli, who became involved at an earlier age and whose activism would be more long term, having been a full-fledged member of the PCI since 1948, as well as the financial backer of the party and some of its key cultural projects at the time.[27] For their part, Maspero's and Andersson's involvement was more peripheral. The former briefly belonged to the French Communist Party (PCF) (1955–1958) and, sometime later, was associated with the Revolutionary Communist League (LCR) (1969–1974), although his activism had more to do with his thinking and relations than with past events.

Nils Andersson became involved in communist youth organizations at the beginning of the 1950s, resulting in his participation in the organization (Swiss committee) and staging of major international communist youth festivals (Bucharest 1953, Moscow 1957). All in all, neither he nor François Maspero—barring a few months—were remarkably active in local communist movements. Later on, they would share certain sympathies for Maoism (especially strong in the case of Andersson), with which they became involved in one way or another through their respective publishing houses in the 1960s, inasmuch as they published its texts after the Sino-Soviet controversy at the beginning of the decade, driven more by their desire to air ideas and debates than by their strict defense of the Chinese cause.[28]

Klaus Wagenbach's political background was different, as were the postwar context and the mainstream debates in Germany. In the mid-1950s, he became involved in socialism through his active participation in the Socialist German Student Union (SDS), the then youth organization of the Social Democratic Party of Germany (SPD). He collaborated with the SPD in the 1965 campaign, drumming up support among writers and intellectuals.[29] Henceforth, he began to drift toward the New Left,[30] participating in some of the key events in its evolution and becoming acquainted with many of those who were destined to play leading roles either in politics (such as

Rudi Dutschke, whose editor he was) or in the underground (such as Gudrun Ensslin and Ulrike Meinhof, who went on to join the German Red Army Faction [RAF]). In 1968 he participated in the International Vietnam Congress, held in West Berlin, a key event for the German New Left at the time, which was also attended by Giangiacomo Feltrinelli (one of the event's financial sponsors) and François Maspero.[31]

The political development that had the greatest impact on the lives and intellectual and publishing activities of three of the four editors—the exception being Wagenbach—was the Algerian War as the culmination of the decolonization processes that had got under way back in 1945. Their stances were the logical consequence of their ingrained antifascism and their experiences during World War II. For Feltrinelli and Maspero, a crucial idea was the liberation of territories "occupied" (both physically and ideologically) by fascism, understood as a struggle against the restrictions on political, cultural, or intellectual freedom imposed by the occupying powers, which implied taking a stance against colonization. They were also years in which the Third-Worldism concept took shape, which would be gradually fleshed out during the 1950s and which would be equally present in the publishing and political activities of the four editors.

This transition from resistance and antifascism to anticolonialism, liberation, Third-Worldism, and, ultimately, revolution was not unique to those four editors, as can be clearly observed in the lives of many other activists at the time. Many were those who trod a similar path, including Francis Jeanson,[32] Henri Curiel,[33] and Adolfo Kaminsky,[34] among others. The activism of the first two began during World War II, after which they soon became involved in solidarity with Algeria and in creating support networks, which would be gradually extended to other struggles as some conflicts came to an end and others broke out. Kaminsky, for instance, began his career in the underground as a forger of documents during the war, something he would continue to do altruistically in all those conflicts that he regarded as popular liberation struggles, until the end of the 1960s.

It is remarkable that not only did they tread similar paths, to a greater or lesser extent, and defend some or other cause depending on the circumstances, but they also formed part of the same sphere of occasionally underground activity, ties that can only be understood in terms of a similar way of interpreting their time on the basis of a common political-ideological position. Therefore, their experiences, as with the ideas that drove and united them, can be understood only in the historical context and time in which they lived. As with many of their contemporaries, the four editors were the product of their times with professional links to or close ties with the aforementioned networks and activists, and can thus be considered (especially Maspero and Andersson) to have more or less formed part of them.

The Algerian issue was a major milestone in their careers both for those who had experienced World War II and for others who, because of their age or for other reasons, had not suffered its brunt, such as Andersson and, for that matter, many other activists at the time who championed the anticolonial and Third World cause as a result of the mobilization against the Algerian War.

In the case at hand, this conflict also served as a catalyst: it was behind the creation of Maspero's and Andersson's publishing houses and would be very present in the one already established by Feltrinelli who, owing to the conflict in Algeria, had made the acquaintance of the Frenchman and the Swiss. By and large, it was what forged and strengthened the ties between the three editors, as can be seen in their personal memoirs and biographies. However, this was not the case with Klaus Wagenbach, who launched his publishing house in 1965, when Algeria had already obtained independence, insofar as neither his biographical details nor his prior experience in publishing reveal any relation to the conflict.

The Publishing Houses

Feltrinelli established his publishing house (Giangiacomo Feltrinelli Editore, GFE) in 1955, after starting out in the cultural sphere in publishing projects linked to the PCI at the end of the 1940s. The first two books he published were clear declarations of intent: *Il flagello della svastica* by the Englishman Edward F.L. Russell, dealing with the Nazi atrocities with which the author was familiar due to his participation in the British courts that had judged them; and *Autobiografía*, the autobiography of the Indian politician Jawaharlal Nehru, the premier of the country's first independent government and one of the founders and leaders of the Non-Aligned Movement (NAM).

They were books that, in the words of Feltrinelli, represented the three principal lines that, thenceforth, would become the publishing house's leitmotif: a consistent and coherent antifascism; the quest for peaceful coexistence among countries with different economic and political structures; and attention to the new forces emerging in the Third World as a result of colonial domination, which sought to insert themselves forcefully into the global political system. In short, an editorial line that broke with those (liberal, Catholic, or Marxist) prevailing in Italian publishing houses at the time, seeking a somewhat heretic mixture that offered a more comprehensive and encyclopedic overview of human activity in which there was room for literature, politics, philosophy, and scientific knowledge.[35]

Antifascism would be a constant in the GFE's catalogue during the following decade. The Third-Worldism (anticolonialist and anti-imperialist at the same time) that Nehru's work represented could not have been more timely and offers us clues about the editor's relationship with his time: the year in which the Bandung Conference was held, the first tentative steps toward the subsequent creation of the NAM, and the outbreak of the Algerian War of Independence (at the end of 1954). If its first books can be understood as reflections of its mission statement in a field already dominated by other actors, the GFE sought to identify with specific political traditions and local struggles and other revolutionary movements abroad: a commitment to new topics, to current debates, and to offering like-minded readers a new stimulus. It did not intend to be just another publishing house.

Algeria would be omnipresent in the GFE's catalogue during the following years: the first book to be published was precisely by Francis and Colette Jeanson (*Algeria fuorilegge*, 1955), both advocates of the Algerian cause in France and key actors in the first networks supporting the North African country. Two other books by Francis Jeanson were published in 1962, one in French for its underground distribution, because it had been banned in France.[36] For the GFE, Algeria was a subject of interest in a broader rationale of knowledge of the prevailing reality, especially in relation to the Third World and liberation struggles. For Éditions François Maspero and La Cité Éditeur (Andersson), in contrast, Algeria would be their principal raison d'être. The advent of both of them cannot be understood outside the context of the Algerian War and, in the case of the latter, it probably would not have existed without it.

Nils Andersson opened the bookshop La Cité in Lausanne in 1957 with the aim of disseminating French literature in French-speaking Switzerland, given the limited scope of Parisian publishing houses in the country and its cultural dependence on France. There was precisely a dearth of the avant-garde literature edited by some publishing houses such as Éditions de Minuit (a non-communist, left-wing, resistance publishing house established during World War II), the unconventional publishing house of Jean-Jacques Pauvert and L'Arche, a French publishing house par excellence specializing in theater, one of Andersson´s greatest passions. In March 1957, he visited all three to conclude agreements with them to distribute their works in Switzerland, after which he opened his bookshop.[37]

It was that relationship with those three Parisian editors, and particularly with Jérôme Lindon (Minuit), that led Andersson to establish his own publishing house two years later. Since 1957 Lindon had begun to publish works on the war and the French repression in Algeria which could not be published in the press given the increasingly more restrictive legislation. Books, which still were not directly affected by the censorship, became yet again, as during World War II, a means of denunciation, criticism, and political instruction. After the publication of the first book in this vein in 1957,[38] in February 1958 Lindon published Henri Alleg's *La Question*, a new account of repression and torture, in this case of a well-known communist journalist with a long intellectual career. The stir caused by the book— which followed in the footsteps of other similar works—the allegations against French operations in Algeria, the intellectual mobilisation, and its huge sales in just a few weeks, led the authorities to ban it. Accordingly, Lindon asked Andersson whether it would be possible for some other colleague to publish it in Switzerland as a way of circumventing the ban.

Andersson himself undertook the task, which posed the challenge of launching his own publishing house starting with Alleg's work, prefaced by a text by Jean-Paul Sartre that had also been censored. In his own words, La Cité Éditeur arose from the need to reject censorship and prohibitions.[39] Until its forced closure in 1967, after Andersson's deportation from Switzerland for his political and cultural activities (which compromised the country's neutrality according to the authorities), La Cité Éditeur had published thirty-eight books in all. Algeria would take pride of place in its catalogue, especially during the initial years. The other two central topics would be Maoism, which had nothing to do with a clear-cut ideological stance but with divulging another version of the Sino-Soviet controversy, an issue that had disappeared from the shelves of communist bookshops; and theater, although from an equally political and revolutionary perspective.[40]

François Maspero's publishing career was similar to Andersson's, although it commenced earlier. In 1955 he opened La Joie de Lire, a bookshop that would soon become the principal benchmark of political publishing in Paris in the second half of the 1950s. And in 1959, at the same time as his Swiss colleague, he established the publishing house bearing his own name: Éditions François Maspero. The first book to be published, *La Guerre d'Espagne*, by the Italian socialist and international brigade member Pietro Nenni, also revolved around antifascism, although the main theme during the initial years would yet again be Algeria, a burning issue in France at the time and the main topic of all intellectual and political debates.[41]

Maspero's intention as a publisher and, therefore, his editorial line was unquestionably political and grounded in the idea of commitment, in "taking sides": his stated intention was not to publish poetry, but books offering accounts of conflicts. His generation was being sent to fight in Algeria and, as an editor and bookseller, he took sides with those opposing it, as he himself testified in court on the networks supporting the Algerian cause in 1961.[42] It was a question of using testimonies to disclose, decry, and reject the indignity of the colonial war and to give voice to the France showing solidarity with the Algerian cause and opposing the occupation.

Between 1960 and 1962 some fifteen books published by Maspero were seized for jeopardizing state security, for questioning the morality of the army, for slander, or for inciting disobedience or desertion. As can be deduced from his memoirs, he soon became a freewheeler. He was not a member of any party, did not have any training or previous experience in the publishing industry, and published what he liked, and, if it were seized, would republish it. His bookshop was attacked several times, and he established ties with networks supporting the Algerian cause and with those European editors with similar inclinations. In a catalogue almost completely monopolized by the Algerian issue during the initial years, after publishing Frantz Fanon's *Les Damnés de la Terre*, prefaced by Sartre (April 1962), he also became a "Third World" editor. In 1961 he had begun to publish the writings of Fidel Castro, followed soon afterward by those of Ernesto Guevara and other works relating to the Latin American revolutionary struggles, which in the following years would bring him in line with the central topics of political debate in the New Left.

Klaus Wagenbach's career commenced very differently—and also later, since he established his publishing house in West Berlin in 1964—as it was unrelated to antifascism or the Algerian War. In 1949 he had started to work as a reader at Fischer, one of the leading German publishing houses at the time, where he learned the trade. After he was sacked in 1963, he decided to open his own publishing house in order to accomplish the idea for which he had lost his job at Fisher: the commitment to supporting and publishing the works of authors of the German Democratic Republic (GDR) as a way of bridging the cultural gap between the two Germanys. This proposal was reflected in the first books that he published: on the one hand, two prose works by literary figures on both sides of the Wall; and, on the other, three books written by members of Group 47 (with which he had close personal ties, including the already popular writer Günter Grass), who thus showed their support for the new publishing house. In its early years, the publishing house would focus on avant-garde German literature and new authors appearing in the GDR, and on rescuing those who had been absent since the end of the war.[43]

Wagenbach's personal background and development differed from those of the other three editors, his initial publishing pursuits being of a local nature focusing on literary renovation on the basis of a new understanding of the German situation stemming from the war. In his milieu it was a revolutionary mission statement, especially with regard to the defense of East German writers and the intended dialogue. It was not until some years later, in 1968, that Wagenbach's editorial line and his role as an editor would coincide with those of Feltrinelli and Maspero. In that case it would be his leftist inclinations—above and beyond any personal ties—that would be the driving force behind his professional career, to such an extent that the conservative press contemptuously called his publishing house the "Baader-Meinhof-Verlag."[44]

Networks, Commitment, and Activism

In view of the above, a crucial assumption can be deduced for the analysis proposed here: the four editors, in addition to others, maintained close ties during those years. Albeit normal in a business context, their relationship went beyond purely professional matters. And, just as they exchanged works, copyrights, author contacts, etc., so, too, did they all maintain similar relations with other editors, who are not in themselves noteworthy. What is of real interest are the reasons behind those relations and their peculiarities.

In this respect, the key lies in the idea of commitment noted by Maspero: people who became committed to one or several causes and pursued their professional careers in terms of these.[45] From this perspective, the relationships between them acquire a new dimension. More than a business activity, theirs was dedicated activism undertaken and transmitted through the professional sphere.

That activism should not be understood in the usual strict sense of the word, that is, in the context of an organization. The four editors, except at certain moments, did not actively participate in political groups, but developed another kind of activism through their commitment to certain causes from a left-wing political-ideological position. The affinity between them was either in a strict or broad sense. An example of this is Maspero's involvement in the Algerian cause, specifically his support for it from an unambiguous perspective of anticolonization, antifascism, and liberation of peoples. But once independence had been achieved, he neither remained linked to it nor liked its drift,[46] and his attention turned to other causes grounded in similar principles.

It is in this sense that we should understand the role played by Feltrinelli, Maspero, Wagenbach, and Andersson (before his expulsion from Switzerland in 1967) until becoming the main editors of the New Left in their respective countries. In their political and publishing activities there were two binding elements: Algeria during the initial stages, which is fundamental to explaining their individual personalities and the ties between them; and Cuba and the revolutionary movement as from the middle of the decade and, primarily, in relation to the most radical activism of the New Left in the wake of 1968.

Andersson and Maspero entered the publishing world because of the Algerian cause. As their biographies and Julien Hage's research both bear out, the exchange of works on Algeria for their sale in their respective bookshops and the Swiss edition of those works seized in France for their underground distribution were both customary practices. They were not only united by their personal contact, which in their case began at the end of the 1950s,[47] but also drew on the underground networks supporting the Algerian cause. The leaders of those networks—Francis Jeanson, Henri Curiel, and Georges Mattei, to name but a few—are mentioned time and again in their memoirs. These people supplied them with most of the texts that they published, including the controversial testimonies of torture and repression with which they scandalized French society at the end of the 1950s. It can be claimed that Maspero and Andersson, together with Jérôme Lindon, were the "officious" publishers of the Algerian cause in France and Europe at the time.

This was confirmed in 1961 when Maspero founded the journal *Partisans*, on whose editorial board Andersson sat. *Partisans'* mission statement left no room for doubt, namely, that of championing democracy, the legal status of individuals and races, liberation from all forms of oppression and alienation, and the socialist revolution; confronting fascists, racists, and colonists; and defending the liberation of the last colonies, with an accent on the Algerian Revolution.[48]

There was room for all of this in the journal's pages, as plainly evinced by its first number: articles on the Cuban Revolution and its path to socialism

(Raúl Castro and Nicolás Guillén), on the Kurdish issue (Gerard Chaliand, also a member of the editorial board), and on the Algerian Revolution (a number of French and Algerian authors). Through *Partisans* Maspero and Andersson would progress toward supporting the national liberation struggles in Latin America and Africa. The nexus between the two editors was anticolonialism and their definition of the situation in Latin America as neocolonial, which in practice juxtaposed it with Africa.

Last, it should be noted that it was Andersson who, in 1963, convinced Maspero to publish Chinese texts, insofar as he had already begun to do so because of his commitment to promoting voices censured for political reasons (in this case, the communists in Moscow's orbit) and for their support for colonized nations, national liberation struggles, and all those who defended that line.[49] And although it is true that Andersson ended up becoming an active Maoist sympathizer, this can be understood as a result of his knowledge of Chinese ideas through his publishing work. This was not the case with Maspero, who published the texts because the French communists censured them and because that was the raison d'être of his publishing house: to overcome censorship and to familiarize his potential readership with all existing political currents. His commitment, one might say, was to political and ideological publishing freedom, rather than to a specific cause.

Feltrinelli became acquainted with Maspero and Andersson during the period of the Algerian War, a subject on which he became a leading authority in Italy at the time, probably thanks to the texts that he received from his colleagues and the aforementioned support networks. Thus, at the beginning of the 1960s we can speak of the existence of a publishing triangle advocating for the Algerian cause formed by Paris, Milan, and Lausanne. That relationship was what led to, for example, a joint publication by Andersson and Feltrinelli in 1961,[50] the assistance that the Italian lent Maspero in circumventing censorship,[51] and their collaboration—occasional at least in the case of Andersson—in offering refuge to those persecuted for their support for the Algerian cause in Northern Italy.[52]

On the other hand, however, the GFE was a commercial publishing house, with a very broad catalogue in which most of its publications had nothing to do with political causes, as was indeed the case with Andersson[53] and Maspero.[54] This opened it up to other spheres, spaces, and relations inherent to the day-to-day running of a publishing house. As a result, in 1962 Feltrinelli came in contact with Wagenbach, still employed as a reader at Fisher, who traveled to Milan accompanied by Günter Grass, who had published *The Tin Drum* with Feltrinelli that same year. That first contact did not occur in any political context, but in a strictly literary and publishing one, as with their next encounter at the 1965 edition of the Frankfurt Book Fair, where Feltrinelli graciously put him in touch with many colleagues and people relevant to his recently launched publishing career.

That was the start of a relationship on which the existing sources do not offer any details, but which was surely intense. As from the mid-1960s Feltrinelli established contacts with the most radical sectors of the Berlin left, with whom Wagenbach was also associated and whose editor he was; he was a friend of Rudi Dutschke, whose works would be published later by Wagenbach, had contacts with small groups, which would subsequently lead to the armed factions, and participated in the Vietnam Congress, held in West Berlin in 1968.[55] They were milieus and spaces in which in all likelihood they met or had ties that went beyond the purely personal and professional relations to be expected during the Italian's trips to Berlin. There remaoins the unanswered question as to the exchange of books and authors and the extent to which they both drew on radical left-wing literature as from 1968, when both published the texts of their respective student movements and extra-parliamentary groups, and when Feltrinelli was already distributing many works on Latin America stemming from the Cuban Revolution throughout Europe.

Their last encounter took place in 1971, when Feltrinelli had already gone underground. In addition, it was Wagenbach, who, in 1972, gave the funeral address at his burial in Milan's Monumental Cemetery.[56] Moreover, it should be noted that he was one of the few editors who dared to attend their friend's funeral.

The Role of Cuba

Cuba was, as from the mid-1960s, the last reference central to this analysis. In a sense, it took up the place held by Algeria until 1962, not only as a main publishing topic and popular cause, but also as a touchstone in the political debate of the New Left and the publications that fueled it. As the 1960s progressed, the Cuban Revolution was interpreted as a process of independence from an imperialist power; it also served as a benchmark for Latin American popular causes by providing a new strategy for liberation and achieving socialism. It therefore became the driving force behind the region's imaginary and, at an international level, picked up where the Algerian cause had left off.

In the most radical sectors of the New Left, all those major political ideas, which years before had shaped its discourse and were now mature by the end of the 1960s, converged: antifascism, a term now applied in a more generic and sweeping fashion than in the postwar years and which would soon be employed to refer to all antidictatorial stances in Latin America; neocolonialism, which, in the discourse of the Latin American New Left, did not refer to the lack of political independence of nations, but to their effective dependence given the international geopolitical and economic climate; anti-imperialism which, following on from the above, referred to the United States and was enmeshed with the criticism against the United States for its military operations in Vietnam, among other things, as a reflection of the discourse of the German radical left in 1968, for instance; the liberation vindicated as a result of the former, the dependence of Latin American countries, and the imperialist domination of the United States in the region; and Third-Worldism, an idea that had emerged in the previous decade in relation to ongoing processes of decolonization and the new geopolitical world order, including Latin America (in the context of decolonized but dependent and dominated territories) and which would be crucial in the 1960s. This last idea also reshaped the forms of struggle employed by European revolutionaries who no longer focused only on their own countries but perceived their own struggles as a way of collaborating with the global revolution—whose epicenter would be located in the Third World—undermining the structures of imperialism and capitalism in the cities.[57]

To all this must be added the ultimate cause, relating to revolution, the major contribution of Cuba and Latin America during the period. By and large, it was championed by all the sectors of the New Left, albeit with differences of opinion as to the revolutionary strategy to be implemented and the role that violence should play in it. The gradual relegation of the concept of "revolution" to armed conflict, upheld and defended by Cuban theoreticians first and foremost, encouraged certain militant sectors to consider its use as a means of achieving that objective, which would have an impact on both Latin America as from the beginning of the 1960s and Europe following 1968.

All these ideas were present in the catalogues of the editors analyzed here, except for Andersson who had to close La Cité Éditeur after his deportation from Switzerland in 1967, just when it was being taken up by European publishers. But, at the time, it was not merely a question of publishing Latin American, especially Cuban, political works. This was already being done by several editors, given the public interest in developments in the region and in some of the leading revolutionary figures, such as Ernesto Guevara. The difference between them here lay in their involvement in the cause, their commitment, and their activism. They became, one might say, the editors of the Cuban Revolution and the Latin American Revolutionary Left in Europe, above all Feltrinelli and Maspero and, to a lesser extent, Wagenbach who received the texts from the former and, as before, was conditioned by the local idiosyncrasies of Berlin.

Both Maspero and Feltrinelli traveled to Cuba and experienced the revolution early on. Maspero made his first trip in 1962, possibly through the contacts already established by some of his close friends with Sartre. As a left-wing editor and representative of activist commitment (to Algeria) at the time, it is reasonable to believe that feelings were mutual. Feltrinelli first traveled to the island at the end of 1963, invited by the Cubans, with a view to editing the memoirs of Fidel Castro in the Sierra Maestra. Henceforth, both would make frequent trips to Havana, particularly from 1965. They attended all the major international political events of the revolution—the Tricontinental Conference in 1966,[58] the first conference of the Organization of Latin American Solidarity (OLAS) in 1967, and the Cultural Conference of Habana in 1968—as well as making many personal trips, albeit for political reasons.[59]

The two editors were present at the ceremonies commemorating the revolution held in July 1967 and, in the following weeks, fully aware of Guevara's dire situation and the first arrests of members of his guerrilla group (including the French intellectual Regis Debray, an author of Maspero and Feltrinelli, alike), both traveled (separately) to Bolivia at the request of the Cuban intelligence. Maspero made two trips, the first a direct assignment according to his memoirs, to familiarize himself with the situation in Bolivia; and the second to lend Debray moral support at his trial, although he was expelled from the country before he had time to see him.[60]

In August 1967 Feltrinelli also traveled to Bolivia to lend Debray his support soon after his arrest, although doubt was cast on the underlying reasons behind his trip; he was also arrested and expelled by the local authorities.[61] At any rate, none of these trips appear to have been coincidental. It was not only the altruistic support of an editor for his author in a predicament, but the odds are that, as Maspero himself implies, they had acted hand in hand with the Cuban intelligence, well aware of the plight of "Che," whose presence in the country would be confirmed soon afterward, in September, leading to the manhunt that ended on October 8.[62]

As editors, Maspero and Feltrinelli had been in contact since the beginning of the decade in relation to the Algerian cause. We know from Cuban sources that they both met again in Havana in June 1968, after they had been summoned, together with the Mexican Arnaldo Orfila (Siglo XXI ediciones), to prepare the international edition of Che Guevara's *The Bolivian Diary*, secretly obtained by the Cubans a few weeks before. Within a few days, they translated the text into their respective languages and, after returning home, published it immediately, for fear that a falsified version would be circulated by the United States beforehand.[63]

The publication of Guevara's work in July 1968 was a bombshell for the facts it included, his persona, and his experiences. Thousands of copies were sold in both countries and, further, Feltrinelli took it upon himself to make it available to any left-wing editor who requested it, such as Rob van Gennep in Holland (who published the first Dutch edition almost immediately) and Wagenbach.[64]

From that moment on, Maspero and Feltrinelli became the publishers of the Cuban Revolution in Europe.[65] Their catalogues would be partially dedicated to the publication of a substantial amount of Cuban and Latin American literature, particularly in the heyday of the region's guerrilla groups in the Southern Cone. In fact, a simple tally of the works by Latin American authors, or those dealing with Latin America, in the catalogues of Maspero, Feltrinelli, and Wagenbach reveals that they were more qualitative than quantitative. In no event did they account for more than 5 percent of the production of the three publishing houses since the year of their founding until 1980. Most important was the significance of books that were published. In this respect, the editors led the field in the publication of Cuban works, including those written by the island's leadership and those relating to the revolutionary proposals emerging there, plus their re-edition time and again during the aforementioned period. The most prominent author was Che Guevara, followed by Fidel Castro.[66] Feltrinelli launched specific collections,[67] published at a loss (i.e., sales didn't cover expenses) and assumed the dissemination of that subject matter as a political obligation, even more so at a moment when he was drifting toward revolutionary activity, a cause for which he would die prematurely in March 1972 while preparing a covert act of sabotage.

Moreover, both were editors of the journal *Tricontinental* (the French and Italian editions of the Cuban internationalist journal). In Maspero's catalogue, the Latin American revolutionary movements were also present through the writings of their main leaders and organizations (Che

Guevara, Regis Debray, Carlos Marighella, OLAS, Fidel Castro, Ricardo Ramírez, Douglas Bravo, etc., many of whom were also published by Feltrinelli, without our knowing as yet how these works circulated among them), an activity that led to different proceedings being initiated against him.[68]

Feltrinelli's death in 1972, the Cuban Revolution's move toward Soviet orthodoxy, and the financial straits of the publishing houses of Maspero and Wagenbach, among other factors, undermined the role played hitherto by the four editors. Maspero would close his publishing house a few years later and, as the decade progressed, Wagenbach would change tack.

Conclusions

Feltrinelli, Maspero, Wagenbach, and Andersson were unique editors of their time and key actors in the process of disseminating thinking and ideology in the context of the New Left in the 1960s. Due to space limitations, we have not been able to examine their catalogues in further detail or perform a more in-depth analysis of their publishing activities in 1968 and the following years, when their endeavors were crucial to promoting the New Left. Our primary aim has been to focus on their careers, to understand their stances and roles as editors, and to investigate an issue that has become a staple of studies of the cyclic dimension of the waves of violence: the transfers and bridges between waves which, we sense, were vital as regards the forms of dissemination employed, among other factors.

They were all remarkable editors given what they represented at the time. Looking at the figures, the reader could be forgiven for thinking that our object of study has been blown out of proportion. As they themselves admit in their memoirs (especially Maspero), their contribution to the publishing scene, in percentage terms, was minimal, except in the case of Feltrinelli. In this regard, Andersson's was an extreme case, when taking into account that La Cité Éditeur published no more than thirty-eight books in a decade, a ridiculous figure for a major publishing house even for shorter periods. On the other hand, it should be borne in mind that they were not the only ones who published certain topics or authors, as was the case with Che Guevara and those books dealing with the Latin American revolutionary movements, which were published by several non-leftist publishing houses for intrinsically commercial reasons.[69]

In light of this, we understand that what is relevant to our object of study is not the quantitative but the qualitative dimension. These editors accomplished, more or less, two key objectives: on the one hand, they represented the political-ideological commitment of part of their generation, given their painful experiences during the previous decades. Taking a specific stance against occupation or repression and torture, as was the case with Algeria, was no coincidence. The memory of World War II, the German occupation, the struggle of the resistance and its human consequences were used to interpret what was happening in Algeria. It was an inevitable correlation, a juxtaposition of situations, which on the other hand leads us to believe that the 1960s, especially in France, cannot be properly understood without those prior experiences. It is therefore no twist of fate that it was precisely in France that certain ideas, positions, or activist and solidarity networks developed, which would then be extended to new causes and would be crucial to the international scope of the New Left wave. In a way and for activities of a certain type, this had its epicenter in Paris, even though it seems that recent research has only just begun to recognize this and to gain a deeper understanding of those elements that made it possible.

Further, the four editors made a vast amount of thinking and knowledge available to potential activists, which, depending on the circumstances, might have influenced the decisions made by different individuals and groups. Obviously, this second stage did not concern them, but the political-ideological evolution of the New Left would not have been possible, at least to extent to which it was achieved, without the publication and distribution of most of the literature that passed through their hands.

As from the end of the 1950s, their endeavors fueled debates, cultivated thinking, or eventually influenced policymakers, while contributing at the same time to build, thanks to all this, the grand ideas with which a sector of the population interpreted the world surrounding them and interacted with it. Thus, through the activities of these editors—among many other elements—there was a transition from antifascism and anticolonialism to liberation struggles, Third-Worldism, and the possibility of revolution. A gradual interpretation of those times and their sociopolitical conflicts is key to explaining a decade of mobilization that ended in the crowning momento of conflict at the end of the sixties. In the long term, this would in turn bring about a profound global political, ideological, and social revival.

That was not the responsibility of the four editors; it would have been too much of a task. But their activities were unquestionably central to the process of political-ideological dissemination, without which it is impossible to understand the mobilizations, the organizations, the plans for renovation or even revolution in the sixties and the early seventies.

Notes

1. On the dissemination and transfer of ideas, see Goodwin and Holley, eds., *The Transfer of Ideas*; Bickerton and Proud, eds., *The Transmission of Culture in Western Europe*.

2. Rapoport, "Modern Terror: The Four Waves." For a more recent review of his theory and central ideas, see Rapoport, "Reflections on the Third or New Left Wave: 17 Years Later."

3. The Dutchman Rob van Gennep and the Spaniard Jorge Herralde, among others, played similar roles in their respective countries, although they have not been included here given the existence of studies of the publishing activities of the former and the particularities of those of the latter in Francoist Spain.

4. Martín and Rey, eds., *Revolutionary Violence and the New Left*.

5. Martín and Rey, "La oleada revolucionaria latinoamericana contemporánea, 1959–1996."

6. Givan, Roberts and Soule, "The Dimensions of Diffusion. Introduction."

7. Gupta, "Waves of International Terrorism. An Explanation of the Process by which Ideas Flood the World."

8. Gupta, "Waves of International Terrorism," 33.

9. Rey and Gracia, "The Role of the Left-wing Editors on the Diffusion of the New Left Wave: The Case of Giangiacomo Feltrinelli."

10. Slobodian, *Foreign Front: Third World Politics in Sixties West Germany*.

11. Martín and Rey, *Revolutionary Violence and the New Left*.

12. Hage, "Feltrinelli, Maspero, Wagenbach: une nouvelle génération d'éditeurs politiques d'extrême gauche en Europe occidentale, 1955–1982."

13. Balestracci, "Klaus Wagenbach und die italienische Literatur in der Bundesrepublik Deutschland 1964–1989."

14. Rey and Gracia, "Role of the Left-wing Editors."

15. Grandi, *Giangiacomo Feltrinelli. La dinastía, il rivoluzionario*.

16. Feltrinelli, *Senior Service*.

17. This had been the case since the beginning of the 1970s, when his actions and death gave rise to differences of opinion on his figure. For an example, see Mattioli, *Morte a Segrate*; Punzo et al., *L'affare Feltrinelli*; Duflot, *Feltrinelli. Le condottiere rouge;* Viola, "Requisitoria Feltrinelli"; Sterling, *The Terror Network*; Angelo Ventura, "Il problema delle origini del terrorismo di sinistra."

18. Cfr. Ruggiero, *Dossier Brigate Rosse 1969–1975*; Scavino, "La piazza e la forza"; Terhoeven, "Germania e Italia nel 'decennio rosso." Feltrinelli also appears in part of the literature on the German Years of Lead, owing to his relationship with Rudi Dutschke and other young people who during those years went underground (Cfr. Kraushaar, *Rudi Dutschke, Andreas Baader und die RAF*.)

19. Maspero, *Les abeilles & la guêpe*; Wagenbach; *La libertà dell'editore. Memorie, discorsi, stoccate*; Nils Andersson, *Mémoire Éclatée*.

20. Valloton, *Livre et Militantisme. La Cité Editeur, 1958–1967*.

21. Mannheim, "El problema de las generaciones," 223–231.

22. In a way, the so-called Algerian generation, to which Maspero belonged, reacted to the government's policy by arguing that the systematic use of repression and torture in a territory "occupied" by colonization, such as Algeria, could be equated with the modus operandi of the Nazis in France.

23. Feltrinelli, *Senior Service*, 31–42; Grandi, *Giangiacomo Feltrinelli*, 97–108.

24. Maspero, *Les abeilles & la guêpe*.

25. Hage, *Feltrinelli, Maspero, Wagenbach*, 137.

26. Andersson, *Mémoire Éclatée*, 23–26.

27. Feltrinelli, *Senior Service*, 43–77.

28. Andersson, *Mémoire Éclatée*: 273–289.

29. Hage, *Feltrinelli, Maspero, Wagenbach*, 278–282.

30. A relevant moment, due to its symbolism, was 1965 when Hans Magnus Enzesberger founded the journal *Kursbuch*, which was destined to become one of the key publications of the German New Left and a disseminator of the ideas coming from the Third World. Wagenbach participated actively in some of the project's phases as its editor.

31. Hage, *Feltrinelli, Maspero, Wagenbach*, 283.

32. Ulloa, *Francis Jeanson. Un intellectuel en dissidence de la Résistance à la guerre d'Algérie*.

33. Perrault, *A Man Apart. The Life of Henri Curiel*.

34. Kaminsky, *Kaminsky, el falsificador*.

35. Feltrinelli, "The future is unwritten," Introduction to *Feltrinelli 1955–2005. Catalogo storico*: III–IV.

36. *Problemi e prospettive della rivoluzione algerina* y *La révolution algérienne*. Furthermore, he had already published *La Rivoluzione Algerina* (Angelo Franza, ed.) in 1959, and *Gli algerini in Guerra* (Dominique Darbois and Philippe Vigneau) in 1961. Cfr. *Feltrinelli 1955–2005*, 3–8.

37. Andersson, *Mémoire Éclatée*, 69–71.

38. *Pour Djamila Bouhired*, a testimony of the tortures to which this young Algerian woman had been subject during the conflict.

39. Andersson, *Mémoire Éclatée*, 100–105.

40. Valloton, *Livre et Militantisme*.

41. According to Hage (*Feltrinelli, Maspero, Wagenbach*, 131–132), many years later Maspero himself had declared in an interview that the Algerian War had indeed encouraged him to become an editor.

42. Maspero, *Les abeilles & la guêpe*, 153–154. See also Andersson, *Mémoire Éclatée*, 106.

43. Hage, *Feltrinelli, Maspero, Wagenbach*, 173–181.

44. The editor personally knew some of the founders and most relevant members of the RAF, including Ensslin and Meinhof, to such an extent, in fact, that it was he who delivered the funeral address in 1976 after the latter's death in prison. Above and beyond his underground activism since the beginning of the 1970s, Meinhof had been, in the words of the editor, the most outstanding left-wing journalist in the 1960s. The Algerian cause was among those that he initially supported (Wagenbach, *La libertà dell'editore*, 43, 55–56).

45. Maspero, *Les abeilles & la guêpe*, 153–154.

46. Maspero, *Les abeilles & la guêpe*, 168.

47. Andersson, *Mémoire Éclatée*, 180.

48. *Partisans*, Paris, September–October 1961, 3–5, "Nous sommes des partisans," by Vercors.

49. Andersson, *Mémoire Éclatée*, 242.

50. *Les Algériens en guerre*, by D. Darbois et P. Vigneau (the alias of Jacques Vignes of the Jeanson network). They had already been touch in relation to the Italian edition of Keramane Jafid's *La Pacification*, first published by La Cité Éditeur and then by Feltrinelli in 1960, although it was not until the following year that they got to know each other personally.

51. Andersson, *Mémoire Éclatée*, 133; Maspero in Valloton, *Livre et Militantisme*, 165–166.

52. Andersson, *Mémoire Éclatée*, 149–159.

53. Andersson published thirty-eight books, mostly dealing with politics except for a few on theater, as well as the journal *African Revolution* (the English-language edition of the Algerian *Revolution Africaine*), renamed *Africa, Latin America, Asia Revolution* as from its third number.

54. This was the case with most of Maspero's catalogue during those years, although it also featured other literary or philosophical works, avant-garde writings, and editions that were hard to find in other general publishing houses. The complete catalogue can be found in Hage, *Feltrinelli, Maspero, Wagenbach*, 754–935.

55. Cfr. Kraushaar, *Rudi Dutschke*.

56. Wagenbach, *La libertà dell'editore*, 111–113.

57. Cfr. "Bommi" Bauman, *Tupamaros Berlin-Ouest ou Comment tout a comencé*, 81–82.

58. Maspero clearly attended the Tricontinental Conference, insofar as his name appears on the list of participants, a fact that he himself confirmed on several occasions. Whether or not Feltrinelli was there is not so clear: although he does not appear on the aforementioned list, several documents and personal notes in his archive offer the impression that he usually attended these encounters in Havana.

59. On Feltrinelli and Cuba, in addition to the aforementioned works by Grandi and Feltrinelli, see the analysis in Rey and Gracia, "The Role of the Left-wing Editors," 89–109. In the case of Maspero, his memoirs barely mention some moments, although further details can be found in Hage's study.

60. Maspero, *Les abeilles & la guêpe*, 202–206.

61. Rey and Gracia, "The Role of the Left-wing Editors," 89–109.

62. So far as we know, Feltrinelli did not personally meet Regis Debray; or at least their personal encounters were infrequent, without them forging any lasting relationship. In any event, this did not stop Feltrinelli from traveling to Bolivia, probably at the request of the Cubans. For his part, Maspero became closely acquainted with Debray, above all after the philosopher's release from prison in Bolivia and his return to Paris. We have been unable to document further relationships between the editors analyzed here

and their authors. If these did indeed exist, it would be an interesting line of research with a view to completing the overview that we have provided here.

63. Valloton, *Livre et Militantisme*, 166–167; Rey and Gracia, "The Role of the Left-wing Editors," 97–98.

64. Hage, *Feltrinelli, Maspero, Wagenbach*, 943.

65. The presence of Latin America in Wagenbach's catalogue was not as strong, for the most part boiling down to Guevara's main writings.

66. The catalogue review was performed using Hague's work in the case of Maspero and Wagenbach, and the edition of the *Catálogo Histórico. Feltrinelli 1955–2005*, released by this publishing house on the occasion of its fiftieth anniversary.

67. The main collection was "Documenti per la Rivoluzione nella America Latina," which totaled forty volumes, including the works of the main leaders of the Cuban Revolution and those of prominent guerrilleros in the region, and even documents drafted by the communist parties sympathizing with the revolutionary approach, as was the case with those of Cuba and Venezuela. They ranged from brief twenty-page documents containing the transcriptions of interviews or the reports of the guerrillas, to 500-page volumes containing party documents.

68. Hage, *Feltrinelli, Maspero, Wagenbach*, 315–319.

69. There are no available print run or distribution figures that would allow us to gain further insights into the scope of the publications to which we have referred in this chapter.

Bibliography

Andersson, Nils. *Mémoire Éclatée*. Lausanne: Editions d'en bas, 2016.

Balestracci, Fiammetta. "Klaus Wagenbach und die italienische Literatur in der Bundesrepublik Deutschland 1964–1989," *Jahrbuch für Internationale Germanistik* 38, no. 1 (2006): 59–80.

Bauman, "Bommi." *Tupamaros Berlin-Ouest ou Comment tout a comencé*. Les Presses d'aujourd'hui, 1976.

Bickerton, David, and Proud, Judith, ed. *The Transmission of Culture in Western Europe, 1750–1850: Papers Celebrating the Bicentenary of the Foundation of the Bibliothèque Britannique (1796–1815) in Geneva*. Bern & New York: P. Lang, 1999.

Cornelißen, C., Mantelli, B., and Terhoeven, P. *Il decennio rosso. Contestaziones sociale e conflicto politico in Germania e Italia negli anni Sessanta e Settanta*. Bologna: Il Mulino, 2012.

Duflot, Jaques. *Feltrinelli. Le condottiere rouge*. Paris: Balland, 1974.

Feltrinelli, Carlo. "The future is unwritten." Introduction to *Feltrinelli 1955–2005. Catalogo storico*, III–VIII. Milano: Feltrinelli, 2005.

Feltrinelli, Carlo. *Senior Service*. Milano: Feltrinelli, 2010.

Feltrinelli Editore. *Feltrinelli 1955–2005. Catalogo Storico*. Milano: Feltrinelli, 2005.

Givan, Rebecca K., Kenneth M. Roberts, and Sarah A. Soule. "The Dimensions of Diffusion. Introduction." In *The Diffusion of Social Movements. Actors, Mechanisms and*

Political Effects, edited by Rebecca K. Givan, Kenneth M. Roberts, and Sarah A. Soule, 1–15. New York: Cambridge, 2010.

González Calleja, Eduardo. *El laboratorio del miedo. Una historia general del terrorismo: de los sicarios a Al Qa'ida*. Barcelona: Crítica, 2012.

Goodwin, C.D.W., and Holley, I.B., ed. *The Transfer of Ideas: Historical Essays*. Durham, NC: South Atlantic Quarterly, 1968.

Grandi, Aldo. *Giangiacomo Feltrinelli. La dinastía, il rivoluzionario*. Milano: Baldini & Castoldi, 2000.

Gupta, Dipak K., "Waves of International Terrorism. An Explanation of the Process by which Ideas Flood the Worlds." In *Terrorism, Identity and Legitimacy. The Four Waves Theory and Political Violence*, edited by Jean E. Rosenfeld, 30–43. London: Routledge, 2010.

Hage, J. "Feltrinelli, Maspero, Wagenbach: une nouvelle génération d'éditeurs politiques d'extrême gauche en Europe occidentale, 1955–1982, histoire comparée, histoire croisée." Doctoral thesis, Université de Versailles Saint-Quentin-en-Yvelines, 2010, 2 vols.

Kaminsky, Sarah. *Kaminsky, el falsificador*. Madrid: Clave Intelectual, 2011.

Knigge, Jobst. *Feltrinelli, sein weg in den terrorismus*. Berlin: Humboldt Universität, 2010.

Kraushaar, Wolfgang, ed. *Rudi Dutschke, Andreas Baader und die RAF*. Hamburg, 2005.

Mannheim, Karl. "El problema de las generaciones," *Revista Española de Investigaciones Sociológicas* 62 (1993): 193–242.

Martín Álvarez, Alberto, and Eduardo Rey Tristán. "La oleada revolucionaria latinoamericana contemporánea, 1959–1996. Definición, caracterización y algunas claves para su análisis." *Navegamérica, Revista Electrónica de la Asociación Española de Americanistas* 9 (2012): 1–36.

Martín Álvarez, Alberto, and Eduardo Rey Tristán, eds. *Revolutionary Violence and the New Left: Transnational Perspectives*. New York & London: Routledge, 2016.

Maspero, François, *Les abeilles & la guêpe*. Paris: Seuil, 2003.

Mattioli, N.M. *Morte a Segrate*. Modena: Settedidenari, 1972.

Neri Serneri, Simone, ed. *Verso la lotta armata. La politica della violenza nella sinistra radicale degli anni Settanta*. Bologna: Il Mulino, 2012.

Perrault, Gilles, *A Man Apart. The Life of Henri Curiel*. London: Zed Books, 1984.

Punzo, M., M. Andriolo, G. Da Rold, L. Fanti, A. Viola, and M. Balbo, eds. *L'affare Feltrinelli. Con una testimonianza di Carlo Ripa di Meana*. Milano: Stampa clb, 1972.

Rapoport, David C. "Modern Terror: The Four Waves." In *Attacking Terrorism: Elements of a Grand Strategy*, edited by. Audrey K. Cronin and James M. Ludes, 46–73. Washington DC: Georgetown University Press, 2004.

Rapoport, David. "Reflections on the Third or New Left Wave: 17 Years Later." In *Revolutionary Violence and the New Left: Transnational Perspectives*, edited by Alberto Martín Álvarez and Eduardo Rey Tristán, 24–64. New York & London: Routledge, 2016.

Rey Tristán, Eduardo, and Guillermo Gracia Santos. "The Role of the Left-wing Editors in the Diffusion of the New Left Wave: The Case of Giangiacomo Feltrinelli." In *Revolutionary Violence and the New Left: Transnational Perspectives*, edited by Alberto Martín Álvarez and Eduardo Rey Tristán, 89–109. New York & London: Routledge, 2016.

Ruggiero, Lorenzo, ed., *Dossier Brigate Rosse 1969–1975. La lotta armata nei documenti e nei comunicati delle primer Br.* Milano: Kaos edizioni, 2007.

Scavino, Marco. "La piazza e la forza. I percorsi verso la lotta armata dal sessentotto alla metà degli anni settanta." In *Verso la lotta armata,* edited by Simone Neri Serneri, 117–205. Bologna: Il Mulino, 2012.

Slobodian, Quinn. *Foreign Front: Third World Politics in Sixties West Germany.* Durham, NC & London: Duke University Press, 2012.

Sterling, Claire. *The Terror Network. The Secret War against International Terrorism.* New York: Holt, Rinehart, and Winston, 1981.

Terhoeven, Petra. "Germania e Italia nel 'decennio rosso': per un'introduzione." In *Il decennio rosso,* edited by C. Cornelißen, B. Mantelli, and P. Terhoeven, 13–49. Bologna: Il Mulino, 2012.

Ulloa, Marie-Pierre. *Francis Jeanson. Un intellectuel en dissidence de la Résistance à la guerre d'Algérie.* Paris: Berg International Éditeurs, 2001.

Valloton, François, ed. *Livre et Militantisme. La Cité Éditeur, 1958–1967.* Lausanne: Éditions d'en bas, 2007.

Ventura, Angelo. "Il problema delle origini del terrorismo di sinistra." In *Terrorismi in Italia,* edited by Donatella Della Porta, 73–151. Bologna: Il Mulino, 1984.

Viola, Guido. "Requisitoria Feltrinelli." In *Criminalizzazione della lotta di clase,* edited by G. Guiso, A. Bonomi, and F. Tommei, 1–154. Verona: Bertani Editore, Verona, 1975.

Wagenbach, Klaus. *La libertà dell'editore. Memorie, discorsi, stoccate.* Palermo: Sellerio, 2013.

6

Solidarity and Diplomatic Work of the Guatemalan Revolutionary Movement in Europe
The Case of the Ejército Guerrillero de los Pobres (Guerrilla Army of the Poor)

ARTURO TARACENA ARRIOLA

Toward a New Revolutionary Phase

In the second quarter of 1967, a document entitled "*Situación y perspectiva del movimiento revolucionario guatemalteco*" (Situation and Prospects of the Guatemalan Revolutionary Movement) began circulating among members of the Guatemalan Revolutionary Armed Forces (FAR). Known as the "Documento de marzo" (March Document), because it was dated March 7, and drafted by Ricardo Ramírez under the pseudonym of Orlando Fernández, it censored the role that the Guatemalan Party of Labor (PGT) had played hitherto in the development of the revolutionary war in Guatemala. It also criticized the direction that the FAR had taken. In principle, it was a reassessment of their performance, although it also outlined a new guerrilla project built around grassroots militants coming from the PGT, the Patriotic Labor Youth (JPT), whose members had been trained in Cuba, and other revolutionaries living in Mexico and Guatemala.

Of the criticisms contained in the "Documento de marzo," the most important focused on underscoring that the war was not being waged along strategic military lines; that a bureaucratic conception prevailed in the political sphere; that there should be a sole command in order to put an end to the dispersion of the regional and zonal guerrillas; and that a "popular" revolutionary war should be developed, something that would be impossible without the participation of the country's Indigenous peoples. In a nutshell, the geographical scope of the war had to be broadened to include the country's northern and western highlands.

It was necessary to divide Guatemala into three "strategic theatres": (1) the area where the enemy had its most important economic interests: the coast and central highlands; (2) the area where the enemy had its nerve centers and seat of power: the capital and other cities; and (3) the area that the enemy deemed "inert," where its interests and ideological penetration were limited and the state apparatus was weaker: the jungle and the country's northern reaches. It was essential to leverage all three at the same time, while always bearing in mind that the last was fundamental, since it was from where the revolutionary army would be able to strategically destabilize enemy forces.

Last, the document emphasized that in the 1960s global political interests, defined by the contradiction between imperialism and socialism, were particularly visible in two regions: Southeast Asia (with the Vietnam-China axis) and the Caribbean (with the Cuba-Venezuela-Guatemala axis), the latter being characterized by "imperialism's backyard." This was even more evident after the invasion of the Dominican Republic in 1965. Regionally speaking, however, Guatemala was the Central American country where the structure of the ruling classes and the ideological and political influence of imperialism were weakest in relation to the population as a whole, taking into account the deep scars left by the political upheaval of the "democratic bourgeois" Guatemalan Revolution of 1944. This portended that imperialism would be willing to intervene massively there.

Despite its geopolitical content, the Documento de marzo did not include any indication as to the international work that the Guatemalan revolutionaries should undertake in order to disseminate and drum up political and diplomatic support for this master plan. Nevertheless, the relations established by Ramírez, as a director of the World Federation of Democratic Youth (WFDY), would facilitate its dissemination.[1]

The "Hour of the Furnaces"

When it came to international dissemination, Aura Marina Arriola, who played an important role in the operational aspects of this new phase, also moved from Cuba to Rome, where she activated previously established international contacts. In Italy, she engaged with the Italian Communist

Party (PCI), the recently founded Il Manifesto, the Italian Socialist Party (PSI), the Proletarian Unity Party (PdUP), and the extra-parliamentary group Lotta Continua, in addition to the country's trade unions. And she did much the same with such outstanding intellectuals as Rosana Rossanda, Giangiacomo Feltrinelli, Alberto Moravia, Renato Guttuso, Lelio Basso, and K.S. Karol.

Arriola also discretely began to weave a network of political relations inasmuch as she was responsible for setting up a clandestine apparatus whose purpose was to receive all comrades leaving Cuba. Accordingly, between 1969 and 1971, a little over two dozen Guatemalan revolutionaries arrived in Mexico. In January 1972, a group of them suddenly entered the jungle of Northern Guatemala with the aim of creating the right conditions for the foundation of what would become the Guerrilla Army of the Poor (EGP). Parallel to this, Arriola also visited France for the purpose of engaging with Artur and Lise London, and the Debrays, and strengthening ties with other French intellectuals such as Costa-Gavras and Michèle Ray-Gavras, Yves Montand, Simone Signoret, and Xavier Langlade, one of the leaders of the Revolutionary Communist League (LCR) responsible for relations with Latin America.[2] At this juncture, the fledgling organization began to put theory into practice as regards political international relations by means of "personal envoys" with a view to whipping up the necessary support for launching its project. Meanwhile, in his *La critique des armes*, Regis Debray co-wrote the chapter on Guatemala with Ricardo Ramírez.[3] It was here that this organizational effort was publicly dubbed the New Revolutionary Combat Organization (NORC) for the first time, although it was noted that the title was only temporary while members decided on a final name. Militants in Guatemala and Mexico had already been using this title since 1970 to refer to the organization in the first contacts made in Guatemala.

The initial guerrilla nucleus efforts in the Guatemalan jungle, and its support structures in Guatemala City and on the south coast, to construct the organization within the country, meant international work took second place, except for occasional contacts with the United States and, above all, Mexico, the organization's rear-guard. It was with its public debut in 1975, now under the official name of the Guerrilla Army of the Poor, that the EGP bought advertising space in the national and international press to promote its political platform and its political-military actions. At the same time, the organization created a press agency called *Compañero*, albeit one whose track record would be erratic. Further, it continued to operate on the international stage both through special envoys sent to talk to representatives of governments and political parties, and through clandestine activities, particularly in Mexico and Central America.

The International Solidarity Boom: The Advent of the "Fourth Leg"

The Christian network supporting the Guatemalan popular movement had meanwhile begun to develop in 1976 as a result of the devastation wreaked in the country's central highlands by the earthquake occurring on February 4, with more than 28,000 victims according to official figures. This solidarity movement would contribute to the efforts to reconstruct the country in the face of the corrupt management of international aid by the National Reconstruction Committee controlled by the Guatemalan army. It would also be connected with the advent of the mass rural movement in Guatemala through the official creation of the Peasant Unity Committee (CUC) on April 15, 1978. It was precisely the support given to this movement and to other expressions of the rural and urban masses that was behind the Guatemalan state's crackdown on the Guatemalan, European, and American priests, nuns, and laypeople who aided them and who, in some cases, had direct ties with the organizations promoting the country's revolutionary movement.

This expansion of European Christian solidarity with Latin America in Europe was fueled, on the one hand, by the ever-closer ties of grassroots Christian organizations with the European Left, from labor party members to Trotskyists. And on the other, the evident boom of social democracy in Western Europe by the end of 1960s not only opened the doors to Foreign Ministries that had previously been the exclusive preserve of conservative parties, but also generally raised the awareness of governments to the despotism of the Latin American military dictatorships. This led to fierce rejection within parliamentary democracies of the U.S.-influenced National Security Doctrine, because it was hitting European citizens (priests, nuns, trade unionists, militants, university students) committed to the poor of the Third World.

This solidarity logic and action would begin to pay off politically in Europe when the popular workers' and peasant movement evolved in Guatemala as of 1977, and when the military activity of the revolutionary organizations took a qualitative leap forward at the beginning of the 1980s, challenging the military government of General Lucas García. The government's harsh reaction, characterized by the "scorched-earth" and a "communist spotted, communist dead" policy, forced many internationalist activists, militants, and their families resident in Guatemala to leave the country with the aim of organizing tours to denounce the situation and raise funds. These included members of different European Christian communities, as well as internationalist doctors and nurses who had become involved in the different expressions of the Guatemalan popular and revolutionary movements. These people were basically Spaniards, Belgians, and Dutch who would support several Guatemalans' individual efforts to create the solidarity network at a continental level.

By pure chance, relating to our political lives at the time, two of us who had founded the EGP, who shared a similar stance on the symbiosis between military and political power, and who had left the organization in 1973 now found ourselves living in exile in Paris. Thus, at the end of 1973 Miguel Ángel Sandoval and I—supported by our comrades and other Guatemalans—began to suggest the necessity of creating an international support network, following the example of the solidarity committees of our comrades in the Southern Cone (Uruguayans, Chileans, Brazilians, and Argentineans). The idea was to create a broad and independent legal structure of solidarity work in order to raise awareness of the region's social movements and disseminate news of the progress of its revolutionary struggles.

What led us to propose such an idea? Well, first and foremost, we both belonged to a group within the EGP that endorsed the view that there had to be a combination of political and military elements in its strategy, and that this second aspect should be prevented from dictating action. It was essential to combat the influence of *foquismo* on EGP's strategy. Hence, we always stressed the need for broader, comprehensive work performed by comrades individually or in groups. Meanwhile, as a result of the crisis stemming from Soviet intervention in Czechoslovakia, the urgency of combating the Stalinist legacy in Latin American revolutionary organizations, often concealed by the organizational approach of "democratic centralism," was left up in the air, thus favoring militarist theses.

Likewise, when we arrived in France, we discovered a global picture that encouraged us to reflect on several elements of a political nature. First, the negotiations on the Vietnam War at the Lutetia Hotel in 1973 showed us how the Vietnamese strategy had focused on the thesis that to achieve the military defeat of the enemy it was essential to undermine it not only on the battlefield, but also in the eyes of public opinion both at home and abroad, dismantling U.S. propaganda depicting itself as the champion of democracy. Since 1968, it had been imperative that diplomacy triumphed because it would pave the way to the reunification of Vietnam. In fact, we were impressed by the solidarity movement that the Vietnamese had created and the favorable reaction of French public opinion. Furthermore, a matter that caught our eye was how, emulating the student movement of 1968, the French Communist Party (PCF) had lost its internationalist hegemony to the momentum of Trotskyist and Maoist solidarity.

The Southern Cone exiles, a product of respective coups in their countries in the framework of the National Security Doctrine championed by Washington, were already organized in solidarity movements that implemented initiatives with French political parties (the French Socialist Party [PSF], the PCF, the Unified Socialist Party [PSU] and the Revolutionary Communist League [LCR]) and trade unions (the General Confederation of Labor [CGT], the Democratic Confederation of Labor [CFDT] and Force Ouvrière [FO]), while maintaining government contacts. These contacts were backed by a solidarity network organized by religious institutions with a Third World vocation, such as Justice et Paix (Justice and Peace), the Association Catholique contre la Torture (Catholic Association against Torture), the Catholic Committee against Hunger and for Development (CCFD-Terre Solidaire), Terres de Hommes and Frères des Hommes; in addition to the journalists Christian Rudel, Claude Bourdet, and Claude Roire, and the lawyer Gisèle Halimi. These groups in turn organized public events to call attention to the situation in Latin America, activities that were supplemented by the participation of Latin American countries and organizations in party festivals—Rouge, La Rose, and L'Humanité—with their own stands. We also started to do the same in Italy at the Feste dell'Unità and in Madrid at the festival of the Spanish Communist Party (PCE) and that of La Rosa of the Spanish Socialist Workers' Party (PSOE).

By then some of the exiles of the Sandinista National Liberation Front (FSLN), including Pablo Centeno, Jorge Alanís, and Enrique Smith, who lived in Germany, and the People's Liberation Forces-El Salvador (FPL), such as Roberto Rodríguez, and Manuel Bonilla, as well as the poet Roberto Armijo, who was named the representative of the Farabundo Martí National Liberation Front (FMLN), had already begun to create their own solidarity committees, encouraged by the existence of the Centre for International Solidarity Studies and Initiatives (CEDETIM), incorporated under Act 1901 as an association in 1965, for the purpose of lending support to national liberation and revolutionary struggles in Asia, Africa, Oceania, and Latin America. The Chileans, Uruguayans, Argentinians, and Nicaraguans had their base at this center, whose heart and soul was François

Gèze, then a Maoist militant, and Michele Griffon, a socialist militant. The Argentinians, who had always supported the Central American cause, included the journalist Carlos Gabetta and the lawyer Rodolfo Matarollo, both members of the Revolutionary Army of the People (ERP), and the *montonero* Jorge Colucci. The center also had the backing of the Chilean Communists Carlos Orellana and Luis Bocaz, the *miristas*, Jaime Castillo and Francisco Peruzzi, and the Brazilian intellectual and member of the LCR, Michael Löwy.

Thus, between 1975 and 1976, we began to lay the foundations for the creation of a committee of solidarity with Guatemala and to organize joint actions at a Central American level (which, as of 1981, was evidenced by the publication of the bulletin *Amerique Centrale en lutte*), bearing in mind that we had to fish for the same party, trade union, university, and ecclesiastical support. At the time, it should be noted, the solidarity network linked to the communists was completely closed to us since it did not favor the option of armed struggle in Latin America; the Communist Parties were very wary of organizations with Guevarist leanings. This meant that our action focused on seeking the endorsement of the socialist and far-Left parties in France and in Europe in general, as well as that of the Christian solidarity networks.

Following a stay in Guatemala from January 1977 to August 1978, I returned to France. The following November, one compañero who had just suffered an attack in which his older brother had been killed, arrived in Paris and stayed briefly with me. I had known him, a member of EGP involved in cultural and mass work, ever since we were boys. He wanted to contact the writer Manuel José Arce, who had gone into exile in France after the army's murder of Manuel Colom Argueta, the Mayor of Guatemala City and leader of the United Front of the Revolution (FUR). That same year, the EGP created the Comisión del Trabajo Amplio de Masas (Commission for Broad Mass Work, COTRAM), and Ricardo Ramírez drafted the EGP's Mass Line with which the broad work had been developed—not without considerable internal contradictions—from 1973 onward as a result of the outbreak of the teachers' strike, the first of its kind in Guatemala since 1962.

In February 1979, this compañero also turned up again in Paris in order to explain the upsurge in peasant, worker, and student protests in Guatemala City, in addition to the subsequent government repression with the selective assassination of the leaders of the belligerent Coca-Cola trade union. His intention was to tour several European countries to denounce the situation and search for contacts, considering that, as a result of Commander Edén Pastora's standoff in the Nicaraguan National Palace, an international campaign in support of the Sandinista Revolution had been launched, which would open spaces of solidarity with the Salvadoran and Guatemalan struggles. Afterward, he traveled to Costa Rica to inform the woman responsible for the organization's international work about the results of his trip. Since she was accustomed to the criterion of clandestine international contacts, which the organization's cadres were normally trained to follow, he began to work in the same way, more covertly, and, therefore, the broader political impact of his tour was lost.

It was not until November 1980 that two Guatemalan representatives of mass work reappeared in Europe: two militants of the Quiché ethnic group and members of the CUC, who participated in the Russell Tribunal hearings held at The Hague (Holland) to denounce the increasingly brutal subjugation of the Indigenous communities of the Guatemalan highlands. The journalist Marco Antonio Cacao, who followed suit, was assassinated by the police after returning to Guatemala.

It goes without saying that the triumph of the Sandinista Revolution on July 19, 1979, had highlighted the importance of international support (interlocutors, funds, propaganda, internationalists, arms, etc.) for a revolutionary war and its success. Consequently, the Nicaraguans acquired a different political-diplomatic status in Europe, thus ensuring the support of their ambassadors for the dealings of Salvadorans and Guatemalans with governments, chanceries, and political parties. That victory encouraged us all to continue to construct *ex officio* the *"cuarta pata del banco"* (literally, the fourth leg of the bench; a colloquial expression to denote a missing essential component of a structure that would allow it to stand).

In 1980, the Parisian solidarity committee for Guatemala finally achieved the legal status of nongovernmental organization (NGO), under the name of Collectif Guatemala, its first chair being the sociologist Nicole Bourdillat, the person responsible at the time for Central America in the Socialist Party (she would later be in charge of all Latin America, with the mathematician Marie Duflo covering Central America). Board members—about twenty of us in all—included the prestigious lawyer Jean-Paul Levy as vice-chair, the activist Dominique Camard, and Michel Liberman of the LCR. Solidarity committees in other European countries in accordance with their own laws followed the example of the Parisian committee.

Aware of the revolutionary situation in Guatemala, the Paris Police Prefecture assigned an inspector to our organization, whose official address was at 67 rue du Théâtre, to keep an eye on our movements and maintain an open channel of communication. This inspector forewarned us that the secretary of the Embassy of Guatemala, who had been transferred from Washington to Paris and was close to the right-wing National Liberation Movement (MLN), attended all our activities in order to draw up a list of the participants. He suggested that we should not respond to the provocation. As a matter of fact, our movements were always monitored by the European secret services, a surveillance that was stepped up as of 1987 in the wake of the talks between the Guatemalan guerrilla and the government.

Meanwhile, the Collectif Guatemala began to publish a monthly bulletin *Guatemala solidarité* (mimeographed at first and then printed, with a run of 250 copies), while publishing booklets, posters, and videos in French, which were then distributed among different collectives throughout the country and, because of the language, also in Belgium, Luxembourg, and Switzerland. The propaganda and study materials of the different mass and armed organizations were translated in each country. Thus equipped, we covered all the public universities, aware that students were the best multipliers since they drew on our materials to cover news on Guatemala in their own publications. In turn, journalists, documentary makers, and film directors started to ask us for contacts with an eye to traveling to Guatemala to interview revolutionary activists and militants in its cities, countryside, and highlands.

Another aspect of international work of great help to us was the dialogue with Amnesty International (AI). Until then, AI had declined to champion the human rights struggle in Guatemala on the grounds that no political prisoners were held there, which was quite true: whoever was arrested for subversive activities was assassinated, an official practice since 1966. At the same time, the humanitarian organization was inclined to defend conscientious objectors, who did not exist in Guatemala either since the levy was obligatory for peasants, above all those belonging to the country's Indigenous ethnic groups. Thanks to the contacts with Nicole Bat, one of the directors of the French section, it was possible to negotiate the involvement of AI in the paradigmatic Guatemalan case at the organization's headquarters in London. Needless to say, the growth and boom of the popular movement favored all this activity when its militants and cadres had to go on tour using this network. Consequently, the committees began to receive people from Justice et Paix, the CUC, the National Committee for Trade Union Unity (CNUS), and all the other major revolutionary Guatemalan organizations.

At a European level, between 1978 and 1979 a large number of solidarity committees emerged in practically all countries with an interest in supporting the cause of the Guatemalan left, attracting many exiles, especially scholarship students. In fact, it was a network that would continue to grow internally in each West European state: Spain, France, Portugal, Belgium, Luxembourg, Germany, Holland, England, Denmark, Sweden, Finland, Austria, Switzerland, and Italy. This led to the creation of the European Coordination of Committees of Solidarity with Guatemala, with the presence of eleven committees, in Amsterdam in November 1979, at the initiative of those responsible for organizing Dutch and Belgian solidarity, all of whom had worked as priests in Guatemala for several years. To give a good example of this work, it is worth noting that the Revolutionary Organization of the People in Arms (ORPA) chose the aforementioned founding meeting to reveal its existence in Europe.

This led the European committees of solidarity with Guatemala to strengthen ties with political parties, trade unions, religious congregations, and human rights movements; and the Central Americans in general—backed by a multitude of Europeans—held joint demonstrations in front of their embassies as well as marching through the streets on special days with the prior consent of the authorities. These demonstrations were massive affairs between 1980 and 1983.

Aura Marina Arriola's stay in Italy during 1980 was also very important. After having abandoned the organization in 1973 and moving back to Latin America in 1976, she returned to Rome for a year before finally establishing herself in Mexico. She was supported in her work by Gabriela and Paolo Mercadini, Patricia Baeza, and Hélène Férraux. As regards to solidarity, the Roman group of Monte Sacro, the International League for the Rights and Liberation of Peoples (LIDLIP), and the solidarity committees of Latina, Cesena, Pescara, Rome, Florence, Bologna, Turin, Lucca, and Milan all stood out. In this last city, the facilitators were Gigi Malabarba and Cristiano and Alice Dan, who published *Quetzal*, a bimonthly journal dealing with solidarity with the Central American struggles.

The joint efforts of the Guatemalan revolutionary organizations and, above all, the civilians close to them, led to the implementation of three initiatives essential to their international work. The first had been the creation, at the end of 1978, of the Democratic Front against Repression (FDCR), composed of sixty-five trade unions and eight central organizations or federations of urban workers, plus peasants, students, and Christians. The second involved the creation in 1982 of the Guatemalan Committee for

Patriotic Unity (CGUP), chaired by the writer Luis Cardoza y Aragón and made up of twenty-four political, intellectual, and social leaders, both Indigenous and non-Indigenous. These personalities began to travel through Europe to now request not only financial and propagandistic support, but also to call for the official recognition of Guatemala's political parties and revolutionary movements struggling against the institutionalized military dictatorship by means of periodic elections. The third initiative was the creation of the Unitary Representation of the Guatemalan Opposition (RUOG), including Rolando Castillo Montalvo, Raúl Molina, Marta Gloria Torres, Frank La Rue, and Rigoberta Menchú, responsible for diplomatic work at the United Nations (UN) and foreign ministries all over the world, whose frequent tours we supported. To this was added the tour carried out in Europe and in other continents by the members of the Human Rights Commission of Guatemala.

The high point of this first phase was the Russel Tribunal's "Session on Guatemala" held in Madrid in January 1983, with the participation of representatives of the country's popular peasant and workers' organizations, plus delegates of its left-wing political parties and revolutionary movements.

All in all, these initiatives put the case of Guatemala on the agenda. People now spoke openly about strategic villages, the massacre of the Indigenous population, and the assassination of workers, Indigenous and student leaders, university professors, journalists, catechists, priests, and nuns.

The Start of the International Work of the EGP and the Guatemalan National Revolutionary Unity in Europe

During the second quarter of 1981, this painstaking international work opened the door to Sandoval's and my re-admission to the EGP and the admittance of new comrades, including Camilo Ospina, one of the main promoters of solidarity in France. The revolutionary organization was interested in capitalizing on the political and social work that we had managed to perform in the area of solidarity in Europe at a moment when its revolutionary activity in Guatemala was on the increase. At the end of that year, Marie and Juana, two cadres of the ORPA, arrived in Paris, where they would work tirelessly. In Spain, Teresa became in turn its official representative. The Guatemalan revolution thus began to place its European activities on a firm footing.

This cumulative work also led the EGP to name an official representative for Europe, a post that fell on my shoulders as of January 1982. At an ad hoc meeting held in Managua (Nicaragua) in April of the same year, the organization created the International Work Team (ETI), which began to function with six cadres. The following year, the number was increased to eight with new incorporations. Our tasks, which covered the United States, Mexico, Costa Rica, Nicaragua, Europe, and Cuba, were defined by collective or individual instructions issued by the National Direction (DN) and the propaganda team. In Europe, we continued to receive every now and again the classic personal envoys on specific missions, who, if necessary, were expected to coordinate with our political contacts. Sure enough, Cuban diplomats also assisted us during the 1980s, especially those at the country's Paris embassy such as the sociologist Aurelio Alonso, formerly one of the editors of *Pensamiento Crítico*.

At this juncture, the EGP bolstered its propaganda commission, run by Mario Payeras, which gave a new impetus to the old international bulletin *Compañero*, which had managed to publish only three issues from 1975 to 1980. Likewise, it breathed new life into *Informador Guerrillero*, some of whose issues were translated into French, English, and Dutch. It appeared monthly for several years with news on the war and the social struggles, plus political analyses of national and international current affairs.

The success of receiving Guatemalan international delegations of the broad revolutionary movement in Europe allowed us to introduce them to different political parties, trade unions, and progressive religious congregations, as was the case of the delegation of the FDCR arriving in Paris in May 1980, which included the doctor Carlos Gallardo Flores, General Secretary of the Democratic Socialist Party (PSD), the lawyer Guillermo Colom Argueta representing the FUR, Miguel Ángel Albizures from the CNUS, Emeterio Toj representing the Committee for Peasant Unity (CUC), and the lawyer Elizabeth Álvarez from the University of San Carlos. François Mitterrand, already President-elect, together with other French politicians, received the delegation at the rue Solferino.

The French socialist leader's victory in the presidential elections opened political and diplomatic spaces to such an extent that Guatemalan intellectuals of the caliber of the writers Luis Cardoza y Aragón and Augusto Monterroso were invited to participate in activities at a European level. Thus, their testimonies served to revive the memory of the Guatemalan democratic period of 1944–1954 during which they had been civil servants and intellectuals. The solidarity of Dominique Eluard, who chaired the committee for the safe return of the writer Alaíde Foppa, who had disappeared in Guatemala City on December 19, 1981, proved to be of vital importance.

Meanwhile, the development of political relations smoothed the way to the reception of the first delegation of the Guatemalan National Revolutionary Unity (URNG) on February 23, 1982—namely, sixteen days after the unification of the Guatemalan revolutionary movements, in which the Cuban government played a significant role. This delegation toured Europe to present the guerrilla movement's achievements. In Paris, they participated in a political rally attended by three thousand people, which the Guatemalans and Salvadorans had organized at the Maison de la Mutualité to denounce what was happening in Central America. It was a political and artistic encounter with which we intended to encourage acts of international solidarity with the Guatemalan people and condemnation of the arrests/disappearances, particularly that of Foppa. The first experience of this type had taken place a year earlier, when, on March 24, 1981, we organized the encounter "6 heures pour El Salvador et l'Amérique centrale" at the same venue full to bursting point.

Different political personalities, including the writer Eduardo Galeano and the magistrate Philippe Texier, participated in the encounter, the most noteworthy address being that of the legendary Artur London, a member of the international brigades and the French resistance, a leader of the Prague Spring, and a friend of Guatemala. In the future, we continued to assist the Guatemalan unity delegations arriving in Europe to establish political contacts.

On October 20, 1982, coinciding with the 38th anniversary of the Guatemalan Revolution of 1944, the Coordinator of the European Solidarity Committees was asked, as the European team handling the economic campaign in favor of the URNG, to help us to raise funds, distribute information kits on the revolution, and denounce the coup regime of General Ríos Montt and his "scorched-earth" policy, as well as the backing that the Reagan administration was now giving him in the midst of its neoliberal counter-revolution.

In parallel, for the Guatemalan opposition, the world of cinema became a weapon both for denouncing the situation and for confirming the state of war, with the making of documentaries such as *Imágenes de una dictadura* (1980) by Paolo Mercadini, *La guerre des mayas* (1983) by Jean-Marie Simonet, *Genocidio en Guatemala* (1983) by Salomón Zetune, *When the Mountains Tremble* (1983) by Tom Siegel, Peter Kinoy, and Pamela Yates, *La otra cara de la guerra* (1984) by Paolo Mercadini, and *Caminos del silencio* (1987) by Félix Zurita. These documentaries were subtitled in several European languages and screened at solidarity events. The space purchased in the European press multiplied in order to demand explanations from the Guatemalan military government, which was increasingly isolated after the burning of the Spanish Embassy in January 1980.

In 1984, the government of Óscar Humberto Mejía Víctores managed to re-establish diplomatic relations with Spain and launched a national and international campaign to suggest that the peasants and students occupying the building had been responsible for the fire. At the trial of Pedro García Redondo, the head of the police commando, held thirty-five years later, in light of the testimonies of two of the policemen involved, it became clear that they had been ordered by the government to start the fire with homemade flamethrowers, despite the demands of those present that they respect the inviolability of the premises of the mission. General Romeo Lucas García had issued the order that they were to be removed from the building dead or alive.

Last, it should be noted that the Guatemalan army's offensive against the revolutionary movement during the period 1982–1983 had a resonance in the European press, the EGP being the most affected by this. First, on August 8, 1983, the day on which General Mejía Víctores ousted General Efraín Ríos Montt in a coup, Commander Camilo, one of the EGP's main leaders, was killed in the capital, a murder attributed to the organization that had allegedly wanted to silence his dissention. One of his circle, a person of Italian extraction working for a NGO in Chimaltenango, toured France, Belgium, Holland, and Italy for several weeks to blame the EGP for his death, after having been broken in prison and set free by the Guatemalan army. I had to refute this version before politicians, unionists, and solidarity committees. Years later, the National Police archives confirmed that Camilo had been killed while fighting at a house in the city and that the following day the country's military intelligence had disclosed that he had been located in the city center in order to claim that he had been ambushed by his comrades. Creating scenarios that relativized its course of action and attributing deaths to common criminals or to guerrilla infighting, which did indeed occur, was a very frequent practice of the country's military intelligence.

Second, as a consequence of that defeat, in January 1984 a split occurred in the organization led by Mario Payeras, backed by several comrades involved in international and mass work. In their letter of resignation, they rightly pointed out that the EGP's military strategy for seizing power has been thwarted and that, henceforth, its political work was now more important and necessary than ever to reach a political solution to the conflict.

Likewise, they declined any responsibility for having lost the initiative and for the military defeats suffered. This split occurred at the same time as that of the "6 de enero" group in the PGT, those resigning predicting the disintegration of the URNG. However, the political-military activity at home and the political work abroad enabled the organization to overcome the crisis. Three years later, its strategic guerrilla fronts were capable of halting the army's important "Final Offensive" and creating a unitary guerrilla front in Guatemala's central highlands.

During 1984, the compañera Mariana had also been sent to Spain for two years as the EGP's representative in the country to reinforce the organization's efforts in Europe. She not only helped us to perform a more precise analysis of the different scenarios, but also broadened the scope of the EGP's solidarity work and, above all, its political relations beyond the Spanish Socialist Workers' Party (PSOE) and the Communist Party of Spain (PCE) and the General Workers' Union (UGT) and the Workers' Commissions (CC.OO.), the two trade unions in their orbit, by reaching out to the country's minority left-wing groups and the Catalan and Basque nationalist parties. Since 1979, I had also been traveling to Madrid to support the solidarity.

Guatemalan Diplomacy under Siege

How was it possible to corner the Guatemalan diplomatic corps in Europe by constructing that *cuarta pata del banco*, or essential missing component? First, our priority was to dismantle the campaign of the Guatemalan government, which was focused mainly on drawing a veil over the reality of the war. This was why we boycotted Guatemala's official participation, headed by the country's Institute of Tourism, at all European tourism shows. Second, by asking citizens to send letters to the Guatemalan government and its embassies demanding respect for human rights, information on those who had disappeared, and an end to the "scorched-earth" policy. Third, by denouncing what was happening in the country using mail, the radio, the press and rallies, as well as by sending the first journalists to Guatemala to write reports on and film the reality in its cities and countryside. Fourth, by making an effort to translate the propaganda of the mass and revolutionary organizations into different languages and to distribute it at public events or by mail to lists of politicians, intellectuals, unionists, ecclesiastics, and artists. Fifth, by raising funds and submitting projects to all kinds of NGOs with the aim of obtaining funding for internal operational, propaganda, and military structures. Sixth, by procuring medical supplies, above all those medicines needed in the highlands that were very expensive and difficult to obtain (for example, treatments for leishmaniosis). Seventh, by visiting different European chanceries, the offices of those prime ministers who allowed their civil servants to receive us, the headquarters of political parties (socialists, communists, greens, liberals, and Trotskyists) and trade unions, as well as the offices of different ecumenical and confessional religious organizations, cultural and artistic committees, and organizations promoting fair trade and environmental protection.

All these activities were facilitated by the chaos, lack of motivation, and corruption of the Guatemalan Foreign Office, which was all very important for the success of Guatemalan revolutionary diplomacy and solidarity. In fact, most of the ambassadors and other members of the diplomatic corps in Europe were not career diplomats, but people appointed by the incumbent government for political or family reasons. They lacked the faintest idea of what it took to represent a Latin American country, but rather used their posts to live the good life and to do business, such as trafficking with the diplomatic corps' preferential exchange rate, the obtaining of honorary consulates, the importing-exporting of goods, the misuse of the diplomatic pouch, the abuse of official per diems, and to influence peddling and its respective commissions. This widespread corruption—save the normal exceptions in different missions, posts, and periods—was already a defining trait of the Guatemalan political establishment and would worsen after the signing of the peace accords. The diplomatic corps' wheeling and dealing lost it the support and sympathy of the majority of Guatemalans studying or working in Europe.

The members of the Guatemalan diplomatic corps meanwhile attended official receptions without necessarily dedicating their time to political lobbying in chanceries, parliaments, party headquarters and, much less, with trade union, or religious leaders. It was unthinkable for them to travel from state capitals to the smaller cities where they had their posts, unless this formed part of their holiday plans. When going about their work, they were unaccustomed to taking buses or trains or using their own cars to travel thousands of miles throughout the year to attend political, media, or cultural events and encounters.

In this context, it was highly significant that, as of 1982, the CUC and other peasant organizations managed to broach and debate on the Indigenous issue at the UN office in Geneva, specifically the Sub-Commission on Prevention and Discrimination and Protection of Minorities of the

Commission of Human Rights. The large work group was led by Rigoberta Menchú with the support of colleagues from the Peasant Unity Committee, the Guatemalan Refugee Support Group (CSARG), and the Altiplano Peasant Committee.

The eyewitness account of Menchú in her book *I, Rigoberta Menchu: An Indian Woman in Guatemala*, which was edited by Elizabeth Burgos and I with the help of Francisca Rivera to transcribe it, was paramount to that leap forward. As is common knowledge, the book was published by Burgos under her name, first in French (Paris, Éditions Gallimard, 1983) and then in Spanish in Cuba (Havana, Casa de las Américas, 1983), where it won the Casa de las Américas' Testimony Prize, before being translated into English by Ann Wright (London & New York, Verso, 1984). I spoke about the process of producing the book in an interview that I gave to Luis Aceituno,[4] in response to a statement made by Burgos a few days earlier to the same newspaper about the book's production, questioning the Nobel Prize Laureate, Juan Mendoza and me, as well as the role played by Danielle Mitterrand herself and the France Libertés Foundation.[5]

Major Challenges Facing the International Revolutionary Work in Europe

Despite the evolution and development of these international fronts, the strategic defeat suffered by the Guatemalan revolutionary movement from 1982 to 1983 with regards to its aim to seize power threw the URNG's international work into turmoil. It gave rise to tensions in solidarity committees and, of course, with governments, political parties, trade unions, NGOs, and the European press. Many European comrades told us, more or less in a few words, that "we support the popular movement as regards its expressions, but we do not necessarily support the URNG. We are in favor of the mass movement's autonomy and also international solidarity." Such an estrangement, which with time turned out to be ideological in many cases, was not easy to swallow. Moreover, this coincided with a change of heart in government circles and global organizations with respect to humanitarian work as a job opportunity for many young Europeans who had hitherto dedicated their time to solidarity activism voluntarily. This meant that many ended up promoting the official lines of action of their respective governments.

For its part, the Guatemalan army started to coerce the representatives of NGOs working in the conflict areas already under its control, many of who distanced themselves from us in order to safeguard their presence as well as their institutional and personal interests, regardless of whether or not our contacts had introduced them to communities and popular organizations. This was also the case with several left-wing European journalists, without mentioning the right-wing press, which was always on the side of the military, and the presidents-elect in the framework of "managed democracy" (1986–1996). For the members of the URNG, the right decision was to respect these stances and attempt to make them understand that the Guatemalan revolutionary movement could cope insofar as it had not been defeated on the battlefield, the military continued to govern in Guatemala and, above all, unjust socioeconomic structures, impunity, and racism still prevailed.

In 1983, I was joined in representing the URNG by the physician Jorge Rosal ("Belisario Aldana"), living in Belgium, and two years later by the sociologist Miguel Ángel Reyes ("Francisco Mendizábal") of the FAR in England. The three of us concurred that the political-diplomatic teams of the URNG should be a model space of revolutionary unity that at the time neither included a military nor, above all, an organizational or financial dimension. As Reyes reflected in retrospect: "To represent the URNG. This was particularly important because it represented the unity of the organizations comprising it and because it was probably the only team embodying this unity that worked and did so in a congenial fashion."[6] Undoubtedly, this was an important element in the success of our mission, accepting in turn that we performed most of our unitary representative work in a singular way. The fact that, as representatives, we were few in number compared to the territorial and political vastness of Europe added to the importance of unity.

Together, we began to visit members of the European Parliament, both in Brussels and Strasbourg, and the UN mission at Geneva, with the aim of lobbying the European governments that were lending military and diplomatic support to the military dictatorship, in order to encourage them to submit motions that shed some light on the ongoing massacres of the Mayan peasant community, the Guatemalan refugees in Mexico, and a harshly repressed popular movement. At different junctures, the support of parliamentarians such as Luciana Castellina (PCI), Gianni Baget-Bozzo (PSI), Enzo Mattina (PSI), Klaus Hänsch (Social Democratic Party of Germany-SPD), Frederick Roll (SPD), Heidi Wieczorek-Zeul (SPD), Janis Sakellariu (SPD), Henry Saby (PSF), Claude Dejardin (Belgian Socialist Party–PSB), Enrique Barón Crespo (PSOE), and Antonio García-Pagán (PSOE) would prove vital. Between 1986 and 1987, García-Pagán sat on the commission responsible for Central America and the Contadora Group. This enabled the European representation to be more dynamic and to redouble its efforts to break the wall of silence regarding the war and repression in Guatemala, which was becoming more intense and widespread.

We highlighted several political aspects: the disastrous consequences of counter-insurgency and, therefore, the prolongation of the military dictatorship in Guatemala which, after having closed spaces in 1963, prevented any democracy in the country and its citizens from playing the role to be expected of them; the dimension of the genocide, with the intensification of the "scorched-earth" policy, the civil defense patrols, and the model villages; and the fact that, even though the URNG's strategy to seize power by force had failed, this did not signify that it had been defeated on the battlefield. All the military campaigns that the Guatemalan army planned periodically were ultimately fiascos due to its incapacity to break the resistance of the guerrillas in their jungle strongholds. The URNG continued to influence the main expressions of popular resistance in the countryside and cities.

Notwithstanding this, by the end of 1985 the work of our support structures in Europe began to feel the effects of the consolidation of the hegemony of the conservative revolution in international relations, observing how this brought pressure to bear on chanceries, political parties, and, above all, the European Parliament to isolate us. It was the Spanish member of the European Parliament Enrique Barón Crespo, who at the beginning of 1986, put "a flea in our ear" when saying, "Look gentlemen, if you repeat my words, I will deny it, but everything about European policy on Central America has changed. Use another strategy, another discourse. Europe is toeing the line of the new diplomacy of the Reagan-Thatcher era. It is necessary to find a new way of driving the project forward, to opt for a political solution." We then conveyed this message to the members of the then International Team of the URNG. Likewise, we all included the information in our individual reports to our respective organizations.

To this political-diplomatic scenario was added the decision of the Guatemalan military to call Constitutional Assembly elections in 1984, with the aim of establishing a "managed presidential democracy"—to wit, one that continued to bar those political parties that professed "communist ideologies" from the country's political spaces. In this respect, Vinicio Cerezo, the leader of the Guatemalan Christian Democracy (DCG) party and president-elect, complained shortly afterward that as president and commander-in-chief he wielded only "30 percent of the power." This political thaw orchestrated by the military led some European activists who had previously condemned the Guatemalan military regime to modify their stance and consider not only establishing closer diplomatic relations with Guatemala, but also to ask for guarantees while operating in the country. In France, the change of heart among several social scientists and members of NGOs was fairly evident, but the militarization continued.

One last aspect that underscored the need to modify our European strategy was that the European governments now obliged NGOs to take into account that, if they received financial aid for their Central American operations, these had to be in line with the foreign policy of their respective countries, which led to a drop in public funding for the region's mass revolutionary organizations. Further, in 1984, what was known as the International of Resistance, an organization defending the forces combating the Sandinista government—that is, the Contras—as well as condemning Central American revolutionary movements on the grounds that their Marxist ideologies and practices undermined the indigenous ethnic groups, gained momentum. This was the shape that the counter-revolution took in the confrontation between the United States and the Soviet Union, which, despite being focused on the Afghan conflict at the time, constantly raised the alarm to the negative effects that the "domino theory" could have in the Central American isthmus for the interests of Western democracy. Thus, some of the European intellectuals who had championed our cause now pointed the finger of blame at us.

Toward a Negotiated Solution

In this context, the URNG began to discuss the possibility of moving toward a negotiated solution to the armed conflict that had begun in 1962 internally, as described by Sandoval in *El sueño de la paz. El inicio del diálogo gobierno-guerrilla* (The Dream of Peace: The Start of Dialogue between the Government and Guerrilla).[7] Now living in Mexico, he participated actively in the contacts that the URNG established with the Mexican government through diplomats such as Jorge Castañeda, Gonzalo Martínez Corbalá, Gustavo Iruegas, and Ricardo Valero, all of whom had been involved in reaching a negotiated solution in El Salvador.

As of March 1987, President Cerezo began to hold discrete talks with the Spanish president Felipe González with an eye to convening the first meeting between the Guatemalan authorities and the representatives of the

URNG. This was helped by the signing of the Esquipulas II Accord by the Central American presidents on August 7, in which they assumed such a possibility at a regional level (Guatemala, El Salvador, and Nicaragua). Two months later, on October 7, a meeting between the Guatemalan government and guerrilla movement was held in Madrid. The official delegation included the vice-president of Congress, Roberto Valle, the deputy, Alfonso Alonso, and the Ambassador of Guatemala to Spain, Danilo Barillas, who were accompanied by military advisors.

Commander Rodrigo Asturias, Luis Bekker, and Sandoval led the delegation of the URNG. Their advisors included our comrade Reyes who, having been a member of the Guatemalan Christian Democracy (DCG), knew both Ambassador Barillas and President Cerezo well. In his essay "La esperanza entre sombras, el proceso de solución política al conflicto armado" (Hope among Shadows, the Process of a Political Solution to the Armed Conflict), Reyes recalls that, once Cerezo had been sworn into office in March 1986, when meeting with him in Costa Rica to explain the need for a negotiated solution to the armed conflict, he had received the reply that "Reagan and the army were against it." Nonetheless, Cerezo accepted the continuation of talks. Consequently, Reyes briefed the commander of the FAR, Jorge Soto García, on putting together a team of negotiators for future meetings, which would be called the Political-Diplomatic Commission. On May 12 of the same year, a second meeting was held in Costa Rica, this time between a government delegation led by Cerezo and that of the URNG, in which it was decided to leave "the channel open." For its part, the URNG took the initiative by publicly declaring that it was "open to political dialogue on peace."[8]

* * *

Nevertheless, as Sandoval has stressed, in the country at the time, "Neither the guerrillas regarded that situation as feasible, nor had the military contemplated it in its different scenarios."[9] We, who were working in the international field, were the ones who more clearly saw the impasse that had been reached and who had the impression that there was now no solution to be had. For the military leaders, a new campaign, this time larger, was the only way forward, as they would show with the "Final Offensive," waged from November 1987 to August 1988. For the revolutionary leaders in the interior, the best option was to continue with the war of attrition with a view to an eventual recuperation in the midterm.

This time, the Guatemalan army fielded 13,000 men, supported by aircraft, helicopters, and heavy artillery, with the aim of torpedoing the political and diplomatic effects of the Madrid talks. The high command sought to annihilate the insurgents, whose guerrilla columns had assembled in the strategic areas of Ixcán, the Tajumulco and Atitlán Volcanoes, and in the extensive areas of the department of Petén. Moreover, it took control of the Communities of Population in Resistance in the jungle and in the highlands in order to undermine their support for the revolutionary movement. The failure of the offensive, which involved the largest contingent of troops during the war, prolonged the armed conflict amidst others ("Pueblo 89," "Avance 90," and "Consolidación de la Paz 92"), reaching a deadlock in which the army continued to suffer casualties and the loss of material, while the guerrillas were now incapable of massively incorporating new combatants.

*   *   *

While talks were being held in Madrid, Rosal and I attended a meeting of the Socialist International held in Vienna (Austria) in October. The Salvadorans Guillermo Ungo and Héctor Oquelí Colindres, respectively leaders of the National Revolutionary Movement (NRM) and the Democratic Revolutionary Front (FDR), accompanied us respectively. In an interview that I gave a journalist in the Austrian capital, I declared that we had received information that the Guatemalan government was prepared to enter into formal negotiations, news that was immediately covered in the Guatemalan press and denied by the government of Cerezo. Obviously, he felt pressured by the protests of the country's business leaders and far-Right political parties, particularly the MLN. We needed to break out of the political-diplomatic isolation in which we were immersed and which the Esquipulas I and II Accords had done nothing but increase. In December 1987, Sandoval called us to a meeting held in The Hague (Holland).

As regards the results of the 1987 negotiations, Sandoval pointed to several ideas worth recalling: first, the meeting that he had held with us to inform us about the content and possibilities of both the Madrid talks and our work in the immediate future had seemed to him the right course of action, above all when bearing in mind that we were resentful of "the disinformation and, especially, a certain disregard [for our work] shown by those in charge of international work and, above all, the guerrilla command"; second, the importance of recuperating the political initiative on the international stage, taking into consideration that, by then, the situation of the struggle could only be explained to chanceries and political parties in Europe and other parts of the world as "part of the framework of the Central American conflict"; third, that the talks would give new impetus to our relationship as a unitary delegation with solidarity organizations, trade unions, and political parties by envisaging a political solution to the Guatemalan armed conflict; and last, that the statements that I had made in Vienna and the fact that the Guatemalan press had covered them showed that "the talks in Madrid had begun to bear fruit at an international level only a few weeks after their conclusion."[10] Throughout 1988, we did not tire of intentionally reiterating our willingness to find a political solution to the war in Guatemala.

In February of that year, Menchú traveled to Geneva to participate in the sessions of the UN Human Rights Commission, where she was heckled by Dr. José Luis Chea Morales, the official Guatemalan representative to the organization, who dared her to visit Guatemala. Chea Morales believed that the RUOG was not in contact with the country's new political reality. The RUOG, deciding to take up the gauntlet, made plans to send two of its members, Menchú and Rolando Castillo Montalvo, to Guatemala to discuss the country's political situation and that of its exiles with representatives of the government, the political parties, the Catholic hierarchy, and the mass movement. On April 7, they arrived in Guatemala accompanied by parliamentarians from Belgium, England, Germany, Mexico, and the United States, plus a number of journalists and representatives of the United Church of Canada. Despite the presence of the national and international press and hundreds of grassroots activists, the national police arrested them as soon as they left the plane; they were taken before a judge and accused of "crimes against the state." The fragility of the "managed democracy" led by Cerezo was again reflected on the front pages of the global press. In the face of national and international pressure, the president ordered their release under the legal pretext of an "amnesty." In Europe, the doors opened again and our cause gained impetus, for it evinced the close interdependence between the dormant state of the war and the popular and revolutionary political-diplomatic activity.

In October 1988, I requested to be transferred to Mexico after ten years of working in the international field, which was granted to me. I was exhausted as a result of traveling through Europe, attending endless appointments, issuing dozens of statements, constantly drafting reports, and combating the skepticism and indifference of so many civil servants and citizens. I wanted to return to Central America to be close to the struggle of my people and to convey my experience in the international field, since

I knew that a negotiated solution would take quite a bit of time due to the positions of both parties on the eve of the fall of real socialism. As that solution became more drawn out, our diplomatic position in Europe was yet again legitimized and the international pressure brought to bear on the Guatemalan state became more focused on achieving a peace agreement.

In Mexico, I started to collaborate directly in supporting the CUC. Little did we know that Rigoberta Menchú had already started out on the path to obtaining the Nobel Peace Prize. The first European politician to mention this possibility was Bettino Craxi, the leader of the PSI, in 1990.

Finally, I believe that in order to understand the political results of that international work, four subsequent events must be recognized that ultimately affected the path of the negotiated solution of 1996: (1) the decision of the URNG in 1989 to opt for Swedish mediation to complete the negotiations successfully, taking as an example the Palestinian-Arab-Israeli negotiations that we had observed; (2) the breakup of the Soviet Union and Vladimir Kryuchkov's failed coup to restore it; (3) the peace accords between the FMLN and the Salvadoran government in January 1992, which stressed the importance of a negotiated solution to the Central American civil wars; and (4) the award of the Nobel Peace Prize to Menchú, which put Guatemala on the global political map due to its triple significance: the recognition of the voice of the American Indigenous peoples, of the popular Guatemalan movement, and of the victims of the country's armed conflict.

The Historical Lesson to Be Learned

It is appropriate to end with the following general reflection: in Guatemala, it is thought that the peace accords were basically reached thanks to armed struggle and the resilience of combatants. Abroad it is conversely held that the revolutionary victory forced the institutionalized politicians and the military to sign those accords. Both stances have their shortcomings insofar as they do not assume that it was due to both realities; moreover, the final outcome was the result of a balanced combination of both, evincing the globalizing dimension of our political-military struggle.

The URNG's political-diplomatic triumph would have been impossible if it had not been for the fact that the Guatemalan army and its allies were incapable of defeating the guerrillas on the battlefield, even though the revolutionary military strategy to seize power had floundered, on the one hand, and that they were isolated and defeated diplomatically. And it is clear that the latter was thanks to the international work of the URNG and the Guatemalan popular movement on two continents (Europe and America), which were backed by a significant part of world opinion that aspired to put an end to the revolutionary struggles in Central America. Even so, in the main, although it is tacitly present in the history of both the EGP and the Guatemalan revolutionary movement, the true worth of that *cuarta pata del banco* is still underestimated. It is therefore hoped these lines serve to give it its due importance.

Notes

This chapter is the product of the author's personal experiences as a representative of the Guerrilla Army of the Poor (EGP) in Europe from 1981 to 1988 and of the Guatemalan National Revolutionary Unity (URNG) from 1982 to 1988.

1. This appeared in No. 15 of *Pensamiento Crítico*, published in Havana in December 1967, together with other texts written by revolutionaries who had been active in the FAR until then. This was the case of Antonio Fernández Izaguirre, who used the pen name Julio del Valle in the essay entitled "Guatemala bajo el signo de la guerra" (Guatemala under the Sign of War), and Aura Marina Arriola, the authoress of "Secuencia de la cultura indígena guatemalteca" (Progression of Guatemalan Indigenous Culture). Likewise, two political statements issued by the FAR were disclosed. Included as background material were the "Discurso del comandante Luis Turcios Lima en la Conferencia Tricontinental" (Speech of Commander Luis Turcios Lima at the Tricontinental Conference) of January 1966; "Breves apuntes históricos del Movimiento Revolucionario 13 de Noviembre" (Brief Historical Notes on the Revolutionary Movement of November 13) by Commander Marco Antonio Yon Sosa; and "La revolución guatemalteca" (The Guatemalan Revolution) by the writer Luis Cardoza y Aragón, alluding to the feat of 1944–1954.

2. For an account of her revolutionary work in Europe, see Arriola *Ese obstinado sobrevivir*. Based on what had been published in Cuba between 1969 and 1971, we raised the possibility of disseminating the main writings of the revolutionary project in Europe—in Italy through the publishing houses Feltrinelli (*Autobiografia di una guerriglia. Guatemala 1960–1968*) and Vangelista Editore (*Guatemala: la via della guerriglia*), and in France through Maspero (*Lettres du front guatémaltèque*)—as well as in Uruguay through Ediciones de la Banda (*Turcios Lima. Biografía y documentos*, 1969), making the most of the writer Eduardo Galeano's arrival in the Central American country in 1967 to prepare *Guatemala, País ocupado*, and in the Mexican journal *Hora Cero* no. 4 (April 1968).

3. Paris, Éditions du Seuil, 1974.

4. "Conversación. Arturo Taracena historiador," interview by Luis Aceituno and Francisco Rodríguez, *El Periódico*, Guatemala, November 9, 1999, 16–17.

5. See the preface by Grandin. *Who is Rigoberta Menchu?* pp. v–xiii.

6. Author's interview with Miguel Ángel Reyes, April 3, 2017.

7. Sandoval, *El sueño de la paz.*

8. Miguel Ángel Reyes Illescas. "La esperanza entre sombras, el proceso de solución política al conflicto armado."

9. Miguel Ángel Reyes Illescas. "La esperanza entre sombras, el proceso de solución política al conflicto armado," 5.

10. Sandoval, *El sueño de la paz*, 149–151.

Bibliography

Álvarez Aragón, Virgilio, et al. *Guatemala Historia reciente (1954–1996) Tomo IV. Proceso de paz y contexto Internacional*. Guatemala: FLACSO, 2013.

Anónimo. *Turcios Lima. Biografía y Documentos*. Montevideo: Ediciones de la Banda Oriental, 1969.

Arriola, Aura Marina. *Ese obstinado sobrevivir. Autoetnobiografía de una mujer guatemalteca*. Guatemala: Ediciones del Pensativo, 2000.

Debray, Regis. *La critique des armes*. Paris: Éditions du Seuil, 1974.

Galeano, Eduardo. *Guatemala, País ocupado*. México: Nuestro Tiempo, 1967.

Grandin, Greg. *Who is Rigoberta Menchu?* London & New York: Verso, 2011.

Morán, Rolando. *Autobiografia di una guerriglia: Guatemala 1960–1968*. Milano: Feltrinelli, 1969.

Ramírez de León, Ricardo; Arriola, Aura Marina. *Guatemala: la via della guerriglia*. Roma: Vangelista Editore, 1969.

Ramírez de León, Ricardo. *Lettres du front guatémaltèque*. París: Maspero, 1970.

Reyes Illescas, Miguel Ángel. "La esperanza entre sombras, el proceso de solución política al conflicto armado," in Álvarez Aragón, Virgilio, et al. *Guatemala Historia reciente (1954–1996) Tomo IV. Proceso de paz y contexto Internacional*, 145–189. Guatemala: FLACSO, 2013.

Sandoval, Miguel Ángel. *El sueño de la paz. El inicio del diálogo gobierno-guerrilla* Guatemala: F&G Editores, 2013.

7

Spanish Internationalists in the Sandinista Revolution

An Approach to the Ambrosio Mogorrón Committee (1986–1990)

JOSÉ MANUEL ÁGREDA PORTERO

Two militants have remained in the Spanish left-wing's collective imagination because they were killed during the Sandinista Revolution in Nicaragua. The first is Gaspar García Laviana, a Catholic priest and commander of the Sandinista National Liberation Front (FSLN), who was killed by the national guard on December 11, 1978, in Departamento de Cárdenas, close to the Costa Rican border on the Southern Front.[1] The other is Ambrosio Mogorrón, who arrived in Nicaragua in 1980. He was a nurse in San José de Bocay until May 24, 1986, when his vehicle ran over a Contra landmine.[2] A few months later, in October, a group of Spaniards who lived in Nicaragua working for the Sandinista Revolution founded the Ambrosio Mogorrón Committee in his memory.

Twenty years after the Cuban Revolution, the FSLN's victory in 1979 was followed by a series of revolutionary measures. The structural reforms introduced in Nicaragua and the clash with Ronald Reagan's administration in the United States over its backing of the Contra guerrillas from 1981 prompted left-wing organizations and groups from all over the world to take a stand on Nicaraguan political developments.

* * *

This chapter sheds light on the global dimensions of the FSLN's revolutionary project. It shows how the FSLN's struggle against the dictatorship of Anastasio Somoza Debayle in Nicaragua and the Cold War in the 1980s provided the context for the emergence of a transnational solidarity network between Europe and Nicaragua.[3]

In Spain, all political parties took a stand on the FSLN´s struggle against Somoza. Spanish left-wing militants and activists got involved in a solidarity network with Nicaragua after its inception in 1978. Nonetheless, the FSLN was not supported only by activists in Spain before and after 1979—Spaniards in Nicaragua were fighting or working for the FSLN as well.

This chapter focuses on the Ambrosio Mogorrón Committee (1986–1990), a truly atypical solidarity committee founded by Spaniards but based in Nicaragua. Among other facets, the committee worked as a sort of intermediary and clearinghouse of the Nicaraguan revolutionary government for the solidarity network created in Spain. In this capacity, the organization became a place of reference for Spanish solidarity groups. Its creation and development show how internationalists built an organization in a host country to manage solidarity relations in the context of the Spanish non-state interaction with the FSLN. The main purpose of this work is to highlight the key importance of the complex network of institutions and groups that made up the basis of the Spanish transnational solidarity network with Nicaragua, revealing as well its internal dynamics.

The chapter thus offers some preliminary findings about the meaning and global dynamics of solidarity with Nicaragua. It argues that the position inside the political system of the parties that offered solidarity conditioned their involvement in the Spanish-Nicaraguan transnational solidarity network. The most important left-wing Spanish parties, despite sharing the Sandinista's ideological framework almost in full, distanced themselves from solidarity work when their own political goals did not fully coincide with those of its Nicaraguan partners. In contrast, activists of parties with less political clout became the most committed members of the transnational solidarity committee, fully embracing the FSLN's ideals and political project.

Additionally, this case study offers interesting findings that go beyond the particularities of this transnational network. For instance, it shows that when the group requesting solidarity is in a strong political position, it is capable of maintaining contacts at different levels with each one of the actors offering solidarity, according to their different political views and interests. Thus, relationships with key actors of the political system (strong political parties) are carried out as interactions between equals. By contrast, relationships—the FSLN's in this case—with marginal (extra-parliamentary) political actors were not direct but channeled through solidarity committees.[4]

The chapter is organized into three sections. The first deals with the Spanish political parties involved in the transnational network supporting Nicaragua at the end of the 1970s and at the beginning of the following decade. The second provides a brief overview of the network's structure in Spain and the institutions created by the FSLN to communicate with it. In the final section, the history of the Ambrosio Mogorrón Committee offers insights into how the activists of these Spanish left-wing parties managed relations between the solidarity network created in Spain and the FSLN in Nicaragua.

Spanish Left-Wing Parties and the Sandinista Revolution (1978–1990)

After Franco's death in 1975, Spain's foreign policy toward Latin America changed. According to Francisco Villar, in the terrain of international relations, a substitution policy was adopted in which Latin America was used as a way of legitimizing the regime. During the Spanish transition, this policy evolved to become an essential aspect of the first democratic governments.[5] In relation to Nicaragua, Adolfo Suárez, the first premier of the newly established Spanish democracy, continued to make loans to the Somoza regime that the latter used to purchase arms. The initiative known as the *Paquete España* (Spanish Package) was heavily criticized by the opposition parties.[6] However, contradicting its earlier policy of selling arms to Somoza, Pedro de Arístegui, Spanish Ambassador in Managua from 1978 to 1980, argues the government also offered the victors of the 1979 revolution in Nicaragua its support.[7] Arístegui himself managed to organize the evacuation of some three thousand people from Nicaragua during the clashes of the final months. The evacuees included Spaniards, Sandinistas, and supporters of the Somoza regime.[8] In July 1979, Mexico and Peru asked the Spanish Ambassador to manage their interests in Nicaragua, since they had severed diplomatic ties with Somoza.[9] Spain then recognized Nicaragua's new government on July 19, the same day Managua was liberated.[10]

Between 1979 and 1981, the government of Adolfo Suárez then went out of its way to effect further political change in Nicaragua. According to a report issued by the FSLN's Department of International Relations (DRI), Spain was the European country that made the largest donations in kind to Nicaragua between July 19, 1979, and November 26, 1980, amounting to $12,224,500, representing 6.4% of total foreign aid. (For comparison, the United States made the biggest contribution as regards both donations in kind [16.8%] and loans [13.5%].)[11] Indeed, the Spanish establishment warmly welcomed the Sandinista Revolution. The idea of overthrowing a prolonged dictatorship like that of Franco appealed not only to the country's left-wing parties but also, as will be seen below, to the center-right represented by the party in power.

The Spanish Left of the 1970s and 1980s can be divided into two types related to their position in the new political regime: on the one hand, the Spanish Socialist Workers' Party (PSOE) and the Communist Party of Spain (PCE), which were able to access the new regime's institutions after obtaining representation in the first democratic elections; and on the other, the extra-parliamentary Left that was located on the margins of the political system. This last term is the one that Spanish historiography employs to refer to the extreme left-wing parties that emerged during the final stages of the Franco dictatorship. These included the Workers' Revolutionary Organization (ORT), the Party of Labor of Spain (PTE), the Communist Movement of Spain (MCE), the Revolutionary Communist League (LCR), and the Communist Party of Spain (Marxist-Leninist) (PCE[m-l]), to name but a few.

The PSOE was Spain's main left-wing political force following the first democratic elections in 1977. During the armed period of the FSLN from 1978 to 1979, the PSOE unofficially showed the organization how to obtain arms in Libya, Algeria, and Lebanon, through personal contacts between the FSLN member Ernesto Cardenal and Javier Nart, the party's representative for Africa and the Arab states.[12]

Until the PSOE's electoral victory in October 1982, these contacts were made via two main channels. Since September 17, 1979, the party had been permanently represented in Nicaragua by the Agrupación Nicaragüense del PSOE (Nicaraguan Group of the PSOE). Its members anticipated the creation of their own federation within the PSOE and intended to act as intermediaries for the cooperation projects that it managed. However, they soon realized that they did not have as much power as they would have liked, and other communication channels were opened.[13]

The second channel, more robust than the first, was routed through European social democratic groups for which the PSOE aspired to act as an intermediary with the FSLN.[14] Felipe González, Secretary General of the PSOE, was named chairman of the Nicaraguan Revolution Defense Committee of the Socialist International (SI) in November 1980, during a meeting held in Madrid. The committee's objectives were "to work for international solidarity and assistance for Nicaragua's development program . . . to spread information about the country and its democratization process . . . to avert intervention in Nicaragua's internal affairs by outside powers . . . [and] to guarantee the respect for Nicaragua's right to self-determination."[15]

The SI was one of the main backers of the revolution during the 1980s. The FSLN participated in its meetings as an observer, although this also led to a dilemma. In February 1982, González then mediated between the Latin American parties, which opposed the FSLN attending a Caracas meeting because the issue of the Central American crisis was on the agenda. Willy Brandt, the president of the SI at the time, decided to postpone the encounter, holding it in Bonn in April instead. The reason for the friction was the critical opinion that, as of 1981, the revolution had been drifting toward an authoritarian regime. In the Declaration of the SI's *Presidium* of April 2, different aspects of the Central American conflicts were analyzed. And although delegates did not focus solely on the case of Nicaragua, support for its cause was nevertheless explicitly ratified. The central idea that can be gleaned from the documents available is that the SI had a global view of the Central American problem, and it believed the solution was not only to be found in Nicaragua, but that a treaty including the United States and Cuba should also be established.[16] In short, the aim of the PSOE and the SI alike was to seek and endorse peace processes in the region.

González traveled to Nicaragua on a number of occasions between 1979 and 1982, but never visited during the years in which the PSOE and the FSLN were government parties in their respective countries. As Spanish Premier, he made his first trip in 1995 to meet with Violeta Chamorro.[17] This was a clear sign of the socialist leader's gradual disaffection with the Sandinista Revolution. Indeed, between 1982 and 1990, according to Francisco Villar, the Spanish government's stance on Nicaragua was that of calculated ambiguity with a view to fostering a relative rapprochement with the United States.[18] Spain did not back Nicaragua's elections held in 1984, on the grounds they lacked democratic credentials. As a matter of fact, the country sent a low-profile representative to attend Daniel Ortega's inauguration in 1985.[19]

In contrast, González supported the 1990 Nicaraguan elections by sending observers.[20] Moreover, Yago Pico de Coaña, General Manager to Latin America of Spanish Ministry of Foreign Affairs, had a dispute in a 1983 meeting of NATO with Luigi Einaudi, U.S. representative, in which the

Spanish government criticized the U.S. point of view regarding Nicaragua.[21] The contact between the PSOE and the FSLN was never broken. Prominent Sandinistas were both officially and not officially received during Felipe Gonzalez's administration.[22] Spain played an important role in contacts and meetings to get the pacification of the region; it even sent troops between December 1989 and December 1991 in the first UN peacekeeping mission commanded by a member of the Spanish armed forces.[23]

In summary, during the 1980s, the PSOE's position vis-à-vis the Sandinista Revolution varied, from firm support in the initial years to an ambiguous distancing during the time the party was in power.

At the time, the Spanish Communist Party (PCE) became fully committed to solidarity with Nicaragua as regards to both politics and cooperation. In the political sphere it enjoyed a peer-to-peer relationship with the FSLN. In 1985, Julio Anguita, Secretary General of the PCE, attended Daniel Ortega's inauguration, and the Sandinistas made a return visit on the occasion of the tribute paid to Dolores Ibárruri, one of the party's most prominent leaders in exile during the Franco dictatorship.[24] In Spain, the PCE also became politically involved by attending the solidarity committees during the initial years. Marcos Ana, a charismatic leader as a result of the time he had spent in prison during Franco's dictatorship, participated in the Nicaraguan solidarity platform in Madrid as head of the party's solidarity department.[25] He also managed aid and cooperation campaigns, such as the one organized after the hurricane that struck Nicaragua in 1982.[26]

In the realm of economic cooperation, Miguel Núñez, another leader of the PCE in Catalonia, created the Association of Cooperation with the South (ACSUR-Las Segovias, in reference to the northern region of Nicaragua). Núñez raised funds for his pilot project in the city of Estelí in 1987, thanks to donations from artists such as Antoni Tàpies and Eduardo Chillida and film director Carlos Saura.[27]

Meanwhile, during Spain's democratic transition, a number of sectors within the PCE did not share the party's stance on the country's political changes. According to them, the new democracy was hampered from the start by the steadfastness of the structures of the previous regime. After realizing it would be impossible to effect far-reaching social and political changes in their country, some communist militants had therefore given vent to their frustrations by embracing internationalism and traveling to Nicaragua. Pedro Ariza, an economic exile living in Germany, for example, described how, after a PCE meeting for émigrés, he decided to travel to Nicaragua to take up arms in 1978. Ariza did not understand why the delegation representing the PCE turned up with the Spanish constitutional flag when the struggle against the Franco dictatorship had been in defense of the republican tricolor. After joining the Southern Front in Costa Rica, Ariza remained in the Sandinista Popular Army for a number of years and still lives in Nicaragua.[28]

During the first months after the victory of July 19, other activists traveled to the country to participate in the revolution. This was the case with Luis Alfredo Lobato, who would later assume post of Secretary General at the National Autonomous University of Nicaragua (UNAN-Managua) and who arrived in the country at the end of 1979 with the help of the Communist Party of Asturias. However, Lobato never wanted to attend meetings or mix with the Spaniards arriving in Nicaragua through the solidarity network. His sole aim was to live the revolution as if he were just another Nicaraguan.[29]

On the other hand, the extra-parliamentary Left was composed of parties that represented the so-called *vía rupturista* within the Spanish transition, namely, those political forces that were against the consensus reached by the mainstream political parties for reforming the Franco's regime. The extra-parliamentary Left called upon citizens to vote "No" in the Spanish constitutional referendum held on December 6, 1978, believing that it kept the structures of the dictatorship in place.[30]

They were very active in opposing the previous regime, but they lacked electoral strength and failed to gain representation in the new democratic parliament after the 1977 elections.[31] The most long-lived and, further, most committed to the transnational solidarity network with Nicaragua, were the Marxist-Leninist-Maoist MCE and the Trotskyist LCR.[32] In the words of Joaquín Alfonso, a member of the Committee for Solidarity with Nicaragua of Zaragoza and a Spanish internationalist, "In Zaragoza, the vast majority came from the LCR and the MC, in addition to the independents. There were also people from the Communist Party of the Peoples of Spain (PCPE's) and the PC-ml."[33]

Both the MCE and the LCR eventually put their electoral defeat behind them and stepped up their commitment to the main social movements appearing in Spain during the 1980s: the peace movement, the movement against compulsory military service, and internationalist solidarity.[34] They gradually lost steam from the end of the 1980s to the beginning of the following decade, due to having backed the "No" vote in the 1986 Spanish NATO membership referendum and, above all, being faced with the fall of the Berlin Wall and the FSLN's election defeat in Nicaragua in February

1990. That was when the two parties initiated a process of merger resulting in a new party, Alternative Left (IA), in 1991.[35]

These parties identified completely with the demands and directives of the FSLN. They were scathingly critical of the PSOE for what they believed was its rapprochement with the United States and its understanding of the Nicaraguan conflict as a struggle between two Cold War Blocs. For them, Nicaragua was involved in a revolutionary transition to democracy even though it did not share the political characteristics of its Western Bloc counterparts; meanwhile, transition in Spain maintained the Franco dictatorship structures. Although they acknowledged González's willingness to enter into negotiations with a view to brokering a peaceful solution to the conflict, they criticized the self-serving objective that, in their view, he was pursuing: to strengthen Spain's position in Latin America.[36]

As has been seen in this brief overview, the involvement of both the parliamentary and extra-parliamentary left-wing parties in the solidarity network related to their position on the Spanish political stage. From the moment when a party comes to power, relationships of solidarity are normally contingent on classic diplomacy and cooperation, conditioned in turn by national and international policy, as occurred with the PSOE. Meanwhile, the PCE, the second most important party, albeit without national government responsibilities, continued to maintain relations with Spanish social movements within the solidarity network, although its political power also allowed it to establish them directly with parties outside the network.

Finally, the Spanish-Nicaraguan relationship also suggests that when a peripheral party does not have government responsibilities, its ideological position is closer to that of the organizations requesting solidarity insofar as it is easier to share objectives. True enough, the ideologies defended by the LCR and the MCE, Trotskyism, and Maoism, respectively, contained elements of proletarian internationalism. But, on the other hand, their close ties with social solidarity movements can also be interpreted as a political strategy for spreading their ideology and, above all, for recruiting militants at home as well. In a nutshell, from any one of the three aforementioned contexts (governing, prominent, or peripheral party), it is clear that national political interests influenced the participation of political parties in the Spanish solidarity network.

The Structure of Transnational Solidarity in Support of the Sandinista Revolution

Transnational solidarity in support of Nicaragua, of which the Ambrosio Mogorrón Committee formed part, was created in Spain in Autumn 1978, when Ernesto Cardenal appointed Ángel Barrajón as the representative of the FSLN for Southern Europe (Spain, Portugal, Italy, and Greece) and the United Kingdom, with headquarters in Madrid.[37] Barrajón was a former Spanish priest who had arrived in Nicaragua in 1969 and had been deported by the Somoza government in 1977 under accusations of having collaborated with FSLN guerrilla forces.[38]

Together, Barrajón and Enrique Schmidt—also appointed by Cardenal as the representative for the rest of Europe—created a network of committees in Western Europe. The European Secretariat, with the two Dutch activists Klaas Wellinga and Hans Langenberg and the German Hermann Schulz, was set up to manage it.[39] By organizing European solidarity committee congresses in support of Nicaragua, the FSLN established guidelines and presented the work undertaken in each country. Sixteen congresses were held between 1979 and 1991, three of which were in Spain: in Madrid in October 1978, in Zaragoza in February 1984, and in San Sebastian in December 1991.[40]

Before the Sandinista victory on July 19, 1979, the network had two goals in Spain and the rest of Europe. On the one hand, the political objective consisted of promoting solidarity among the main political parties and Spanish society as a whole. According to Barrajón, the organizations that initially lent the greatest amount of support included the PSOE—through Luís Yañez, a member of the international relations department—the trade unions and peripheral parties like the MCE.[41] To engage Spanish society, the Nicaraguans residing in Spain organized and created twenty-one committees throughout the country. Their tasks involved giving talks on the situation in Nicaragua, staging awareness raising events and, chiefly, catching the attention of the Spanish press.[42]

The second objective was economic and military in order to maintain the struggle against Somoza. The parties and committees contributed to raising funds for the FSLN. Barrajón traveled to Lebanon with Javier Nart to purchase arms from the Palestinian Liberation Organization (PLO). In June 1979, a plane was chartered from Beirut to Costa Rica, but it never arrived at its destination.[43] During the meetings Cardenal attended in Europe, a number of people offered to participate in the armed struggle in

Nicaragua, but the FSLN turned them down, as its main objective was to obtain political support, money, and arms.[44]

By the spring of 1979, the committees in Spain were already connected, albeit modestly. There were two main coordinating groups: the committee run by Barrajón in Madrid, and the Comité de Solidaritat de Catalunya amb Nicaragua (Catalan Solidarity Committee in Support of Nicaragua or COSOCAN), based in Barcelona.[45] The dissemination of information is one of the main goals of any network.[46] The COSOCAN, together with other committees, managed to publish three bulletins whose aim was to inform Spanish society about the Nicaraguan Revolution and to present the Sandinistas in a favorable light.[47]

Following the Sandinista victory on July 19, Barrajón returned to Nicaragua on August 12 to participate in the revolutionary process, as did many of the Nicaraguan activists who had sat on Spanish committees since their inception.[48] And from the end of 1979, there were important changes to the solidarity network formed prior to the revolution. On the one hand, the Nicaraguans who had returned home were replaced by Spaniards, and on the other, three coordinating committees grouping together all the Spanish committees were now created.

Despite their differences, all left-wing parties in Spain participated in the committees, but, as the 1980s progressed, it was the extra-parliamentary Left that gradually gained control of them, particularly the MCE and the LCR.[49] Documents from the mid-1980s nevertheless refer to the rivalry between both parties over the control of the committees, co-ordination committees, and work brigades in Nicaragua. In 1987, for example, when the LCR accused the MCE that its opinion on a housing project in El Salto had not been taken into account, the depth and ongoing nature of the rift was laid bare:

Problems with the MC:
1. Their criticism of us: we have managed to push the project through despite being in a minority on the committees and despite the refusal of the leadership of the MC. . . .
2. Actions of the MC: they have done their utmost to obstruct us (above all in the state coordinating committee . . .
In 1985, the brigades were organized all but exclusively by the MC. . . . Asturias has not accepted the "El Salto" project since the MC holds an ample majority on that committee.[50]

For these two parties, desperately in need of activists, the transnational network in support of Nicaragua was an important recruitment pool in which to "fish" for support:

> To Promote and Organize Solidarity Work with Nicaragua
> Work guidelines and criteria
> 4. In this task it is also possible to recruit for both the party and the JCR [Young Communist Revolutionaries] . . .
> 5. Political groundwork needs to be undertaken with the brigade members before, during, and after their stay in Nicaragua . . . that they continue to be activists in their brigades in Nicaragua, that the party continues to exist for those brigade. . . . [51]

Meanwhile, in Item 6 of the same document, the Central Committee of the LCR deplored the fact that activists preferred working in Nicaragua to carrying out tasks for the solidarity network in Spain. All the revolutionary movements in Central America during the 1980s had an enormous appeal for left-wing militants, particularly for those whose expectations of social change had not been met, as occurred with the extra-parliamentary Left. Thus, many activists sought to participate in a process that they considered truly revolutionary ("6. We should politically convince ourselves that the solidarity work with Nicaragua is basically here and not in Nicaragua . . . we should avoid the current propensity to go and live in Nicaragua as a personal choice . . ."[52]).

As to the committees' structural organization, figure 7.1 shows the preeminent position of Sandinistas in the network. The FSLN created different institutions to encompass and manage this solidarity network. Before 1979, each different "tendency" into which the FSLN was divided (Prolonged People's War group, the urban proponents of the Proletarian Tendency, and the Insurrectionist Tendency) had its own international commission. After July 19, they were merged into a single body, the Department of International Relations (DRI), run by Julio López during most of the 1980s. This department was responsible for direct contact with ideologically like-minded political parties abroad.

Moreover, relations with solidarity committees from all over the world were managed though other institutions under its aegis. DRI gradually began to take over these tasks. In August 1984, for example, the Nicaraguan Committee in Solidarity with the People (CNSP) took charge of communication with the European committees.[53] In 1987, due to the state compression process implemented in Nicaragua, all the organizations dependent on the DRI were brought under the umbrella of the Consejo Nicaragüense de Solidaridad, Amistad y Paz (Nicaraguan Council of Friendship, Solidarity and Peace or CNASP), until the Sandinista's election defeat in 1990, when communication channels were again managed by the DRI, led at the time by Henry Ruíz.[54]

Since the FSLN controlled a state, when establishing contacts with NGOs it became the linchpin of the network. In order to manage this support, it created the Ministry of External Cooperation, under the control of Henry Ruíz, and the Augusto César Sandino Foundation (FACS), a major NGO in March 1980.[55] These organizations were responsible for drafting cooperation projects for the committees and assessing the actions of the NGOs operating in Nicaragua.[56]

The Catholic Church does not appear in figure 7.1 (mainly because of the need to limit this chapter strictly to political committees), although the Church was a key piece in solidarity with the Sandinista Revolution. In fact, the Catholic Church had its own network, different from the one analyzed here, managed in Nicaragua by the Antonio Valdivieso Ecumenical Center.[57]

In Spain, the Coordinadora Estatal de Solidaridad con Nicaragua (State Solidarity Co-ordinating Committee in Support of Nicaragua, CESN) was created in Barcelona in 1980. It served as an umbrella organization for committees from all over the country, overseeing relations with the Nicaraguan embassy and the European committees and coordinated state campaigns.[58]

A short time later, two other coordinating committees were created. These divisions were based on the different nationalist identities that existed in the country: the Basque and Catalan coordinating committees. In the rest of the country regional co-ordinating committees were also created, the difference being that all, except the Basque and Catalan, assumed the CESN campaigns and projects, although also with nuances between the two.

The Coordinadora Vasca de Solidaridad con Nicaragua (Basque Solidarity Co-ordinating Committee in Support of Nicaragua or CVSN), established in 1983, functioned autonomously regarding the FSLN, European relations, and brigades until 1987. During this time, as with the others committees controlled by the MK and the LKI (the Basque equivalent to the MCE and the LCR, respectively), it was divided into the Komité Internazionalistak and Askapena, close to the so-called Basque National Liberation Movement, to wit, the political and social movement organized by the

NICARAGUA   SPAIN   EUROPE

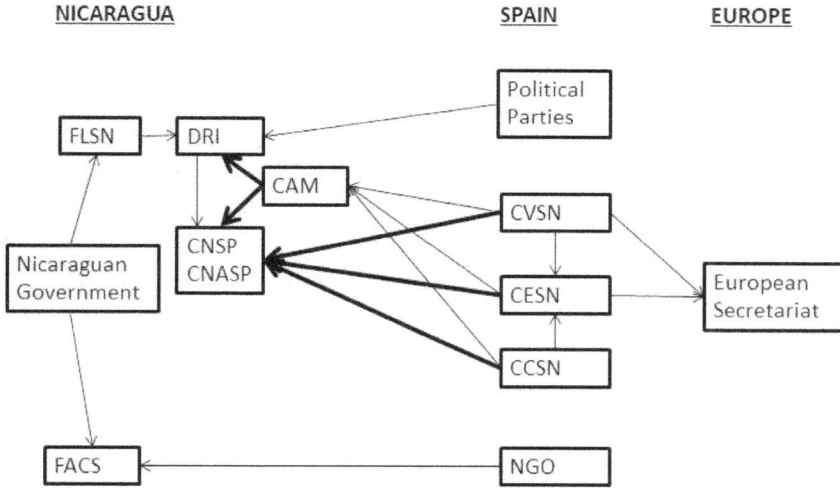

Figure 7.1. Diagram of the Spanish Transnational Solidarity Network (TSN) in support of the Nicaraguan Revolution

Basque nationalist Left.[59] The latter dissociated itself completely from the Spanish network, off its own bat establishing ties with the FSLN and organizing the Basque internationalists arriving in Nicaragua as of 1987.

In Catalonia, the Coordinadora Catalana de Solidaridad con Nicaragua (Catalan Solidarity Co-ordinating Committee in Support of Nicaragua, CCSN) was created in 1984. This organization did indeed remain under the aegis of the CESN. In fact, owing to its potential, it was given the task of politically coordinating campaigns throughout the country, until 1989. Nonetheless, the CCSN acted independently as far as the brigades and co-operation projects were concerned.[60]

The chief objectives of this network were to inform the Spanish public so it would support the revolution, and to challenge U.S. propaganda targeting the Sandinistas. However, it also managed to raise substantial funds for undertaking cooperation projects in Nicaragua. Throughout the decade, the committees began to work with other countries besides Nicaragua, and several committees merged, creating more general groups or committees of solidarity with Latin America (COSAL). They saw in state cooperation a better way to get funds, and some of them went on to found their own NGOs, with ideas more in tune with those of the beneficiaries. These were Mugarik Gabe, created by the CVSN, and Entrepueblos by the CESN and the CCSN.[61]

As can be seen in figure 7.1, the Ambrosio Mogorrón Committee (CAM) occupied a position midway between the coordinating committees and the Sandinista institutions. Although the coordinating committees held meetings in Spain and Europe with members of the DRI and the CNSP, the CAM's privileged position allowed it to obtain and distribute first-hand information on the latest developments in Nicaragua. Additionally, the reception of brigades for cooperation projects provided it with the opportunity to control the people arriving through the committees. Similarly, as will be seen below, the organization of the internationalists in situ also helped to forge closer links between Spain and Nicaragua.

The Ambrosio Mogorrón Committee (1986–1990)

The Ambrosio Mogorrón Committee is central to understanding the connections between Nicaragua and the solidarity committees in Spain. The committee was created by Spaniards involved in solidarity work in Nicaragua. The Ambrosio Mogorrón belonged to the Spanish network as a committee integrated into the CESN, but owing to its special situation, that is, unfettered access to information and contacts with the Sandinistas, it occupied a prominent position within it between 1986 and 1990. As Joaquín Alfonso said, "Afterwards, and we haven't spoken about this, in 1987 and 1989, alike, there was a very important solidarity committee, the Ambrosio Mogorrón, which was a sort of Spanish internationalists' collective in Nicaragua itself."[62]

The key figure in the committee was Pablo Otero, born in Brazil to a Spanish mother, who settled in Galicia (Spain) at the beginning of the 1970s, before soon joining the groups championing the Latin American revolutionary struggles. He arrived in Nicaragua in 1983 as a brigade member anxious to live the revolution, before taking up residence there on a permanent basis the following year. He worked as a journalist for *Barricada Internacional* and was the coordinator of the Ambrosio Mogorrón from October 1986. In 1989, he handed over the baton to José Miguel Benítez, with whom he never lost touch. The reason behind this change was that Otero was spending progressively more time in Barcelona in order to print and distribute the Spanish-language edition of *Barricada Internacional* for Europe.[63]

The Ambrosio Mogorrón Committee´s members included Spanish internationalists working in government or FSLN organizations: *Barricada*

Internacional, the Nicaraguan Institute of Mining (INMINE), the Central American University, the National Institute of Technology, the Ministry of Housing and Human Settlements, and others. Since most of them lived many miles away, they only occasionally visited Managua, where the organization was based, to attend assemblies at which important decisions were made. According to Otero, the committee was open to everyone, irrespective of their political leanings: "there were all sorts in the Committee, from people belonging to the ICI to veterans or internationalists like ourselves; there were people who came from the committees and people who had nothing to do with the committees."[64]

In the daily work of preparing press kits with information on the revolution, receiving brigades arriving from Spain and attending meetings with the DRI, Otero and Benítez were assisted by Spaniards who turned up intermittently at the committee's headquarters during that period. There were many brigade members who had decided to stay on after their allotted time.[65] Before the Sandinista victory, there had been, as already noted, Spaniards fighting in the ranks of the FSLN in Nicaragua. However, they began to arrive in greater numbers after Somoza had been ousted from power. At first, they were mainly members of the PSOE and the PCE, followed later on by activists belonging to the extra-parliamentary Left.[66]

It was not until 1983 that the first Spanish internationalist organization, the Unión de Residentes Españoles en Nicaragua 'Gaspar García Laviana' ("Gaspar García Laviana" Spanish Residents Union in Nicaragua), was created in Nicaragua by Miguel Ángel Martínez and Isaías Barreñada, both members of the PCE who had arrived from Mexico in the middle of the same year.[67] The DRI asked Martínez and Barreñada to attempt to establish contact with the committees in Spain in order to organize the work brigades.[68] But the CESN denied that the Unión de Residentes was their representative in Nicaragua, thus scuppering the initiative. The reason behind this was the struggle in Spain between the parties of the extra-parliamentary Left for the control of the Nicaraguan transnational network. The PCE controlled the Unión de Residentes, but the extra-parliamentary Left called the shots as regards to the committees. In the words of Otero, "The first to pose, or accept, the challenge, or to answer the requests of the Front to organize themselves a bit more, who got things moving in that respect were the people of the PCE who were there at the time. And the first coordinator of that Unión de Residentes Españoles en Nicaragua was Miguel, a chap from the PC. Miguel occupied this post until two things happened:

firstly, many more people began to arrive and the newcomers were also from other organizations, from the MC, some from the LCR, but above all from the MC, independents, Basques . . ."[69]

At the end of 1983, Martínez and Barreñada traveled to Spain, where they were appointed by the Central Committee of the PCE as its representatives in Nicaragua. Their task involved meeting with the DRI to address issues affecting them both and preparing the arrival of brigade members and party leaders.[70] Since representing the PCE was seen as incompatible with coordinating the Unión de Residentes, it was Jorge Martínez, a member of the MC, who managed to garner the support of the internationalists in order to continue with the project,[71] where he remained in charge until September 1986.[72]

Martínez's primary task was to keep in regular contact with the committees. This was achieved through the party, which then submitted the proposals arriving from Nicaragua to the committees.[73] The Unión de Residentes thus became a more political organization. Furthermore, the arrival in Nicaragua of militants of the extra-parliamentary Left helped to strengthen relations between the internationalists and the activists participating in the solidarity campaigns in Spain.

As has been shown, party affiliation was one of the main elements in the relationship among the Spaniards working in both dimensions of transnational solidarity. A prominent party like the PCE was unable to establish closer ties with the committees since it did not control them. The way in which this more stable communication channel was opened was through its party contacts, rather than its solidarity actions. This reflects the struggle between the different political groups to manage the participation of the Spanish social movements in the network: "because in Spain, rather than helping us, it caused further problems, because everything came through the MC. Obviously, any initiative that they put forward here in the committees was rejected by those of the LCR, those of the PCE, those at the embassy, everyone rejected those initiatives and ultimately became partisan brigade members."[74]

The next development was the forging of closer links between the committees and the CAM. Otero, a former militant of the LCR, took over from Jorge Martínez and managed to integrate the Unión de Residentes (the CAM since the end of 1986) into the TSN's structures in Spain.

To counter the uncontrolled influx of internationalists and Spanish brigade members in Nicaragua between 1979 and 1986, the CNSP decided to use this group to impose order, a task given to Otero:

The Nicaraguans have begun to be interested in and anxious about organizing the Spaniards in Nicaragua. . . . they started to consider that Spanish solidarity had developed in an odd way, something that hadn't happened in any other region of the world, because it was an anarchistic, crazy, compelling rigmarole . . . that is what the international brigades are like, they appear from all over the place, they're all international brigades. . . . And so, one day, when I was in the area minding my own business, they rung me and said, "But didn't you come from one of those committees from abroad." "Yes." "But do you . . . ?" "No, no, I have nothing to do with the committees, the truth is I was fully involved in the solidarity movement with Latin America abroad, not with Nicaragua . . . and so I've some idea about it." So, well, my first experience was an assignment for the DRI. . . . [75]

The mandate that Otero received was to allow all those people who wanted to express their solidarity with the Sandinista Revolution to participate in the committees, in an attempt to break the partisan control that the extra-parliamentary Left exerted over them. Thus, the Ambrosio Mogorrón Committee followed the foreign policy doctrine of the FSLN, though extrapolating it to solidarity.[76] As Otero remembered: "It was essential to open up to a load of other movements and even promote this. Because there were political groups that didn't want to participate in the committees since they saw them as the private reserves of the League or the MC, and that, however, there was a lot of potential in doing just that."[77]

The strategy implemented by Otero to achieve the objectives with which he had been entrusted was to become a committee within the CESN in Spain, thus avoiding the previous disputes over its representation in Nicaragua.[78] But this solution was not problem-free; the CESN distrusted the discretion that the Ambrosio Mogorrón would enjoy in its relations with the FSLN. Otero explained: "What we asked was to be just another committee within the state coordinating committee. . . . And they said, 'Yes, one more committee but . . . you'd be another committee with information, you'd have mechanisms and all that stuff.' Because that also implied something else: when we'd said that we didn't want to be representatives, we weren't then under the orders of the state coordinating committee."[79]

The FSLN's mandate to open up the solidarity committees to all the political currents that wanted to lend their support clashed with the control that the extra-parliamentary left exercised over them. The Ambrosio Mogorrón's entry in the network, with such a strong position due to the fact that it operated in situ, was seen by the Sandinistas as a way of participating in the Spanish network.

In March 1987, the Ambrosio Mogorrón and the CESN reached an agreement not on issues of representation but on providing the brigades in Nicaragua with information and support.[80] The Ambrosio Mogorrón was even given a symbolic monthly expense allowance of $100.[81] This did not, however, spare it from future tensions. Mikel Soler, a member of the CCSN in charge of the secretariat of the CESN, traveled to Nicaragua to meet with the CNSP in July 1987.[82] "As things stood," Otero recalled, "at the DRI they were told, 'Look, stop this nonsense, do what you like, but here you've got to handle those guys because we can't cope, we can't attend to the needs of the brigades, we can't send the information you're asking us for as quickly as you'd like, so you'll have to do so through them. . . . '"[83]

This did not help to iron out the problems. In 1988, the CESN sent another letter to the CNASP to inform it that the Ambrosio Mogorrón was not its representative in Nicaragua.[84] The issue of exchanging information was also a continuous source of discord.[85] As Pablo Otero explained, "we obeyed the secretariat (CESN) which did a good job of controlling the people of the League and the MC, they shared the work and that was what interested us. They'd tell us, 'Send us the information and we'll pass it on to the committees.' And we'd reply, 'No, as we're just one of the committees of the co-ordinating committee, we'll send it to everyone, to the secretariat, of course, but also to the committee in Jaen, or to the one in Galicia, or to the one in Zaragoza, or to the one in Valencia or to any other committee' . . . for us that was non-negotiable."[86]

As can be seen, relations between the internationalists working in areas requesting solidarity and the activists participating in the offering side of the network were strained for two reasons: first, because of differences in how the process was perceived. The greater involvement of the internationalists and their connections with the beneficiary country meant that the activists lost some control over the network in Nicaragua, hence the antagonism. Second, the activists fully embraced the political objectives of those requesting solidarity, while with respect to the society offering it, the political parties controlling the network also pursued their own.

The CAM's activities basically comprised three tasks that the internationalists belonging to this committee undertook: to provide the committees with first-hand information on recent developments in Nicaragua; to make known the position of the FSLN as regards the current political situation after attending the meetings with the DRI; and to receive the brigades arriving from Spain. As Otero explained: "We created a team recognizing that the battle we'd have to wage in Spain was going to be unambiguous and hard: one, to bring as many people as possible to Nicaragua to get to know the process; and two, to inform."[87]

Other European groups also held their own encounters in Nicaragua. The Germans called their meetings "Sunday Circles," although these had more to do with personal networking than with organizational tasks.[88] For their part, the U.S. activists usually frequented the Casa Ben Linder.[89] Unsurprisingly, given its factional history, differences of opinion existed within the Spanish community. Basque solidarity with Nicaragua was organized as a resident's collective in 1988, with Mertxe Brosa as its representative.[90]

The first two tasks could be combined, since the objective was the same: to keep the committees informed about the political situation in Nicaragua and the FSLN's stance in this respect. This allowed the activists to launch advocacy campaigns in their national media and lobby the main political parties.

Having learned from the previous mistakes of the Unión de Residentes, Otero decided to send the Spanish solidarity committees information directly, instead of leaving the task up to the CESN. The partisan control exercised over the state-coordinating committee by the MC and the LCR was thus circumvented, as well as making the CAM responsible for sending reliable first-hand information to the committees. In Otero's words, "since we had contact and the capacity to get into contact with practically all the committees in Spain, we bypassed the state coordinating committee, the secretariat, and sent it directly. So, we started to send all our communiques directly to the committees. . . . those coordinating the committees never liked our initiative."[91]

Around 1989, the Ambrosio Mogorrón modified its legal status to become a Non-Governmental Organization (NGO). The purpose was none other than the legalization of its headquarters in Barcelona after having opened an office there, attached to that of *Barricada Internacional*, from where it distributed its publications among the committees and applied for state subsidies that enabled it to widen its scope of action in Nicaragua.[92] This change of status also involved a change of name to Movimiento 'Ambrosio Mogorrón' de Cooperantes de los Pueblos ("Ambrosio Mogorrón" Movement of Volunteers of the Peoples, MCP).[93]

Another direct source of information emanating from the Sandinista institutions were the periodic (more or less fortnightly) meetings between the representatives of the European solidarity network and the CNSP or the

CNASP. After these encounters, Ambrosio Mogorrón's members, basically Otero or Benítez, its coordinators, drafted reports that were then sent to Spain using brigade members or people returning home as couriers.[94]

The Ambrosio Mogorrón Committee put together several press kits (some of which were monothematic) containing information on the revolution appearing in the Nicaraguan press, which it then sent to Spain, where they were distributed among the different committees by its Barcelona office. There is a document that lists the information, published as of July, which was already available in October 1989.[95] But the most curious case was the recording of short radio reports on the situation in Nicaragua and their broadcasting via telephone answering machines. Activists in Spain would call the Ambrosio Mogorrón's number in Nicaragua and then record their reports, which did not usually last for more than two minutes.[96] In the twenty-first century, the flow of information is much quicker and more dynamic, but at the end of the twentieth century, imagination was the key when sending any physical object from one side of the Atlantic to the other.

The committee also became a very important means of support for the brigades arriving in Nicaragua. Its tasks included picking brigade members up from the airport of Managua, taking them to the Arlen Siu hostel, organizing the political talks given by a variety of Sandinista, Salvadorian, and Guatemalan organizations and, lastly, ferrying the brigades to their work locations. Owing to this and its preeminent position in the network, managing the contacts between the two countries comprising it, the Ambrosio Mogorrón was able to control which brigades should be allowed to come to Nicaragua and when, as well as deciding on their number and composition. Joaquín Alfonso Marín remembers being received by Pablo Otero when he traveled to Nicaragua in 1987: "They undertook many bridging and co-ordination tasks. We had close ties with the Ambrosio Mogorrón at the time. In 1989, when I was coordinating with Ulfrido, we always tried to get Pablo Otero to give brigade members the first talk on the situation in the country."[97]

Some brigade members stayed on—which was prohibited by the regulations circulated by the DRI—to perform support work for the Ambrosio Mogorrón or in their brigade's work location. These people constituted a variable mass of activists who frequented the committee to lend a helping hand. Once they had returned to Spain, they were very valuable inasmuch as they could share their experiences with new brigade members and supply activists with first-hand news on the situation in Nicaragua. The main bridge that the Ambrosio Mogorrón managed to build with all the committees in Spain was based on information. This information came from three sources: that supplied by the Sandinista institutions, that collected by the committee itself in Managua, and that provided by brigade members returning home.

Conclusions

In light of the above, the first assumption made at the beginning of this chapter has been confirmed. National politics does have an influence on the parties offering solidarity in a transnational solidarity network. Additionally, they establish different relationships with the beneficiary country, depending on their position within the network.

In the case of the Spanish network, two important years marking the evolution of activities should be recalled: 1979 and 1982. Before July 19, 1979, contacts between Spanish political parties and the FSLN had been personal, basically thanks to those that FSLN member Ernesto Cardenal established with the members of political organizations that could potentially help it to reach its objectives. The PSOE and the PCE, both prominent political parties in Spain but without any say in the running of the country, embraced the Sandinista Revolution with the greatest enthusiasm. Once the FSLN had overthrown Somoza, these two parties established a relationship of political solidarity with the organization. The PCE managed to take a dual stance, participating in grassroots committees thanks to the power that it still wielded over the country's social movements, while building bridges with the FSLN by other means.

It was the rest of the left-wing parties in Spain, namely, the extra-parliamentary Left, without a power quota, which stood in for the Nicaraguans returning home to participate in the revolution. The MCE and the LCR, first and foremost, vied for control over the social movement for solidarity with Nicaragua. The political ideology of the FSLN was all but fully embraced by these peripheral parties. The reasons behind this included their ideological proximity and the creation of a space in which to engage social masses potentially susceptible to their political ideas.

In short, two levels were established: political solidarity at a party level, offered by both the PSOE and the PCE; and the level represented by those Spanish social movements in favor of the Sandinista Revolution, at which the PCE also participated, but which was ultimately controlled by the extra-parliamentary Left.

The second major milestone occurred in 1982 when the PSOE won the general elections and formed a government. Thereafter, the main left-wing party in Spain changed tack, from offering plenty of solidarity to offering tepid support depending not only on its own political interests but also on those of the state. When political groups manage to obtain parcels of power, they tend to distance themselves from the party requesting solidarity, making the objectives of transnational solidarity networks dependent on their own. With this change, a third level was created within the Spanish relationship with Nicaragua: state relations.

The other assumption relating to the capacity of the FSLN to organize a transnational solidarity network can also be considered to have been borne out. Through the Spanish internationalists living in Nicaragua and the Ambrosio Mogorrón Committee, the FSLN organized and established direct communication channels with social solidarity movements in Spain.

The Spanish internationalists living in Nicaragua reproduced the partisan battles being fought back home. But their commitment to the network shifted from defending the political objectives of their parties of origin to complete identification with the FSLN. It could be argued that a transfer of militants occurred from one side of the transnational network to the other. As Alfonso Marín reflected: "They're sensations difficult to describe but they tie you down. They make you identify with those people, feel furthermore that their cause is just. Ask yourself who could be so frightened of those people if all they want, after all, is to be happy. There's no need to resort to revolutionary theories or ideologies. . . . From the start I came to the conclusion that I wanted to stay on. Nicaragua's the place where I've felt most free. Free and involved in something that was changing. The relationship with people and with the Nicaraguans."[98]

The FSLN was able, thanks to its political clout, to use these internationalists not so much to take full control of the network, but to organize it. First-hand information and structures for receiving brigades were the means that the Ambrosio Mogorrón Committee mainly employed to this end. The committee occupied a prominent position in the transnational network in support of Nicaragua because, first, it was not associated with any Spanish political party in particular and, second, because it fully empathized with the Sandinista Revolution, constituting moreover the principal channel through which first-hand information arrived in Spain on a regular basis.

Another prominent feature of the political power of the Sandinistas was their flexibility when establishing contact along the 1980s with the SI and the PSOE; at a second level, they kept in touch with the PCE due to the strong political affinity between them; and, additionally, at a social movement level through the committees.

All in all, transnational solidarity in support of Nicaragua involved all the Spanish political Left, establishing different levels of communication according to the ongoing developments in both countries. The Spanish internationalists, who had first fought for the cause before supporting the revolutionary process, fully identified with the Sandinistas. Initially, they had taken their political flags with them to Nicaragua, but afterward their ties with the Nicaraguan people led them to feel and behave like one of their number.

Notes

1. Radio Televisión del Principado de Asturias. *Gaspar. Misionero y comandante sandinista*, 13.

2. Valencia, Jesús. *Euskal Herria internacionalista*, 215–220; and Ágreda and Helm, *Solidaridad con la Revolución Sandinista*, 12.

3. The concept *transnational solidarity network* is taken from theories of transnationalism. In Keck and Sikkink, *Activists beyond borders*, 8, it is possible to find the concept *transnational advocacy network*. In Bob, *The Marketing of Rebellion*, 2, the author provides a definition of transnational advocacy network. However, Tarrow in *The New Transnational Activism*, 44, used a wider concept that he called transnational social movements. Transnational solidarity network is a modification of these. Following the definition of "solidarity" from Waterman, *Globalization, Social Movements and the New Internationalism*, 52, transnational solidarity network is a network where the sense of belonging to the same frame of offerer and receiver of solidarity are closer than in the transnational advocacy network or in a transnational social movement.

4. No serious studies have been published yet on the Ambrosio Mogorrón Committee or on Spanish solidarity with the Sandinista Revolution. For further information, see Ágreda Portero, "Un acercamiento al Comité de Solidaridad con Nicaragua de Zaragoza, España (1978–1990)" and Ágreda and Helm's comparison between West German and Spanish networks, "Solidaridad con la Revolución Sandinista. Comparativa de redes transnacionales, los casos de Alemania y España." Nonetheless, the memoirs of individuals involved in the process are available. For example, Perales, *Los buenos años. Nicaragua en la memoria*, or Corrales, *Nicaragua: una paseo entre volcanes*. With respect to institutional relations, Belén Blázquez Vilaplana's book dealing with the connection between Felipe González, the leader of the Spanish Socialist Workers' Party (PSOE), and the Central American crisis in general and that of Nicaragua in particular during the 1980s, is also important. See Blázquez Vilaplana, "La proyección de un líder político: Felipe González y Nicaragua 1978–1996." Historical research on transnational solidarity networks with Central American revolutionary processes is quite recent. In relation to Western Europe, the first study to be published was conducted by Kadelbach in 2006 on the Swiss brigades in Nicaragua: *Les Brigadistes Suisses au Nicaragua (1982–1990)*.

Regarding the United States, Héctor Perla studied how a number of Americans—and not Nicaraguans, as claimed in the conservative press—participated in a campaign against their own government which was providing the Contras with financial aid and military support: "Heirs of Sandino. The Nicaragua Revolution and the US Nicaragua solidarity movement." With regards to Latin America, Adrián Jaén's master's thesis has dealt with the participation of the Costa Rican Left in the armed conflict triggered by the Sandinista victory: "Movimientos sociales y solidaridad política: la participación de la izquierda costarricense en la Revolución Sandinista." On the other hand, Paula Fernández has studied the brigades created by the Communist Party of Argentina. This is one of the most novel approaches insofar as it combines different ideas of solidarity with Marcel Mauss's gift theory. See Fernández, *Nicaragua debe sobrevivir*.

5. Villar, Francisco. *La proyección exterior de España*, 117, 184.

6. Blázquez, "*La proyección de un líder político*," 158.

7. Arístegui, *Misión en Managua*, 32.

8. Arístegui, *Misión en Managua*, 193.

9. Arístegui, *Misión en Managua*, 190, 206.

10. Blázquez, "La proyección de un líder político," 166.

11. Departamento de Relaciones Internacionales. *Avances de la Revolución Popular Sandinista*.

12. Nart, *Nunca la nada fue tanto*, 33.

13. Archivo de la Fundación Pablo Iglesias, 1991. 2160. 068-G. 1. 003. Internacional.

14. Nart, *Nunca la nada fue tanto*, 31.

15. Archivo de la Fundación Pablo Iglesias, Archivo Comisión Ejecutiva Federal, Box 6, Folder 16.

16. Archivo de la Fundación Pablo Iglesias, Archivo Comisión Ejecutiva Federal, Folders 5 and 15.

17. Blázquez, "*La proyección de un líder político*," 137.

18. Villar, *La transición exterior de España*, 100–101.

19. Blázquez, "*La proyección de un líder político*," 212.

20. Blázquez, "*La proyección de un líder político*," 149.

21. *El País*, September 30, 1983. elpais.com/diario/1983/09/30/internacional/433724420_850215.html (Accessed 7 November 2018).

22. The visit can be verified in the whole book of Blázquez. *La proyección de un líder político*.

23. The visit can be verified in the whole book of Blázquez. *La proyección de un líder político*.

24. Archivo del Ayuntamiento de Zaragoza, Fondos del Partido Comunista de Aragón, Box 26542, Debate Comunista Internacional, *Temas Internacionales*, nos. 19 and 25.

25. Archivo del Ayuntamiento de Zaragoza, Fondos del Partido Comunista de Aragón, Box 26542, Debate Comunista Internacional, *Temas Internacionales*, no. 23.

26. Archivo del Ayuntamiento de Zaragoza, Fondos del Partido Comunista de Aragón, Box 26559, Internacional.

27. Núñez, *La Revolución y el deseo*, 338.

28. Interview with Pedro Ariza, August 2, 2015, Managua, Nicaragua.

29. Interview with Luis Alfredo Lobato Blanco, August 17, 2015, Managua, Nicaragua.

30. Laiz, *La izquierda radical en España*, 318.

31. Laiz, *La izquierda radical en España*, 295.

32. Interview with Joaquín Alfonso Marín, December 27, 2014, Utebo, Spain.

33. Interview with Joaquín Alfonso Marín.

34. Laiz, *La izquierda radical en España*, 320.

35. Caussa and Martínez, *Historia de la Liga Comunista Revolucionaria*, 64–65.

36. Roitman, *La política del PSOE en América Latina*, 6, 107, 140, 141.

37. Skype interview with Ángel Barrajón, March 8, 2016.

38. Interview with Ángel Barrajón.

39. Interview with Klaas Wellinga and Hans Langenberg, October 15, 2017, Utrecht, Holland.

40. On the Madrid congress: International Institute of Social History. Arch 01007 Archief Nicaragua Komitee Nederland. Folder 72. Para el congreso de Zaragoza: Archivo del Ayuntamiento de Zaragoza, Fondos del PCA, Box 26560. Para el congreso de San Sebastián: Archivo Komite Internazionalista de Donostia.

41. Interview with Ángel Barrajón.

42. Interview with Ángel Barrajón.

43. Nart, *Nunca la nada fue tanto*, 72; and Cardenal, *La Revolución perdida*, 172–175.

44. Ágreda and Helm, "Solidaridad con la Revolución Sandinista," 12.

45. Interview with Ángel Barrajón.

46. Keck and Sikkink, *Activists beyond Borders*, 9.

47. Armed Movements Documentation Centre, CeDeMA, *Nuestra lucha*. No. 1 May 1979; Archivo del Ayuntamiento de Zaragoza, Fondos del PCA, Boxes 26560 and 26555, *Nicaragua en lucha*. No. 1 July–August 1979. No. 2 October–November 1979. No. 3 February 21, 1980. No. 4 undated and *Boletín Informativo Sandinista*. No. 1 May 1980. No. 2 September 1981.

48. Interview with Ángel Barrajón.

49. Agreda, "Un acercamiento al Comité de Solidaridad con Nicaragua de Zaragoza."

50. Archivo de la LCR de Zaragoza, Informe de la facción de solidaridad de la LCR, 6 May 1987.

51. Archivo de la LCR de Zaragoza , Boletín Interno no. 12 Actas del Comité Central, October 1986, 5.

52. Archivo de la LCR de Zaragoza, Boletín Interno no. 12 Actas del Comité Central, October 1986, 5.

53. Archivo del Comité de Solidaridad con América Latina de Asturias (ACOSAL), 20 August 1984, "Carta del CNSP a los comités" (Letter from the CNSP to the committees).

54. Archivo del Comité de Solidaridad Internacionalista de Zaragoza (ACIZ), Box 3, Folder CAM, Document 14, May 7, 1990, "Síntesis de la reunión celebrada entre el DRI y los Comités de Europa" (Summary of the meeting held between the DRI and the European committees).

55. Fundación Augusto César Sandino, *Memoria 15 años de trabajo*.

56. Archivo del Comité de Solidaridad con América Latina de Asturias (ACOSAL).

"Proyectos presentados por la Fundación Augusto César Sandino a los comités de solidaridad en Europa de enero de 1981 a octubre de 1981" (Projects submitted by the Augusto César Sandino Foundation to the European solidarity committees from January to October 1981).

57. The participation of religious personnel in the Sandinista Revolution deserves an in-depth research that goes beyond this chapter. In Nicaragua, the roles of the above-named Gaspar García Laviana and Ángel Barrajón could be studied in conjunction with those of Pedro Casaldáliga, José María Vigil, Domingo Urtasun, or Xavier Gorostiaga, among many others.

58. Archivo de la Casa de Nicaragua de Barcelona.

59. Valencia, *Euskal Herria Internacionalista*, 89.

60. Archivo Casa de Nicaragua de Barcelona.

61. Mugarik Gabe, www.mugarikgabe.org; Entrepueblos, www.entrepueblos.org

62. Interview with Joaquín Alfonso Marín.

63. Interview with Pablo Otero, December 12, 2015, San Pere de Ribas, Barcelona, Spain.

64. Interview with Pablo Otero.

65. Interview with José Miguel Benítez, September 9, 2017, Barcelona, Spain.

66. Interview with Pablo Otero.

67. Interview with Isaías Barreñada, February 25, 2018, Madrid, Spain.

68. Archivo del Comité Internacionalista de Zaragoza (ACIZ), Box 3, Folder CAM, Document 1, 1983, "Carta de la Unión de Residentes a los comités."

69. Interview with Pablo Otero.

70. Interview with Isaías Barreñada.

71. Interview with Pablo Otero.

72. ACIZ, Box 4, Folder CAM, "Carta de la Unión de Residentes a los comités," Managua, October 1986.

73. Interview with Pablo Otero.

74. Interview with Pablo Otero.

75. Interview with Pablo Otero.

76. Pozas, *Nicaragua (1979–1990) Actor singular del pragmatismo y protagonismo de la revolución sandinista en la escena internacional*, 248.

77. Interview with Pablo Otero, December 12, 2015, San Pere de Ribas, Barcelona, Spain.

78. ACIZ, Box 5, Folder CAM, "Carta de la Unión de Residentes a los comités," October 1986.

79. Interview with Pablo Otero.

80. ACIZ, Box 4, Folder CEOP and CESN, Document 29, March 1, 1987, "Acuerdo de la Coordinadora Estatal de Solidaridad con Nicaragua."

81. ACIZ, Box 4, Folder CEOP and CESN, Document 31, April 26, 1988, "Carta de la comisión técnica del CESN al CAM. ."

82. ACIZ, Box 1, Folder CESN, July 24, 1987, "Cartas de la comisión técnica a Patricia Elvir, Orlando Castillo y Pablo Otero."

83. Interview with Pablo Otero.

84. ACIZ, Box 4, Folder CEOP and CESN, Document 29, March 1, 1988, "Carta del CESN a Patricia Elvir por la representación del CAM."

85. ACIZ, Box 5, Folder CAM, Document 8, October 19, 1989, "Carta de José Miguel Benítez al CESN."

86. Interview with Pablo Otero.

87. Interview with Pablo Otero.

88. Ágreda and Helm, "Solidaridad con la Revolución Sandinista. Comparativa de redes transnacionales," 14.

89. Interview with Pablo Otero.

90. Archivo Comité Internazionalistak de San Sebastiá, "Carta del Colectivo de Residentes Vascos al CNSP," 1988.

91. Interview with Pablo Otero.

92. Interview with Pablo Otero.

93. Archivo del Comité de Solidaridad Internacionalista de Zaragoza, Box 3, Folder CAM, Document 9, November 1989, "Carta desde Barcelona a la CESN firmada por Pablo Otero."

94. Interview with José Miguel Benítez, September 9, 2017, Barcelona, Spain.

95. ACIZ, Box 3, Folder CAM, Document 6, October 1989, "Los materiales informativos del Colectivo Ambrosio Mogorrón."

96. Interview with Pablo Otero.

97. Interview with Joaquín Alfonso Marín.

98. Interview with Joaquín Alfonso Marín.

Bibliography

Ágreda, José Manuel. "Un acercamiento al Comité de Solidaridad con Nicaragua en Zaragoza, España (1978–1990)," coloquios "Redes internacionales de apoyo y solidaridad con grupos, actores y movimientos político-sociales latinoamericanos," *Nuevo Mundo Mundos Nuevos*, 2016. nuevomundo.revues.org/69639

Ágreda, José Manuel, and Christian Helm. "Solidaridad con la Revolución Sandinista," *Naveg@merica* 17. revistas.um.es/navegamerica/article/view/271921

Blázquez Vilaplana, Belén. *La proyección de un líder político: Felipe González y Nicaragua 1978–1996*. Sevilla: Centro de Estudios Andaluces, 2006.

Bob, Clifford. *The Marketing of Rebellion. Insurgent, Media and Intenational Activism*. New York: Cambridge University Press, 2005.

Cardenal, Ernesto. *La Revolución Perdida*. Managua: Anamá, 2013.

Caussa, Martí, and Ricard Martínez i Muntada (eds.). *Historia de la Liga Comunista Revolucionaria (1970–1991)*. Madrid: La oveja roja, 2014.

Comité de Solidaridad con América Latina (COSAL). *El fusil de la ternura. Homenaje poético a Gaspar García Laviana*. Valle del Nalón: COSAL, 1986.

Corrales, Xavier. *Nicaragua: un paseo entre volcanes*. Valencia: Universidad Politécnica de Valencia, 2004.

De Arístegui Petit, Pedro. *Misión en Managua*. Barcelona: Ediciones B, 1989.

Departamento de Relaciones Internacionales. *Avances de la Revolución Popular Sand-*

inista. Informe preparado por el departamento de relaciones internacionales del Frente Sandinista de Liberación Nacional, Managua: DRI, enero 1981.

FACS. *Memoria 15 años de trabajo, 1980–1995,* Managua: Fundación Augusto César Sandino, Managua, noviembre 1985.

Fernández Hellmund, Paula. *Nicaragua debe sobrevivir. La solidaridad de la militancia comunista argentina con la revolución sandinista (1979–1990).* Buenos Aires: Ediciones Imago Mundi, 2015.

Jaén España, Adrián. "Movimientos sociales y solidaridad política: la participación de la izquierda costarricense en la Revolución Sandinista." MA Thesis. San José de Costa Rica: Facultad Latinoamericana de Ciencias Sociales, 2013.

Kadelbach. *Les Brigadistes Suisses au Nicaragua (1982–1990).* Doctoral thesis. Fribourg: Université de Fribourg, 2006.

Keck, Margaret E., and Kathryn Sikkink. *Activists beyond Borders.* Ithaca, NY: Cornell University Press, 1998.

Laiz, Consuelo. *La izquierda radical en España durante la Transición democrática.* Madrid: Tesis doctoral de la Universidad Complutense de Madrid, 1993.

Nart, Javier. *Nunca la nada fue tanto.* Barcelona: Editorial Península, 2016.

Núñez González, Miguel. *La Revolución y el deseo: Memorias.* Barcelona: Península, 2002.

Perales, Iosu. *Los buenos años. Nicaragua en la memoria.* Barcelona: Icaria, 2005.

Perla, Héctor "Heirs of Sandino. The Nicaragua Revolution and the US Nicaragua solidarity movement." *Latin American Perspectives* 36, no. 6 (2009): 80–100.

Pozas Pardo, Víctor Santiago. *Nicaragua (1979–1990) Actor singular del pragmatismo y protagonismo de la revolución sandinista en la escena internacional.* Bilbao: Tésis doctoral de la Universidad del País Vasco, 2000.

Radio Televisión del Principado de Asturias. *Gaspar. Misionero y comandante sandinista.* Gijón: Radio Televisión del Principado de Asturias, 2008.

Roitman Rosenmann, Marcos. *La política del PSOE en América Latina.* Madrid: Revolución,1985.

Tarrow, Sidney. *The New Transnational Activism.* Cambridge: Cambridge University Press, 2005.

Valencia, Jesús. *La ternura de los pueblos. Euskal Herria Internacionalista.* Navarra: Txalaparta, 2011.

Villar, Francisco. *La transición exterior de España. Del aislamiento a la influencia (1976–1996).* Madrid: Marcial Pons, 2016.

Afterword

The Americas, North and South

VAN GOSSE

I approach this volume with humility, as someone who has written about and participated in the "North American front" of solidarity but has little expertise on how Latin America's Revolutionary Left engaged with the rest of world.[1] Tanya Harmer and Alberto Martín Álvarez have carefully delineated how this volume engages with the new Global Cold War history from the point of view of Latin Americanists. I will offer some thoughts as a U.S. historian and a former solidarity activist.

Viewed from the perspective of solidarity work inside the imperial subject, these chapters illuminate the exceptional character of American politics, its absences (or differences). At no point since the 1940s has a recognized "Left space" existed within U.S. political institutions and the nation's public sphere, or for that matter in mainstream historiography; the long history of solidarity with Latin American revolutions, including its most significant expression, the "Central America movement" of the 1980s, is obscure to most U.S. historians, including those who study the Cold War (reflecting the limitations of diplomatic history). Certainly, there have been many consequential left movements inside the United States, but they operated on the margins, fighting for recognition, a fundamental marker of difference with Western Europe and Latin America, the subjects of the chapters herein. No political party in the United States (let alone a ruling party, like the Spanish PSOE or the French Socialists) has ever put its organizational resources and diplomatic capacities at the service of exiled revolutionaries advocating armed struggle, as documented by José Manuel Ágreda Portero's examination of Spanish solidarity with Sandinista Nicaragua, which included the PCE, and Gerardo Leibner's essay on the Italian

Communists' relationship to Brazilian guerrilla groups.[2] The only parallel would be the long relationship between the Congressional Black Caucus (the main social democratic grouping within the U.S. Democratic Party) and Cuba's revolutionary government. On occasion, individual members of Congress have advocated against U.S. interventions in Latin America and engaged with leftist exiles. Senator Edward Kennedy helped lead the effort to expose human rights abuses by the Brazilian junta in the late 1960s, and Iowa Representative (later Senator) Tom Harkin declared "yo soy Sandinista!" at a rally in Washington, DC, in late July 1979, celebrating the triumph over Somoza. As recently as January 30, 2019, thirty-nine members of Congress sent a letter to Secretary of State Michael Pompeo decrying U.S. interference in El Salvador's upcoming presidential elections. But that is hardly the same as putting a large national party's apparatus and its associated institutions, whether a daily newspaper like *L'Unità* or *L'Humanité* or a national trade union federation like Italy's CGIL or France's CGT, behind a foreign movement. In the United States, the AFL-CIO, given its long history of collaboration with the Central Intelligence Agency, was an enemy rather than an ally of solidarity organizers in the 1960s, 1970s, and 1980s. Further, even the best-organized exile representation, like that of the Salvadoran FMLN, was frozen out of major media outlets in the United States except at points of extreme crisis, such as the general offensive of November 1989.[3]

Another point of basic difference between the United States and the rest of the world is periodization. The chapters in this book focus primarily on the 1960s and early 1970s, the high tide of *foquismo* and urban guerrilla warfare in Brazil, Venezuela, Guatemala, Uruguay, and Argentina. Those movements had few if any connections to left politics in the United States, then emerging from McCarthyism's repressive fog. New Left anti-imperialism centered on the vast anti–Vietnam War movement, although James N. Green has rediscovered the history of the surprisingly effective movement in the early 1970s to expose the Brazilian junta's state terror.[4] The fullest U.S. engagement with revolution in the Americas came later, in the post-Vietnam era of the 1980s, when a broad "solidarity and anti-intervention" movement challenged the Reagan Administration's wars in Central America. That movement was powered by the reaction to the overthrow of Unidad Popular in Chile in 1973, as well as the Venceremos Brigades that sent thousands of young North Americans to Cuba from 1969 on, and was unaware of the flurry of enthusiasm for the Cuban Revolution in the late 1950s and early 1960s.[5]

A third distinction is how antifascism linked Latin America and the rest of the world at a personal level—for instance, that the Brazilian guerrilla leader, Rene Carvalho, was the son of a man who had fought in Spain with leaders of Italy's PCI. The United States furnished a substantial number of combatants for that antifascist struggle, but after 1945 the veterans of the Abraham Lincoln Brigade were disdained outside of the ghettoized world of the U.S. Left, versus the enormous prestige accorded those former combatants in postwar Europe.[6]

Finally, we should consider the editors' distinction between a broad "New Left" and a clandestine or insurrectionary "Revolutionary Left." Even at the sixties' apogee, the United States never had much of a Revolutionary Left. Max Elbaum's brilliant *Revolution in the Air: Sixties Radicals Turn to Lenin, Mao, and Che* analyzes the efforts of several thousand activists to build a New Communist Movement, meaning an authentic Marxist-Leninist party to supplant the "reformist" Communist Party USA. His account of the many "pre-party formations" of the 1970s, *grupitos* as Fidel Castro would have called them, documents the legacy of that movement, and Elbaum's sober judgment is that its strategists disastrously misjudged the revolutionary potential of the U.S. working classes during the Nixon years.[7] If the extent of repression is the measure of an organization's impact, one could make a stronger case for the Black Panther Party for Self-Defense as briefly the vanguard of a North American Revolutionary Left circa 1967–1973. That organization did have international ties, notably to Algeria and Cuba. However, the BPP succumbed very quickly to targeted state disruption, disastrous "Custerism" (a term invented by its Chicago leader, Fred Hampton, himself a victim of police terror, to indict suicidal armed confrontations), and the gangsterism fostered by its founder, Huey P. Newton, in the later 1970s.

Having noted all the above, the largest operational difference in the practice of solidarity was that the discourse of leftist *compañerismo* across Europe and the Third World was emphatically secular, whereas in the United States the deepest connections were faith-based, involving not only left Catholics, especially the religious like the Maryknolls, but also via extensive missionary work by mainline Protestants, including Episcopalians, Methodists, Presbyterians, Lutherans, and American Baptists.[8] Otherwise, there were limited commonalties in the Global North, to invoke an anachronism. The importance of left-wing publishing houses in disseminating key texts from Latin America's Left, as outlined in Eduardo Rey Tristán's chapter, had parallels in the United States, such as Grove Press, along with respected liberal magazines like *The Nation* and *The Progressive* and the key radical weekly, *The Guardian*. In general, however, intellectuals have less social weight in the United States than in Europe, so the rosters of scholarly and literary luminaries who publicly aligned themselves with one or another Latin American movement had less impact.

For a scholar of the United States, the least familiar aspect of these chapters is their descriptions of partisan maneuvering at the level of regimes, as in James G. Hershberg's examination of the fight for Cuba's support between Luis Carlos Prestes of the Brazilian Communist Party and Francisco Julião's Peasant Leagues, and how that competition became a factor in the Castro government's relationship to João Goulart's administration before the 1964 coup. Conversely, because of their temporal focus on the 1980s, the most familiar narratives in this collection to a North American activist are Arturo Taracena Arriola's memoir of his years as a European representative of Guatemala's EGP and Ágreda Portero's analysis of Spanish solidarity with the Frente Sandinista at the height of the Contra War. These two accounts resonate strongly. Like any long-time El Salvador activist, I knew the diplomatic representatives of the FMLN, who played a similar role to the Guatemalans in Europe, and was well aware of the many North Americans coming and going from Nicaragua. Indeed, one can envision a volume made up entirely of oral histories akin to Arriola's essay, which would illuminate, as he does so well, the inner life of revolutionary organizations engaged in transnational political-military struggles.

More generally, this volume points toward further areas for exploration. First, many of its chapters allude to Mexico's vital role since the 1950s as the principal rear-guard for exiled revolutionaries in the Americas. The Mexican state's carefully calibrated nonalignment between the United States and Cuba and its relation to its domestic (or domesticated) Left badly needs unpacking, since Mexico City was a central transit point in the hemispheric and trans-Atlantic transmission belts that kept Latin America's Revolutionary Left alive. In that connection, all of these chapters suggest the urgency of a truly multinational history of the Cold War Left, or maybe a "Left diplomatic history," to break out of the various national binaries (the United States and Cuba; Cuba and Nicaragua; Cuba and Mexico). Inevitably, histories of Latin America's Left since 1959 must be Cuba-centric. Classics like Jorge Castañeda's *Utopia Unarmed* and Piero Gleijeses's deep explorations of the Cuban Revolution's commitment to African liberation underscore the global reach of *fidelista* internationalism. But there is more to this history than just Cuba. Michal Zourek's uncovering how the Czechoslovak secret service moved revolutionaries into and out of the Americas hints at how many other countries in the socialist bloc were involved, and Blanca Mar León's excavation of Cuban diplomats' working the interstices of Third World and Communist diplomacy to manage the Tricontinental Conference underscores the centrality of state actors in supporting internal subversion. One can envision similar volumes focused on the Anglophone world, stretching from the United Kingdom to Ireland, Canada, Australia, and also Jamaica, Grenada, Kenya and Nigeria, and even India. What about connections across the Global South? Did exiles and representatives of movements in Latin America go to Dar es Salaam, Algiers, or Tripoli? Certainly, the role of the Vietnamese is worth exploring: there are strong hints that Salvadoran and Nicaraguans received training there, and perhaps others earlier.

Raising such a wide range of topics for future scholarship suggests the inherent limitations of "movement" histories, including my own. To fully interrogate solidarity among Latin American revolutionaries and the Left in a particular country such as France, Italy, Spain, or the United Kingdom, we should assess the full spectrum of that particular country's Left in its domestic and international contexts, and all of its foreign or "internationalist" relations. Each of these countries had significant Socialist (or Labor) and Communist parties, and each had a spectrum of New Left groups. The conventional parties had their own distinct foreign relations (e.g., the relative closeness to or distance from the Soviets of a particular Communist party, ranging from the PCF's extreme orthodoxy to the PCI's "polycentrism," with an equivalent variation regarding the U.S. among Socialists). The New Left groups were more or less Maoist (as in France) or workerist (as in Italy) or Trotskyist (as in the United Kingdom). But even this mapping would be only a beginning, because one must also consider the significant role of other state actors, not merely the Soviets and the PRC with their mirror-facing tendency to support opposing factions with training, financing, propaganda, and ideological aid, but other relatively autonomous actors, such as the GDR's intelligence services, never merely appendages of the KGB. The archives of the Democratic Republic of Vietnam's various missions would be especially helpful here, since the DRV conducted foreign policy independent of any great powers.

A final thought: Piero Gleijeses's books on Cuba in Africa are the model for a deep interrogation of multiple state and non-state actors in the North and South, across radically different parts of a continent, from Algeria to Angola. Gleijeses has a protagonist in the Cuban Revolution, but from

there he builds out a web of relations involving many others of every political coloration. This is the future task for those of us seeking to historicize
the long, still-unfinished arc of Latin America's revolutionary movements
operating in the world.

Notes

1. My scholarship that touches on the larger world includes "Ronald Reagan in Ireland, 1984" and "Unpacking the Vietnam Syndrome: The 1973 Coup in Chile and the Rise
of Anti-Interventionist Politics."

2. The Communist Party USA was much smaller than its European counterparts and
hobbled by the sectarianism (if not national chauvinism) of its paramount figure after
1959, General Secretary Gus Hall, who perceived himself as the hemisphere's leading
Marxist-Leninist.

3. For the militants of the Committee in Solidarity with the People of El Salvador
(CISPES), including this author, it was a brief moment of triumph when one of the
FMLN-FDR's Diplomatic Representatives, Francisco Altschul (later Ambassador to the
United States), appeared on the influential television news program *Nightline* (ABC) at
the height of the fighting in San Salvador.

4. See Green, *We Cannot Remain Silent*.

5. The most comprehensive treatment of the Venceremos Brigades is in Latner, *Cuban
Revolution in America*; for the earlier period, see Gosse, *Where the Boys Are* and "'El
Salvador Is Spanish For Vietnam.'"

6. Kirsten Weld is writing a history of the Spanish Civil War's impact in Latin America, which will be invaluable in exploring this connection.

7. Readers may note the lack of mention of the Weather Underground, which reflects
my perspective that they were little more than a media phenomenon.

8. It may be there were equivalent patterns of Christian solidarity in Europe, but they
are not cited in these essays. This topic requires further investigation, as part of querying
conventional categories of what is "Left" or revolutionary.

Bibliography

Latner, Teishan A. *Cuban Revolution in America: Havana and the Making of a United
    States Left, 1968–1992*. Chapel Hill: University of North Carolina Press, 2017.
Gosse, Van. *Where the Boys Are: Cuba, Cold War America, and the Making of a New Left*.
    New York: Verso, 1993.
———. "'El Salvador Is Spanish for Vietnam': The Politics of Solidarity and the New Im-
    migrant Left, 1955–1993" in *The Immigrant Left*, eds. Paul Buhle and Dan Georgakas.
    Albany, NY: SUNY Press, 1996.
———. "Unpacking the Vietnam Syndrome: The 1973 Coup in Chile and the Rise of
    Anti-Interventionist Politics," in *The World the Sixties Made: Politics and Culture in*

Recent America, eds. Van Gosse and Richard Moser. Philadelphia: Temple University Press, 2003.

———. "Ronald Reagan in Ireland, 1984: A Different Cold War?" *Journal of American Studies* 47, no. 4 (2013): 1155–1174.

Green, James N. *We Cannot Remain Silent: Opposition to the Brazilian Military Dictatorship in the United States*. Durham, NC: Duke University Press, 2010.

Contributors

About the Editors

Tanya Harmer received her PhD in international history from the London School of Economics and Political Science (LSE). She is associate professor at the LSE, where she specializes in the history of the Cold War and Latin America, with particular focus on Chile and Cuba. Her research interests include revolutionary movements, anti-communism, inter-American relations, solidarity, exile, and gender. She is the author of *Allende's Chile and the Inter-American Cold War* and *Beatriz Allende: A Revolutionary Life in Cold War Latin America* and co-editor with Alfredo Riquelme of *Chile y la guerra fría global*.

Alberto Martín Álvarez holds a PhD in Latin American Studies from the Universidad Complutense de Madrid. He is distinguished professor in the Department of Public Law at the Universitat de Girona (Spain). He has been full professor at the Instituto Mora (Mexico City) and visiting researcher at several universities and research centers in Europe and Latin America. He is cofounder and coordinator of the Revolutionary New Left International Research Network on Political Violence. He has undertaken extensive research on the origins and development of the Salvadoran revolutionary Left. His publications include *Latin American Guerrilla Movements: Origins, Evolution, Outcomes* (co-edited with Dirk Kruijt and Eduardo Rey), *Revolutionary Violence and the New Left: Transnational Perspectives* (co-edited with Eduardo Rey), and the monograph *From Revolutionary War to Democratic Revolution: The Farabundo Martí National Liberation Front (FMLN) in El Salvador.*

About the Contributors

José Manuel Ágreda Portero is a PhD student in the department of contemporary and Latin American history at the Universidad de Santiago de Compostela (Spain). He is developing a research project on Spanish networks of solidarity with the Nicaraguan Revolution. His recent publications include "El Frente Sandinista de Liberación Nacional, 1961–1979: reflexiones para su análisis" in *Naveg@merica*; "Una aproximación a la historiografía sobre el Frente Sandinista de Liberación Nacional, 1961–1979" in *Historiografías*, revista de teoría e historia; "¿Sandino sandinista? Una aproximación a la evolución ideológica de la Revolución Nicaragüense (1926–1979)" in Patricia Calvo González, ed., *Discursos e ideologías de derechas e izquierdas en América Latina y Europa*; and with Christian Helm, "Solidaridad con la Revolución Sandinista," in *Naveg@merica*.

Van Gosse is professor at Franklin & Marshall College and a political activist. His research centers on the history of radical movements, the New Left, and American democracy. He received his PhD from Rutgers University and has published widely since then. His books include *Native Sons: Black Politics in America, From the Revolution to the Civil War*; *Rethinking the New Left: An Interpretive History*; *The World the Sixties Made: Politics and Culture in Recent America* (co-edited with Richard Moser); and *Where the Boys Are: Cuba, Cold War America and the Making of a New Left*.

James G. Hershberg received his PhD from Tufts University and is professor of history and international affairs at George Washington University in Washington, DC. His research interests include the Cold War and the nuclear arms race. His principal publications include "New Evidence on Soviet-Brazilian Relations and the Cuban Missile Crisis," *Journal of Cold War Studies*; *Marigold: The Lost Chance for Peace*; "The Cuban Missile Crisis," in Westad and Leffler, eds., *The Cambridge History of the Cold War*; "The United States, Brazil, and the Cuban Missile Crisis, 1962," *Journal of Cold War Studies*; and *James B. Conant: Harvard to Hiroshima and the Making of the Nuclear Age*.

Gerardo Leibner received his PhD in Latin American history from Tel Aviv University, where he is now associate professor. His research interests include the history of Latin American communism, revolutionary politics and ideas across the Atlantic, the Italian and Latin America Left, oral history, and social movements. His principal publications include *Camaradas y Compañeros: Una historia política y social de los comunistas del Uruguay*; *El Mito del Socialismo Inígena en Mariátegui. Fuentes y Contextos Peruanos*; and "Women in Uruguayan Communism: Contradictions and Ambiguities, 1920s–1960s," *Journal of Latin American Studies.*

Blanca Mar León is a PhD candidate in history at El Colegio de México and research professor at the Autonomous Universidad of Mexico City (UACM). Her research interests include the Cuban Revolution and the Afro-Asian Movement, international relations of the Cuban Revolution, and the Cold War in Latin America. Her publications include "Economía y migración: las crisis y reformas económicas y sus efectos en el proceso migratorio cubano (1990–2013)" in Martínez Pérez, ed., *Cubanos en México. Orígenes, tipologías y trayectorias migratorias (1990–2013)*; "La Revista Cubana durante el período de entreguerras, 1935–1938" in Pita González, ed., *Redes Intelectuales transnacionales en América Latina durante la entreguerra*; and "El espacio de la utopía: los unamitas y la Revolución Cubana" in Andrés Kozel et al., eds., *El imaginario antimperialista en América Latina.*

Eduardo Rey Tristán is full professor of Latin American history at the University of Santiago de Compostela, Spain. After completing his PhD on guerrilla movements in Uruguay, he has specialized in political violence and contemporary Latin American revolutionary movements. He has carried out long-time field research in the Rio de la Plata region and Central America. He is cofounder and coordinator of the Revolutionary New Left International Research Network on Political Violence. He has published monographs, articles and book chapters in several European and American countries, including *La Izquierda Revolucionaria Uruguaya, 1955–1973*; *Revolutionary Violence and The New Left: Transnational Perspectives* (co-edited with Alberto Martín); and *Latin American Guerrilla Movements. Origins, Evolution, Outcomes* (co-edited with Dirk Kruijt and Alberto Martín).

Arturo Taracena Arriola holds a PhD in history from the École des hautes études en sciences sociales (EHESS). He is researcher at the Centro Peninsular en Humanidades y Ciencias Sociales (CEPHCIS) of the Universidad Nacional Autónoma de México (UNAM). His research focuses on state-building processes, social and regional history, ethnicity, and memory. Among his recent publications are *André Cornette. Relato de un viaje de*

México a Guatemala en el curso del año de 1855; Guatemala, la República Española y el Gobierno Vasco en el exilio (1944–1954); La polémica entre Eugenio Fernández Granell, la AGEAR y el Grupo Saker-ti: Desencuentros ideológicos durante la 'primavera' democrática guatemalteca; with Roberto García Ferreira, *La Guerra Fría y el anticomunismo en Centroamérica* ; and with Omar Lucas Monteflores, *Diccionario Biográfico del movimiento obrero urbano de Guatemala, 1877–1944.*

Michal Zourek holds a PhD in Ibero-American studies from the Faculty of Arts, Charles University in Prague. He is lecturer in the Department of Territorial Studies of the Faculty of Regional Development and International Studies, Mendel University in Brno, Czech Republic. His research interests include the study of communist secret services in Latin America, Latin America's New Left, the Soviet Bloc's cultural policies, and intellectual history. His publications include *Checoslovaquia y el Cono Sur 1945–1989: Relaciones políticas, económicas y culturales durante la Guerra Fría;* with Josef Opatrný, Matyáš Pelant, and Lucia Majlátová, *Relaciones entre Checoslovaquia y América Latina 1945–1989: En los archivos de la República Checa; Československo očima latinskoamerických intelektuálů 1947–1959;* and *Praga y los intelectuales latinoamericanos.*

Index

Westad, Odd Arne, 3
WFDY (World Federation of Democratic Youth), 228
Wright, Ann, 243

Xavier Pereira, Zilda Paula, 172, 178, 186, 196n36, 196n46
Xiuquan, Wu, 145

Yañez, Luís, 261
Yates, Pamela, 239
Yazid, Mohamed, 80, 98n47

Yofre, Juan, 30, 34, 38, 39
Yon Sosa, Marco Antonio, 84, 251n2

Zedong, Mao, 27, 104, 109–10, 126, 137–47, 150, 162n197, 163n208, 164, 283
Zetune, Salomón, 239
Zhen, Peng, 144–45
Zhou Enlai, 139
Zolov, Eric, 7
Zourek, Michal, 13, 16, 284
Zurita, Félix, 239